Withdrawn

EUROPE ON THE MOVE

The **European Science Foundation** is an association of its 54 member research councils, academies and institutions devoted to basic scientific research in 20 countries. The ESF brings European scientists together to work on topics of common concern, to co-ordinate the use of expensive facilities, and to discover and define new endeavours that will benefit from a co-operative approach.

The scientific work sponsored by ESF includes basic research in the natural sciences, the medical and biosciences, the humanities and the social sciences.

The ESF links scholarship and research supported by its members and adds value by co-operation across national frontiers. Through its function as a coordinator, and also by holding workshops and conferences and by enabling researchers to visit and study in laboratories throughout Europe, the ESF works for the advancement of European science.

This volume arises from the work of the ESF Network for European Communications and Transport Activities Research (NECTAR).

Further information on ESF activities can be obtained from:

European Science Foundation
1 quai Lezay-Marnésia
67080 Strasbourg Cedex
France

Tel. 88 76 71 00
Fax 88 38 05 32

Europe on the Move

Recent Developments in European Communications and Transport Activity Research

Edited by

PETER NIJKAMP

Avebury

Aldershot · Brookfield USA · Hong Kong · Singapore · Sydney

© European Science Foundation 1993

All rights reserved. No part of this publication may be reproduced, stored in a retrieval system, or transmitted in any form or by any means, electronic, mechanical, photocopying or otherwise without the prior permission of the publisher.

Published by
Avebury
Ashgate Publishing Limited
Gower House
Croft Road
Aldershot
Hants GU11 3HR
England

HE
242
.E88
1993

Ashgate Publishing Company
Old Post Road
Brookfield
Vermont 05036
USA

British Library Cataloguing in Publication Data

Europe on the Move: Recent Developments in
European Communications and Transport
Activity Research
I. Nijkamp, Peter
388.094

ISBN 1 85628 547 2

Printed in Great Britain by Ipswich Book Co. Ltd., Ipswich, Suffolk

Table of Contents

Preface

The period of the eighties has witnessed an increasing European interest in social science based approaches to communications and transportation research, not only in various research institutes but also in international institutions (like the EC, ECMT, OECD etc). This interest has even exhibited an accelerated pace after the recent drastic socio-economic and geo-political changes in Europe. Consequently, there is much scope for European-oriented communications and transportation research.

The Network on European Communications and Transport Activity Research (NECTAR) found its origin in the recognition that existing scientific research in Europe in the area of transportation, communications and mobility could be considerably improved and made more effective, if a cross-national platform for exchange of information and for scientific cooperation among European scholars in this field would be created. It was expected that by means of external stimuli (e.g., funding of overhead costs or seed money for new activities), a self-organising process among scientists would take place that would lead to a significant upgrading of European research in the transport field and that would also create a bridge between historically separated social science and engineering approaches. The NECTAR Network which served to promote international scholarly cooperation was a result of the path breaking efforts of the European Science Foundation (Strasbourg).

The objectives of the Network were:

- to promote collaboration between transport researchers in different European countries;
- to foster strategic research (including more appropriate methods) and to place emphasis on future-oriented approaches;
- to focus on critical issues in transport and communications research and to initiate new research directions;
- to shape a multi-faceted and multidisciplinary framework for advanced research;
- to improve the transfer of knowledge and experience in this broad field, in particular to the benefit of countries which have a short tradition and relatively less experience in transport research;
- to create a seedbed for young promising scholars.

This Network has generated a wide range of deliverables and spinoffs. One of these products has been the collection and presentation of papers on the theme 'Europe on the Move' presented at an international symposium in Amsterdam (March 1992). The present volume contains a representative sample of presentations at the above meeting. I wish to thank the European Science Foundation for financing this venue, the Royal Dutch Academy of Arts and Sciences (Amsterdam) for offering hospitality to his symposium, and the Netherlands Institute for Advanced Study (Wassenaar) for creating the right atmosphere for preparing this meeting. This book would not have come into being without the uninterrupted assistance provided by Jody Kersten and the editorial skills of Marnix de Romph. Finally, I wish to thank all my NECTAR friends with whom I have shared as Network chairman a wonderful and creative time in the past five years.

Amsterdam/Wassenaar, 1992 Peter Nijkamp

List of Contributors

Andersen, Bjorn	Department of Transport More and Romsdal College 6400 Molde Norway
Banister, David	Planning and Development Research Centre, The Bartlett, University College The Bartless/Wates House 22 Gordon Street London WC1H 0QB England
Barrett, Sean	Department of Economics Trinity College, University of Dublin Department of Economics Dublin 2 Ireland
Berechman, Joseph	The Public Policy Programme Tel Aviv University Faculty of Social Sciences 69978 Ramat Aviv Israel
Bovy, Piet H.L.	Ministry of Transport and Public Works Rijkswaterstaat Postbus 1031 3000 BA Rotterdam The Netherlands
Capello, Roberta	Instituto di Economia Politica Università Bocconi Via R. Sargatti 25 20136 Milano Italy

Capineri, Cristina	Dipartimento di Storia Sezione Geografia Universita degli Studi di Firenze via Piccolomini 3 Siena 50123 Firenze Italy
Fischer, Manfred M.	Department of Economic and Social Geography Vienna University Augasse 206 1090 Vienna Austria
Gérardin, Bernard	European Investment Bank Technical Advisory Service 100, Blvd Konrad Adenauer L-2950 Luxembourg
Giannopoulos, George A.	University of Thessaloniki Civil Engineering Department Transport Research Unit 540 06 Thessaloniki Greece
Gillespie, Andrew	Newcastle PICT Centre CURDS University of Newcastle Newcastle upon Tyne NE1 7RU England
Himanen, Veli	Technical Research Centre of Finland Road and Traffic Laboratory Itatuulentie 2 02100 Espoo Finland
Holm, Einar	Department of Human Geography University of Umea 90187 Umea Sweden

Janssen, Ben J.P.
NEA, Transport Research and Training
Schouwburgring 91
5038 TK Tilburg
The Netherlands

Jones, Peter M.
Transport Studies Group
Oxford University
11 Bevington Road
Oxford OX2 6NB
England

Kokkota, Stavroula
Laboratory of Railways and Transport
5 Iroon Polytechniou Street
157 73 Athens
Greece

Maarseveen, Martin van
Department of Management Studies
University van Twente
Dept of Management Studies
P.O. Box 217
7500 AE Enschede
The Netherlands

Maggi, Rico
Sozialökonomisches Seminar
Universität Zürich
Ramisstrasse 71
8006 Zurich
Switzerland

Masser, Ian
Department of Town and
Regional Planning
University of Sheffield
6 Clairemont Place
Sheffield S10 2TB
England

Nijkamp, Peter
Department of Regional Economics
Free University of Amsterdam
De Boelelaan 1105
1081 HV Amsterdam
The Netherlands

Orfeuil, Jean-Pierre	Institut National de Recherche sur les Transports et leur Sécurité 2 ave du Général Malleret-Joinville BP 34 94114 Arcuel Cedex France
Padjen, Juraj	Ekonomiski Institut Zagreb Trg. J.J. Kennedy 7 41000 Zagreb Croatia
Rammer, Christian	Department of Economic and Social Geography Vienna University Augasse 206 1090 Vienna Austria
Ratti, Remigio	Istituto Ricerche Economiche Cantone Ticino 6501 Bellinzona Switzerland
Reggiani, Aura	Università di Bergamo Facolta di Economia e Commercio Via Salvecchio, 19-24100 Bergamo Italy
Reichman, Shalom	Passed away in October 1992
Rietveld, Piet	Department of Regional Economics Free University of Amsterdam De Boelelaan 1105 1081 HV Amsterdam The Netherlands

Rossera, Fabio	Centre for Economic Research Canton Ticino 6501 Bellinzona Switzerland
Rus Mendoza, Ginés de	Department of Applied Economics Universidad de Las Palmas de Gran Canaria Saulo Toron 4, Tafira Baja Las Palmas de Gran Canaria Espagne
Salomon, Ilan	Department of Geography The Hebrew University of Jerusalem 91905 Jerusalem Israel
Stern, Eli	Ben Gurion University of the Negev Dept of Geography P.O. Box 653 84 105 Beer Sheba Israel
Svidén, Ove	Drive SECFO Rue de Trèves 61 B 1040 Brussel Belgium
Viégas, José	CESUR, Instituto Superior Técnico Avenida Rovisco Pais 1000 Lisbon Portugal
Wandel, Sten	University of Linköping Logistics and Transport Systems Department of Management and Economics 58183 Linköping Sweden
Wegener, Michael	University of Dortmund Institut für Raumplanung Postfach 500500 D-4600 Dortmund 50 Germany

This book is dedicated to

Shalom Reichman,

one of the founding fathers of NECTAR

CHAPTER 1

CHALLENGES TO EUROPEAN TRANSPORT POLICY ANALYSIS

Peter Nijkamp

1.1 The European Scene

Our world shows clear signs of socio-political re-orientation and economic-technological restructuring. Especially in recent years we witness that the world economy is in full dynamics. Traditional patterns of competition - within national borders - are increasingly being replaced by vigorous competition on a multi-national and even worldwide scale. "Intra-country" competition is being replaced by "inter-trade-block" competition, since traditional boundaries disappear; this takes place in Europe and will take place in other parts of the world as well. Countries within such trade-blocks are becoming part of an economic **network**. To maximize the competitiveness of such a network, and thereby maximize its socio-economic potential and performance, the quality of infrastructure is of critical importance, as transport has become an important component of modern production structures and processes, inter alia because of intensified division of tasks between firms (in different countries).

Furthermore, the European countries are increasingly also showing signs of an integrated economy, in which trade barriers are more and more removed and spatial interactions are increasing. The full exploitation of a nation's competitive advantage in an open international economic system has long been recognized as an important key force for maximizing national economic growth. Over the past decades a succession of agreements (e.g. the General Agreement on Tariffs and Trade - GATT) and trading unions (notably the European Community and the Benelux Union) have developed which have attempted to remove (or at least reduce) the effects of various tariff, quota and subsidy systems and other protectionist measures which have been introduced at various times by national governments in furtherance of their individual economic growth.

Because of this globalization trend and other socio-economic factors (including the need for higher and sustained economic growth), transportation in Europe has grown enormously, especially in recent years. As the supply of infrastructure - for various reasons - followed this trend only partly, existing infrastructure bottlenecks have been accentuated. This is a very serious problem, since economic development and infrastructural development have always been strongly interlinked, as is shown by hundreds of years of European history. The full benefits of the foreseen Internal European Market will only be reaped in case of effective (physical and non-physical) infrastructural adjustments in Europe. What is needed in this context, is European - and **not** national - thinking and action in infrastructural policy, based on knowledge of past successes and failures in infrastructural planning and of the future needs of the economy, the people living in Europe and their (increasingly threatened) (natural) environment (see also Masser et al., 1992).

Unfortunately, interest in the European scale of networks has until recently not yet been very significant, as transport policy and planning is seldom performed from this perspective. National frontiers have always provided a clear physical barrier between countries despite growing transport demand. Intra-European transport infrastructure networks have not followed this rising trend and show nowadays various bottlenecks in terms of missing links and missing networks (see Nijkamp et al., 1993). The emerging Internal Market between the twelve members of the European Community has put the focus of European politicians and industry on issues of socio-economic harmonization in order to remove distortions to free competition between industries in the various member states, and as a result increasing consideration is now given to transportation.

The major difference between a (more or less) nationalistic and a European approach to infrastructure network planning can best be described in terms of its economic effects. Nationalistic infrastructure planning means focussing on the way in which national infrastructure building companies, vehicle producers and transportation companies are given a competitive advantage at the cost of their foreign counterparts. As other countries will use the same tactics, in most cases however, all parties will be losers in this way, since efficient economies of scale are not reached and large sums of public investments are wasted; one of the reasons being that external competitors (e.g., Far Eastern or American companies) - while having large home markets - may then outperform European companies.

If the focus however would be on the European potential - the need to respond efficiently to the increased intra-Community demand - and if (public) infrastructure investments would be 'pooled' to develop European infrastructure networks, then scale economies can be reached and costs saved, as factors of production would then be equally available. This means developing an innovative European strategy for European transport, incorporating strategic long term issues such as sustainable mass transport systems, given the urgent transport capacity and environmental needs of our society.

1.2 Networks in Europe: A Historical Sketch

Transport and communications infrastructure has played a critical role in the history of Europe, not only many centuries ago but also in recent years. The European political and economic system has increasingly evolved from a set of relatively independent states into a collection of interacting economies connected by means of various types of network infrastructures.

Historically, major transitions in the European economic system were always accompanied (or even induced) by major changes in transport and communications infrastructures. Four main transport and logistic revolutions in the history of Western Europe can be distinguished, each of them characterized by the emergence, adoption and implementation of a new type of international infrastructure. These four revolutions are (see Andersson and Strömqvist, 1988):

- the Hanseatic period (from the thirteenth to the sixteenth century), in which waterways (inland and coastal transport links) emerged as a new logistic system connecting cities along rivers and coastal areas;
- the 'Golden' period (from the sixteenth century to the seventeenth century), characterized by a drastic improvement in sailing and sea transport and by the introduction of new banking systems, through which trade to the East Indies and West Indies was stimulated (with Lisbon, Antwerp and Amsterdam as major centres);
- the Industrial Revolution (from the middle of the nineteenth century onward), in which the invention of the steam engine generated new transport modes (sea transport, railways) which also created new market areas (e.g., North-America);
- the period from the seventies in our century, which is marked by informatization and flexibilization; in this framework JIT (just-in-time) systems and MRP (material requirements planning) are evolving as new management principles. The rapid developments in the area of new information technology have also led to the emergence of integral logistics. This may mark the beginning of a new era (the 'fourth logistic revolution').

Economic development and infrastructure development are thus mutually dependent driving forces. Therefore, the European economy will remain critically dependent on well functioning networks as catalysts for future development. There is nowadays however, a growing awareness that the current European infrastructure network is becoming outdated, without being replaced by modern facilities which would position the European economies at a competitive edge. Missing networks emerge, because transportation systems are developed in a segmented way, each country seeking for its own solution for each transport mode without keeping an eye on the synergetic effects of a coordinated design and use of advanced infrastructures. Another reason for missing networks is the focus on hard ware and the neglect of soft ware and organizational aspects as well as financial and ecological implications (see Nijkamp and Blaas, 1993). Cabotage, protection of national carriers, segmented European railway companies, and lack of multi-modal transport strategies are but a few examples of the emergence of missing networks. A European orientation of all transport modes is necessary to cope with the current problems of missing and competing networks. At the same time there is a clear need for sustainable transport solutions which are compatible with environmental requirements.

1.3 Europe on the Move: Megatrends

European economies have never been in a static situation, but always in a state of flux. Despite inertia, older infrastructures are constantly being replaced by more up-to-date networks to respond to new developments in the transport and communications sector (the 'overlapping generations' model).

In recent years a series of drastic changes can be observed in Europe's transport and communications. At the same time the fear is growing that our current networks are far from satisfactory in fulfilling the needs for a European-oriented infrastructure. Such changes concern all modes relating to **commodity** transport, **passenger** transport and **services/information** transport. Each of these three issues will briefly be described.

The European integration will lead to high volumes of freight transport. Far reaching changes in **commodity** transport include:

- **dematerialization**: the trend towards high value and low weight commodities, requiring flexible and varied transport modes.
- **customization**: the tendency to produce more tailor-made goods in more diverse and smaller product series leading to a decrease in the role of bulk transport.
- **informatization**: an increasingly important role of new information technology and (both internal and external) logistics management which places more emphasis on the coordination of physical transport (e.g., door-to-door transport).
- **globalization**: a world-wide orientation of modern transport, accompanied by the emergence of transnational transport companies which also generates many new international trade patterns.
- **integration**: the rise of combined transport of previously competitive modes leading to new demands for transhipment facilities (e.g., road-rail or road-air).

European developments have also drastic implications for spatial mobility of people. In the area of **passenger** transport various megatrends are arising:

- **grey revolution**: a reduction in the growth of population leading to an aging society with much leisure time and hence a high geographical mobility.
- **individualization**: a tendency towards more, but smaller and alternative types of households creating an additional demand for more mobility.
- **new welfare state**: an (expected) trend of gradually rising income levels per capita, accompanied by a higher female labour force participation and flexible working hours thus leading to a rise in car ownership and car use (for both business and personal purposes).
- **suburbanization**: an ongoing rise in commuting distance and in urban sprawl implying a rapid rise in motorization of our society.

Finally, our society moves towards an information society. Important developments in the field of **information services** include the following:

- **fourth logistic revolution**: a trend toward integral logistic systems, thus leading to the need for just-in-time (JIT) concepts, an increase in delivery frequencies and an increase in road haulage (based e.g. on preprogrammed routing and logistic platforms).
- **telematics**: an increasingly important role of telecommunication and information in transport, leading to an intensification of physical and human interactions in space (telematics may act as both a generator of and a substitute for

physical transport).

The conclusion which can be drawn from the above megatrends is evident: transport and communications become more intensive, not only locally/regionally, but also internationally. The potential offered by modern information technology and logistic systems will lead to a re-orientation of conventional transport systems. The need for reliability, flexibility and multi-modality in modern transport systems requires advanced infrastructure networks. The presence of bottlenecks and missing networks in Europe is at odds with a balanced, competitive and sustainable European development after the economic integration.

The expected integration benefits will only come into being if Europe becomes an open and flexible network in which transport and communications infrastructure provides efficient connections between all regions and states in Europe. Consequently, the opportunity costs of missing networks are extremely high. There is much evidence from the literature that productive investments and social overhead investments (notably infrastructure investments) need each other to arrive at a balanced economic development of nations and regions (Bruinsma et al., 1991). It seems thus plausible that the spin-off effects of new infrastructure investments - provided they are tailor-made with respect to local- and regional-economic needs - are significant. Nevertheless they need a careful scientific investigation, as will be shown in the next section.

1.4 The Critical Role of Infrastructure in Europe

Transport and communications provide a stimulus for economic development (exchange of commodities, division of tasks, specialization etc.). According to the Cecchini Report presented to the European Commission any additional economic growth is critically dependent on the physical exchange capacity of Europe.

Improvements in transport and communications systems are thus a critical success factor in generating highly significant dynamic integration effects. And there is an urgent need for such a strategic improvement. Even nowadays we see already that - from a geographical viewpoint - Europe is in fast motion. The action radius of commuting is structurally rising, the volume of commodities transported nationally and internationally is increasing, and airline activities for both passengers and commodities are booming. In a recent publication this mobility drift in Europe has been described as the 'Euro-mobile' phenomenon (see Nijkamp et al., 1991).

Transport policy favouring a free movement of persons and commodities in the EC is a sine qua non for a single market. The removal of existing barriers is of great importance for obtaining the highest dynamic integration benefits from a network economy. In recent years transport in most European countries has exhibited clear signs of **devolution** leading to a less intensive involvement of central governments. This devolution appears to be a uniform phenomenon, although in various countries and cities it manifests itself in different forms, e.g., deregulation, decentralization and privatization.

In this context, the first and most noticeable observation is that there is a striking **parallel movement** of transport infrastructure policies in most European countries in the past three decades: a period of expansion in the 1960's, a period of contraction in the 1970's and an era of selective expansion in the 1980's, in which the direction of selection is strongly governed by either market forces or by decentralization principles. Countries with a more liberal policy model and/or with severe deficits in the public budget are apparently the first ones to advocate privatization - in combination with deregulation - of transport policy, not only in the airlines sector and the freight sector, but also in the public transport sector. Among all these countries significant differences still exist, as the intensity of economic stagnation and of monetarist policies may drastically vary. In some countries local autonomy rather than privatization can be observed as a political ideology. Altogether however, the hypothesis of a financially-driven devolution ideology is reasonably valid in many European countries.

A second observation to be made here is that European transport policy should not only be focused on an improvement of the intra-EC network infrastructure, but also increasingly on **external links** of this network. An open EC has the highest benefits for both the Community itself and the world economy as a whole. Thus the improvement of cross-frontier routes is extremely important, such as the Trans-European Motorway, or the Scandinavian links. In the near future also major links to East-European countries have to be envisaged. There is also a strong case here for cooperation between non-member countries which provide (transit) links between EC-members, such as Switzerland, Austria and the former Yugoslavia. It goes without saying that a balanced transport policy is of critical relevance for regional equilibrium in the Community. The current tendency toward major fast links is not by definition beneficial to all regions. Extensive evaluation research will be necessary here to provide policy-makers with adequate guidelines.

A third major observation is that a major stimulus for new advanced infrastructure policy is given by **information technology** (information, telecommunications and micro-electronics). Physical distribution is increasingly relying on informatics-related activities. That holds true for containerization, fast trains and airlines. Accessible and internationally coordinated information systems are becoming a major vehicle for a further improvement of the transportation and logistics network in the Community. A necessary condition for the further penetration and success of such information systems is standardization, and this policy issue is one of the most crucial corner stones of European transport policy. JIT principles and multi-modal logistic chains will never become fully operational without sufficient European standardization. Thus the potentials and the barriers in European infrastructure need a thorough scientific analysis, in which various countries would need to participate.

1.5 Shades on the European Transport Scene

The European transport system is in general the circulation system underlying the European economy. Unfortunately, thus far hardly any coherent view on the functioning of the European transport system has developed. Instead of a systemic view in which the transport sector would be looked at from the viewpoint of coherence and positive synergetics, policy-makers and planners have tended to develop segmented solutions to emerging bottlenecks by looking for specific local or modal solutions without due regard to the connectivity of the transport system across different regions, sectors and modes. One of the main frictions in European transport policy is the absence of a strategic view on the 'wholeness' of the European transport system at all geographic levels.

Despite the increasing trend of JIT systems and related concepts, the actual practice of both commodity and passenger transport is disappointing and often frustrating. Severe traffic **congestion** phenomena at the urban or metropolitan level (e.g., Athens, Rome, Paris), unacceptable delays in medium and long distance transport during peak hours, unsatisfactory service levels of European railway systems and public transport in general, unreliable airline connections due to limited airport capacity, and the slow technical and institutional renewal of air traffic control in Europe; all these phenomena illustrate the difficult situation faced by the European transport sector. And there is no clear perspective for a drastic improvement of this situation. On the contrary, it is increasingly claimed that a free European market (from the year 1993 onward) and a further deregulation of the European transport sector may lead to unacceptable accessibility conditions - caused by congestion in major regions - in Europe.

Another important factor will be **environmental policy**. In contrast to the deregulation trend regarding transport, environmental policy is critically dependent on regulations and interventions at both the supply and demand side. In particular, technical restrictions are likely to be imposed, such as limited (or even zero) emission levels for motorcars or maybe even a selective prohibition of the use of certain transport modes. Recently, even various pleas for a car-less city have been voiced. Transport policy makers in most European countries find themselves in extremely complicated situations. A large number of interest groups, ranging from multi-national companies to local environmentalists are urging them to take action, but often in quite different directions. On the one hand it has become obvious that the environment poses its limits on the volume, character and pace of the extension of transport infrastructure. On the other hand, many business firms in Western Europe are concerned about their competitiveness in a global context due to an inadequate infrastructure.

Inadequate infrastructure affects European business life in several ways. First, the relatively slow development of sophisticated telecommunication infrastructure in Europe may curtail the possibilities to offer new services. Moreover, it may limit the possibilities to speed up international trade in an efficient way. And third, the restricted capacity of inland transport networks may cause higher production costs in Europe and affect global competitiveness.

For these reasons Europe must improve its transport and communications infrastructure to increase its competitive power, while at the same time sufficient care should be given to environmental considerations. This raises an extra difficulty, as due care is usually incompatible with swift action. Short term solutions, as advocated by some business-oriented interest groups, tend to rely heavily on a further massive extension of the European motorway system. This option may make sense in Southern and Eastern Europe, but for Western Europe this option does not seem viable in the long run. Since supply tends to generate its own demand (the 'Law of Say'), network extensions beyond the level of relieving unacceptable bottlenecks will create a new era of congestion at a higher level. Furthermore, this scenario will also be detrimental to a balanced spatial development of urban areas and the environment in Western Europe.

In conclusion, Europe is facing a major development constraint, in that its infrastructure network is highly segmented, whilst policy strategies to build a multi-modal European-oriented infrastructure network are just beginning to emerge. The European infrastructure development is thus coping with important restrictions which deserve a full-scale scientific investigation.

1.6 Transport Policies in Europe

The way in which governments can influence international transport costs are numerous. In most countries it is still the national government which provides - directly or indirectly - the major components of infrastructure, such as ports, airports, glass fibre networks, railway tracks, etc. Despite deregulation, the provision and presence of infrastructure itself gives power, because through its very location or capacity the infrastructure can influence the magnitude of a country's trade. The power to charge for the use of the national transport or communications infrastructure offers a further device by which a government may attempt to influence trade. Apart from more direct measures and institutional arrangements which also serve to influence the costs of international transport (and thus violate the principle of laissez faire), governments may also intervene, again in numerous different ways, to protect their own domestic transport industries from external competition. For instance, cabotage is in particular often viewed in the same way as the 'dumping' of goods in a market and is the subject of particularly severe restrictions in many European countries.

In other countries, the production of transport products (including the supply of consultancy and civil engineering expertise as well as that of cars, lorries, aircraft and other vehicle manufacturers) is regarded as very important (often for reasons of domestic economic stability and protection of traditional sectors rather than on the grounds of strict economic efficiency). The government intervention then restricts the working of the free international market. For instance, domestic industries may be protected by design standards, quota systems and tariff regimes.

It is thus no surprise that international transport agencies call for more national deregulation. Although agencies such as the European Conference of Ministers of Transport (ECMT), EC, Benelux, etc., fulfil an important function as a discussion platform in policy preparation, it is still very difficult to get all member countries on the same policy wave length. European history teaches us that it is difficult to harmonize so many different interests and that, after a compromise has been reached about joint policy formulation, the implementation - and above all the maintenance of the solution developed - is often neglected.

Clearly, the field of international transport and communications is often characterized by ad hoc and partial policy measures. Government actions tend sometimes to be taken more in response to crisis situations, rather than as part of a coordinated and preventive policy programme, that is strategic, holistic and pro-active in nature. As a result, there is a 'long list' of **policy issues** in the European setting, which deserve more attention in the future. Here we will present a representative sample of these issues:

- From an overall European perspective, **transport scenario analysis** seems to be highly relevant, particularly from the viewpoint of world trade, notably free trade, protectionism, global trade flows and shifts in economic importance of regions and continents.
- **The role of the government in a deregulated market** with respect to access, competition, financing/subsidising, safety and risks is an important issue. The effects of deregulating deserve a thorough analysis in order to remove monopolistic tendencies and to ensure a competitive market. This is particularly relevant for railway companies. They have the potential to operate in a more commercial way in combination with a high quality offered in terms of speed, reliability and comfort.
- As far as commodity transport is concerned, **deregulation of freight transport** (e.g., scope and impacts on modes) deserve also full scale attention in the near future.
- In view of the international importance of transport infrastructure and freight transport, possibilities of developing **coastal transport and roro** (roll on roll off) **transport** in Europe as a partial solution to infrastructure shortcomings have to be explored more intensively.
- The consequences of the **massive (auto)mobility growth** (the 'Euro-mobile' phenomenon) are evident: on a European scale we have to face the problem of endless traffic jams and inaccessibility in and around urban areas. A main side effect is the serious **environmental impact.** Two different kinds of policy measures deserve analytical attention here:
    1. **Variabilisation of costs of car use** as a compensation for environmental costs. Although several experiments have been done with navigation systems and dashboard mounted video display screens (especially in Japan), a practical European cross-frontier programme of electronic traffic aids on congested trunk roads is still missing (although the DRIVE programme of the EC seems to be promising in this respect).
    2. **Improvement of public transport.** It is plausible to assume that for long distance transport (notably railway and automobile transport) most likely the environmental decay will not count as an argument in the

choice between these two different modes, unless public transport will improve substantially its quality (in terms of fares, punctuality, comfort, etc.). Some important necessary conditions are: liberalisation of the European transport market, a reduction of the monopoly positions of (notably) railway companies (which implies a separation between infrastructure holding companies from transport operations); and (ex ante) evaluations of new transport projects in light of their environmental effects.

Design of **management information and computerized planning systems**, and satellite control of trains and vehicles under the condition of integration of national and international databases is urgent.

From 1993 onwards, the **reduction of border formalities and avoidance of customs delay** in both passenger and freight transport are also important items on the list of policy priorities. Harmonisation of combined transport technologies in person transport and in freight distribution seems in this respect to be the main precondition in which telematics plays a crucial role.

- The **geographical potential** of infrastructure should be fully recognized. In this respect gateway areas (seaports, telematics 'ports' etc.) and peripheral (problem) areas deserve common international attention, because it has become evident that each of these types of regions in Europe faces more or less similar problems.

From the foregoing exposition it has once more become clear, that the transport system performs the same kind of function to the European economy as the blood circulation performs in the human body. There are however, also big differences between them, since the human body has a number of sophisticated control systems trained to cooperate with one another and is therefore able to achieve a high-level performance, whereas the 'European network body' lacks coherent materialization and coordination, since sometimes even basic transport functions do not exist (or perform very poorly), whilst major parts of this body compete with each other rather than complement each other.

Finally, it should be noticed - particularly when considering policy choices - that transportation is a derived demand. Transportation is not an aim in itself, it serves 'higher' economic goals related to the requirements of a network economy. Efficient access to economic activities and social facilities is the major service provided by infrastructure networks and - irrespective of the type of mode - this is the main goal of a European-oriented transport policy.

1.7 European Transport and Communications Research: A Missionary Calendar[1]

The above observation and analysis have brought to light the existence or

---

1 The author wishes to thank Terence Bendixson for his stimulating input for this part.

emergence of four major core research areas which would deserve intensified research efforts in the European transportation and communications field in the years to come. These areas are:

- the simultaneous occurrence of integration and disintegration trends in Europe.
- the trend towards strong competition among key actors (industries, metropolises) in Europe as a result of many new European network configurations.
- the strategic importance of new infrastructures and new technologies as competitive weapons (European and world-wide).
- the increasing stress between the drive to economic progress and spatial mobility on the one hand and the need for safeguarding the environment and quality of life on the other hand.

These four issues will now be considered in more detail.

1.7.1 Integration and disintegration in Europe

The disappearance of the iron curtain has led to a widening of Europe which will have far reaching economic, spatial and political consequences. It has led to both re-integration (Germany) and disintegration (USSR, Yugo-Slavia, Tsjecho-Slovakia) at the same time. The completion of the internal market in Europe by 1993 has created an 'open arena' for business life in Europe connecting countries and regions which in former times were isolated. At the same time now, when national borders tend to vanish, we observe a strong tendency towards more regional-economic, -political and -cultural identity and even autonomy (Spain, Italy, Belgium, the UK).

The reconstruction and bonding of a greater and more open Europe of more than 500 million people is an enormous task. It will necessitate high levels of investment supported by the European Regional Development Fund (EFDF) and the European Investment Bank (EIB). Such issues will be of great importance in the Fourth Framework of the European Community. This will imply that questions about the direction, size and geographical distribution of infrastructure investment, regional development and environmental protection all arise. Many open questions will then come to the fore. Should the cities and countries of central Europe see the West as models to be followed? Or does the new concern for sustainable development require them to shape their future economic, regional-urban and infrastructural trajectory in new ways?

And will the citizens of Poland or Hungary - to mention a few - accept a future which is not a copy of what they have seen as an ideal model for many years? Is it realistic to assume that the rise in spatial mobility will also conquer all countries in central and east Europe? Will the view on the new Europe as the homeland of many cities, regions and nations be strong enough to cope with the threats of monopoly power and protectionism? And which are the critical success factors which will ensure that the new Europe will not lose its momentum during the present difficult transition period? And - last but not least - what is the mission of a European-oriented transportation planning which aims both to alleviate the transaction costs of European restructuring and to exploit the competitive advantages of European cities, regions and nations?

1.7.2 Competition in European networks

The current European dynamics may - from a spatial-economic viewpoint - be characterized by two complementary forces: a drive towards an open economic network and a drive towards more competition between regions and/or industries.

Recent developments in Europe add a new dimension to the interaction between transport and communications networks and spatial development:

- New, faster transport networks (high-speed rail and air) create new spatial concentrations of accessibility in Europe
- The difference in accessibility between West and East will remain large despite the re-integration of East-European transport networks
- New telecommunication networks such as ISDN and satellite communication create areas of high informational accessibility at nodal centres.

The combined effect of these developments will be a polarisation of accessibility on the continent and an increase in the locational advantage of the regions in the European core over those at the periphery. Policies to improve Scandinavian sea crossings or the conversion of the Spanish mainlines to standard gauge are not likely to offset this polarising tendency. The European Community has realised the risks associated with increasing spatial disparities in Europe and in the Maastricht agreements it calls explicitly for the utilisation of trans-European networks to promote cohesion in and between the regions in the Community.

Clearly, the network concept is analytically not an unknown concept (e.g., in mathematical topology, electrical engineering, or operations research), but its functioning and implications in a European economic setting need to be investigated more thoroughly. This leads to a series of important research questions. Concepts like the European 'blue banana' are interesting and creative thought experiments, but need to be substantiated with solid research and proper policy strategies. Is, for instance, a European network economy beneficial to lagging or peripheral regions? Is the European network economy compatible with environmental quality standards? To what extent does a network configuration provide a new geo-political structure impacting on national or regional socio-cultural identities in Europe? Is a network system determined by the spatial organisation of multinational European firms or does the network shape the linkage patterns of such firms? Is a European network concept a realistic idea, if it is not supported by coordinated European policy strategies for sophisticated transnational infrastructures? If a European network cannot be built up simultaneously but needs same phasing of activities over a time span of some 20 years, isn't there a real danger of the emergence of a Europe with two speeds? What type of transnational infrastructure agencies have to be envisaged for coordinating such activities? And who decides on the types and modes of network infrastructures to be developed? And, last but not least, will the emerging European network generate sufficient comparative advantages to be internationally competitive?

1.7.3 New technologies and new infrastructures

Transport and new technologies are interwoven in two complementary ways. First, transport and infrastructure shape a geographical form which determines to a large extent location patterns of industries and households. More efficient transport systems favour the competitive position of firms in such a network and hence favour the cities or regions linked to such a network. This means that transport infrastructure is particularly important on access and communication. This holds in general true for most high tech firms, so that communication and transport networks may be regarded as catalysts for high tech development, an assumption which is supported by many empirical facts.

In the second place, new technologies have also an impact on the degree of sophistication of a network. This does not only hold for the airline or rail transport sector, but also for the road transport sector. The impact of modern logistics and telematics on transport behaviour and the efficiency of transport movement is increasing.

From a policy point of view, the role of transport for spatial development has become central for transport and telecommunication policy of the Europe Community at a time when new highspeed rail, motorway and advanced telecommunication networks are about to fundamentally transform the map of Europe. In addition, the unconstrained tendency to ever more transport and mobility causes serious social and environmental imbalances so that the identification of feasible policies to curb this trend is a highly desirable goal.

All such developments lead to intricate future oriented research questions. A few of them will be posed here. Is it plausible to assume that high tech infrastructures favour economies of scale and may therefore induce the emergence of 'hub and spokes' systems? Is it possible to develop realistic future scenarios for the impact of telecommunication on the transport sector and the spatial behaviour of people or organisations? Will telematics ever have a significant impact on spatial mobility or will it at the same time favour further urban sprawl? Will the car industry be able to develop new technologies which will make the car compatible with ecological and spatial constraints? Or will the car play an even more important role as an extension of the office and the home (including telephone, fax, pc, video and tv)? Do such new technologies discriminate between different regions in Europe? Which are the social implications of teleworking on family life or on female labour force participation?

1.7.4 Transport and environmental sustainability

Environmental costs imposed by the transport sector are high and increasing, despite extensive legislation at the European and national levels. Clear policy directions need to be given to the transport industry so that production processes can be cleaned up, and so that more environmentally benign transport modes can be encouraged. The private sector contribution would complement that of the public sector in giving priority to public transport and cycling within cities, and in encouraging energy efficient urban forms. In general, one may claim that private sector contributions have an important role to play in supplementing the public sector investment in transport and communications infrastructure. Various forms of partnership must be established between funding agencies, between sources of European capital (e.g., the European Investment Bank and the European Bank for Reconstruction and Development) and between national governments, as the levels of capital required for investment in Europe are often too a large for a single agency.

It should be noted that economic concepts are clear in that the user and the polluter should pay the full costs of travel including all externalities. However, there are many problems with the implementation of such concepts, as the public acceptability is low and international agreements are difficult. For instance, any such implementation would ideally have to be fiscally neutral, otherwise the policy would be inflationary and could lead to increases in unemployment.

The needs for sustainable mobility and a compact city design are concepts recently introduced by the European Community. However, the necessary massive investments in transport and communications networks, particularly on a regional and international basis, are likely to increase journey lengths and levels of mobility. These outcomes are inconsistent with the objectives put forward by the EC (e.g., in the Green and White Paper).

It goes without saying that the social costs incurred as a result of modern transport systems generate many research questions. Examples are the following. Do current European developments open a possibility for finding politically acceptable ways of internalizing transport's external costs? Is it possible to charge the wide range of external costs - road casualties, noise, gas emissions, severance of communities, destruction of wildlife and so on - in a meaningful way to the user? Which policy strategies can be envisaged to ensure sustainable development (new car technologies, strict regulations, road pricing, parking policy, physical planning etc.)? And if a system of directly-debited road user charges is canvassed as the best instrument for internalizing congestion (and other) costs, what are their likely side effects? And how would such a system impact on urban form and (re-)location behaviour of people and firms? Which are the likely impacts of telematics (e.g., route guidance or advance booking of parking spaces)? Are there sufficiently strong economic arguments for reducing traffic congestion by contriving a shift in urban travel from car to public transport? And for which target groups will a particular form of public transport service be the most suitable means? Is it possible to reconcile the need of low-income people for low fares with the desire of car owners to travel at a standard to which they are accustomed? Would it be feasible to have differential segments in public transport - high quality high price services for the affluent and cheaper utilitarian ones for lower income people? Or should telematics and information technology - rather than public transport - be seen as a high quality alternative to ban travel? And, last but not least, is our way of living, working and moving compatible with the justified desires of Third World people for a higher level of sustainable development in which they rightly wish to have a fair share?

1.8 Scope of the Book

In Section 1.7 a set of intriguing research questions on the European communications and transport activity scene has been raised, seen from the observations made in the preceding sections. The complexity of current transport and infrastructure issues in Europe requires some modesty among researchers, as not all above research questions can be adequately tackled. Nevertheless, in various fields significant and remarkable progress has been made in depicting and understanding European transport and communication systems. This book brings together - in a systematic way - a representative set of studies and results focusing on the European transport and communications scene. Most questions formulated above are - explicitly or implicitly - dealt with in these contributions, although an unambiguous answer to each individual question may be difficult to disentangle from these research results. Nevertheless, they form a representative collection of current transport and communications research in Europe nowadays.

The book has the following logical and coherent structure. It starts with a depiction of **megatrends** in European Communications and Transport Activity by focusing in particular on long range scenarios (up to the year 2020), the impacts of new (transport) technologies on spatial organisation, the foreseeable rise in mobility of Europeans, the implications of technological and social developments for in-home/out-of-home interactions, and the changes in the position of border areas in a widening Europe.

The next set of contributions deals with the effects of **new informatics, telematics and logistics.** Particular attention is devoted to the impact of information provision on commuters behaviour, the possibilities of advanced road transport informatics and telematics, and finally the consequences of product channel logistics and logistic platforms.

The consequences of both megatrends and new technologies provoke various important **policy questions**, which are discussed in the third part of the book. Issues addressed here are: European transport infrastructure policy, the impact of deregulation in the transport sector, the question of optimal public transport provision, the constraints imposed by environmental sustainability objectives, and finally the scope for adequate technology policy in transportation networks.

In the final part of the book various interesting **analytical advances** are presented, such as the relevance of non-linear dynamics in relation to micro behavioural modelling, new ways of analyzing communication and interaction behaviour in Europe, and the spatial dimensions of information and telecommunications demand in various European countries.

All such contributions serve to show that the European scene offers a rich research laboratory for transportation scientists. The wealth of potential new research directions is for the time being almost unlimited. This book aims to present only a limited but interesting and balanced sample of such scholarly attempts.

References

Andersson, A.E. and U. Strömqvist, The Emerging C-Society, **Transportation for the Future** (D.F. Batten and R. Thord, eds.), Springer, Berlin, 1989, pp. 64-82.

Bruinsma, F., P. Nijkamp and P. Rietveld, Infrastructure and Metropolitan Development in an International Perspective, **Infrastructure and Regional Development** (R.Vickerman, ed.), Pion, London, 1991, pp. 189-205.

Masser, I., O. Svidén and M. Wegener, **The Geography of Europe's Future**, Belhaven, London, 1992.

Nijkamp, P., J. Vleugel, R. Maggi and I. Masser, **Missing Transport Networks in Europe**, Avebury, Aldershot, U.K. 1993.

Nijkamp, P., and E. Blaas, **Impact Analysis and Decision Support in Transportation Planning**, Kluwer, Boston, 1993.

Nijkamp, P., S. Reichman and M. Wegener (eds.), **Euromobile**, Gower, Aldershot, 1991.

PART A

MEGATRENDS IN EUROPEAN COMMUNICATIONS AND TRANSPORT ACTIVITY

CHAPTER 2

EUROPE 2020: LONG-TERM SCENARIOS OF TRANSPORT AND COMMUNICATIONS IN EUROPE

Ian Masser, Ove Svidén and Michael Wegener

2.1 Introduction

Towards the end of the 20th century, Europe is facing fundamental political, economic and social changes. After the collapse of the socialist systems in eastern Europe, the west European model of a federation of democratic countries with market economies is becoming more and more attractive. During the coming decade, the European Community may grow to the world's largest economic region with more than 500 million consumers. The completion of the Single European Market in 1993 and further steps towards a monetary union will create new economic opportunities of still unknown magnitude. At the same time the European countries are facing the same long-term socioeconomic developments as other countries of the world such as the globalisation of the economy, the emerging information society, the deepening gap between North and South and the aggravating risks for the global climate.

Given this background, **transport** and **communications** play an important role in shaping the future of Europe. Efficient transport and communication links between suppliers, producers and consumers within regions as well as between regions and across national boundaries are vital for the growth and global competitiveness of the European economy. Transport and communications are indispensable for modern lifestyles based on high levels of mobility and personal interaction. Transport and communications are essential for binding the regions and countries together and reducing the disadvantage of the peripheral regions against the core. In line with the growth in gross national product, in the last two decades passenger transport in Europe has almost doubled, goods transport increased by two thirds and telecommunications has grown by a factor of five.

The unconstrained growth in transport, however, has created severe technical, social and environmental problems, especially in the most industrialised regions in North-West Europe. Urban trunk roads, motorways, air corridors and airports are notoriously congested. Transport-induced energy consumption, air pollution, noise intrusion and accidents continue to grow despite all efforts to reduce them. There is a widespread feeling of crisis (see for instance Nijkamp et al., 1990; Group Transport 2000 Plus, 1990; European Round Table of Industrialists, 1991; and Commission of the European Communities, 1991).

At the same time, there is a serious lack of transport and communications infrastructure in the less developed regions of the Mediterranean and eastern Europe. If the large economic disparities between these regions and the more affluent core regions of Europe are to be reduced, massive transport investments are necessary. Even greater sums are required to bring the transport and communications infrastructure of east Euro pean countries up to west European standards. The gap between core and peripheral regions will be further deepened by new levels of transport and communications infrastructure. The emerging European high-speed rail network in combination with new transnational links such as the Channel Tunnel, the new transalpine rail lines and the Öresund and Belt crossings as well as new telecommunication networks such as ISDN will first connect the large agglomerations and further increase the peripherality of regions that are not connected.

In the face of these conflicting tendencies, the future of transport and communications in Europe is extremely uncertain. Will the forces dominate which promote further expansion of transport infrastructure? Or will policies to reduce interregional disparities be pursued? Or will those groups who for environmental reasons are opposed to unconstrained growth win majority support?

These are the issues discussed in this paper. It reports on a scenario writing project undertaken by the authors as part of the Network for European Communications and Transport Activity Research (NECTAR) of the European Science Foundation. In this project, long-term scenarios of transport and communications in Europe were developed in order to identify relevant fields for future transnational research projects from a European perspective and to discuss alternatives for an integrated European transport and communications policy. The project covered nine separate fields of activity ranging from population and lifestyles to regional development and urban form. Three component scenarios representing different policy directions were developed for each of these fields. A structured questionnaire was used to solicit responses to seed scenarios and background information provided by the project team from the international membership of NECTAR. A full presentation of the seed scenarios and background information and the results of the survey is contained in Masser et al. (1992).

2.2 Socioeconomic Trends

2.2.1 Introduction

Transport and communications are secondary or derived human activities that cannot be seen in isolation from the social, economic and political development of a society. Therefore, in order to assess the future development of transport and communications, it is necessary to take account of concurrent developments in other major fields of human activity with which transport and communications interact. For this study, the following nine fields were selected:

- **Population**: Changes in fertility, mortality and migration and their impacts on the overall age structure of the population.
- **Lifestyles**: Changes in household size and composition, labour force participation and activity patterns.
- **Economy**: Economic structural change to a postindustrial society and its impacts on industrial organisation and reorganisation.
- **Environment**: The use of energy, air and land resources and factors governing human well-being, safety and protection from noise and physical disturbance.
- **Regional Development**: Growth and decline processes in central and peripheral regions of Europe and the spatial disparities resulting from them.

- **Urban and Rural Form**: Changes in the internal structure of regions and the relationship between cities and their hinterlands.
- **Goods Transport**: Changes in the volume and directions of raw materials, bulk cargo, energy, food and industry production movements.
- **Passenger Transport**: Changes in personal mobility, the volume and intensity of trips and the use of different modes of travel.
- **Communications**: The emergence of the information society, restructuring of telecommunications and information handling.

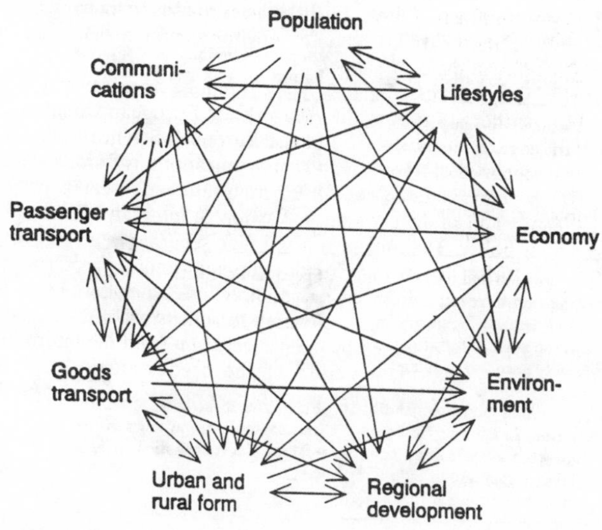

Figure 1 The nine fields investigated in the study and their interaction

These nine fields are not independent of each other. In the real world they overlap and are linked by an intricate cobweb of mutual interdependencies: population and economy interact on the labour market, consume environmental resources, determine regional development and urban/rural form and generate flows of goods, passengers and information which in turn co-determine the process of spatial development, affect the environment and give rise to new mobility patterns and lifestyles.

Figure 1 highlights the most important of these interactions. It is seen that goods transport, passenger transport and communications are influenced by most other fields but themselves influence only some of them.

In the following section therefore, the major social and economic change processes currently taking place in the first six fields in Europe are briefly described. Table 1 summarises these trends and their consequences for transport and communications.

Table 1 Socioeconomic trends and their impact on transport and communications

Field	Socioeconomic trends	Implications for transport and communications
Population	Decline of birth rates;new international migration from eastern and southern Europe; ageing of the population.	Growing demands for transport and communications; increased demand for public transport; relative decline in private car usage.
Lifestyles	Decreasing household size; higher labour force participation of women; new lifestyles; shorter work hours.	Higher car ownership, increasing mobility; increasing use of personal telecommunications; more leisure and tourist trips.
Economy	Decline in manufacturing and agriculture, growth of service activities; reorganisation of production and distribution; liberalisation, internationalisation.	Growth of goods transport, mostly by road; integrated logistic systems; increased use of business telecommunications; increased international passenger and goods transport; deregulation.
Environment	Energy use and emissions of transport increase; growing land demand for transport; traffic noise and traffic safety unsolved problems.	Speed limits, stricter emission standards, car restraint, pedestrianisation, improved public transport; more rigorous traffic restraint policies likely.
Regional development	Increasing interregional disparities in Europe; fastest growth in core regions; relative decline in old industrial and peripheral regions.	Further concentration of transport and communication flows in core regions; decentralisation policies?
Urban and rural form	Counterurbanisation in Northwest Europe, continued urban growth in the South; new city hierarchy; intraregional dispersal; reurbanisation?	Increasing congestion in largest cities; rigorous traffic control; coexistence with car in smaller cities; public transport policies.

2.2.2 Population

The most important demographic trend in most European countries is the decline in fertility (see Figure 2). If only natural change is considered, most European countries are likely to experience a fall in population in the next decades. The decline is likely to be most pronounced in countries such as Germany where the fertility rate has already reached a very low level. The most fundamental impact of declining birth rates - in conjunction with increasing life expectancy - is the progressive ageing of the population. It is estimated that in western Europe the proportion of persons over 65 years will increase from 13 percent in 1985 to more than 20 percent in 2020, with increasing tendency beyond that year. Countries like Sweden and Germany are likely to be the leaders.

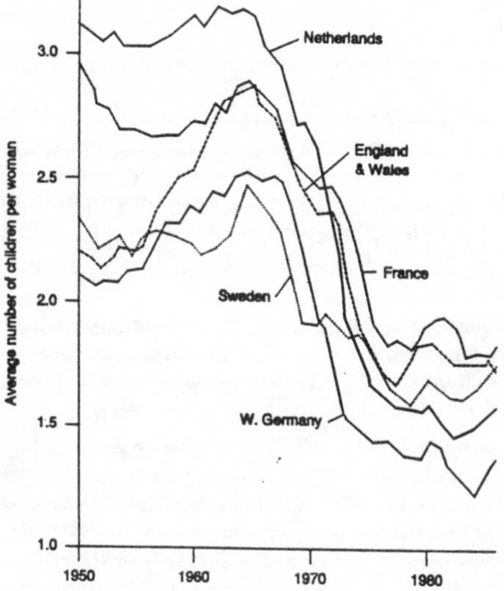

Figure 2 Birth rates in selected European countries, 1950-1986 (adapted from Bourgeois-Pichat, 1981)

The ageing of the population throughout Europe is likely to have important impacts on social and economic life in the 21st century. A considerable increase will be required in health and social services in all countries to meet the demands of old people. There will also be relatively fewer children in schools and there will be a surplus of jobs for school leavers. As the proportion of elderly in the population rises, there will also be increased demands on public transport and a relative decline in private car usage especially in urban areas, unless new types of cars suited for elderly people are developed.

If only present trends are taken into account, it is unlikely that the population decline in most countries would be offset to any significant extent by international migration. The number of guest workers in most European countries has declined over recent years and restrictions on Commonwealth immigration in the U.K. have reduced the flow of immigrants to that country. Nevertheless, work-related immigration into the major receiving countries is still substantial. Moreover, the impact of recent developments in eastern Europe is likely to spark a new wave of international population movements. Germany would be the most obvious beneficiary from such developments, but all west European countries may be affected.

In addition there remains the more fundamental question whether the affluent European countries will be able to shield themselves against immigration from their less affluent southern neighbours where the demographic transition has not yet started, i.e. population growth is still high. It is hard to imagine that the countries of the European community will be able to completely deny their people access at a time of open borders and international cooperation.

The growth in population will have obvious impacts on the demand for transport and communications. The ageing of the population will bring an increase in demand for public transport and a relative decline in private car usage.

2.2.3 Lifestyles

In all European countries the size of the average household has fallen substantially. This trend reflects a number of demographic, social and economic factors such as the decline in overall fertility over this period and the increase in the proportion of old people in the population, the decline in three-generation families and the reduction in the proportion of married couples in the population, an increasing overall affluence, growing economic independence of women and young people and the decline of traditional peasant agriculture.

Further declines in average household size can be anticipated between 1990 and 2020 as the effects of demographic, social and economic factors work through the population. The impact of such trends is likely to be particularly pronounced in wealthy countries with very low fertility and ageing populations such as Germany, but most apparent in absolute terms in southern European countries such as Italy where fertility levels are falling and traditional peasant societies are being replaced by urban cultures.

With households becoming smaller, more women tend to work. Up to eighty percent of all households in inner cities are one-or-two person households: young workers, students, pensioners, yuppies ('young urban professionals') or dinks ('double income no kids') or affluent 'senior citizens' of the 'silver' generation. The darker side of the demise of the large family is the fragmentation of the activity spheres of the individual. The liberation from the traditional bonds of family, neighbourhood or community may facilitate a richer set of transient attachments for the young and active at the same time, as cultural diversity is increasing as a result of greater international mobility, but it can also mean isolation and loneliness for the old and sick, polarisation of interests and discrimination against ethnic, cultural or social minorities. The ideal of the pluralist, multicultural, tolerant and cooperative society has yet to demonstrate its viability.

Another factor works in the opposite direction, i.e. decreases labour force participation. As societies become more affluent, social security and pension schemes make it unnecessary that old people work for their livelihood. This creates financial problems in an ageing society because a smaller number of economically active people have to support a growing number of pensioners.

A consequence of the ageing society, but more importantly of new technologies in manufacturing and services, is a marked increase in free time. If automation increases productivity faster than output grows, labour becomes redundant. This can lead to unemployment, but can also be turned into reductions of working hours per day, per week, per year or per lifetime. This has happened in all industrial countries since the abolition of sunday work, and although there are still large differences between the work time regimes in individual European countries, it is safe to say that by the year 2020 both the eight-hour work day and the five-day work week will be a thing of the past. Also there will be a great diversity of work hour arrangements ranging from flexi-time to teleworking from the home via computer link. The price to be paid for all this will be a certain fragmentation and unpredictability of work schedules subject to the requirements of continuous production processes or shop opening hours, but also a new flexibility and scope for self-determination, a trend accentuated already today by the increase in the number of workers involved in job sharing, sabbaticals and early retirement programmes.

One of the effects will be an enormous increase in the amount of time devoted to leisure activities. To meet these demands, it is likely that there will be a massive expansion of the leisure industry. By 2020 leisure activities may account for as much as 40 percent of all land transport (in terms of kilometres travelled) and 60 percent of air transport. The growing diversity of lifestyles will be reflected in the emergence of new types of specialist tourist markets. A further boost to international tourism can be expected after 1992 with the removal of many of the existing institutional barriers to movement.

In summary, all the above trends point into the direction of more mobility and more intensive communication. Singles and dinks tend to own more cars and make more trips per capita than large families, working women travel more than housewives and mothers, and a large part of the leisure time gained is spent on moving to a wide range of spatially dispersed activities. The fragmentation of the family multiplies the need for interaction with other people and places. To keep up with the accelerating pace of changing fashions and attractions requires to be linked to a network of continuous information exchange and communication.

2.2.4 Economy

Throughout Europe the decline in traditional manufacturing industries has been compensated for by the expansion in service activities, while agricultural employment declined, and this trend is likely to continue, in particular in the countries in southern Europe where agricultural employment is still relatively high (see Figure 3).

However, behind the shift in employment are more fundamental changes in the total organisation of production and distribution. The introduction of computerisation in manufacturing has brought a new flexibility of production. This has become possible by an increasing vertical integration of the production process from supply to delivery by computer control and telecommunications. Earlier steps in the assembly chain are contracted out to outside suppliers who have to synchronise their operations and delivery with the main production schedule ('just-in-time') increasingly over long distances.

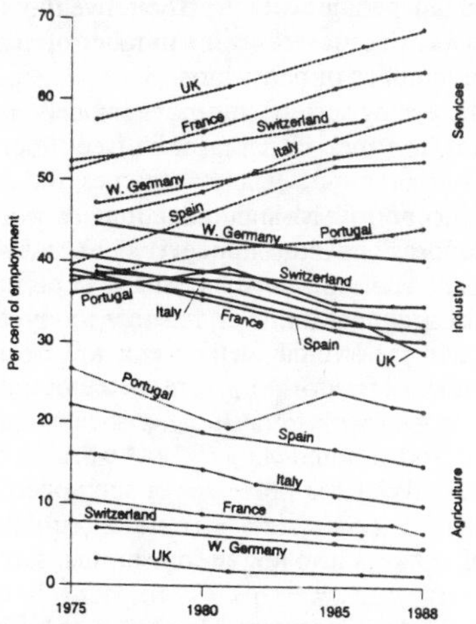

Figure 3 Economic structural change in selected European countries, 1975-1988

This transition also changes the character of work. Ever more sophisticated machines take over more and more of the repetitious and monotonous tasks at the assembly line, so that part of the human becomes more supervisory. Where manual work is still required, the traditional division of labour is replaced by more comprehensive work packages to increase job satisfaction and responsibility. The proportion of jobs requiring higher skills is growing as is the number of staff employed in research and development and sales. Workers who are not able to adjust to the new skills are becoming redundant. For the remaining work force, individual work hours are decreasing with rising productivity, but continuous production jobs require more shift work or work on Saturdays.

Another characteristic of the postindustrial economy is a polarisation of firm sizes. On the one hand there are very large corporations which continue to become even larger. In addition to the vertical integration referred to above, they employ a strategy of horizontal integration by acquiring smaller companies to diversify into fast-growing high-tech products or services. Large companies increasingly become multi- or transnational in order to compete on the world market and to exploit labour cost differentials between individual countries. On the other hand the number of small companies is increasing rapidly. Empirical studies have shown that much of the employment growth in recent years has been due to small and medium-sized firms with innovative product or service ideas. In many countries special subsidy programmes have been set up to promote the establishment of new promising companies. Technology centres are set up as incubators for innovation-oriented enterprises, which later move out to new technology parks and enterprise zones to attract investors with reliefs from taxes and environmental regulations. Technopolis programmes imitating the Japanese example are other technology-oriented policies directed to small and medium-sized firms, although in most countries the bulk of high-tech promotion funds go to the big companies of the military-aerospace complex.

The growth in the service sector does not in all cases compensate for the industrial job losses. The surplus manufacturing workers do not have the skills required for the new high-level financial and consulting services nor can they compete with cheap temporary unskilled labour hired by retail and fast-food outlets. Especially in the wealthier countries, skilled personal services are becoming more and more unaffordable for the majority of the population, with the effect that the alleged 'service society' is gradually turning into a 'self-service society'.

These changes of the economy have significant implications for spatial structure and goods transport: Industrial locations more than ever depend on good transport access to suppliers and markets. Information-intensive industries, in particular of the highest level, tend to concentrate in the agglomerations and so contribute to their congestion. The logistics revolution results in substantial further growth in road goods transport. The completion of the Single European Market in 1993 leads to a dramatic expansion in international exchange and thus growth in both passenger and goods transport.

2.2.5 Environment

Environmental problems are becoming the most important issue in transport. About 25 percent of all final energy consumption is transport-related. Transport-related air pollution is responsible for between 60 and 95 percent of carbon monoxide (CO) and carbon dioxide (CO_2), between 30 and 60 percent of nitrogen oxides (NO_x) and nearly all lead emissions. Despite more energy-efficient and cleaner cars, in absolute terms transport-generated energy use and emissions have increased due to increasing numbers of cars and trucks and the trend to longer trips, higher speeds and larger vehicles. In the densely populated western Europe, land consumption for transport infrastructure is a serious problem. In agglomerations, railways and roads may occupy one fifth and more of the total developed area. The most obnoxious environmental impact of transport is traffic noise. Despite great advances in automobile safety, transport continues to demand its death toll.

The European countries have reacted to the growing negative impacts of transport by various measures such as speed limits, stricter emission standards or car restraint measures and pedestrianisation. The three-way catalytic converter, which requires unleaded petrol, is able to clean some 80 percent of the remaining CO and NO_x, but unlike in the US and Japan, the adoption of this technology is slow and very uneven in Europe (see Figure 4). The Netherlands pioneered a particular combination of car traffic restraint and street design in residential areas, which quickly spread to other countries, most notably Germany, Britain and Scandinavia. In West Germany, 'area-wide' car restraint, which includes the scaling down of trunk roads and extensive speed-limit areas of 30 kmh, are widely applied and are accepted by the population.

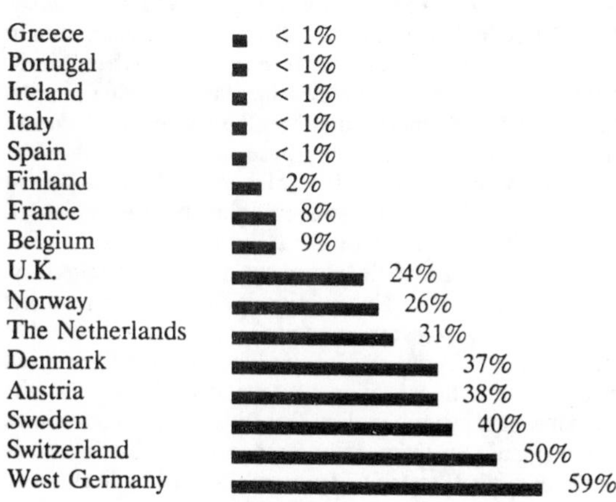

Figure 4 Share of unleaded petrol sold in selected European countries in 1989

The other obvious approach to make urban transport ecologically less harmful is to promote or revitalise public transport. Therefore many cities invest in improvements to their existing or in new public transport systems or experiment with new fare systems to attract more passengers.

The problem is that except in the largest cities the operation of public transport systems without heavy subsidies is impossible. However, in many countries it is beginning to be felt that the car and public transport should no longer be considered as competing but as complementing components of urban transport and that therefore a part of the costs for public transport should be financed by the general public just as the costs for roads.

2.2.6 Regional development

The differences in income, employment, infrastructure and provision of services between the regions of Europe are still enormous, and they are likely to become more pronounced: The regions in the core of Europe will continue to benefit from economic structural change and the integration of Europe, although the old industrial regions will continue to decline. The peripheral regions will grow, but less than the core regions. The differences in income and employment between the regions in Europe can be linked to four factors:

First, centrally located regions tend to be more industrialised and economically more successful than the predominantly agricultural regions at the European periphery. Second, urban regions continue to be more productive and affluent than rural regions. Just as in the early days of industrialisation, cities are the incubators of innovation where capital and specialised skills come together to produce new technologies and products. A third factor in the economic success of a region is its industrial heritage. Regions that led the first cycle of industrialisation based on raw materials and heavy industry such as north-west England, Nord-Pas-de-Calais in France and the Saar and Ruhr regions in Germany suffer under the decline of their major industries. Due to their outdated infrastructure, polluted environment and lack of urban amenities they fail to attract enough of the growing high-tech manufacturing and information-based service industries to compensate for their decline in traditional employment. These new industries select regions with quite different locational characteristics such as high-skill labour, access to international transport and communications networks, availability of business-oriented services and attractiveness in terms of housing, education, culture and recreation. The fourth factor is the growing dependency of regional development on world markets. As production technologies develop and wage levels in Europe rise, low-skill manufacturing processes may have to be exported to low-wage overseas regions, but may return in the form of the fully-automated factory. But even within Europe labour cost differentials between countries induce a growing internationalisation of economic activities in the form of separation of high-skill and low-skill processes within multinational corporations.

The most likely scenario of regional development in Europe looks like Figure 5: There will be a zone of intensive development stretching from south-east England across the Channel through Benelux, south-west Germany and Switzerland to Lombardy (the 'Blue Banana'), where it meets with another growth zone developing along the Mediterranean (the 'Sun Belt'). With the exception of the Ile de France, centres outside these zones will be at a relative disadvantage.

Current transport and communications policies are likely to reinforce these tendencies. There is still a vast discrepancy between the transport infrastructure in core and peripheral countries. The new high-speed rail links and motorways will largely follow present transport corridors and so further improve the accessibility of the core regions at the expense of the periphery. Deregulation of air transport will enhance the position of the present major airports serving as hubs routing flights to secondary airports and concentrating traffic in the core regions. Advanced telecommunications will be available first where high-volume demand will make them profitable, and this will be again in the existing centres.

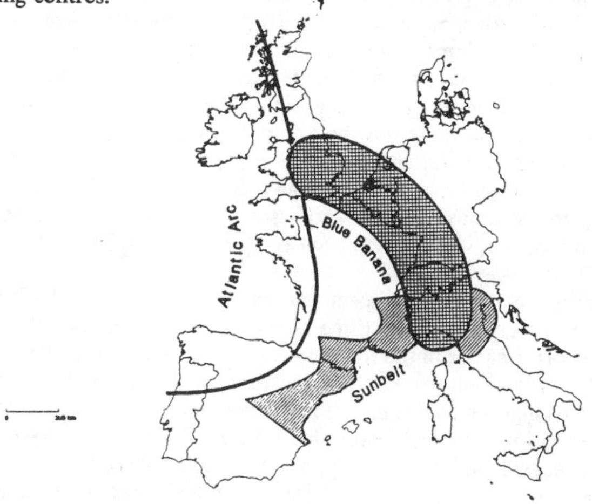

Figure 5 The most likely growth of Europe: the 'Blue Banana' and the 'Sunbelt' (RECLUS, 1989)

2.2.7 Urban and rural form

The 1950s and 1960s were a period of rapid urban growth all over Europe. High birth rates, continued rural-to-urban migration due to mechanisation of agriculture, and a first wave of international labour migration from southern to northern Europe resulted in massive urban expansion, mostly in the form of new satellite towns or large high-rise suburbs. In the 1970s the urbanisation rate started to decline. Cities were facing a decline in population and later also of employment, first in their inner cores, later also in their suburbs and eventually in the whole urban area. At the same time smaller cities at the urban fringe started to grow. Counterurbanisation tendencies are found primarily in the most industrialised countries in north-western Europe, whereas in the Mediterranean and east Europe the urbanisation process prevails. However, not all cities in a country follow a common pattern. The new urban hierarchy divides cities across national boundaries into 'successful' and 'unsuccessful' cities. Successful cities are the two 'global' metropoles London and Paris and the small number of 'Euro-Metropoles', which flourish with the intensification of international trade and information flows, some regional centres with a favourable combination of locational factors and the large number of small towns at the fringe of large agglomerations. All other cities are the losers, with old industrial cities and remote rural towns suffering most from urban decline.

The common experience for both winner and loser cities has been spatial deconcentration. The evolution of transport systems made the expansion of cities over a wider and wider area possible. In particular the diffusion of the private automobile after the war brought low-density suburban living into the reach of not only the rich. However, suburbanisation was not caused by the car, but is a consequence of the same changes in socio-economic context and lifestyles that were also responsible for the growth in car ownership: increase in income, more working women, smaller households, more leisure time and a consequential change in housing preferences. The results are generally considered to be negative: longer trips, more energy consumption, pollution, accidents, excessive land consumption and problems of public transport provision in low-density areas. All over Europe cities have undertaken efforts to revitalise their inner cities, in some cases with remarkable success. Recent figures suggest that the exodus from the inner city may have passed its peak and that there may be a 'reurbanisation' phase.

The impacts of these trends in urban development on transport and communications are: The largest cities will suffer under increasing congestion and will have to resort to rigorous measures of traffic control. Smaller cities are likely to be more successful in peaceful coexistence with the car, whereas suburbia everywhere will continue to depend on the car.

At the other end of the urban-rural spectrum, small rural towns and villages in agricultural regions are threatened by one of three developments: In the wider hinterland of agglomerations, in resort areas or in the mountains they lose their rural character by the outer wave of urban sprawl, most notably in the form of second homes of people living in cities. In areas of high-intensity agricultural production, they suffer from what may be called 'industrialisation without urbanisation' with agro-factories dispersed over a monofunctional plain, severe pollution problems and a distinct lack of amenities. In remote regions at the European periphery, finally, their very existence is threatened by depopulation and the collapse of the agricultural economy altogether, with irreparable ecological consequences.

2.3 Trends in Transport and Communications

The demand for transport and communications will be determined by the socioeconomic trends outlined. Below, the resulting trends for transport and communications in Europe are discussed.

2.3.1 Goods transport

The general trend of goods transport in Europe in the past has been growth. Since 1970 goods transport has increased by two thirds. This growth has been unevenly distributed over modes: Traffic on waterways and railways stagnated whereas road goods transport more than doubled.

Inland Waterways

Sea transport along the coasts and on inland waterways today is only used for bulk goods. Roll-on/roll-off ferries connect the Mediterranean islands, the British isles and Scandinavia with the European continent. The contribution of inland waterway traffic to total goods transport varies between countries depending on their endowment with navigable rivers and canals. In the future the completion of the Rhone-Rhine, Rhine-Main-Danube and Oder-Elbe-Danube canals will improve the market for water transport.

Rail Freight

Europe has a well developed rail system for goods transport. Without railways the rapid industrialisation of Europe in the 19th century would not have been possible.

Today railway goods transport is losing ground against the truck. On average railways attract less than 20 percent of all goods transport and much less in countries such as Great Britain, Italy and the Netherlands. National railway companies are making great efforts to halt the erosion of their market share by streamlining services, direct over-night freight connections and aggressive freight rates or by promoting various forms of combined road and rail transport such as 'piggyback' trains or swapbody systems. However, against the unsurpassed speed and flexibility of the truck none of these policies have been really successful.

Without a basic improvement of its competitive situation, railway goods transport is facing further decline. Client-specific services, further progress in standardisation and containerisation, new freight centres and computerised freight information systems may improve the situation. Many see the introduction of high-speed rail as a possible turning point. The Single European Market will increase average transport distances and reduce custom procedures and thus may offer new opportunities for rail or multimodal road-rail transport. In particular transit countries like Switzerland and Austria are considering combined transalpine links such as the 'moving motorway' through the Gotthard and Lötschberg base tunnels.

Trucks

Trucks are at present the dominant mode of goods transport in Europe. In Britain, the homeland of the railway, the truck has replaced goods transport by rail almost altogether. There are several reasons for this. The road network provides accessibility to all corners of the continent. Year by year the road network has been expanded in line with the growing economy, while rail networks in all countries have been constantly reduced. Moreover, with low diesel prices and taxes and roads being financed by the government, truck transport has never had to cover its true social and environmental costs, in contrast to the railway which has to finance its own infrastructure.

However, the success of the truck is mainly due to its unsurpassed advantage in door-to-door speed, flexibility and reliability. Modern market economies with their multitude of interdependencies and a dispersed settlement structure could not exist without efficient, unbroken, door-to-door transport links. Logistic systems linking supply, production and distribution processes substitute warehousing functions by 'justin-time' delivery and hence rely on flexible small and medium- sized vehicles. Increasing value per ton makes it more and more important to have a driver with responsibility for the whole transport process. Even long-distance sea and rail transport are not possible without regional road transport at their start and end.

In the future, all these trends favour the truck. The value of goods transported increases as the standard of living rises and products are becoming more complex. Advances in information processing and telecommunications give rise to new possibilities for complex logistics systems including multimode transport. The logistics revolution within industries is spreading out to inter-industry transport.

It has been estimated that goods transport by road will grow by 30 percent due to the Single European Market and the growing internationalisation and deregulation it will bring about. This is likely to present serious congestion problems on motorways, in particular in transit countries as Switzerland and Austria. There will be a relative decline in road infrastructure investments, though peripheral countries will still have a strong interest in new road infrastructure. New roads will face increasing environmentalist opposition.

Air Freight

Air transport is the fastest, youngest and fastest growing goods transport mode. Air freight will continue its upward trend with the growing internationalisation of the European economies. Deregulation of air transport will lead to greater competition and reduced freight rates.

2.3.2 Passenger transport

The last two decades have seen an enormous growth in personal mobility. Since 1970 passenger transport in Europe has almost doubled.

Car

Today about 80 percent of all passenger-km in Europe are made by car. This has been accompanied by suburban sprawl around cities, making inhabitants depend on the automobile. The car has become an established and necessary part of life for most families. The success of the car is due to the freedom of movement and almost universal usefulness it offers. It is equally good at short as on long distances, it can be used for carrying people and goods, it requires no mode changes and only minimal planning before starting a journey. Consequently, all forecasts have notoriously underestimated the growth of car ownership and even in the countries with the highest car ownership no saturation is in sight, though the highest growth rates are now in east European countries.

However, in densely populated areas the automobile has already shown its ultimate limits in the form of congestion and unacceptable levels of pollution and noise. In many countries it has become apparent that the solution to urban traffic problems can no longer consist in further expanding the road network but in a synergetic mixture of a variety of policies such as taxation, user charges, traffic restraint, pedestrianisation, and promotion of public transport.

Urban Public Transport

In many countries it is beginning to be realised that the car and public transport should no longer be seen as competing but as complementary components of urban transport and that therefore part of the costs of public transport should be financed by the general public just as the costs for the road infrastructure.

Because of their high costs, commuter rail lines and subways have remained reserved to large cities. For smaller and regional centres, light rail transit (LRT) systems offer affordable solutions with the same service quality as subways. In some countries LRT systems are operated by private companies. Buses serve as feeder to LRT or rail stations, but still are the only mode in small towns and rural areas. The greatest problem for public transport is the provision of adequate service in low-density suburbs or rural areas. In many countries new demand-responsive systems such as dial-a-bus or various forms of paratransit are being experimented with.

Long-Distance Rail

With its dense railway network and generally short distances between its major centres, Europe is ideally suited for rail travel. Eurocity and Intercity trains provide reasonably efficient, comfortable and reliable, though slow, service between the main cities in Europe. For the 1990s, a new network of high-speed trains is envisaged, although problems of compatibility between national systems still have to be solved. Figure 6 shows the currently planned high-speed rail network in western Europe:

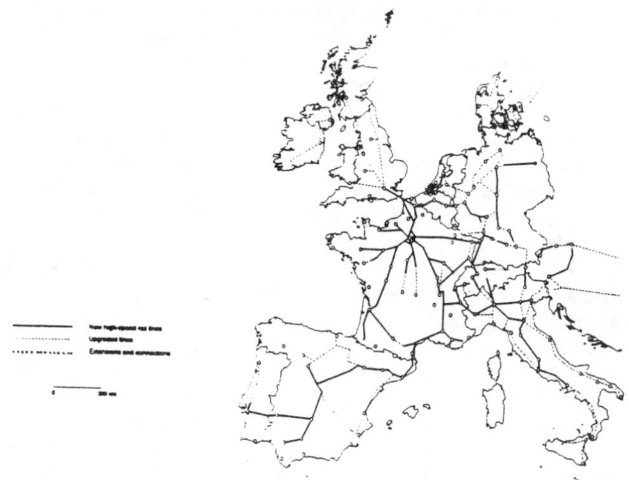

Figure 6 The future high-speed rail network in Western Europe

Trains will run at speeds between 160 and 300 kmh, partly on special tracks. Already existing high-speed trains such as the French TGV and the new German ICE successfully compete with domestic airlines. The German **Transrapid**, a linear-motor MAGLEV system, still has to find a domestic application.

The renaissance of the train in long-distance travel will be greatly enhanced by several megaprojects, by which traditional topographical barriers will be removed or substantially reduced: the Channel Tunnel, the two transalpine base tunnels under the St. Gotthard and Lötschberg mountains, and the bridges across the Storebælt and the Öresund.

Besides investing in faster trains, many national railway companies are trying to attract more passengers by aggressive marketing, special discounts and new combinations of services.

Air Travel

During the last decade airline operations in Europe have experienced steady growth rates of five to ten percent per year. Compared to the US and Japan, airline networks and services are still in the beginning of their market penetration and far from saturation.

However, the future development of air travel in Europe will be largely determined by capacity restrictions of airports and air corridors which already today suffer from peak-hour congestion. The pending deregulation of passenger air travel will increase competition between carriers on major routes and lead to the creation of airline-specific hub-and-spoke systems to discourage interlining. Reduced fares and a variety of special discounts will stimulate the demand for air travel at the expense of rail.

2.3.3 Communications

There has always been a strong interdependence between telecommunications and economic development. Today telecommunication technologies such as telephone, telefax and computer-to-computer data exchange are indispensable for commercial transactions, industrial logistics and multimodal transport systems.

The growth of the European telecommunications market has been stupendous. The newest and most impressive diffusion phenomenon is the explosive proliferation of facsimile machines. Other new technologies such as packet-switched and value-added networks are spreading steadily, others have experienced uneven acceptance in some countries (e.g. videotext), while others fail to pick up their market as originally expected (e.g. video conferences).

Telecommunication may be a substitute for travel. However, the change from traditional business and working styles has been slower than many observers had anticipated. More fundamental and clearly observable are the impacts of telecommunications on goods transport, where they are at the heart of the logistics revolution.

The newest telecommunications technology in Europe is the Integrated Services Digital Network (ISDN). ISDN will replace various current telecommunications systems by simultaneously transmitting voice, data, text and images. All industrialised European countries are presently developing pilot versions of ISDN using conventional telephone lines working at a speed of 64K bits per second (narrowband ISDN). In many countries narrowband ISDN is already available in major cities. Narrowband ISDN is only capable of transmitting voice, data, text and slow-moving monochrome images. In a second phase transmission speeds of multiples of 64K bits using fibre optics (broadband ISDN) are planned.

A question still largely unresolved is whether the new telecommunications networks will promote spatial concentration or deconcentration. It seems certain that the more sophisticated systems will be introduced first in regions where demand will make them profitable. This will reinforce the already dominant position of central regions. On the other hand, once widely available, such systems will reduce the locational disadvantage of remote regions.

On the intraregional scale, the diffusion of the technology will be faster, so the equalising effect is likely to be dominant. This means that outlying parts of a metropolitan area should become relatively more attractive compared with the core, hence the metropolitan area will decentralise more. However, it is also possible that the need for face-to-face contacts will outweigh this decentralisation tendency in favour of the traditional centre.

2.4 Scenarios

Some of the above trends are powerful processes that cannot easily be changed by human intervention. Others are observable but can potentially be influenced by policy action. Others are very uncertain and cannot easily be predicted.

In the project, alternative scenarios were developed for the nine fields presented above. For each field three seed scenarios representing different policy directions were designed:

- **The Growth Scenario (A).** The first scenario shows the most likely development of transport and communications if all policies emphasised economic growth as the primary objective. This would most probably also be a high-tech and market-economy scenario, with as little state intervention as possible. This scenario might be associated with the political ideals of many current conservative governments in Europe.
- **The Equity Scenario (B).** The second scenario shows the impacts of policies that primarily try to reduce inequalities in society both in terms of social and spatial disparities. Where these policies are in conflict with economic growth, considerations of equal access and equity are given priority. This scenario might be associated with the policy-making of social-democrat governments.
- **The Environment Scenario (C).** The third scenario emphasises quality of life and environmental aspects. There will be a restrained use of technology and some control of economic activity; in particular where economic activities are in conflict with environmental objectives, a lesser rate of economic growth will be accepted. This scenario might be associated with the views of the Green parties throughout Europe.

The relationship between the three paradigms is illustrated by the triangle in Figure 7. Each of its corners represents one of the paradigms growth, equity or environment. The present situation is at the centre of the triangle; the triangle area represents the

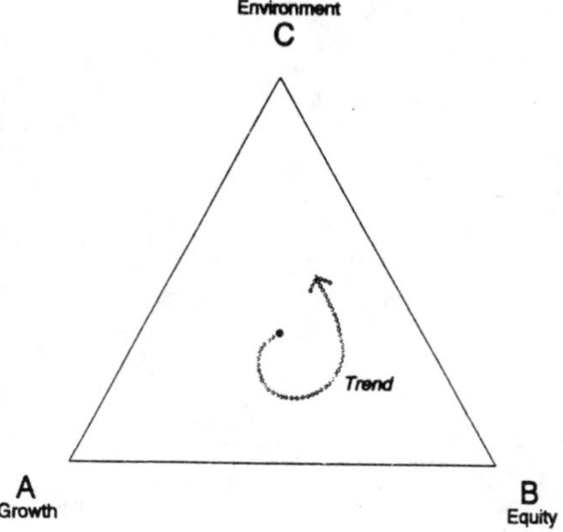

Figure 7 The three paradigms

domain of possible changes from the present state. The line starting from the centre is the trajectory from the present to the future: it may bend in response to technical breakthroughs, new organisational patterns or political decisions.

A structured questionnaire was used to solicit responses to the seed scenarios and trend information from the international membership of NECTAR. Responses were received from sixty experts from eighteen European countries representing a wide range of disciplines, age groups and professional or academic affiliations.

2.5 Which Scenario?

Growth, equity and environment are three partially conflicting paradigms that will influence the future geography of Europe. Which of them will be the most powerful?

Figure 8 gives the answer. Here the responses are represented in a triangular coordinate space the corners of which are associated with the three paradigms as in Figure 7. Each group of responses can be located in this coordinate space as a pair of points indicating the 'most likely' and 'most preferred' scenarios, respectively. The 'most likely' scenario is indicated by a hollow circle and the 'most preferred' scenario by a solid circle. The greater the distance between the two circles, the greater the dissatisfaction of the respondents with the existing trends.

The result is unequivocal. There is an overwhelming consensus that the growth scenario is by far the most likely and that if present trends continue the market economies of western Europe will continue on their growth path.

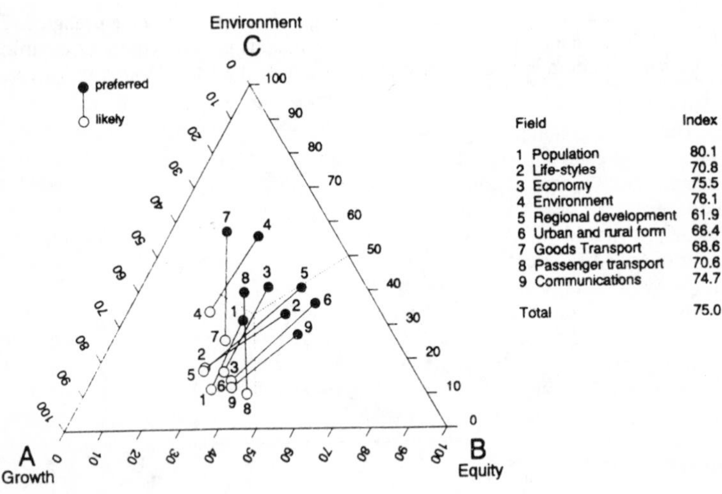

Figure 8 Field scenarios evaluated

However, there was also disagreement. Is this not a too naive extrapolation of existing trends? The consequences of the unconstrained growth scenario are so negative that it is hard to believe that there would be no action by national and European governments. So a great number of modifications of the growth scenario were suggested, some of which were taken from the other two scenarios. The modifications and suggestions tended to endorse the growth scenario but added some more moderate notes. Nevertheless the outlook remains rather gloomy. If the experts are only partly right, the most likely scenario of transport and communications in Europe is a veritable horror scenario. It presents a continent with an unprecedented level of material wealth and technological perfection yet with unparalleled spatial disparities between its regions and cities, congested roads and a collapsed public transport system, a disappearing countryside and a devastated environment. Are there no alternatives?

The majority of respondents felt that a fundamental change in values and policy making was required. Both the equity paradigm and the environment paradigm found their followers, but clearly the environment paradigm turned out to be the winner. The 'most preferred' scenario hence is a combination of the equity and environment scenarios.

Table 2 shows the essential characteristics of the two scenarios, the 'most likely' and the combined target scenario side by side.

2.6 Choices for Europe

Are there conclusions to be drawn from this analysis that might be useful for decision makers in Europe? The first conclusion is that transport and communications policy cannot be separated from economic, regional, urban and environmental policy. The second is that European policy makers are at the crossroads where two fundamentally opposed directions of political action can be selected. Table 3 confronts these two fundamental options.

The one direction (on the left-hand side of the table) follows the paradigm that because of the global competition, Europe must do everything possible to modernise its infrastructure and manufacturing equipment and hence promote growth. Underlying this philosophy is that only a growing European economy can pay for the investments necessary for this global race. However, planning for growth in one of the already richest regions of the world means widening the gap between the industrialised and developing countries with unpredictable consequences for the future. In a competitive economy it also means condoning spatial polarisation, because modernisation is most efficient in the most advanced and most affluent metropolitan regions in the European core. Condoning spatial polarisation, however, means accepting growing disparities between the core regions and the regions at the European periphery, which may benefit from the growth of the centres, but inevitably will grow less than these. Further polarisation also means more agglomeration diseconomies in terms of congestion, land speculation and environmental damage.

The other direction on the right-hand side of Table 3 would be to promote an ecologically sustainable and socially equitable future at the expense of economic growth. This strategy would not only work towards a peaceful solution of the imminent conflict between the developing and the industrialised countries, but also avoid many of the negative aspects of spatial polarisation and environmental degradation inevitably associated with continued economic growth.

For planners and decision makers responsible for transport and communications following the second option would imply:

Table 2 Summary of likely and preferred scenarios

Field	Most likely scenario	Most preferred scenario
Population	Low birth rates, ageing society; growth-financed social security; non-EC foreign labour without citizenship.	Crisis of social security system overcome by immigration from developing countries; government support of young families.
Lifestyles	Singles and 'dinks' model for lifestyle: refficiency, mobility, telecommunication, consumption; declassification of less able.	Change of values: solidarity in stead of competition; renaissance of the family; participation in community affairs emphsised.
Economy	'Fortess Europe' economic empire; income disparities between European core and periphery and within European countries.	Europe government promotes sustainable development; taxes on luxury goods, rigorous emission standards; alternative technologies.
Environment	Serious congestion and transport-generated pollution; massive land consumption for new motorways, high-speed rail lines and airports.	Europe leader in environment-conscious policy making; use of fossil fuels constant; heavy taxes on car ownership and petrol; public transport growing.
Regional development	Further concentration of economic activities in the European core; agglomeration diseconomies; economic decline in peripheral regions.	Decentralisation programmes and strict land use control in urban areas; incentives for location in perpheral area; decentralisation of transport infrastructure.
Urban and rural form	Spatial segreation of social groups in cities; suburbanisation of manufacturing; disappearing countryside.	Disincentives for location in large cities; financial aid for small cities; land speculation curbed; car restraint policies.
Goods transport	Dramatic increase in road freight transport, toll motorways and bridges; rail freight service disappeared.	Restriction and taxation of road freight; air freight regulated; promotion of ecological vehicles for distribution.
Passenger transport	Highly mobile society; dominance of individual automobility; local public transport declining; competition between car, high-speed rail and air.	Car use constrainted; renaissance of public transport; clean cars provide harmless mobility for dispersed society.
Communications	Massive use of fibre-optics and satellite communications; 'information society' changes lifestyles; dominance of large cities reinforced.	Use of telecommunications for equalising information in central and peripheral locations; flat telecommunication fares.

Table 3 Summary of choices for action

Field	Growth	Equity/Environment
Population	Continue to permit non-permanent immigration of workers from non-EC countries without giving them full citizenship.	Permit controlled permanent immigration from non-EC countries; improve support for families and working parents.
Lifestyles	Continue to promote competition and egoism in education and economic life.	Support families to reverse decline in households size; promote shift in values from individual to collective goals.
Economy	Continue to serve needs of transnational companies; continue to deregulation of economy; continue protectionism against developing countries.	Promote small and medium-sized companies; promote equalisation of incomes and social security within Europe; promote economic cooperation with Africa.
Environment	Continue to settle for lowest common denominator for environmental standards; continue to promote high-speed transport infrastructure.	Plan for sustainable development; adopt environmental standards of most advanced countries; redirect transport investments to peripheral regions.
Regional development	Continue to let capital flow to already prosperous central regions; continue to concentrate transport and communication in infrastructure in core regions.	Promote decentralised system of regions with autonomy to develop their endogenous potential; promote deconcentration of infrastructure.
Urban and rural form	Continue to promote winner cities by concentration of high-level infrastructure and not intervening in destructive competition of cities.	Promote small and peripheral cities through modern infrastructure and government agencies; contain urban sprawl in agglomerations.
Goods transport	Continue to reward road freight transport through low taxation and motorway construction.	Reduce road freight transport by taxation and regulation; invest in combined road/rail transport; reduce volume of goods.
Passenger transport	Continue to promote car traffic through low taxation, road construction, dispersed settlements structures and neglect of railways.	Discourage use of cars by taxation and road-pricing; substantially improve the attractiveness of public transport; promote reurbanisation and mixed land use.
Communications	Continue to promote concentration of telecommunications infrastructures in core regions.	Subsidise telecommunications in peripheral regions; introduce flat fare telecommunications fares.

- In **goods transport**: to reduce freight transport on roads through fair taxation of trucks taking account of damage of trucks to roads and environmental costs following the 'user-pays' principle, to immediately introduce rigorous environmental standards for trucks and traffic restrictions for trucks in environmentally sensitive areas and congested areas in cities during rush hours or at night in residential districts, to substantially invest in combined road/rail transport facilities and services and to reduce the volume of freight by the relocation of heavy process industries, the regulation of excessive just-in-time logistics schemes and the promotion of regional, short-distance distribution networks.
- In **passenger transport**: to discourage the use of cars by a differentiated system of taxation, user fees and road pricing taking full account of the environmental and social costs of car driving in general or in particular areas or times of day, while at the same time substantially improving the attractiveness of public transport by new investments, enhanced service and competitive fare structures (acknowledging the fact that public transport is a public good that needs to be subsidised); and to improve the spatial association of residences, work places, shopping areas and public facilities by promoting reurbanisation and mixed land use.
- In **communications**: to promote telecommunications in peripheral regions by subsidising investments for telecommunications infrastructure and introducing flat rate (not distance-dependent) telecommunication charges - this is the decentralisation option available to dampen the growth of the largest agglomerations by establishing equivalent service, culture and information work opportunities in small cities and peripheral regions.

Unfortunately national governments and the European Commission today predominantly follow the first, the growth option. However, more and more planners and decision makers begin to realise that the rich countries in the world cannot continue to base their culture on the self-propelling dynamics of unconstrained growth. It would be a great challenge for Europe to demonstrate that there is a future that is both equitable and in balance with nature without excessive and destructive material growth.

References

Bourgeois-Pichat, J., Recent Demographic Change in Western Europe, **Population and Development Review**, vol. 7, 1981, pp.19-42.

Commission of the European Communities, **Europe 2000: Outlook for the Development of the Community's Territory - a Preliminary Overview**, Office for Official Publications of the EC, Luxembourg, 1991.

European Round Table of Industrialists, **Missing Networks: a European Challenge: Proposals for the Renewal of Europe's Infrastructure**, European Round Table of Industrialists, Brussels, 1991.

Group Transport 2000 Plus, **Transport in a Fast Changing Europe: Vers un Reseau Européen des Systèmes de Transport**, Group Transport 2000 Plus, Brussels, 1990.

Masser, I., O. Svidén and M. Wegener, **The Geography of Europe's Futures**, Belhaven Press, London, 1992.

Nijkamp, P., S. Reichman and M. Wegener, M. (eds.), **Euromobile: Transport, Communications and Mobility in Europe**, Avebury, Aldershot, 1990.

RECLUS, **Les Villes 'Européennes'**, Rapport pour la DATAR, La Documentation Française, Paris, 1989.

CHAPTER 3

TRANSPORT, COMMUNICATIONS AND SPATIAL ORGANISATION: CONCEPTUAL FRAMEWORK AND FUTURE TRENDS

Roberta Capello and Andrew Gillespie

3.1 Introduction[1]

Few changes are having a greater impact on the ability of firms and countries to compete in global markets than the recent and on-going revolution in telecommunications and transport. The new capabilities of information processing and transmission, as well as the enhanced mobility of people and the movement of freight, are profoundly altering features upon which the competitiveness of firms and the comparative advantages of regions depend.

The key forces generating a new industrial and spatial structuring are embodied in the radical technological changes currently underway in the telecommunications and transport industries. Communications and transport networks can be regarded as the 'carriers', in both literal and symbolic senses, of new systems of industrial and spatial organisation.

The idea of communications and transport as the carriers of new industrial and spatial forms is of course not new. Many commentators have drawn attention to the historical association between advances in transport and/or communications technologies and changes in the nature of society, changes in the way the economy is organised, and changes in spatial structure and organisation (see, among others, Giaoutzi and Nijkamp, 1988; Soekka et al., 1990; Nijkamp et al., 1990; Brunn and Leinback, 1991; Brotchie et al., 1991; Hepworth and Ducatel, 1991).

In one sense, the very existence of the city can be understood as the spatial response to the severe limitations upon the movement of people, goods, and information which prevailed before, and during the early stages of, the industrial era (see Moses and Williamson, 1967; Walker, 1981). As Schaeffer and Sclar (1975, p.8) put it, "to avoid transportation, mankind invented the city".

In contributing to this debate, our approach contains a number of points of departure from conventional approaches:

(1) first of all, this study is based on a simultaneous analysis of both transport and communications. The analysis of technological innovation which we develop proceeds on the basis of a strong interrelationship existing between transport and telecommunications technologies, an interrelationship witnessed for example by a host of IT applications applied to the transport sector. This relationship goes well beyond simple technological linkages and manifests itself in the joint capacities these technologies have to impact on the spatial structure of the economy;

---

1 This paper is the result of research work by the two authors, R. Capello, who wrote sections 3.1, 3.4 and 3.5, and A. Gillespie who wrote sections 3.2 and 3.3.

(2) secondly, the analysis is based on a constant awareness that, although technological changes in telecommunications and transport are the catalyst for spatial dynamics, they are only necessary but not sufficient conditions for these dynamics. The reason for this assumption is twofold:
- technological changes are developed and generated on the basis of economic, industrial and institutional forces governing their development trajectories. By this we mean, for example, the institutional changes governing the telecommunications sector, which acts in effect as a "gatekeeper" for the development of new information technologies.
- even with a rapid development and diffusion of these new technologies, changes in spatial structure and organisation only take place if they are accompanied by modifications in locational preferences at the level of the firm. This is also true at an industrial level, where locational patterns reflect the industrial and economic equilibria arising from interlinked locational preferences;

(3) another distinct feature of the present study is that despite most frequent analyses trying to capture a direct link between technological changes and spatial patterns, this study stresses the interrelationship between technological changes, new organisational forms of production and spatial trajectories. The organisational variable is regarded as a fundamental and crucial "bridge" to capture the linkages between technological changes and spatial dynamics. The relationship between these three variables are neither linear nor unidirectional, being best regarded as a circular set of interconnections, making the definition of the original causes of changes not easy to define (see section 2 below);

(4) the present study adopts a two level approach, a micro and a macro level, for studying changes in organisational and spatial structures, related respectively to the firm and the industrial system as a whole;

(5) a final characteristic of the analysis is that no single, unique trajectory of change in the industrial and spatial structures can be identified for the future. The development trajectories for these industrial and spatial structures are obviously related to the development of transport and telecommunications technologies, but these in turn depend on the development trajectories of some other crucial elements, including technological innovation, the diffusion and application of technologies throughout the industrial system, and the institutional framework within which diffusion takes place - concerning for example the structure of markets and how they are regulated, standards issues, etc.

These elements can follow a number of different development paths, each of them leading to a different pattern of usage of transport and telecommunication technologies and consequently to the constitution of different industrial and spatial structure scenarios. For these reasons, in this paper we refer to different possible scenarios in the development of the industrial and spatial structure and we consider which of them is most likely to take place, given some key considerations. Before considering these scenarios, however, the next section explores in rather more detail the complex nature of causality in the relationships between transport and communications and spatial organisation.

3.2 Understanding the Interrelationships and the Circular Nature of Causality

As established in the previous section, our concern in this paper is with the nature of the interrelationships between transport and communications on the one hand, and organisational and spatial structures on the other, during a period of major structural change, change which is affecting all of these elements, and the relationships between them, simultaneously. With so many simultaneous changes taking place, understanding the direction(s) of causality is by no means straightforward. In this section, we begin to 'unpack' the complex interrelationships at work, and in so doing attempt to establish the framework which we will use in the following section for presenting a range of future transport and communication scenarios.

Table 1 Major areas of innovation in transport and communication

MODE / MOVEMENT OF	(PHYSICAL) TRANSPORT	(ELECTRONICS) COMMUNICATION
INFORMATION	Express Courier services	High speed fax Electronic mail Computer networks (e.g. for CAD) Videotex/Teletex
PEOPLE	High speed trains Road informatics Information and booking systems	Work stations with slow-scan video images Video-conferencing
GOODS	Logistical systems	EDI Facsimile trasnmission of printed materials Computer networks for just-in-time delivery

One of the driving forces affecting both transport and communications is of course technological innovation (Table 1). The interesting aspect analysed in this paper is that technological innovation is not only affecting the development of transport and communications but also the interrelationship between them. New complementarities, as well as some new substitution possibilities, are being created by innovations in the physical movement of information, people and goods over transport networks, and their electronic communication over telecommunications networks.

From the point of view of our objectives in this paper, however, the significance of the types of technological innovation considered above lies in the way they interact with, or modify, or limit, the behaviour of organisations and, in the longer term, the spatial organisation of the economic system. The complex nature of the interrelationships between these various elements, particularly as concerns causality, can best be illustrated by means of examples. Below three such examples are used to demonstrate the relationships between changes in transport/communications, organisational behaviour and spatial structure. Each has a different causal 'starting point', for there is no single direction of causality, the different elements being bound together in a web of two-way interactions.

Example 1: Technological innovation

The first example starts with a technological innovation, EDI, which is, simultaneously, both a transport/communication innovation, affecting the flow of information associated with the movement of goods, and an organisational innovation, affecting the relationship between customer and supplier. EDI can have significant implications for the behaviour of the firm and for organisational structure more generally; it can contribute to improving the internal efficiency of the firm, through automating existing labour intensive procedures; it can improve the competitive position of adopters, by speeding up their response to customer orders; and, in the longer term, through reducing transaction costs, it can even shift the boundary of the firm by affecting the 'make or buy' decision (see Williamson, 1975).

EDI can also be expected to have implications for the spatial organisation of production systems; by reducing one element of transaction costs, and by improving the overall efficiency of the transactional system, EDI is likely to contribute to the spatial extension of production linkages and, hence, to the viability of global production systems. Further, as EDI becomes more widely adopted and centrally embedded into the organisation of production, the ability of locations to support sophisticated electronic communications for EDI will become a prerequisite for inward investment. In the longer term, therefore, it can be suggested that EDI will affect, at a variety of scales from the urban-rural to the international, the relative locational attractions of different places for productive investments.

Finally, the 'wheel comes full circle' (appropriately enough, given the nature of the example), with these EDI-led organisational and spatial adaptations imposing new requirements upon the transport system, for example to support larger volumes of long distance freight movement.

Example 2: Organisational change

Our second example, based on an actual firm (documented in more detail in Capello and Williams, 1990), breaks into the transport/ communication/ organisational behaviour/ spatial organisation web of interrelationships at a different point; it starts not with a technological innovation but with a perceived need for organisational change. The firm in question, which produces agricultural fertilisers and pesticides, recognised that its marketing effort was inconsistent and fragmented. The existing marketing effort was dispersed around its many production sites, and the firm decided to centralise the marketing function into three sites.

The re-organisation of the marketing function within the firm thus had an explicit spatial dimension, and at once imposed new requirements upon the firms' communications infrastructure. A new computer communication network was implemented, linking the head office with the three new regional sales and marketing offices. At the same time the pattern of business travel within the firm changed substantially, both between the head office and the three marketing centres and between the sales offices and the firm's customers.

Example 3: Spatial restructuring

The final example, like the second an actual firm (documented in more detail in Goddard, 1990), starts from the need to re-organise the spatial structure of the firm, this time in response to a geographical shift in the firm's markets. The firm, based in the north of England and making timber doors and window frames, saw its existing northern market contract substantially with the demise of council-house building in the 1980s. Southern markets were growing vigorously with the boom in 'do-it-yourself', but serving these markets necessited meeting much shorter order-to-delivery cycles than the firm was capable of with its existing production organisation.

The geography of the firm's production organisation was completely restructured, without having to close existing sites or open new ones, and a computer network implemented in order to support a very different set of inter-linkages between the firm's production sites and with its final markets. As a result of this reorganisation, patterns of movement of both intermediate and final products have changed completely, and the volumes of movement substantially increased. The higher transport costs have, however, been more than compensated for by production economies of scale and by the firm's improved responsiveness to customer orders which the computer network has made possible, resulting in increased market share and improved competitiveness.

As these examples demonstrate, there is no single direction of causality in the complex interactions between transport, communications, organisational behaviour and spatial structure. The circle by which they are interconnected can be broken into anywhere, in the sense of a change in any one element of the system then affecting each of the other elements. The 'starting point' adopted in any examination of these interrelationships is nevertheless significant, indicating a choice, a conceptualisation of the main dynamics of the system of interconnections under investigation.

A familiar, indeed conventional, approach to understanding the types of interrelationships with which we are concerned would be to focus on the 'impacts' of new technology; starting therefore with the major changes taking place in the technologies of transport and communications, and following through their impacts upon organisational behaviour and spatial organisation, an approach adopted for example in the EDI case outlined above.

In the remainder of this paper, however, we choose a different starting point, reflecting the conceptualisation with which we started of transport and communications as 'carriers' of particular paradigms of industrial and spatial organisation. Our contention is that Europe is moving towards a new paradigm of industrial and spatial organisation, one which is different in certain key respects from the model of growth which has been hegemonic in Europe since the 1950s, and which we labelled in the introduction as 'Fordism'. Just as transport and communications developed along certain paths during the Fordist era, helping indeed that paradigm to be realised, to be viable, so a new paradigm of economic organisation, a successor to Fordism as it were, will make new demands upon the transport and communications system.

It follows that if we wish to try and understand what transport and communications will be like beyond the immediate and relatively predictable future, say in Europe 2020, then it will be necessary to attempt to understand first what type of industrial and spatial organisation will be prevailing at that time. If we are right in our contention that the present period of restructuring is indicative of a new paradigm of economic organisation, then a reading of what it is that is new about that paradigm (and indeed what it is that is not), at least as it is likely to effect the demand for transport and communications, will be an essential starting point.

This is not of course to deny the strong element of circular causality that we have discussed above, for future developments in transport and communications will no doubt facilitate forms of industrial and spatial organisation which are not currently viable. Our belief, however, is that starting with the changes now occurring in such organisation, and tracing through their implications for transport and communications, will prove to be a better choice in predictive terms than starting with a new technolgy-led prediction of transport and communication in the year 2020, and then trying to read off the 'impacts' they are likely to have on economic and spatial organisation.

We are surely all too familiar with the inadequacies of futurological predictions based on the supposed power of new technologies to 'transform' society and its spatial organisation. The strong element of wishful thinking behind such predictions often seems to be motivated by a sense of frustration with the complexities and perceived inadequacies of society as it is presently constituted. Rather than grappling with these complexities in the real world, how much easier it is to envisage a new society, constituted around the liberating potential of new technology. The field of transport and communications research is not unfamiliar with this type of discourse, which can be regarded as harmless or dangerous depending on your point of view; either way, it is not science, or social science, and should be left to the science fiction shelves.

Our own conceptual preference is then to start not with the impact of changes in transport and communication on economic and spatial organisation, but rather with the less superficially exciting, albeit more challenging, task of considering the implications of changes in economic and spatial organisation for transport and communications.

3.3 Transport and Communications and the Spatial Structure of Fordism

3.3.1 Introduction

The concept of 'Fordism' is a broad and far-reaching attempt to capture the essential characteristics of what the French Regulation School defines as a distinctive 'model of development' under capitalism. According to Leborgne and Lipietz (1988), a model of development involves a conjunction of three sets of relationships; firstly a 'technological paradigm', a set of general principles which govern the evolution of the organisation of labour; secondly, a 'regime of accumulation', the macro-economic principle describing the long-term compatibility between levels of production and of consumption; and, thirdly, a 'mode of regulation', the forms of individual and collective adjustment which enable the regime of accumulation to be sustained.

Fordism is one such conjunction, which Mathews (1991, p.125) suggests "is now seen as the dominant political-economic framework of the twentieth century". This framework or growth model became established in the United States in the inter-war period and diffused to Europe in the period of post-war reconstruction, producing 'a twenty-five year golden age' of capitalism (see Lipietz, 1986), but which has since the 1970s sustained a number of interrelated set-backs which have undermined its continued viability.

The dominant 'technological paradigm' under Fordism can be summarised as one of mass production and Taylorist work organisation, the 'regime of accumulation' that of a mass consumption counterpart to mass production, and the 'mode of regulation' as the combination of collective wage bargaining, the hegemony of large corporations, Keynesian demand management and the welfare state (see Leborgne and Lipietz, 1988; Boyer, 1988). Our concern below is only with the first of these three interlocking elements, that which deals with the organisation of the Fordist system of production. We begin by outlining the main features of this system, paying particular attention to its spatial organisation, before considering Fordism's transport and communications requirements (see Table 2 for a summary and a comparison with the two scenarios presented in section 3).

3.3.2 Fordist industrial and spatial organisation

The basic rationale behind mass production was the reduction of cost by standardising the production of parts, and the use of repetitive methods to substitute for skilled labour. Piore and Sabel (1984) characterise the rise of the mass production system as a first 'industrial divide', differentiating it from craft and batch production methods. Although these previously established forms of industrialisation continued to co-exist with Fordist mass-production, the enormous productivity improvements which the latter made possible rapidly came to dominate in those sectors, such as cars and consumer durables, for which mass markets could be developed. As articulated by Scott (1988): "These sectors, in their classical form, are distinguished by a search for massive internal economies of scale based on assembly line methods, technical divisions of labour and standardisation of outputs. The Fordist elements of the system comprise, in their essentials, the deskilling of labour by means of the fragmentation of work tasks while inte- grating the human operator into the whole machinery of production in such a manner as to reduce to the minimum discretionary control over motions and rhythms of work" (p.173).

The technical embodiment of Fordist production principles, the semi-automatic assembly line (see Aglietta, 1982), can be seen as a device not only for increasing output but, as importantly, for gaining control over the pace and organisation of production, combining the technical requirements of a shift from batch to flow production with a new drive for management control (see Mathews, 1991).

This form of 'hard automation' proved very successful in achieving high rates of productivity growth for standardised, mass produced goods. An appropriate vehicular analogy for Fordist production organisation at this micro-level would be the steamroller; a large, rather cumbersome, but crushingly efficient piece of machinery designed for and dedicated to a particular task, and extremely difficult to deflect once it is in motion. These same characteristics, however, proved rather less effective when the erosion of mass markets and the need for constant product innovation required not a steamroller but an adaptable all-terrain vehicle!

At the level of the industrial system as a whole, Fordism was characterised by large, vertically-integrated firms. Partly this stemmed from the internal economies of scale in production associated with its technological basis, but of considerable importance too was the need to co-ordinate and re-integrate the considerable technical division of labour which Fordism engendered. Quite simply, this co-ordination and re-integration task was more effectively handled, and with lower transaction costs, by the corporate hierarchy than by the external market.

The spatial form of the Fordist system of production organisation was of course integral to that system, for, as Walker (1988, p.385) argues, "it is impossible to separate the organisational from the geographical", as "capitalist organisation is constituted in and through spatial relations". At the broad regional scale, Allan Scott (1988) has described the spatial form of Fordism, at the peak of its development, as:

> "associated with a series of great industrial regions in North America and western Europe, as represented by the Manufacturing Belt of the United States and the zone of industrial development in Europe stretching from the Midlands of England through northern France, Belgium and Holland to the Ruhr of West Germany, with many additional outlying districts at various locations. These locations were the locational foci of propulsive industrial sectors driving forward, through intricate input-output connections, dense systems of upstream producers" (p.173).

The geography of Fordism was associated in particular with major metropolitan regions, for it was the large city that provided the agglomerations of labour required for mass production. However, although this spatial form characterised what we might describe as 'early' Fordism, its spatial expression evolved and changed over time. Schoenberger (1988, p.255) suggests that this evolutionary tendency involved a shift from "initial massive industrial agglomerations in the core to decentralisation and increasing dispersal of production towards the periphery".

This shift reflects an internal dynamic within Fordist production which, more so than any previous form of industrialisation, came to use space and spatial differentiation as active elements of accumulation (see Harvey, 1987). The Taylorist principles of work organisation embodied in the Fordist mass production system involved a constant search for ways of improving profitability through the division of labour. The 'technical disintegration' of the production process, into separate shops within a plant and then into an interplant division of labour, was so sharp that it could be increasingly realised as a 'territorial disintegration' (see Leborgne and Lipietz, 1988), in which different plants could be optimally located according to the type of labour they needed.

The spatial form of the industrial system thus underwent significant changes with the evolution of Fordism. The earlier form of geographical specialisation based on sectors became a functional specialisation associated with the increasing refinement of the division of labour within the firm, with certain regions coming to specialise as centres of corporate control, others as concentrations of research and development, others as semi- or un-skilled production 'branch plants' (see Hymer, 1972; Lipietz, 1975; Massey, 1984). The 'spatial division of labour' within 'late' Fordism soon became international as well as interregional, as the progressive deskilling of elements within the production process enabled the large vertically integrated Fordist corporation to take advantage of even cheaper unskilled labour in the Third World periphery (see Frobel et al., 1980; Lipietz, 1986).

3.3.3 Fordism's transport and communications requirements

The increasingly complex spatial organisation of production which evolved under Fordism imposed very considerable requirements upon the transport and communications system (Table 2). Indeed, it is clear that the pattern of production characterised above as 'late Fordism', with its high degree of territorial disaggregation and dispersed production, would not have been viable without significant innovation in both transport and telecommunications. As noted by Frobel et al. (1980, p.36), in their analysis of the new international division of labour, this form of industrial development is predicated upon "a technology which renders industrial location and the management of production itself largely independent of geographical distance".

How, and to what extent, were these requirements met? In the transport field, significant improvements have taken place since the 1960s which have benefited exactly the type of long-distance, regular, standardised commodity flow demanded by the (late) Fordist production system (see Pedesen, 1985). Containerisation, and the long-distance motorway networks which have so facilitated freight movement by truck, can be regarded then as the necessary transport concomitants of Fordist production organisation. As Van Hoogstraten and Janssen (1985) have argued in the case of the Netherlands:

> "it is more than contingent that the generalisation of the network of motorways, spread from the western part of The Netherlands over the rest, has run concurrently with the decentralisation of production".

In addition to the routinised long-distance movement of intermediate and final production, Fordism also required that reliable systems of voice communication be in place to permit the long-distance control and co-ordination of spatially dispersed production. Beyond voice telephony, the advent of computer networking in the 1970's clearly further facilitated the process of decentralisation. Thus according to Perrons (1981, p.251), "neo-Fordist labour processes, based on electronic information systems with automatic feedback mechanisms...meant that locations in peripheral areas were technically feasible".

Table 2 **Mean features of the past industrial and spatial organisation and of the two possible future scenarios: infrastructure requirements and policy options**

TYPES OF ORGANISATION / FEATURES AND POLICY OPTIONS	FORDIST ORGANISATION	FLEXIBLE SPECIALISATION SCENARIO	LOCAL-GLOBAL SCENARIO
INDUSTRIAL ORGANISATION	Economies of scale	Economies of scope	New equilibrium between economies of scale and scope
Micro	Mass production	Small batch production	Diversified mass production
	Hard automation	Soft automation	Systems automation
Macro	Vertically integrated systems	Vertically disintegrated systems	Quasi-vertical integration Network firms
	Large firms dominated	Firms network	Asymmetrical but stable linkage arrangements between producers and suppliers
SPATIAL ORGANISATION	Spatial division of labour within multilocational enterprises	Spatial clustering	New management of territory (same geography of the economic space of the firm with different functional locations) New logistical platforms
TRANSPORT AND COMMUNICATION PATTERNS	Long distance intermediate product movement to assembly sites	Long distance final product movement to markets	Long distance movement of both intermediate and final products
	Regional functional specialisation	Short distance intermediate product movement	Increase in horizontal inter-corporate information flows
INFRASTRUCTURE REQUIREMENTS	Reliable long distance goods transport of standard quantity predictable in advance Reliable long distance communications	Frequent face-to-face contacts Long distance flexible final product movements Increased short distance frequent intermediate transport system	Long distance air-freight and other long distance goods movements coupled with short distance frequent delivery road based on local systems Long distance computer networks
POLICY OPTIONS AND PRIORITIES		Development of regional transport system and digitalised local networks	Development of long distance transport and computer networks

The vertically integrated nature of Fordist production organisation places considerable emphasis on intra-corporate flows of information. One of the main requirements of Fordism in terms of communications infrastructure is, in consequence, the provision of point-to-point voice and computer networks by means of leased circuits. The evidence concerning the geography of computer networking in the U.K. shows that such networks are indeed used almost exclusively for intra-organisational communication (see Daniels, 1987), and suggests further that the use of dedicated private circuits is highest in those regions most clearly associated with the type of decentralised branch plant production associated with the late Fordist spatial division of labour (see Diamond and Spence, 1989).

The Fordist system of production organisation thus placed very considerable demands on transport and communication infrastructures and networks. Leaving aside the (rather sterile and probably unresolvable) question of whether the requirements of Fordism stimulated the necessary innovation and infrastructure investment, or whether this innovation and investment 'led' the development of new forms of production organisation which evolved in order to exploit the new opportunities, it can be concluded that Fordism is clearly associated with major improvements in long-distance transport and communication.

Without such improvements, it is evident that the model of decentralised production organisation that we have characterised above as late Fordism would not have been viable, for this model demanded both the efficient long-distance movement of intermediate goods as well as final production, and the space transcending control and co-ordination of complex multilocational enterprises.

3.3.4 The crisis of Fordist production organisation

There is by now a substantial body of literature on the reasons why the Fordist system of mass production ran, in the 1970s and 1980s, into increasing problems. Some see the break up of mass markets due to changing consumer taste as the key; others the undermining of Fordism's production heartlands by the rise of low wage industrialisation in the Third World; others again the technical rigidities of Fordist production organisation itself.

The idea of Fordism reaching limits determined by its own internal logic is associated in particular with the French Regulation school, following and building upon the work of Aglietta (1982). He concentrated on the limits of Taylorist task fragmentation, and on the technical limitations of the assembly line in a period of unstable market conditions. Roobeek (1987) sees Fordism as coming up against a series of problems of control, problems which include not only the control over the labour process within the factory but also control over the complex spatial divisions of labour which Fordist production organisation had engendered.

Although improvements in transport and communications had been instrumental in the emergence and evolution of Fordist production organisation, there were clearly limits to the Fordist system's ability to transcend space and to overcome distance. As with so many of the other charcteristics of Fordism, these limits became critical when more volatile and segmented market conditions necessitated much greater flexibility and responsivesness. Responses to the crisis of Fordism would thus need to address, inter alia, the limitations imposed by spatial organisation and by transport and communication systems. It is to these responses, to the possible successors to Fordism, that we now turn.

3.4 Transport and Communications and the Possible Successors to Fordism

3.4.1 A re-invigorated 'neo-Fordism'?

One significant possibility which needs evaluating is that developments in transport and communications networks and systems can help to resolve the crisis of Fordist production organisation. Following Piore and Sabel (1984), Rubery et al. (1987) argues that competitive success now depends not on achieving economies of scale in established mass markets, but rather on securing new markets, developing new competitive strategies for meeting changing demand requirements, and increasing the responsivesness of the organisation to market changes. One of the present authors has suggested elsewhere (see Gillespie and Williams, 1990; Gillespie, 1991) that developments in telematics offer important possibilities of achieving a more 'flexible Fordism'.

The scope for establishing a re-invigorated form of neo-Fordism has been considered in a number of recent contributions (see, for example, Leborgne and Lipietz, 1988; Mathews, 1991). However, even if some of the control and co-ordination problems of Fordism can be overcome by means of innovation in transport and communications systems, there remain questions over the long term viability of Fordist principles of production organisation. As Mathews (1991, p.131-132) contends:

> "Fordism, with its Taylorist fragmentation of jobs, deskilling and divorce of conception from execution, is becoming less and less relevant. It was 'productive' and 'efficient' only under the very special conditions prevailing within mass production".

In the new reality of segmented, rapidly changing markets, in which a considerable competitive premium is placed upon product innovation and upon responsiveness to market shifts, the hierarchical fragmentation of the Fordist system of production organisation is simply no longer optimal. This of course is not to deny that 'Fordist' enterprises can adapt to the changing circumstances, and re-establish the basis for profitable production, as many clearly have been able to do. We would argue, however, that in so doing they have shed many of the key defining characteristics of Fordism. In the remainder of this paper, we turn our attention to two different interpretations of a post-Fordist industrial future, and to the transport and communication implications of these competing scenarios.

3.4.2 The 'Flexible Specialisation' scenario

3.4.2.1 Industrial and spatial organisation

The 'flexible specialisation' model of industrial organisation was formulated by Piore and Sabel (1984), drawing upon an interpretation of developments in the so-called 'Third Italy'. Conceptually, this model rests on the assumption that the economic weaknesses of Fordism need to be overcome, and a new industrial and spatial structure of the economy established, possessing a number of different, indeed oppositional, characteristics to that of Fordism. Thus if Fordism was primarily concerned with mass production and mass consumption and with the exploitation of economies of scale, the flexible specialisation scenario rests on the idea of product customisation, volatility of markets and demand, and the exploitation of economies of scope (Table 2).

Because of its oppositional view to Fordism, this school of thought is heralding, indeed often celebrating, a 'post-Fordist' future, one which marks a radical change and a break with the previous model of industrial development. It is at once evident that the 'second industrial divide' predicted by Piore and Sabel conceptually implies the development of a new industrial order, in which the industrial and spatial forces of equilibrium are related to quite different economic and industrial features and to new corporate strategies. Moreover, associated with the flexible specialisation scenario is the potential for the different development pattern of transport and communications systems, because of the different transactional and relational economic structures they will be required to support.

The generation of this scenario will thus have profound implications for both the micro and the macro level. At the micro level, the emergence of the 'flexible specialisation' system rests on the assumption that mass production will be replaced by an industrial organisational model concerned rather with small batch production, regarded as a more suitable model of production organisation for dealing with dynamic markets, displaying both high levels of vulnerability and volatility of demand.

A consequent outcome of batch production is the exploitation of economies of scope rather than the traditional economies of scale (directly concerned with mass production and consumption). Economies of scope are those economies of joint production resulting from the use of a single set of facilities to produce, or process, more than one product, under dynamic market conditions (see Chandler, 1986; Teece, 1980; Jelinek and Goldhar, 1983).

Moreover, the flexible specialisation scenario will generate a radical shift of demand away from mass consumption products in favour of differentiated, personalised outputs. Demand for a variety of products will increasingly replace demand for cheap and standardised products, and this will create more scope for the development of small, specialised firms. Demand needs will then more and more generate a process of customisation of products, thus rejecting the idea of mass production and favouring a more differentiated production model.

In this scenario, the functional specialisation of Fordism will be substituted by functional integration, conceptually overcoming once again the limits of the present structure. It has in fact long been recognised by organisation scholars that the profound functional specialisation of the large enterprise, designed to achieve economies of scale and higher professional know-how, presents the risk of internal segmentation and bureaucratisation, and in particular a loss in terms of the efficient exploitation of information arising from everyday operations in each department (see Camagni, 1988). A functional integration model can, it is argued, overcome this inefficient and rigid structure, a structure which is completely inadequate in periods of high market volatility. Cross-functional work can generate useful synergies between functions, especially in terms of innovation.

The model of the large hierarchical firm, designed to be the most efficient industrial model of production, will increasingly give way to more decentralised organisational forms, in which the transfer of intermediate responsibility to lower levels in the organisation takes place, assisted by the capabilities of the new technologies. By facilitating online remote communication and decision-support, these technologies can help to decentralise decision-making processes to peripheral areas and to lower organisational levels.

All of these changes in intrafirm organisation are supported and fostered by developments in so-called "soft" automation, by which is meant automation technologies consisting of a high percentage of software components and with a high reprogrammability capacity. The exploitation of economies of scope can be achieved only through the use of reprogrammable technologies, able to produce a variety of products with the same capital resource.

Major changes will also affect the industrial system as a whole, and, once again, the new rules governing the industrial and spatial structure of the economy will have characteristics that are opposed in many ways to those that prevailed under Fordism.

The large firm model of the vertically-integrated firm, with its strongly centralised decision-making power, will be substituted by vertically-disintegrated systems, based on a series of specialised medium-sized and small firms. Under this scenario we can thus envisage a radical segmentation of markets, reconstituted into "firm networks": a group of small and medium sized firms, legally independent from one another, but very much vertically-integrated within a particular production process through co-operative-interfirm linkages. Moreover, these interfirm linkages are likely to be based on single sourcing relationships (see Burns and Stalker, 1979; Antonelli, 1988).

On the basis of the characteristics of this industrial system it is relatively easy to configure its future spatial structure. The high degree of specialisation of interlinked firms will lead towards the development of complementary regional and urban systems, specialised in different final products and based on local specialised labour market needs (see Moulaert and Swyngedouw, 1988).

A spatial clustering will be the expected consequence, characterised by frequent linkages taking place over short distances; the development of specialised local areas, or 'industrial districts', such as Prato and Silicon Valley, in which the industrial system is governed by a high level of product specialisation, can be regarded as contemporary exemplars of the flexible specialisation scenario (see Becattini, 1988; Scott, 1988; Camagni and Capello, 1990).

3.4.2.2 Transport and communications patterns and infrastructure requirements: policy options and priorities

The picture of the industrial and spatial system drawn above is the basis for the configuration of possible transport and communications development patterns, their future infrastructure requirements and appropriate policy options to support this scenario (summarised in Table 2).

The high specialisation level achieved by firms and production areas will generate long distance final product movement to markets, because of the highly spatially segmented market division. For intermediate goods, conversely, the spatial clustering phenomenon and the development of local industrial districts will result in short distance intermediate product movements (cf. Pedersen, 1985).

Another consequence of the spatial clustering and of the development of local districts is the frequent, short-distance movement of people involved in meetings; frequent face-to-face contact can be regarded as essential for generating and maintaining the cooperative and trust-based relationships upon which the flexible specialisation model of production organisation rests. For sales and marketing activities, conversely, long distance travel is to be expected, necessary because of local (urban and regional) product specialisation and of the high degree of market segmentation.

Vertically disintegrated systems require a well developed information axis, around which both inter- and intracorporate information flows will be transmitted. These information flows, both intra- and intercorporate, will be used primarily to transport horizontal information, i.e. information among functions at the same level in the hierarchical structure, or, in the case of intercorporate information flows, among firms at the same level in the production chain. This type of highly specialised and disintegrated production system requires a strong mechanism to ensure synergies, both between functions and firms, resting on a well-developed information system.

These patterns of transport and communication - of goods, people and information - require a future implementation of transport and communications systems able to cope with and support the new industrial and spatial structures. Unpredictable, fluctuating quantities of goods movement, for example, require a highly flexible transport system, able to cope with frequent movements of small quantities, rather than with the predictable, less frequent, larger volumes of transported goods that characterised Fordism.

The highly disintegrated local districts' model will thus increase both short distance, frequent, intermediate product movements as well as long distance, frequent, final product movements, and will necessitate reliable, frequent, regional interconnected passenger transport networks, efficient local telephone and fax networks and local computer networks.

Considerable effort is already being made in Europe to up-grade and improve long-distance transport and telecommunication networks. Consequent to the above discussion, however, a further important policy priority in the future development of transport and communications infrastructures would be to focus on the upgrading of local and regional transport and communications systems; the development of regional and metropolitan light railway networks, for example, or local digital telematics networks.

The Sprint project, developed in the Prato area (a local district in Italy), provides an interesting example of the latter. The attempt has been to create a local digitalised computer network, interconnecting all economic agents of the area and providing them with a local intercompany networked information axis (see De Braband and Manacorda, 1985; Mazzonis, 1985; Rullani and Zanfei, 1988; Zanfei, 1986). The failure of the Sprint project can be explained, first, by its premature appearance in an area without a developed telematics culture and, second, by the threat it posed to the established power relationships embodied in the existing transactional structure (see Camagni and Capello, 1993; Capello and Williams, 1992). However, in the 'flexible specialisation' scenario of the future such limits will be likely to be overcome, both by a diffused telematics culture and by profound changes in the division of labour, in which more symetrical and synergetic horizontal linkages will become established.

The development of this scenario will inevitably heighten the tension between the frequent freight movements required and the capacity of the road network to absorb such movements. Consequently, policy priorities should also be given to projects designed to improve roads at regional and national levels.

3.4.3 The 'Network Firm' or 'Global-Local' scenario

3.4.3.1 Industrial and spatial organisation

Some doubts must remain over the prospects for both the 'neo-Fordism' and the 'flexible specialisation' scenarios. While the first rests on the assumption that the 'crisis of Fordism' can be internally resolved and overcome, and a new or at least modified regime built upon the old industrial and spatial organisation, paradoxically the flexible specialisation scenario is based on the over-idealistic view that a completely different industrial and spatial structure can be developed, with completely opposite features from those of Fordism (see Amin and Robins, 1990 for a critique of the empirical and theoretical validity of the flexible specialisation scenario). Whereas the neo-Fordism view thus maintains that little of importance has changed, the flexible specialisation view maintains that little of importance remains. Our own view lies somewhere between these oppositional extremes. On the basis of empirical evidence supporting it, a third and more likely scenario can be envisaged, which we term the 'network firm' or 'global-local' scenario, built on the assumption that the inadequacies of Fordist mass production are overcome, but with less radically oppositional outcomes than those predicted (advocated?) by the flexible specialisation school.

This intermediate position is likely to appear both at micro and macro levels (Table 2). At the micro level, instead of envisaging the exploitation of either economies of scope or of scale, a new equilibrium between the two will be more likely. In fact, the development of economies of scope stem from the exploitation of reprogrammable production technologies, which require very substantial capital investment, thus necessarily requiring large scale production to be economically viable; ie. the exploitation of economies of scale. Thus, instead of completely substituting for economies of scale, economies of scope will rather complement and co-exist, exploited not only in the 'information handling activities sphere' (see Jonscher, 1983), but also in the area of production activities (see Capello and Williams, 1990).

Moreover, empirical evidence suggests that the development of new industrial systems strengthens a 'quasi-vertical integration' as the most efficient organisational form of production. There are various intermediate forms of 'quasi-organisation' that are assuming an ever more important role as an alternative to full vertically-integrated or vertically-disintegrated production systems. In the terminology of Williamson (1975), these intermediate forms of organisation will arise between the two opposite alternatives of "make or buy", and can be described as the "make-together" alternative (see Camagni and Rabellotti, 1988).

The "make-together" type of organisational form rests on the need to create synergies and complementarities through partnerships, due in part to the increased complexity and specialisation of products and markets. The traditional models of the large, vertically-integrated company on the one hand, and of the small, autonomous, single-phase firm on the other, will be replaced by a new type of large 'network firm', with strongly centralised strategic functions and extending in several directions, and by a new type of small enterprise, integrated into a multicompany local network. Across the network, a system of constantly evolving power relationships governs both the dynamics of innovation and the appropriability of returns to the partners involved.

The 'network firm' will be attracted towards diversified mass production, which is the result of the contemporary exploitation of economies of both scope and scale, and by 'systems automation'; i.e. not isolated 'islands of automation', but rather integrated automation systems, through local area networks (LANs) or wide area networks (WANs). Moreover, the integration process will take place between currently stand-alone procedures, with the positive consequence of an automation of intersphere and interfunction procedures. At the level of bureaucratic procedures, then, functional integration is likely to occur. The 'network firm' will inevitably centralise control at the level of strategic functions, but with the implementation of modern technologies, control over bureaucratic and routinised functions will be decentralised.

The industrial system coming out of this scenario is a reinforcement and generalisation of the concept of the 'network firm', consisting of large firms, leading in their respective market specialisation, competing with a host of smaller firms. At the level of suppliers, the existence of a 'network firm' will generate asymmetrical but stable linkage arrangements, the asymmetry depending necessarily on the unequal division of power among competing firms.

With respect to spatial organisation, the outcome which can be envisaged from this scenario is far less dramatic and severe in its changes than the one suggested above by the 'flexible specialisation' scenario. Despite the widespread assumption that the intrinsic capacities of new transport and communications technologies will reshape the geography of firms, it can be argued that the spatial extent of firms will remain, or at least could remain, largely the same.

This assertion is backed by empirical evidence, which suggests that a very different spatial organisation can be achieved without the relocation of activities (see Goddard, 1991). On the contrary, what will change is the way in which firms exploit their economic space, putting in place a new management of territory within the existing locational parameters of the firm (see Williams and Taylor, 1991). In particular, following efficiency and effectiveness aims, firms will try to rationalise their fixed locational assets by physically integrating previously disjointed functions, thereby achieving better economic performance.

Another way of using and exploiting territory more effectively is through the development of new logistical systems, which may well lead to adjustments in the geography of corporate space. The development of central locations for stored goods helps in rationalising materials purchases and intermediate goods movements, the efficiency of which derives from highly computerised storage systems (see Ruijgrok, 1990).

3.4.3.2 Transport and communications and infrastructure requirements: policy options and priorities

A different development pattern emerges from this third configuration of a possible industrial and spatial system (Table 2). This scenario requires long distance movement of both intermediate and final products, accompanied by an increase in short distance final product movement, co-ordinated through new logistical systems. The consequence is a more intense movement of both intermediate and final products from production sites to storage centres and from them to the final market. Globalisation of markets strengthens this phenomenon, augmenting the spatial distribution of products and thus their physical movements.

A rather strong pressure for long distance business travel derives from this scenario, necessitating high volumes of movement between firms and (spatially diffused) customers, and between functions of multi-site firms (each of which is expected to be located in one place, avoiding duplication and thus inefficiency). The 'network firm' scenario additionally implies a high volume of business travel associated with cooperative agreements, which may well be international in scope, complemented by well developed and advanced satellite-based video-conferencing systems.

Moreover, the "make together" form of organisation implies a high volume of information transmitted between firms, in the form of horizontal intercorporate information flows. At the same time, high volumes of vertical intercorporate information flows characterise this scenario, corresponding to the information requirements for asymmetrical but stable linkages with suppliers. Intensive intracorporate information flows will also be necessary in order to develop the types of 'new management of territory' outlined above, involving the relocation of part functions in one place, thus rationalising decision-making processes. It is clear that with such a relocation of activities in space, firms will need a constant flow of information, both horizontally (to develop decision making processes) and vertically (because of the decentralised control system).

From the above discussion, a simple consideration comes immediately to mind concerning the infrastructure requirements associated with this scenario. In an industrial and spatial system based on intense long distance movement of people, goods and information, a wide range of transport and communications systems infrastructures will be necessary, including air-freight systems, short distance frequent-delivery road based local systems, high speed trains, air passenger travel, long distance computer networks, and advanced personal communication services (i.e. videoconferencing, electronic mail).

Some clear policy priorities emerge from this scenario and from these infrastructure requirements. All policies enhancing long distance transport and communications infrastructures are this respect useful and efficient policies. The development of international computer networks with Electronic Data Interchange (EDI) applications will be required to deal with the mass of information associated with the new logistical platforms, as will the implementation of ISDN (the Integrated Services Digital Network). With respect to this scenario, then, a top-down policy approach to the development of advanced networks, rather than the bottom-up local network approach embodied in the previous scenario, is much more effective and efficient, dealing with the implementation of international 'information highways' rather than local telematics networks and applications.

This scenario has then clear implications for the development of transport and communications infrastructures. Not only is this new industrial and spatial scenario built on the assumption that long distance, reliable transport and communications networks are implemented, but it rests on the idea that these networks have to be 'integrated networks', both geographically and technologically speaking.

The integration of these networks permits the development of the industrial and spatial system outlined above, for a 'quasi-vertically integrated' form of organisation requires both an advanced communications infrastructure and a highly reliable complementary transport system.

The integration has to take place at both a geographical and technological level. At a spatial level, we are referring primarily to international networks, designed for long distance transport and communications. Networks which are confined to national territories, whether for the movement of information or people, will be of limited use in sustaining the types of industrial organisation predicted under the network firm or global-local scenario. Technological integration is clearly vital for the development of international interconnected networks. Standards problems have to be overcome, both in the telecommunications and transport arenas, in order for genuinely border-less infrastructures to be developed.

With respect to this issue, a group of international experts have developed a project on 'Missing Networks in Europe' for the Round Table of Industrialists, primarily concerned with identifying the discontinuities which exist in international networks, both in transport and communications sectors. The result has pointed out that both telecommunications and transport networks could perform much better if missing networks were addressed, at five different levels (see Maggi et al., 1992):

- hardware (physical infrastructure)
- software (logistics and information)
- orgware (institutional and organisational setting)
- finware (financial and funding arrangements)
- ecoware (environmental and safety effects)

The interest in avoiding 'missing networks' becomes more crucial once a spatial and industrial system is envisaged in which economic transactions are developed primarily at an international scale and where synergies among firms take place globally.

3.5 Conclusions and Policy Recommendations

Of the three scenarios presented above, the most likely appears to be what we have described as the 'network firm' or 'global-local' scenario. There are few grounds for expecting that the Fordist model could be re-invigorated, even if some of its limits and weaknesses could be overcome. Once the nature of markets and of the regulatory system has shifted, as they have clearly done with Fordism, there are few reasons to suggest that the old system with its attendent model of production could return. However, the 'rejection' of the Fordist model for the future does not need to lead to accepting the directly opposing model envisaged in the 'flexible specialisation' scenario. This scenario is idealistic but unrealistic, with little empirical evidence to suggest that we are moving towards this kind of regulatory system. On the contrary, the empirical evidence suggests rather a third kind of scenario, an intermediate model of production between the assumed rigidity of Fordism and the anticipated flexibility of 'post-Fordism'.

Some clear policy recommendations for the transport and communications infrastructure can be drawn, on the assumption that the 'global-local' scenario is the one most likely to be represented in Europe "2020".

The transport and communications infrastructure requirements of this scenario go well beyond the geographical and technological integration of networks. The 'global-local' scenario rests on the assumption that a complete integration between transport and communication networks will be developed. The increasing importance of standardisation and harmonisation refers not only to the two sectors separately, but also to their co-integration. The strength of infrastructural development in this scenario is related to the implementation of technological and geographical integration of elements in both the transportation and communication systems.

Spatial planning of transport infrastructure needs therefore to be developed in conjunction with the territorial planning of communications infrastructure. An efficient and reliable logistical system requires a contemporary existence of both advanced telecommunications systems and transportation networks. Integrated logistical systems require information systems and communication facilities that lead to improved control possibilities and to more efficient deliveries of stored goods in time and space (see Ruijgrok, 1990).

A final consideration concerns the need for integrated transport and communication systems to be developed in conjunction with broader spatial (urban and regional) planning. Only in this way will transport and communication networks be developed on the basis of the real needs and necessities of the newly emerging industrial and spatial system. This assumption refers to the idea that transport and communication technologies in themselves are not sufficient forces for generating indigenous local economic development. On the contrary, they have to be thought of as strategic instruments to be exploited with reference to broader spatial economic planning. In this way, supply-driven transport and communications projects with little or no connection to real demand requirements and needs can be avoided, and the future development of these leading technological infrastructures can be conceived rather in terms of their contribution to the creation of an integrated economic system for 'Europe 2020'.

References

Aglietta, M., **Regulation et Crises du Capitalisme: l'Experience des Etats Unis,** Calmann-Levy, second edition, Paris, 1982.

Amin, A. and K. Robins, The Re-emergence of Regional Economies? The Mythical Geography of Flexible Accumulation, **Society and Space: Environment and Planning D**, 8(1), 1990, pp.7-34.

Antonelli, C. (ed.), **New Information Technology and Industrial Change: The Italian Case,** Kluwer Academic Publishers, London, 1988.

Aydalot, P. and D. Keeble (eds.), **High Technology Industry and Innovative Environments: The European Experience**, Routledge, London, 1988.

Becattini, G. (ed.), **Mercato e Forze Locali: il Distretto Industriale**, Il Mulino, Bologna, 1988.

Boyer, R., Technical Change and the Theory of 'Regulation', **Technical Change and Economic Theory** (G. Dosi, C. Freeman, R. Nelson, G. Silverberg and L. Soete, eds.), Frances Pinter, London, 1988, pp.608-630.

Brotchie, J., M. Batty, P. Hall and P. Newton (eds.), **Cities of the 21st Century**, Halstead Press, Longman, Cheshire, 1991.

Brunn, S.D. and T.R. Leinbach, **Collapsing Space and Time: Geographic Aspects of Communication and Information,** Harper Collins Academic, London, 1991.

Burns, T.J. and G.M. Stalker, **Direzione Aziendale ed Innovazione**, Franco Angeli, Milan, 1979.

Camagni, R., Functional Integration and Locational Shifts in New Technology Industry, **High Technology Industry and Innovative Environments: The European Experience** (P. Aydalot, and D. Keeble, eds.), Routledge, London, 1988, pp.48-64.

Camagni, R. and R. Capello, Towards a Definition of the Manoeuvring Space of Local Development Initiatives: Italian Success Stories of Local Development - Theoretical Conditions and Practical Experience, **Global Challenge and Local Response** (W. Stohr, ed.), Mansell, London, 1990, pp.328-353.

Camagni, R. and R. Capello, Nuove Tecnologie di Comunicazione e Cambiamenti nella Localizzazione delle Attivita Industriali, **Nuove Tecnologie dell'Informazione e Sistemi Urbani** (S. Lombardo, ed.), La Nuova Italia Scientifica, Rome, 1993 (forthcoming).

Camagni, R. and R. Rabellotti, L'Innovazione Macro-Organizzativa nel Settore Tessile-Abbigliamento, **Sviluppo e Organizzazione**, 108, 1991, pp.2-8.

Capello, R. and H. Williams, Nuove Strategie d'Impresa, Nuovi Sistemi Spazial e Nuove Tecnologie dell'Informazione come Strumenti di Riduzione della Incertezza, **Economia e Politica Industriale**, 67, 1990, pp.43-70.

Capello, R. and H. Williams, Computer Network Trajectories and Organisational Dynamics: A Cross-National Review, **The Economics of Information Networks** (C. Antonelli, ed.), Elsevier, London, 1992, pp.347-362.

Chandler, A., Scale and Scope: the Dynamics of Industrial Enterprise, research paper, 1986 (mimeo).

Daniels, W.W., **Workplace Industrial Relations and Technical Change**, Frances Pinter, London, 1987.

De Braband, F. and P. Manacorda, Scenario Telematico e Territorio: Lettura di un 'Esperienza in Corso, Research Report, October 1985.

Diamond, D. and N. Spence, **Infrastructural and Industrial Costs in British Industry**, Report for the Department of Trade and Industry, HMSO, London, 1988.

Frobel, F., J. Heinrichs and O. Kreye, **The New International Division of Labour**, CUP, Cambridge, 1980.

Giaoutzi, M. and P. Nijkamp (eds.), **Informatics and Regional Development**, Avebury, Aldershot, 1988.

Gillespie, A.E., Advanced Communications Networks, Territorial Integration and Local Development, **Innovation Networks: Spatial Perspectives** (R. Camagni, ed.), Belhaven Press, London, 1991, pp.214-229.

Gillespie, A.E. and H.P. Williams, Telematics and the Reorganisation of Corporate Space, **Telematics, Transportation and Spatial Development** (H.M. Soekkha, P.H.L. Bovy, P. Drewe and G.R.M. Jansen, eds.), VSP, Utrecht, 1990, pp.257-274.

Goddard, J.B., The Geography of the Information Economy, PICT Policy Research Paper No 11, **Programme on Information and Communications Technologies**, ESRC, London, 1991.

Harvey, D., Flexible Accumulation Through Urbanisation: Reflections on Post-Modernism in the American City, **Antipode**, 19, 1987, pp.260-286.

Hepworth, M. and K. Ducatel, **Transport in the Information Society**, Belhaven Press, London, 1991.

Hoogstraten, P. van and B. Janssen, New forms of Industrialisation and Material Infrastructure in the Netherlands, 1985 (mimeo).

Hymer, S. The Multinational Corporation and the Law of Uneven Development, **Economics and World Order** (J. Bhagwati, ed.), Free Press, New York, 1972, pp.113-140.

Jelinek, M. and J. Golhar, The Interface Between Strategy and Manufacturing Technology, **Columbia Journal of World Business**, Spring, 1983, pp.26-36.

Jonscher, C., Information Resources and Economy Productivity, **Information Economics and Policy**, n. 1, 1983, pp.13-35.

Leborgne, D. and A. Lipietz, New Technologies, New Modes of Regulation: Some Spatial Implications, **Society and Space: Environment and Planning D**, 6, 1988, pp. 263-280.

Lipietz, A., Structuration de l'Espace, Probleme Foncier et Amenagement du Territoire, **Environment and Planning A**, 7, 1975, pp.415-425; English translation in: **Regions in Crisis** (J. Carney, R. Hudson and J. Lewis, eds.), Croom Helm, Beckenham, Kent, 1980, pp.60-75.

Lipietz, A., New Tendencies in the International Division of Labour: Regimes of Accumulation and Modes of Regulation, **Production, Work, Territory: The Geographical Anatomy of Industrial Capitalism** (A.J. Scott and M. Storper, eds.), Allen & Unwin, Boston, 1986, pp.16-40.

Maggi, R., I. Masser and P. Nijkamp, Missing Networks in Europe, **Transport Reviews**, vol. 12, no. 4, 1992, pp. 311-321.

Massey, D., **Spatial Divisions of Labour**, Macmillan, London, 1984.

Mathews, J., Mass production, The Fordist System and its Crisis, **Understanding Technology in Education** (H. Mackay, M. Young and J. Beynon, eds.), Falmer Press, London, 1991, pp.109-144.

Mazzonis, D., A Project for Innovation in Prato, paper presented at the workshop of San Miniato, November 28-30, 1985.

Moses, L. and H.F. Williamson, The Location of Economic Activity in Cities, **American Economic Review**, 57, 1988, pp.211-222.

Moulaert, F. and E. Swyngedouw, A Regulation Approach to the Geography of the Flexible Production System, **Society and Space: Environment and Planning D**, 7, 1988, pp.327-345.

Nijkamp, P., S. Reichman and M. Wegener (eds.), **Euromobile: Transport, Communications and Mobility in Europe**, Avebury, Aldershot, 1990.

Nijkamp, P. and I. Salomon, Future Spatial Impacts of Telecommunications, **Transportation Planning and Technology**, vol. 13, 1989, pp.275-287.

Pedersen, P.O., **Communication and Spatial Interaction in an Area of Advanced Technology - with Special Emphasis on the Goods Transport**, Paper presented at the ESF Workshop on Transport Planning in an Era of Change, Zandvoort, April 1985.

Perrons, D., The Role of Ireland in the New International Division of Labour: A Proposed Framework for Regional Analysis, **Regional Studies**, 15, 2, 1981, pp.81-100.

Piore, M. and C.F. Sabel, **The Second Industrial Divide: Possibilities for Prosperity**, Basic Books, New York, 1984.

Roobeek, A.J., The Crisis in Fordism and the Rise of a New Technical Paradigm, **Futures**, 19(2), 1987, pp.217-231.

Rubery, J., R. Tarling and F. Wilkinson, Flexibility, Marketing and the Organisation of Production, **Labour and Society**, 12, 1, 1987, pp.131-151.

Ruijgrok, C., Recent Developments in Logistics, Information Technologies and Spatial Systems, **Informatics and Regional Development**, (M. Giaoutzi and P. Nijkamp, eds.), Avebury, Aldershot, 1988, pp.103-110.

Ruijgrok, C., Telematics in the Goods Logistics Process, **Telematics, Transportation and Spatial Development** (H. Soekkha, P.H.L. Bovy, P. Drewe and G.R.M. Jansen, eds.), VSP, Utrecht, 1990, pp.187-195.

Rullani, E. and A. Zanfei, Networks between Manufacturing and Demand: Cases from Textile and Clothing Industries, **New Information Technology and Industrial Change: The Italian Case** (C. Antonelli, ed.), Kluwer Academic Publisher, London, 1988, pp.97-114.

Schaeffer, K.H. and E. Sclar, **Access for All: Transportation and Urban Growth**, Pelican, Harmondsworth, Middlesex, 1975.

Schoenberger, E., From Fordism to Flexible Accumulation: Technology, Competitive Strategies, and International Location, **Society and Space: Environment and Planning D**, 6, 1988, pp.245-262.

Scott, A.J., Flexible Production Systems and Regional Development: The Rise of New Industrial Spaces in North-America and Western Europe, **International Journal of Urban and Regional Research**, 12, 2, 1988, pp.171-186.

Soekkha, H.M., P.H.L. Bovy, P. Drewe and G.R.M. Jansen (eds.), **Telematics, Transportation and Spatial Development**, VSP, Utrecht, 1990.

Teece, D., Economies of Scope and Scope of the Enterprise, **Journal of Economic Behaviour and Organisation**, 1, 1980, pp.223-247.

Walker, R.A., A Theory of Suburbanisation, **Urbanisation and Planning in Capitalist Society** (M. Dear and A. Scott, eds.), New York, 1981, pp.383-430.

Walker, R.A., The Geographical Organisation of Production Systems, **Society and Space: Environment and Planning D**, 7, 1988, pp.377-408.

Williams, H.P. and J. Taylor, ICTs and the Management of Territory, **Cities of the 21st Century** (J. Brotchie, M. Batty, P. Hall and P. Newton, eds.), Halstead Press, Longman, Cheshire, 1991, pp.243-305.

Williamson, O., **Markets and Hierarchies: Analysis and Antitrust Implications**, Free Press, New York, 1975.

Zanfei, A., I Vincoli alla Diffusione delle Tecnologie dell'Informazione in alcune Esperienze di Applicazione della Telematica, **Economia e Politica Industriale**, no. 50, 1986, pp.253-289.

CHAPTER 4

A BILLION TRIPS A DAY: MOBILITY PATTERNS OF EUROPEANS

Piet H.L. Bovy, Jean-Pierre Orfeuil and Ilan Salomon

4.1 Introduction[1]

Transportation and communications are two systems which play a major role in the forthcoming transition of Europe. They facilitate the movement of people, goods and information among regions. Serving as lubricans for European integration, these systems are of crucial economic importance. However, they also bear heavy costs in terms of safety, environmental economic and social impacts upon some parts of Europe.

The travel patterns of the 413 milion Europeans with (within OECD-Europe) demonstrate how transportation is related to the basic processes of economic activity in Europe, as well as how the movement of Europeans generate some of the negative impacts of transportation. By understanding the travel patterns of Europeans, their commonalities and differences, it may be possible to formulate expectations about future developments and to identify the reasons why transportation policies which are successful in one country fail to accomplish their goals in another.

In looking into European travel patterns we have initially focused on two major questions:

(1) Is Western Europe different with regard to travel behaviour from two other advanced economies, namely North America and Japan?
(2) Are travel patterns differing among European countries?

While is was relativily easy to establish positive responses to both questions, it became evident that addressing the causes for such differences is more complicated. Thus, in a joint effort we have obtained a detailed description and analysis of travel patterns in a large number of West-European countries. These shed light on the idiosyncracies of the transportation systems and travel patterns in each country. Based on these, we have selected a number of topics which were identified to be of interest in discussing travel patterns across countries. These topics include:

- Demographic factors
- Income
- Geographical patterns of commuting
- Policy issues related to travel patterns.

---

1 The subject of this paper is addressed in more detail in a forthcoming book titled: **A Billion Trips a Day: Tradition and Transition in European Travel Behaviour**, Kluwer, Boston, Mass.

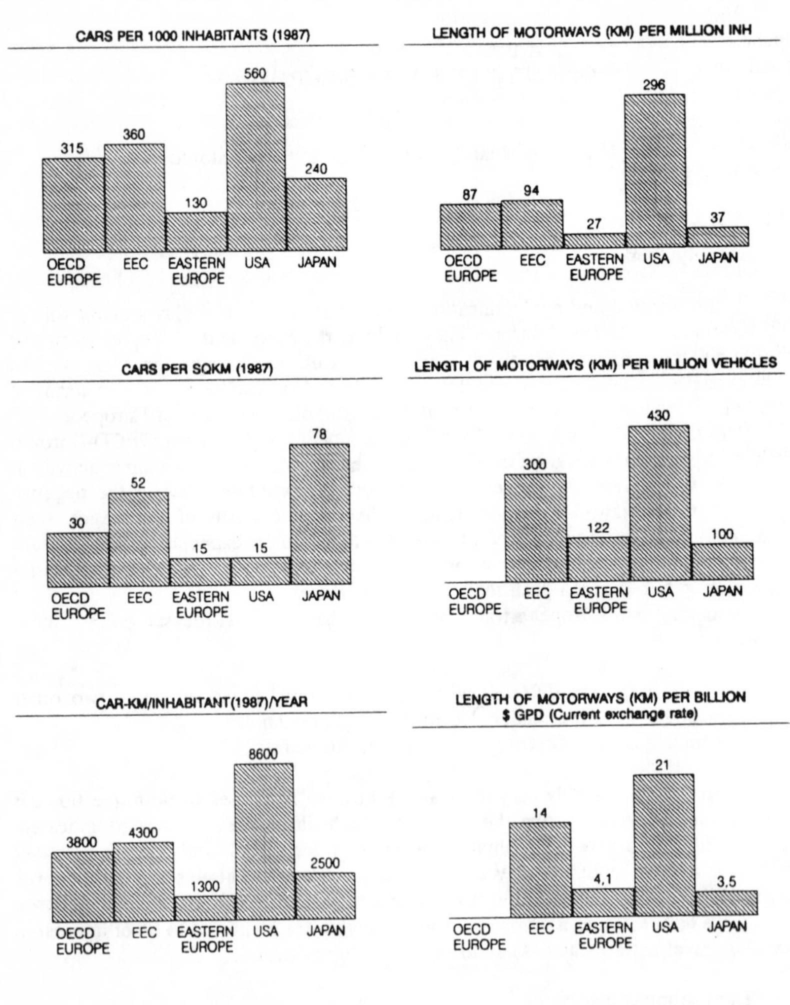

Figure 1 **The European difference: cars and motorways**

Sources: ECMT (1990, 1991a), Japan Road Association (1990), Koshi (1989), Linster (1989), US DOT (1990).

4.2 European Travel Patterns: A Satellite's View

European travel patterns are different from those of the North-Americans and the Japanese. The main differences may be explained by geography (density and distribution of settlements), culture (Europe being in an intermediate position between the holistic approach of Japan and the individualistic culture of American pioneers), and the domestic economic context (pricing policies, infrastructure investment) mirroring the different cultures. Comparing Europe to other parts of the world helps in shaping the west-European identity.

4.2.1 Car ownership

Looking at the **car ownership** level in the five 'blocks' (OECD-Europe, EEC, Eastern Europe, U.S.A. and Japan) makes clear that Europe is still far from the U.S. level (Figure 1). Inversely, the European rate is much higher than the one of Eastern Europe, and more suprisingly, of Japan, despite its higher GDP per inhabitant (Figure 2) and the power of its car manufacturers. On the other hand, the car density, expressed in cars per square-kilometer, is the highest in Japan (which may explain the suprisingly low car ownership caused by the extremely high population density), followed by Western Europe.

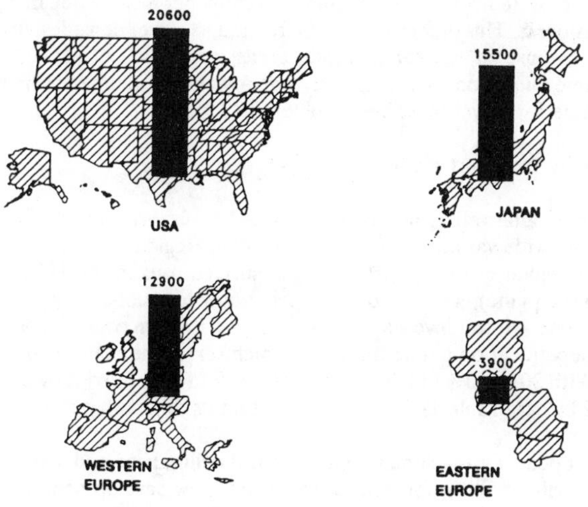

Figure 2 **Gross domestic product per capita (1989: U.S. $ converted in current purchasing power parities)**
Sources: OECD (1991), Encyclopedia Universalis (1990), the Statesman's Book 1990/91.

Compared to these high densities, the U.S.A. and Eastern Europe show much lower values - the second one indicating that Eastern Europe could become a potential growing market for car manufacturers if the economic background would improve. Such a process already started in the former GDR where exploding increases of car ownership occurred. On the other hand, the very high car densities in highly developed countries have initiated traffic calming strategies (in a broad sense) in Western Europe and Japan today.

4.2.2 Travel distance

With respect to **travel distances**, an inverse relationship with density can be expected due to the larger set of opportunities accessible within shorter distances. Similarly, higher income and/or lower prices for transport are expected to be associated with longer trips. In addition, time budget and travel time budget limit our ability to cover the accessible space, unless technological - or other system management - improvements allow travelling longer distances in a given time.

Confining the analysis to mechanized road and rail transport, the comparison between Eastern and Western Europe, Japan and the U.S.A. support the above expectations: with low densities, high income and low prices for transport, North-American residents travel on longer distances. With low levels of income and car ownership as well, Eastern Europe residents have the lowest mobility level, despite densities which can compare with their Western counterpart.

Further, despite higher income, global mobility per head in Japan is only 77% of that of EEC residents. This difference may be related to higher densities, specific policies to discourage the use of the car in urban areas, poor level of services of the road network and time allocation. With impressive work week duration and very short periods for holidays, time for travel must be a problem in Japan.

4.2.3 Alternative transport modes

The use of **alternative, mechanized ground transport modes** (Figure 3) clearly demonstrates the wide variations among these global Regions. The car has become the nearly exclusive mode of transport for ground surface trips in the U.S.A. (leaving the longer trips to the plane), with 3% of the market only for public transport and 10% for soft modes. Inversely, lower levels of car ownership in Eastern countries and Japan make people more dependent on public transport, which serves the majority of the market in urban areas. With 30 to 50% of trips in soft modes, 5 to 25% of trips by public transport and 35 to 50% by car (Table 1), Europe tries to find its own path between individualism and collectivism.

The European approach may indicate that the pluralistic and manifold urban and technological tradition allows for transitions towards new developments (cars, airplanes, high speed railways, maglev, etc.), but only within the framework set by the medieval city, and urban developments typifying Western Europe today. The high population densities in Europe give rise to environmental awareness and actions. Thus, in Europe, the old but well experienced solutions (walk, bike, tramway, railway, e.g.) are revitalized under special circumstances and/or - within well-suited segments - encouraged by official policies and realized in very specific parts of Europe (countries, regions, cities) only, which again is in accordance with the European pluralism.

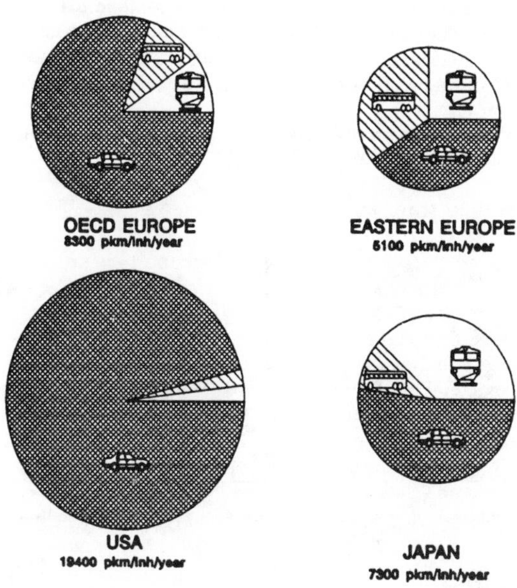

Figure 3 **The European difference: modal shares**
(Area of the circles proportional to total passenger Km/inhabitant/year)

4.2.4 Household expenses

The share of **household expenses** devoted to transport and communications in EEC countries is 15%. It equals the U.S.A. share but differs significantly from the 9.5% in Japan (1985 figures). The shares obviously depend on the global budgets of the households (related to the global GDP of the country they belong to), the intensity of their travel and the relative prices of the various transport functions, compared to general consumption. A cautious EEC study (EUROSTAT, 1986) using conversion in a standard currency (purchasing power parities) enables one to separate a relative volume effect (the level of transport and telecommunications use, compared to the total consumption) and a relative price effect (price for travel, compared to the general price level in the country). Figure 4 shows the position of the U.S.A and Japan compared to Europe (set to index=100).

Overall, the relative price for transport and communications is higher in EEC countries than in the U.S.A. and Japan as well (Figure 4b). The relative volume of transport and communications is much higher in the U.S. but lower in Japan (Figure 4a).

A detailed analysis by function shows that the **relative prices** of the car market are the highest in Europe (Figure 4b). This means that a European has to work more to buy a car than a Japanese or an American. Driving a car is also much less expensive in the U.S., while a bit more expensive in Japan. The relative price of public transport is the highest in the U.S.

a) RELATIVE VOLUME INDEX OF HOUSEHOLD EXPENDITURE FOR T C M FUNCTIONS (1985)
(Volume deflated by the general consumption index Base: 100 for EEC)

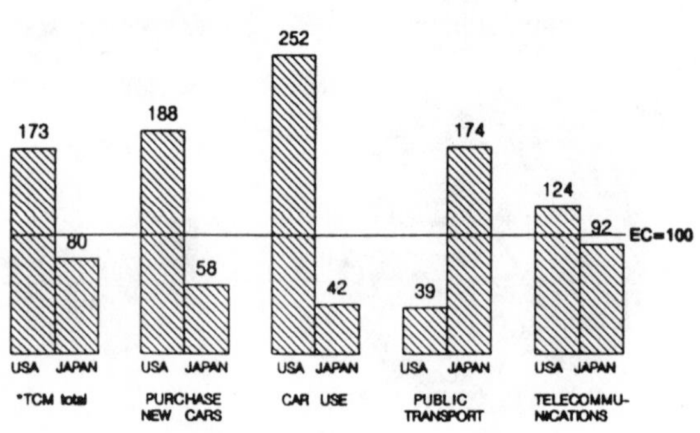

b) RELATIVE PRICE INDEX OF T C M FUNCTIONS (1985)
(Price deflated by the general price Index Base: 100 for EEC)

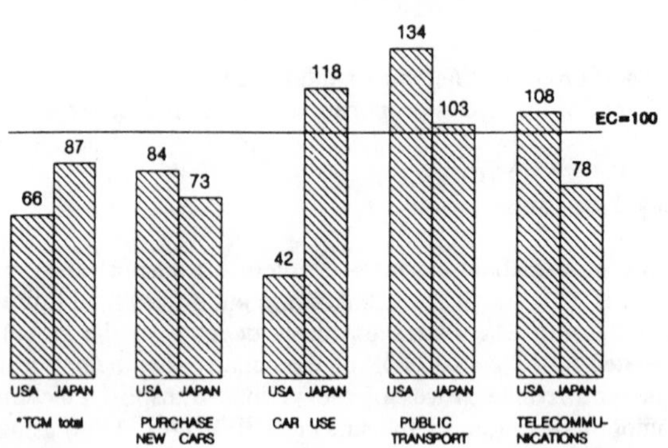

*TCM = Transport, communication and mobility

Figure 4 The European difference: volume and price for mobility
Source: Author's calculation from EUROSTAT (1986).

4.2.5 Volumes

With regard to the **relative volumes** (Figure 4a), the differences are very clear: Europe is in an intermediate position for all items. The U.S.A. is at the top for car purchase, car use and telecommunication, and Japan for public transport. Very low prices for the car system in the U.S. (low taxes and few tolls) go together with a high level of car use and high levels of fares for public transport services. Inversely, low performance levels for road infrastructure in Japan and high levels for public transport services go together with a modal behaviour more oriented towards railways.

Table 1 The European difference: safety, environment, and modal split in urban areas

	OECD Europe	EEC	East-Europe	USA	Japan
Road casualties/ million inh. (1988)	138	142	104	189	109
Transp. Energy Consumption Ton oil equiv/ inh.	0.73	0.70	0.30	2.0	0.57
NOx emission (Kg/inh) (1985)	20	19	-	35	6
Noise: % population exposed to LEQ>65dBA	15	12	-	7	30
Modal share trips urban areas:					
% Car	30-50	30-50	10-20	87	10-30
% Public	5-25	5-25	50-60	3	15-30
% Soft modes	35-50	35-50	30-50	10	50-60

Sources: ECMT (1990,91a), EUROSTAT (1989,90), Gombert (1990), Japan Road Association (1990), Linster (1989), Pucher (1988), OECD (1991).

4.2.6 Costs and benefits

A comparison between gasoline prices and fares for urban public transport suggests huge differences between Western and Eastern Europe, and between Europe and the U.S.A. as well, with Western Europe in an intermediate position (see Pucher, 1990).

The benefits of transportation systems to users and society are counter-balanced by a variety of social burdens, such as negative impacts on safety and the environment (see Table 1). Despite poor road networks Eastern Europe and Japan experience the lowest level of road fatalities, in relation to their lower use of car. Inversely, the U.S.A. has the highest one, despite the highest provision on safe motorways. The very low fuel prices observed in the U.S.A. are correlated with the highest level of car and truck usage,

Table 2 The Western Europe differences

	population (million)	Density Inh/Sqkm	GPD/ Capita PPP's (1989)	Cars/ 1000 inh.	Personal mobility Km/Inh/Y (1000')	% Road public transp.	% Rail public transp.
Austria	7.6	90	13,407	353	9.9	17	10
Belgium	9.9	324	13,587	353	8.7	12	7
Denmark	5.1	119	14,594	311	12.3	16	8
Finland	4.9	15	15,030	347	11.0	16	6
France	55.6	102	14,565	395	11.5	6	9
Germany	61.1	246	14,985	457	10.2	8	6
Greece	10.0	76	7,253	144	2.2	22	9
Irland	3.5	51	8,984	212	-	-	-
Italy	57.3	190	13,902	396	10.2	13	7
Netherlands	14.7	356	13,709	348	9.7	7	7
Norway	4.2	13	16,663	401	11.2	9	5
Portugal	10.3	110	7,360	155	7.2	11	8
Spain	38.7	77	10,263	264	-	-	-
Sweden	8.4	19	15,533	401	11.3	9	7
Switzerland	6.5	158	17,695	421	12.8	5	13
Turkey	51.4	66	4,484	23	2.1	48	6
U.K.	56.9	223	14,345	331	9.3	8	6
OECD Europe	413	94	12,100	308		11	7

Source: ECMT (1990), EUROSTAT (1990).

4.2.7 Concluding remarks

The comparison shows that mobility developments do not necessarily follow a one-dimensional track, the direction of which is determined by economic wealth. Political will can create conditions in Europe (settlement patterns, urban design, public transport supply, travel pricing, etc.) with which high levels of personal mobility can be maintained by keeping the negative societal impacts at acceptable standards. The former East-block countries have to be convinced to avoid the mistakes made by their Western counterparts in the past: urban sprawl, neglect of public transport and slow modes, as well as too low prices for accessibility.

4.3 Travel Patterns of Europeans: Cross-National Comparisons

4.3.1 The European diversity

The diverse situations which pertain to travel are also of great interest (Table 2). For example, the **densities of settlements** are quite low in Nordic countries (46 inhabitants per sqkm from Ireland to Finland), intermediate on the Mediterranean arch (97 inhabitants per sqkm from Portugal to Turkey), high in Central Europe (229 per sqkm from the U.K. to Austria), with a maximum in the so-called 'blue banana', the international megapolis that spreads out from Glasgow to Milan, through London, the Randstad, the Ruhr and Switzerland to Nothern Italy.

The differences in **wealth** are even stronger: the Gross Domestic Product per capita (at current exchange rates) of Switzerland is eighteen times that of Turkey; using purchasing power parities reduces the gap to a ratio of 1 to 4. On average, wealth is high in Northern and Central Europe (14,600 $ per capita at PPP's value) against 9,000$ only in the Mediterranean rim; agriculture contributes to 19% of the employment in Mediterranean countries, against only 4% in Central and Northern Europe.

A good example of the implications of the economic differences are the variations in car ownership rates and motorized mobility (kilometers traveled in car and public transport per capita and per year). Variations in economic situations are correlated with the number of cars per capita which is eighteen times higher in Switzerland than in Turkey, while the motorized mobility is six times higher.

In cross-country comparisons within Europe, income appears to be more important than densities. Inversely, economic development cannot be considered as the only determinant of travel behaviour. The decrease of the share of public transport in combination with higher incomes and higher car ownership rates is not a fully relevant explanation for the European space. With high car and gasoline prices, the Danes are more public transport oriented than the residents of poorer countries. Constant efforts in Switzerland for railway improvements make the Swiss residents the heaviest rail users. The environmental concern provides the same results in Austria. The intensive use of bikes in The Netherlands may explain the (relatively) low level of motorized mobility. It is noteworthy however, that there seems to be a lower limit for the transport share at 14%, probably in relation to the share of the population without any access to the car which also seems to have a minimum level (i.e., about 25% of the households).

4.3.2 Evolution in mobility since 1970

Full time series are available for thirteen European countries from 1970 to 1987. Their analysis reveals common trends and important differences as well (Table 3).

By and large, the growth of personal mobility per capita is only slightly higher than that of GDP (+2.5% per annum, compared to +2.4% for GDP). The share of the private car is increasing from 79% to 83%, in relation to the differences in the growth rates: +2.8% for car mobility versus 1.3% for public transport. On average, the growth of car traffic (+3.0% per annum) is slightly higher than that of personal mobility by car: the car occupancy rates are on a decreasing trend, in relation to decreasing household

Table 3 Annual rates of growth over the 1970-1987 period for GDP and travel demand per inhabitant (in %)

per inhabitant	GDP	Perskm total	Perskm private modes	Perskm public modes	Car-km
Belgium	+2.1	+1.4	+2.0	-0.4	+3.2
Denmark	+2.0	+2.3	+2.0	+3.6	+1.6
Finland	+2.9	+2.5	+2.9	+1.6	+3.9
France	+2.3	+2.7	+2.8	+1.9	+2.9
Germany	+2.5	+2.1	+2.5	+0.3	+3.4
Italy	+2.0	+3.6	+3.8	+2.9	+3.4
Netherlands	+1.8	+2.4	+2.8	+0.2	+3.4
Norway	+3.7	+3.5	+4.1	+0.6	+5.3
Portugal	+3.0	+5.8	+6.8	+2.9	+6.6
Spain	+2.3	+3.3	+4.0	+1.7	+5.5
Sweden	+1.8	+1.8	+1.7	+2.1	+2.3
Switzerland	+1.1	+2.8	+3.0	+1.6	+3.1
Turkey	+3.3	+3.5	+6.0	+2.1	+6.7
U.K.	+2.0	+2.3	+3.0	-0.9	+2.5
OECD Europe	+2.4	+2.5	+2.8	+1.3	+3.0

Sources: ECMT (1990), OECD (1985, 1991).

sizes and increase in multicar ownership, with three exceptions only: Denmark and Italy, two countries with high car-related costs, and the U.K., probably in relation to the decrease of the public transport supply and patronage.

Looking at each country separately - or to specific clusters - reveals interesting differences:

The growth of personal mobility is lower in Central or Northern Europe than in Mediterranean countries, in relation to lower economic growth and lower growth of car ownership. In some of the Northern countries (Belgium, Germany, Finland, Norway), the growth of personal mobility is even slightly lower than that of the GDP. In such context, the position of Switzerland, with a high growth rate of personal mobility, is surprising.

Important differences can be observed in the relative growth of car and public transport mobility. Only two countries, Denmark and Sweden, experience higher or nearly equal growth rates for public transport than for car mobility. Quite an opposite evolution is observed in Belgium and the U.K., with a negative growth rate for public transport, and to some extent in Germany and Norway, with very low growth rates for public transport, compared to car mobility. As far as other countries are concerned, the evolution, though at a lower pace, is in favour of the car.

It may be interesting to refer here to a modelling exercise trying to quantify and explain at an aggregate, country level the contribution of the main factors (population dynamics, gross economic development, employment, car ownership, fuel prices, etc.) to mobility development using a multiplicative model and elasticities (see Van Maarseveen, 1991). The results of this analysis corroborate the qualitative findings given above. They show also that similar mobility developments in some countries exist, independent of fairly different changes in background factors.

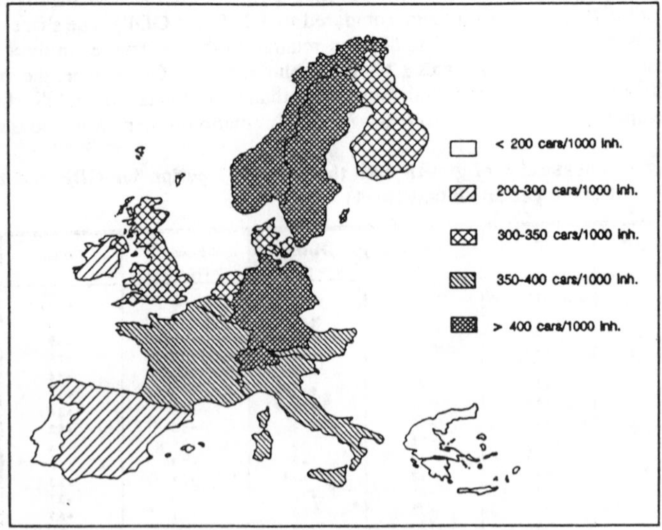

Figure 5 Cars per 1000 inhabitants in Western Europe

Source: ECMT (1990), EUROSTAT (1990).

4.3.3 Aggregate mobility indicators

Mobility indicators are defined for the whole population or for specific groups according to social characteristics. They include indicators related to social interaction, spatial interaction and quality of transport service.

The mean **number of trips** (per capita and per day) is often considered the prime indicator of the level of personal mobility in a country. It has grown in the past, in relation to urbanization and economic development. In the most affluent countries of Central Europe, it is now in a steady state, despite changing factors such as the development of quick lunch at the workplace, the modernization of the retail activities and the ageing of the population. The mean number of daily trips per capita is now in the range 2.5 to 3.5 in most European countries. It must be noted that there is no automatic link between the number of out-of-home activities and the number of trips because of trip chaining. The ratio between the number of out-of-home activities and the number of trips gives an indication of the capability of minimizing the trip numbers, given an activity program.

A disaggregation by purpose suggests three 'packages' of approximately equal importance: the mandatory mobility, including work, school and business-ralated trips; the mobility related to the consumption and household's management (shopping, escorting childeren, personal business); and the 'free' mobility, including visits to friends and relatives and all kinds of leisure trips. The proportions of these three functions in the different countries depend on the demographic structure of the population (proportions of students, workers, housewives, retired) and of the national income. The share of leisure trips (in the wealthier countries more than half of the total distance travelled) increases with the economic development.

Defining mobility through **travelled distances** provides a very different point of view on mobility, which is of prime importance for urban planners and transport network managers, since costs, fares, network occupancy, contribution to congestion or environmental damaging are more dependent on the total distance travelled than on the number of trips. Some philosophical - but important - discussions arose lately among the research community on the choice of the 'right' indicator for mobility levels: some people consider that longer distances reflect a growth of the destination choice set, and must be, as such, considered as a progress in mobility and positively valued. Others consider the number of activities as the right indicator of social interaction, and the growth of distances being an indication of failures in urban planning - such as, for example, suburban locations without any shop or school within walking distance - which should be negatively valued. These discussion points out the status of mobility, as a free activity depending on personal decisions or a constrained activity depending on land use patterns.

Whatever the answer is (probably a combination of the two opposite paradigms), we have to note that the level of mobility, in the sense of travelled distances, has never been so high in the European countries, with travelled distances in the range 25-35 km per capita and per day for the most developed European countries (Table 4).

Table 4 Daily European mobility in brief

Country	Trips/ day (#)	Dis-tance/ Day (km)	Travel time/ day (min)	%-Modal Shares (trip based/distance based)			%-Purpose distribution (trip based)		
				Soft	P.T.	Car	Mand.	Serv.	Discr.
Austria ('83)	2.9	22	67	40/8	19/34	42/58	40	30-41	18-29
Finland ('86)	3.1		71	31/6	12/19	57/75	33	34	33
France ('84)	3.1	21	53	41/8	8/17	51/75	38	36	26
Germany ('82)	2.9	30	69	41/8	14/25	45/57	39	32	30
Israel(*) ('84)	3.0	-	-	37/-	31/-	32/-	43	28	29
Netherlands ('87)	3.4	33	71	47/16	5/12	47/72	29	25	46
Norway(*) ('85)	3.4	32	71						
Sweden ('83)	3.6	25	-	38/5	12/20	50/70	36	16	48
Switzerland ('84)	3.3	29	70	46/10	12/20	42/70	36	34	30
UK ('86)	2.8	23	-	37/9	14/19	49/72	30	40	30

(*) : Urban population only
- : not available
Soft: soft modes, ie walk, bike, moped
PT : Any kind of public transport
Car: car driver + car passenger

Mand: mandatory trips: work, school, professional trips
Serv: service trips: shopping, escorting children
Disc: discretionary trips: visits to friends and relatives, leisure

Measuring **travel time** is a key for mobility analysis. Congestion is a problem in most of the large European conurbations, and most of the transport investment is devoted to time savings; the relative speed of modes is a key element for modal competition and individual choice behaviour; the total daily travel time per capita is one of the most steady parameters characterizing mobility (about one hour), with lower variations through time and space than travelled distances, for example (Figure 6): in those countries where consistent time series are available on this phenomenon, the average total travel time evolves much more slowly than travelled distance or modal split for example. An evolution towards longer distances, the development of leisure trips which take place mainly out of rush hours and, more importantly, the increasing role of the car (see for example Figure 6) may explain this (rough) stability at an aggregate level. The development of congestion and our inability to implement right solutions to face this problem questions however the future of that stability.

Modal shares are dependent on demography, culture, national income, types of settlement, urban policy and specific policies towards bike or public transport, for example. As a result, important differences may be observed from one city to another one, from a suburban location to a central city, and, at the aggregate level, from one country to another. When expressed according to trip numbers, the first position is occupied either by car or by soft modes, with the lowest share for public transport. When expressed according to trip-kilometers, the car has a predominant position in all but one country with 70-80% of the market. Then come the public transport means, with 10-20% of the market, and then soft modes with 5-10% of the market.

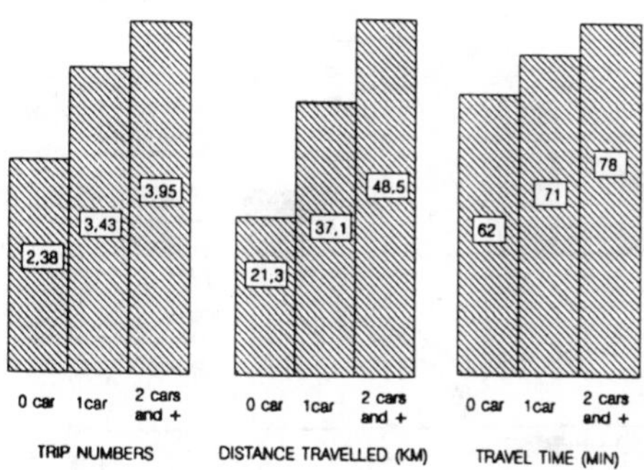

Figure 6 **Mobility, distance and travel time according to the motorization of the household (urban areas, persons 13-74 years of age, Norway, 1985)**

Source: Tretvik (1988).

4.4 Structural Determinations of Personal Travel Behaviour

4.4.1 Gender, age, position in the life cycle

One can expect great differences in mobility patterns for men and women, in relation to family roles, job involvement, as well as license holding or personal access to a car.

Trip numbers of men and women exhibit only low differences, ranging from a few percents in France, the U.K. or The Netherlands to 20% in Germany or Israel.

The figures are much more contrasted for distance: women travel 40% less than men (Figure 7). Three factors (at least) may explain this difference: personal business often takes place in the vicinity of the home; a lower access to car prevents from traveling longer distances, given a travel time budget; commuting distances are lower for women, even for comparable types of jobs and professional status.

Findings in France confirm this uniformity at a given level of car ownership (see Hivert, 1989). The annual kilometrage for economically active drivers exceeds that for retired persons when both have cars. When the total home/place of work kilometrage is subtracted, a comparison between economically active and retired persons gives a much more balanced picture (Figure 8).

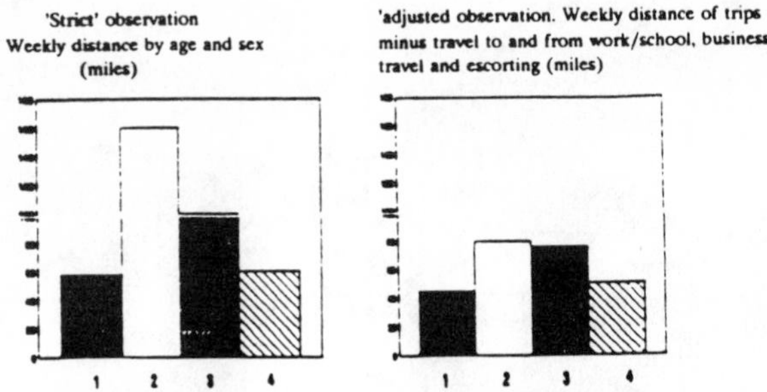

Inclusion of car access. Weekly distance of trips
minus travel and to and from worl/school, businnes travel and escorting (miles)

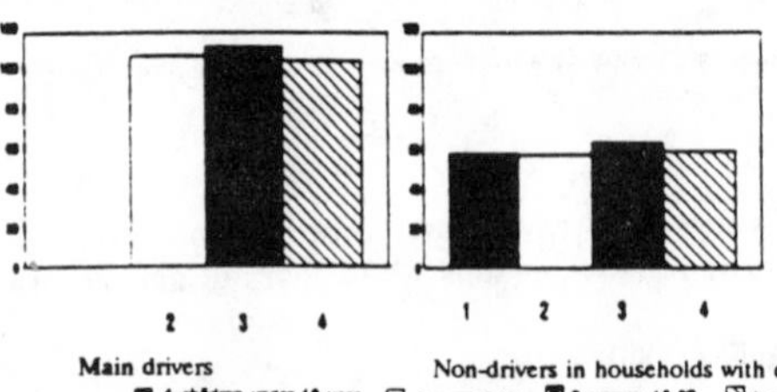

Figure 7 **Weekly distances travelled by various population categories (United Kingdom, 1985/86)**
Source: Author's calculations based on D.O.T, (1988).

DISTANCES TRAVELLED PER DAY (KM)
SWITZERLAND, 1984

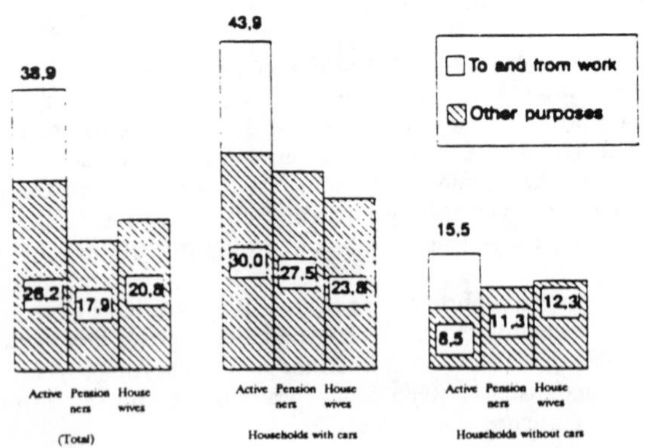

Figure 8 **Distances travelled by various population categories**
Source: Author's calculations based on EVED, (1986).

PARIS CONURBATION

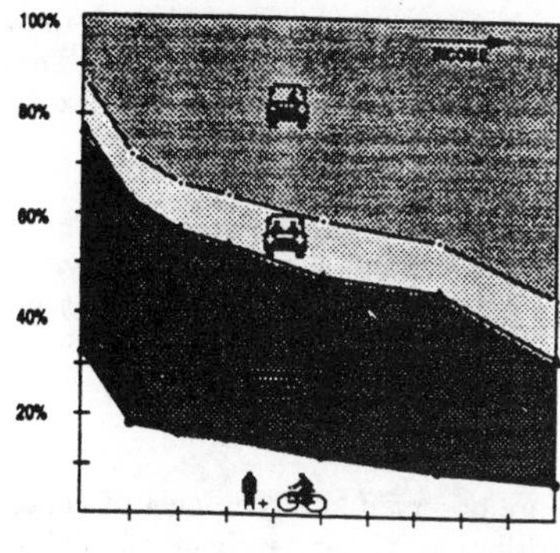

THE NETHERLANDS

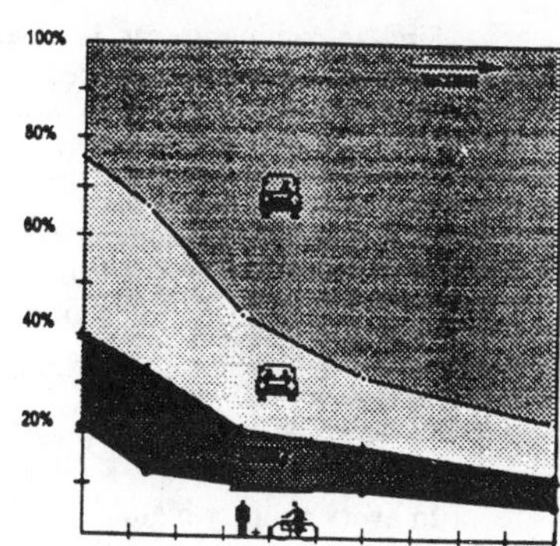

In the 2 cases, the income of the highest income group is 6 times the one of the lowest income group

TRAVEL INTENSITIES ACCORDING TO THE INCOME OF THE HOUSEHOLD

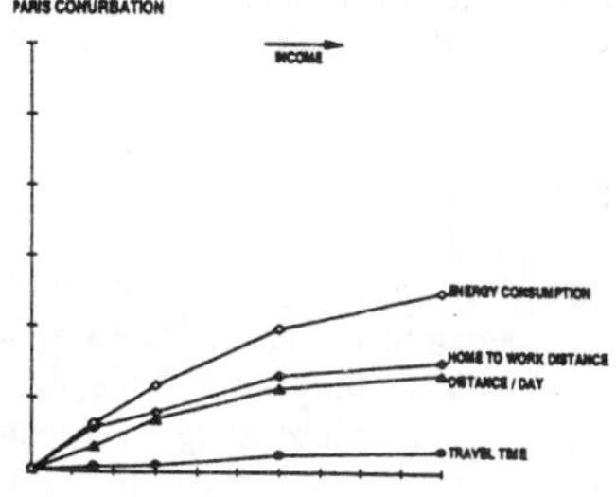

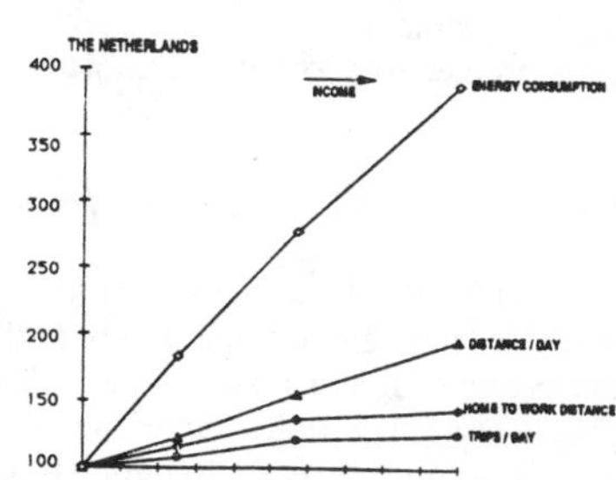

In the 2 cases, the income of the highest income group is 4 times the one of the lowest income group

Figure 9 **Mobility characteristics (passenger/km based) acording to the income of the household**

Source: CBS-OVG.

Similar comments can be made about the use of modes: differences between population categories are reduced when car ownership is taken into account. They do not, however, disappear and the remaining differences can probably only be explained by the working population's tight schedules and pensioner's misgivings about difficult traffic conditions.

In terms of travel and modal use, there are accordingly fewer differences in behaviour between an economically active person and a pensioner when both have access to cars than between two economically active persons when one of them has no car available.

4.4.2 Level of education and income

In every country higher mobility levels are observed in higher level of education groups. This positive correlation is not surprising, as higher levels of education are positively correlated with income.

High car ownership rates in every social group could however question the link between mobility and income. The reality is quite different: whereas the trip numbers increase only slightly with income, the distances travelled do increase sharply, as well as the share of car driving: taking The Netherlands and France as examples (Figure 9) shows that total travelled distances are doubled, distances traveled in soft modes, public transport or as a car passenger are halved, while car driving is seven times higher.

The growth of travel with income might be explained from a specific growth on non-necessary trips, such as social visits or leisure trips. The right explanation is basically different: the growth is mainly explained by higher numbers of commuters, higher business mobility and longer commuting distances. This last point observed in many countries is currently discussed from a theoretical point of view: some people argue that looking for higher income forces households to seek in larger areas for jobs (because higher income jobs are scarce), while other argue that higher disposable incomes allow for a greater freedom in the choice of a suitable residential area.

4.4.3 Residential location and geographical patterns of travel

The effects of residential location on mobility patterns may be studied at three levels at least: the first one refers to the size of the conurbation, and the second one to the position of the residence in relation to the city center. Both levels differentiate people according to their access to urban amenities, such as jobs, shops, or leisure places as well as to their access to public transport networks, with important effects on private mode ownership. Finally, an important role is played by the spatial and size distribution of settlements within a country.

A European analysis of these topics has to be very careful, since geography suggests no clear evidence of common urban structures in Europe: comparing multicentric urban regions such as the Randstad or the Ruhr areas with a highly centralized one such as the Ile-de-France region may seem meaningless. The analysis of transport supply and mobility patterns exhibits however some common features.

First of all, analyses of trip lenghts and distances travelled on a typical day suggest a U-shape (see e.g. Figure 10) according to the size of the area of residence: long distances are observed first in rural communities, then in the greatest conurbations, while shorter distances are observed in medium-sized cities. This seems to indicate that from a mobility point of view medium-sized cities offer attractive conditions.

Separating now the central parts of the conurbations from the suburban ring suggests huge differences in travel needs (Table 5): the distance travelled by suburban dwellers ranges from two or three times that of comparable persons (same family size and income) living in the central parts of the cities. These important travel needs can only poorly be met by public transport, in relation to a poor level of service in less urbanized areas (Table 6). As a consequence, ownership and use of private modes are essential to meet the demand (Germany: Hautzinger, 1989; France: Hivert, 1991) and distances travelled by car appear thus to be much higher for low density dwellers.

As regards land use patterns and their effect on mobility, studies from France and The Netherlands suggest to embody further analysis in a broader perspective.

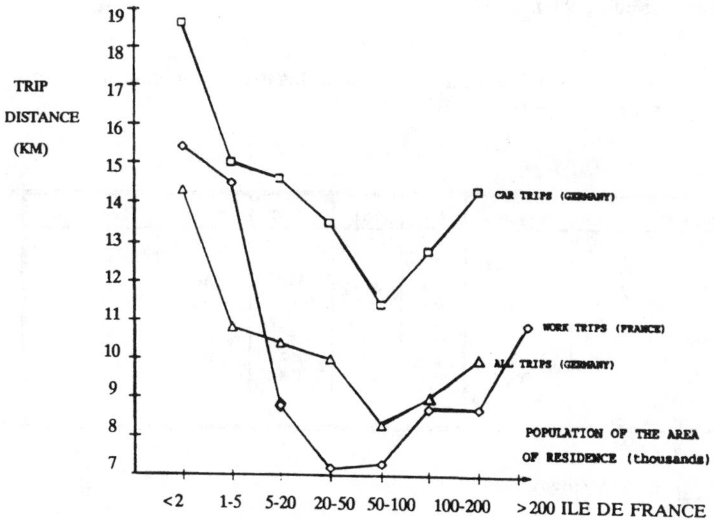

Figure 10 Trip length according to the population of the area of residence

Source: Hautzinger (1989).

Table 5 Total distance travelled per weekday (persons over 6, Toulouse)

	Central city	Inner suburbs	Outer suburbs with amenities	Less densely populated Outer suburbs
Total distance traveled (km)	7.6	11.4	13.9	15.9
Distance with car (km)	4.6 60 %	7.8 68 %	10.5 75 %	13.5 85 %

Source: Orfeuil (1983).

Table 6 Level of service of public transport according to the population of the area of residence (Switzerland)

Urban size (1000')	Less than 2	2-10	1-50	50-100	100-200	More than 200
Access time to next stop:						
Less than 2 mn	20%	19%	30%	39%	32%	41%
6 mn or more	38%	43%	24%	16%	12%	10%
Headways (in peak hour						
5 mn of less	1%	2%	13%	25%	43%	67%
More than 10 mn	98%	94%	62%	17%	15%	8%

Source: EVED (1988).

More precisely, three major trends emerge:

(1) An increasing attractivity of low density areas - rural places, small towns, other suburbs - for housing, espacially for high income households. For example, in the U.K., the average level of income is higher in rural areas than in urban ones.

(2) An increased concentration of 'high level' jobs in the biggest conurbations, of a European size and standard, including airports or high speed train services. As an example, the Ile-de-France or Lyon authorities expect a huge demographic expansion, and make plans accordingly, while the average demographic growth of French population is expected to be very low.

(3) An important movement of suburbanization of jobs, stores or even leisure places:

also golf courses or a Disneyland require space. Table 7 shows the contrasted dynamics of employment between core cities and their suburban ring.

The combination of the reinforcement of hierarchy of spaces, together with jobs scattering and residential suburbanization induces new spatial interactions in travel.

Table 7 Evolution of employment in European conurbations (yearly percentage change)

Conubation	(years)	Core city	Ring of suburbs
Antwerp	(74-84)	-0.7	+0.4
Bremen	(61-83)	-0.7	+0.5
Copenhagen	(70-83)	-0.3	+3.2
French cities	(75-82)	-0.5	+0.9
Hamburg	(61-83)	-0.8	+1.9
Hannover	(61-83)	-0.7	+1.1
Liverpool	(78-84)	-2.6	+3.1
London	(71-81)	-1.1	+0.1
Milan	(71-81	-0.9	+1.9
Paris	(75-82)	-1.1	+0.9
Rotterdam	(75-84)	-1.1	+1.5
Ruhr Area	(61-83)	-0.8	+0.2
Stuttgart	(61-83)	-0.5	+1.2

Source: London: DOT (1986b); Paris: Bessy (1989); French cities: Madre (1991); others: Jansen (1988).

Conurbations attract commuters from larger and larger areas. In France, the proportion of workers commuting over more than 50 km (one way) has grown by 32% in seven years; 160.000 workers have their job located in the inner part of the Paris conurbation without living in the Ile-de-France region, which means a commuting distance longer than 100km. Similar figures (see Jansen, 1988) can be observed in The Netherlands: taking Amsterdam as an example shows a decline of internal trips (-33%) and inversely a considerable growth of external trips (+115%) from 1960 to 1981 in the evening peak hour. In Germany (see, Verkehr in Zahlen, 1990), the annual growth rates of car traffic in inner cities are only 60% of those of regional traffic. Measuring traffic volumes at cordons leads to the same conclusion in Amsterdam, Rotterdam, London or Paris: the more peripheral a cordon, the larger the growth in car traffic.

As can be seen from Table 7, an important development of travel within the suburbs (tangential trips) may be observed too, in relation to the development of jobs, stores and leisure places.

More suprising perhaps is the steady growth of the number of outgoing commuters living in the core city of large conurbations, with for instance an average yearly increase of 5% in the four Dutch metropolitan areas. 'Reverse commuting', observed in Paris too (23% of the residents of Paris city actually work in the suburbs), is probably the result of an increased attachment to the chosen residential location, the development of multi-activity within the households, an increasing specialization of the economy and specific features of the housing market: in the Ile-de-France, for example, the longer the stay in a flat, the lower the rent. 'Reverse' commuters are encouraged by little congestion too. Ironically, the reverse commuters increase the imbalance and thus indirectly induce more congestion for 'normal' commuters.

As a result, mobility patterns evolve towards further spatial diffusion, more complexity, longer distances, higher shares for car and peak developments at the regional scale.

Despite their (relatively) small share in the total number of trips, the regional trips (exchanges between the less urbanized parts and the metropolitan areas, or intercity trips) account for the larger part of traffic volumes, because of their greater length. Furthermore, such distances require either rail services (not always available or suitable for all trip types) or a car route choice including the use of the quickest parts of the highway/freeway network, resulting in specific congestion in the neighbourhood of cities.

4.4.4 Synthesis

Can we derive from our observations a simple behavioural framework combining the demand and supply sides into a dynamic approach? The answer is positive: a scheme including only income, price and speed may explain our transport evolution. The available income is the root of the evolution. Quicker modes are generally more expensive than slower ones. Higher incomes allow the consumer - who devotes approximately a steady time budget to travel - to look for quicker modes. This hypothesis of a link between income and speed is strengthened by our cross-sectional comparisons between countries, between 'wealthy' and 'poor' people within countries, and by longitudinal data as well. So does the link between the 'value-of-time' and income. This 'search for speed' is not only a 'private affair' of the consumer: each time a consumer shifts towards a faster mode, it reinforces its competitiveness.

4.5 Travel Behaviour and Transport Policy

4.5.1 Expert opinions on policies

The evolution of European travel depends on the evolution of such key factors as European demography, wealth and level of car ownership. As an example, important growth rates of car traffic are forecasted in France, Germany, The Netherlands, and the U.K. Inversely these forecasts are used to plan new investments, to evaluate the effects of new regulations, to direct travel behaviour towards acceptable (desirable) paths, and especially to alleviate congestion in urban areas. A global expert survey among members of the Network on European Communications and Transport Activity Research (NECTAR) has provided interesting views on this topic: in the more developed countries, major policy tools will be first classical traffic management, followed by gasoline taxes and road investment, and then higher densities and public transport development. Surprisingly, road pricing and route guidance are not ranked very high. Not surprisingly in less developed countries, investment (road and public transport) comes first, followed by gasoline taxes and traffic management (Table 8).

We sketch some examples of these interactions between transport policy and travel behaviour.

Table 8 **Expert estimated shares of the contributions (%) of specific policies to alleviate congestion in the nineties**

	Western-central Europe	Less developed Europe
Financial tools		
. Road pricing, tolls for tunnels, bridges...	6	7
. Gasoline tax...	14	15
. Less company cars, lower income tax savings for commuting....	4	2
Traffic management		
. General traffic management: parking, bike lanes, pedestrian zones.....	20	10
. Employer-based management: carpool, flextime, telework...	6	7
. Electronic information, route guidance...	4	2
New capacities		
. Public transport...	10	17
. Road investment...	14	20
Land use		
. Discourage new office building in congested areas...	2	0
. Orientation of the development towards medium size cities...	0	5
. More compact cities as opposed to urban sprawl...	12	7
Truck		
. Efforts to keep trucks out of congested areas	7	7

Remark: Experts had to quote what will appear in their country and not what should be done in their opinion.

Source: ESF expert survey (1991).

4.5.2 Transport prices and their effect on demand

The analysis of transport prices is a cumbersome activity: the difference may range: from one to three as a usual ratio for cars depending on the type of car; car taxes and per kilometer gasoline consumption vary in large proportions too; the unit price depends also on car occupancy; moreover, company cars and employer's subsidies may cut down the user's prices. Public transport fares vary according to people for social goals, according to the user's habits for commercial purposes and do not always depend on distance; nobody in the same plane pays the same fare, and that situation is also rapidly taking place for the railways.

There is ample evidence that travel prices with private modes have generally decreased, whereas public modes generally show opposite tendencies, see e.g. France and Germany (Table 9). With the exception of railways, the growth rates of real prices are quite parallel: real prices for air transport and gasoline are decreasing, and inversely real prices for urban and regional public transport are increasing.

Table 9 Long term evolution of real prices for transport (1966-1988)

	France	Germany
Gasoline/liter	- 15%	- 15%
Car ownership, maintenance and use	+ 5%	+ 2%
Railways/km	- 12%	+ 20%
Air/km	- 17%	- 38%
Urban and regional public transport	+ 25%	+ 35%

Source: Orfeuil and Zumkeller (1991).

Such evolutions may be questioned from the point of view of their effects on congestion and the environment as well, especially in the prospects of the 'greenhouse effect'. That is perhaps the reason why rises of gasoline taxes are on the agenda in Germany, The Netherlands and some Nordic countries.

Goodwin (1992) has made a comprehensive overview of the international literature on the effects of prices and fares on travel behaviour. The results (Table 10) exhibit important differences between the short term and the long term: elasticities are low in the short term (one year or less), but higher in the long run (typically five to ten years):

Changes in travel behaviour need time, because travel behaviour changes come through many different and complex processes such as generation, replacement, residential choice, evolution of car fleet etc.

As regards gasoline prices, for example, the difference between long term and short term adjustments is observed in France with short term (one year) elasticities of -0.26 and long term (ten years) elasticities of -0.88 (see Orfeuil, 1990). The difference is explained by several factors: there are time lags in the evolution of public transport supply (one-two years) and also in the response of the demand (two to five years); splits towards smaller cars are linked to the replacement rhythm of the car fleet (around 10% every year only); more energy efficient car brands are available only three to five years after the price rise, and so forth.

Table 10 Summary of elasticities with respect to price and fares

Demand	With respect to	Short term	Long term	Ambiguous
Fuel Consumption	Gasoline price	-0.27	-0,73	-0.48
Car Kilometers	Gasoline price	-0.15	-0.30	-0.39
Car ownership	Gasoline price	-	-	-0.21
Public transport	Gasoline price	-	-	+0.34
Car kilometers	Toll			-0.45
Bus demand	Public transport fares	-0.3	-0.65	-0.41

Source: Goodwin (1992).

A comparison of European countries shows a significantly different car cost structure (car prices, taxation, tolls), with Denmark e.g. having high fixed costs (because of the car taxes), while Italy shows very high variable costs (due to fuel taxes and tolls). It appears that these pricing differences between countries lead to a completely different pattern of car ownership and car use, with low ownership e.g. in Denmark combined with a high kilometrage per car, whereas in Italy a high level of ownership of small, fuel-efficient cars is apparent with a relatively low kilometrage per car.

4.5.3 Developing urban public transport

A decline of public transport patronage is generally expected from such adverse factors as growing car ownership rates or suburbanisation. There is however, some evidence, both in the U.K. and in France, that the public transport patronage is deeply related to the supply.

A comparative study in the U.K. (see Appleby, 1985) demonstrates, on a cross-sectional basis, a very tight link between bus trip rates and the provision of services (see Table 11).

As the level of service depends on relative densities, some doubts may arise on the conclusions to be derived. Taking the densities into account actually weakens the specific effect of bus provision, but does not invalidate the conclusions in comparable areas from the point of view of densities: the better the service, the higher the bus trip rate per person. Furthermore, the higher trip rates are mainly due to the higher level of 'current bus users' (those who take the bus at least once a week), with the higher level of bus trips per user in the second position only. It may be observed too that the level of bus use (with the level of service) is higher for people with a driver's license or with cars in their households than in non-motorized households. Quite similar results hold for France (see Massot, 1991) with respect to urban areas served by urban bus networks. On a cross-sectional basis, a 10% higher level of supply leads to a 6% higher level of current bus users (at least once a week) and a 7% higher level of demand. The difference in demand levels is the lowest for pupils and students (4%) and for people without a driving license (5%). Inversely, it is the highest for persons holding a driving license and having a car available (9%). Limiting the analysis to workers with car access shows the importance of travel times: decreasing the bus travel time by 10% for commuting leads to a 7% growth in bus patronage. Consistent conclusions may be derived from both English and French observations: developing public transport not only improves travel conditions of current bus users, but attracts new users as well.

Table 11 Bus use in relation to the level of service (U.K. 1979)

Bus frequency	Approx. hourly		Half hourly		Higher than half hourly	
Walking time (mn) to bus stop	< 6 mn	6-13 mn	< 6 mn	6-13 mn	< 6 mn	6-13 mn
Bus trip rates (per person/week)	1.76	1.12	2.36	1.90	3.45	3.13
% bus users (at least once a week)	33%	24%	43 %	39%	53%	48%
Bus journeys as a % of motorized modes	14%	8%	19%	15%	30%	28%

Source: Appleby and Jones (1985).

4.6 Outlook

At this moment still large differences exist with respect to mobility patterns in European countries, mainly due to differences in background conditions such as demography, income, prices. We expect that governmental policy actions at the EC and country level as well as market forces will lead to much less differences in these conditions and thus to a convergence in mobility behaviour among the Europeans.

Despite the burden that our current mobility already imposes upon society and the environment now, still higher levels of mobility may be expected in the future in all European countries, and in particular between them. Especially the less developed countries in our region will exhibit a catch-up demand with respect to car ownership and use. However, also the countries with a already high level today will continue to grow because of demographic and income forces. At the European level, average growth figures of 50% or more in the next 20 years are foreseen.

Our analysis reveals that there is however enough potential to limit this growth and its negative impact. Car-related taxation measures e.g. can effectively influence demand and supply at the car market towards a fuel-efficient and environment-friendly car park. Electronic road pricing can efficiently redirect road users in space and time in order to make maximum use of available road capacity by minimizing congestion. Public transport has to play its role too: in particular improvements in service density, service frequency and service quality, if parallelled by appropriate urban development, should make the car or plane superflous for many trips.

Acknowledgement

The authors wish to thank the other members of the NECTAR Working Group on Transport Behaviour and Modelling for their contributions: Ben Jansen, Terje Tretvik, Eli Stern, Peter Jones, Dirk Zumkeller, Claus Heidemann, Einar Holm, Mart Tacken, Ali Turel, Martin van Maarseveen, Anna Vitorino, Arild Hervik, Kostas Petrakis.

References

Appleby, L. and P.Jones, **Investigating the Consequences of Different Levels of Bus Service Provision**, TSU Paper 278, Oxford, 1985.

Centraal Bureau voor Statistiek, The National Travel Survey in The Netherlands, 1988.

Department of Transport, National Travel Survey: 1985/1986 Report, Part 1, An Analysis of Personal Travel, HMSO, London, 1988a.

Department of Transport, Transport Statistics for London, **Statistic Bulletin**, (88) 51, HMSO, London, 1988b.

Department of Transport, International Passenger Report, HMSO, London, 1990.

ECMT, Statistical Trends in Transport 1965-1987, ECMT, Paris, 1990.

ECMT, Prospects for East-West European Transport, ECMT, Paris, 1991.

Encyclopedia Universalis, Chiffres du Monde 1989, Paris, 1990.

EUROSTAT, Parités de Pouvoir d'Achat et PIB Réel, Luxembourg, 1986.

EUROSTAT, Statistiques de Base de la Communauté, 27ème édition, Luxembourg, 1990.

EVEB Stab für Gesamtverkehrsfragen, Verkehrsverhalten in der Schweiz 1984, Bern, 1986.

EVEB Stab für Gesamtverkehrsfragen, Système d'Indicateurs de Coûts et d'Advantages Sociaux des Transports en Suisse, Bern, 1988.

Gombert, M., **La Consommation des Ménages en 1989**, INSEE Résultats 58-59, INSEE, Paris, 1990.

Goodwin, P.B., A Review of New Demand Elasicities, **Journal of Transport Economics and Policy**, May 1992, pp.155-169.

Hautzinger, H. and B. Tussaux, **Verkehrsmobilität und Unfallrisiko in der Bundesrepublik Deutschland**, IVT, 1989.

Hivert, L., J.P.Orfeuil and P.Troulay, **Mobility and Car Ownership: Some Conclusions from National Statistical Surveys**, RTS English, Issue n° 2, Arcueil, 1987, pp. 63-74.

Hivert, L. and J.P.Orfeuil, **Le Parc Automobile des Ménages en 1988, INRETS, 1990**, 1989.

Jansen, G.R.M. and T. van Vuren, Travel Patterns in Dutch Metropolitan Areas: The Importance of External Trips, **Transportation**, 1988, pp.91-108.

Japan Road Association, **Road Handbook 1990**, 1990.

Koshi, K., Les Principales Tâches du Transport au Japon, **Défi et Ouverture sur l'Avenir**, OECD, Paris, 1989.

Linster, M., **Faits et Chiffres de Base in Session Ministérielle sur les Transports et l'Environnement**, CEMT, Paris, 1989.

Maarseveen, M. van, and M.Kraan, A Comparative Analysis and Reconstruction of Mobility Developments in EC-countries 1970-1985, **Colloquium Vervoersplanologisch Speurwerk - 1991 - De Prijs van Mobiliteit en van Mobiliteitsbeperking** (Tanja, P.J., ed.), CVS, Part 1, Delft, 1991, pp.207-225.

Madre, J.L and J.P.Orfeuil, **Evolution des Lieux de Résidence, des Lieux d'Emploi et des Migration Domicile-Travail en France**, ICTB 1991, Quebéc, 1991.

Massot, M.H., **Le Rôle de l'Offre de Transport en Commun sur leurs Usages dans les Villes Sans Site Propre**, ICTB 1991, Québec, 1991.

OECD, Historical Statistics 1960-1983, OECD, Paris, 1985.

OECD, OECD in Figures, Supplement to the OECD Observer n° 170, June-July 1991, 1991.

Orfeuil, J.P., **Structure Urbaine et Consommation d'Énergie: Le Cas de Toulose**, INRETS, Arcueil, 1983.

Orfeuil, J.P., Prix et Consommation de Carburant dans les Transports Routiers de Voyageurs, **Revue Transport**, n° 341, Mai-Juin 1990, Paris, 1990, pp. 127-139.

Orfeuil, J.P. and D.Zumkeller, **Transport Prices, Transport Policy in View of Sustainability: Warnings from Germany and France**, ICTB 1991, Québec, 1991.

Pucher, J., Urban Public Transport Subsidies in Western Europe and North America, **Transportion Quaterly**, vol. 42, n° 3, 1988, pp.109-128.

Pucher, J., A Comparitive Analysis of Policies and Travel Behaviour in the Soviet Union, Eastern and Western Europe, and North America, **Transportion Quaterly**, vol. 44, n° 3, 1990, pp. 93-108.

Tretvik, T., **Shifts in Travel Behaviour from 1970 to 1985 in Norwegian Cities**, Sintef, The Norwegian Institute of Technology, 1988.

U.S. DOT, **National Transport Statistics**, Washington D.C., 1990.

CHAPTER 5

TECHNOLOGICAL AND SOCIAL DEVELOPMENTS AND THEIR IMPLICATIONS FOR IN-HOME/OUT-OF-HOME INTERACTIONS

Peter M. Jones and Ilan Salomon

5.1 Introduction

During the second half of the twentieth century, the widespread acquisition of one transport technology - the motor car - has precipitated a major dispersion of land use patterns in many Western countries, and has led to a significant increase in motorised trip-making (both in terms of trip numbers and length). It has also generated many new types of transport-linked activities; for example, 'going for a drive in the country', or shopping in bulk at supermarkets.

Advances in information technology (see Baer, 1985), coupled with changes in socio-demographic and social structures, are likely to lead in the coming decades to major changes in lifestyles, and radically different patterns of use of both space and time. One consequence of all these developments is a likely shift in the nature and the overall balance of activities carried out inside and outside the home. This, in turn, will affect the ways in which homes are used, and has implications for residential design, the levels and patterns of trip making, and decisions about residential location.

One clear example from the U.K. of the interrelationships between events outside and inside the home was evident during the oil shortages and coal strike in the winter of 1973/74. Road traffic counts taken at five West London sites showed a significant reduction in car journeys:

> "Car journeys into London have fallen by about nine per cent on weekdays since the petrol crisis, but the main reduction has been in weekend trips for social, shopping and pleasure purposes. Surveys by the Greater London Council over a twelve week period from mid-November to early February showed a reduction of twenty two per cent on Sundays and eleven per cent on Saturdays." (Planning No 54, 8/3/74)

At the same time, others were benefiting from the increased time spent at home:

> " 'We have noticed a remarkable increase in viewing during the past three weeks' says Cyril Bennett, programme controller of London Weekend Television. 'Figures for London alone are up ten per cent over last year, which means one and a half million more viewers; this is doubtless due to petrol and other shortages'." (Sunday Times Business News 16/12/73)

While other businesses must have suffered from a reduction in custom (for example, restaurants located in rural areas and relying on urban cliental).

The broad interactions between in-home and out-of-home activities have not been studied extensively by social scientists. This is probably, in part, a result of the fact that the (arbitrary) division of the social sciences is broadly coincident with the division between out-of-home activities (studied in geography, travel behaviour, social psychology) and in-home activities (covered, in part, by the sociology of the family, communications, etc.). Pratt and Hanson (1991) emphasize the need to recognize intra-household arrangements as a major theme for explaining the interaction between households and society, including the roles individuals play in the paid labour force, but this integrated approach is the exception.

In recent years, there have been a number of developments which give an added importance to bridging the academic divide between studies of in-home and out-of-home activities. In particular, the concern to reduce the volume of car travel, in order to save energy and cut down on congestion and pollution, has led to a growing interest in tele-commuting, tele-shopping, etc. and other ways in which activities formally undertaken outside the home can be transplanted into the home environment. Such developments may have wider energy implications than are currently recognised; for example, savings in travel fuel may be offset by greater energy use within the home, and might in the longer term encourage more dispersed land use patterns that negate any short term traffic benefits.

The objectives of this paper are to establish the importance of in-home/out-of-home interactions, as a subject for study in a research and policy context; to raise issues about the changing relationships between in-home and out-of-home activities, and to discuss some of their implications. First, we set out a general conceptual framework for addressing these issues (section 2). Next, we illustrate some of the complexities of the interactions involved (section 3), and go on to identify some of the forces at work which affect the balance of use of facilities inside and outside the home (section 4). Finally, in section 5, we identify a number of specific issues for further research.

5.2 Conceptual Framework

The "home" is a physical entity which provides shelter, but it also "symbolizes the social space which differs in quality from the work place and the 'instrumentalized' relationships that prevail in general 'outside'" (see Nowotny, 1982). Boundaries of various types define the home and its functions for the dwellers, their visitors and the passers-by. Various categories of boundaries exist, including symbolic, social/psychological and physical, and they may either be clearly demarcated (for example, in the case of a high rise building) or may be blurred by the presence of semi-public activity in gardens and neighbourly activities in the street and surrounding area.

The nature of the boundary between home and non-home has been discussed by several authors. Both Ahrentzen (1987) and Hall (1989), in discussing the option of working at home, emphasize the consequential blurring of the boundaries which separate work and home roles, and the psychological and social consequences that may follow. Hall also cites Richter (1984) on the importance that some workers attach to the need for a temporal transition time between home and work - a minimum commuting time.

In general, the home serves as a separator from the outside, in a large number of senses. In the case of a 'protective' home environment, we can characterise some of the key features dichotomising home/non-home as shown in Figure 1. In practice, the actual dimensions at play for each individual may be a subset of these or may include others as well, and in some homes the polarities may reverse (e.g. privacy and security may be attributes of non-home rather than home).

It is likely that individuals will differ in their preference for the two poles of the various dimensions. For example, one person may prefer the relative information deprivation while another may prefer the outside over-stimulation (in fact what to one may be over-stimulation, might be a desired level for another). Personality traits are suggested to play a major role in differentiating between preferences for the two types of activities. Much of the research effort, it seems, must be directed in this direction.

Individuals may also vary in the way in which they treat the separation function of the home: some may strengthen the boundary, both physically and symbolically; while others may allow a blurring of the distinction between the two environments, by "opening" the home selectively to activities typically done outside, or vice-versa. In this

INSIDE	**BARRIER**	**OUTSIDE**
information deprivation	< >	over-stimulation
control of info intake	< >	unstructured info
narrow-band information	< >	richness
symbolic identity	< >	anonymity
security	< >	no defense
privacy	< >	public
physical comfort	< >	physical discomfort
controlled environment	< >	uncontrolled
responsibility for immediate environment	< >	indifference
home roles	< >	outside roles

Figure 1 The home/non-home boundary interface

way some (controlled) blurring of the distinction can take place. Nowotny (1982) observes that, over time "the home has been successively and successfully invaded by that opposite, the public space".

Having considered some of the many subjective and objective attributes that collectively define the characteristics of, and the boundary between, ‘home’ and ‘non-home’, Figure 2 sets out a broad framework within which the changing relationships between in-home and out-of-home activities can be considered.

First, there are the physical and institutional environments within which these relationships operate, and which influence the **supply** of activity and travel facilities. These environments are represented by three categories In Figure 2:

(i) The stock of residences, characterised both by their location and their design (including their size, configuration, etc) and the range of facilities available within the home environment; here we include the availability of cars, which in many ways represent a mobile extension of the home.

(ii) The stock of all non-residential land uses to which household trips might be directed, including work places, educational establishments, shopping and entertainment centres, medical facilities, etc.

(iii) Communications linkages between and among the residential and non-residential land uses. These include both physical transport networks and systems (road, rail, etc) and various forms of telecommunications. Their significance depends on the degree of physical separation between 'home' and 'non-home'.

Over time, technological advances, together with changing demands by consumers and increases in disposable income, result in improvements to communications links and the variety and quality of land uses. In general, the overall effect is to increase the range of choice: communication links become more diverse and faster, the range of non-residential land uses increases, and the variety of facilities available within the home also grows.

Matching these changes in supply are changes in **demand**, brought about by modifications to living patterns and socio-demographic characteristics among the population. Here we can trace three main factors at work:

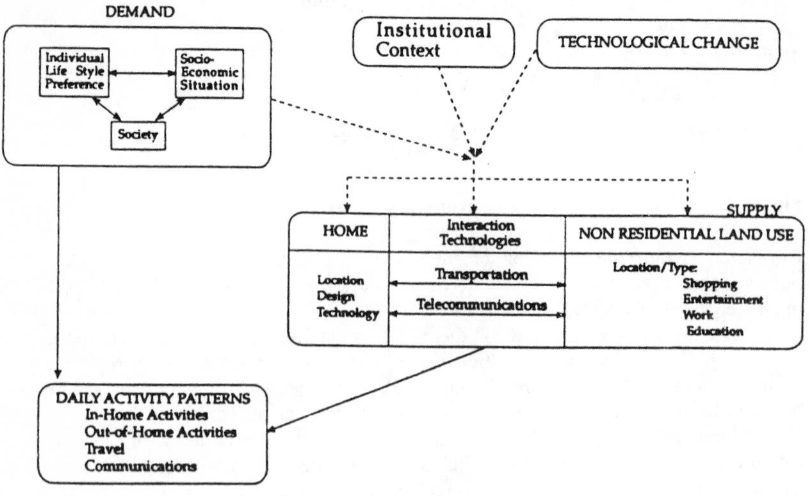

Figure 2 A framework for analysing in-home/out-of-home interactions

(i) Changes in the demographic composition of the population; these affect the general balance between children, economically active and retired adults, and the more detailed distribution of the population among life cycle stages, plus average household size, etc.

(ii) Changes in roles in society, partly resulting from (i), but also due to institutional, cultural, social and economic changes (eg move towards greater sharing of parental duties among couples).

(iii) Changes in lifestyles, partly affected by (i) and (ii), but also relating to changing aspirations, living standards, cultural developments, etc. - and new opportunities afforded by developments in technology itself.

On a day-to-day basis, the **behaviours** that we observe - the daily activity patterns - lie at the intersection between these demand and supply factors. While in the longer term, changes in living patterns and advances in technology interact to produce new patterns of supply, including new urban forms and opportunities for satisfying aspirations. However, while supply opportunities and disposable incomes increase, the total time available for activities remains fixed, and can serve as an increasingly binding constraint on behaviour.

This whole process is in a continual state of flux, with the speed of change constrained on the one hand by the capacity for new investment and the ability to adapt existing land use and communications infrastructure; and on the other, by personal habit and inertia, and the rate at which individuals can adapt to changing circumstances. Here the speed with which people learn how to master new technologies, and the degree of complexity that they are willing to master, are proving to be growing constraints in the design of products for the domestic technology market.

5.3 Complexities of In-Home/Out-of-Home Interactions: Some Examples

The choices that individuals typically confront between performing a similar activity in the home or outside it might, at face value, be seen simply as a binary choice between two alternative locations. However, these choices are usually more complex. The performance of an activity at home or outside it may be associated with differences in the costs, effort expended, gratifications gained and in the factors involved in the choice process itself.

In order to gain some insights into the choice process and the factors which affect it, it is useful to consider some examples of such trade-offs.

5.3.1 In-home/out-of-home recreation

Many recreational activities can be undertaken either within the home boundary or outside. Concerts, films, and spectator sports nowadays have in-home remote-viewing options (or imitations?). There are indications that these in-home options are gaining ground, substituting for out-of-home attendance and the associated travel that is involved. In Israel in 1969, for example, 63% of the population visited a cinema at least once a month, and 27% did so four or more times a month. By 1987, the number of people doing this had declined to 42% and 6%, respectively (CBS, 1990, Table 26.3). By 1989 in the USA, VCR and Cable TV had achieved a penetration rate of 61% and 53% of all households, respectively (see Carey, 1989), and in the same year 59% of U.K. households had a VCR [European Marketing Pocket Book, 1991 Edition]. Robinson (1981) reports that while the total time that Americans spend on leisure activities has not changed dramatically between 1965 and 1975, a significant increase in time devoted to television watching was observed at the expense of other activities.

The difference in location of an activity between in-home and outside also implies that the nature of the experience may be very different - although the objective information content might be the same. For example, viewing a film at home or in the cinema may fulfil different aspirations, which go beyond the immediate function of 'seeing a movie'. While the content of the film may be the same in the cinema, on the television or the VCR, the environment in which it is being observed is perceived very differently, not simply in terms of differences in the size of the screen, etc.

Watching the film at home avoids the costs associated with 'going out'; namely travel, cinema tickets, snacks and, when necessary, baby-sitters. Staying at home is often the effortless default situation. But, staying home often implies a more limited experience, and can deprive the viewer of the opportunity of seeing other people and of being seen. In addition, the attention span may be more limited, or may be broken: the film or concert may be disrupted by other household members, by telephone calls etc.

5.3.2 Work and tele-commuting

Tele-commuting refers to the option of working directly from home, some or all of the time. It has gained considerable attention in recent years as a measure which could potentially reduce peak-period traffic congestion (see Nilles, 1988).

Although empirical evidence on this type of in-home activity is still relatively scarce, it seems that the individual's decision to adopt this work arrangement depends on more than narrow economic considerations. The costs of travelling, in terms of time and expenses, are traded off against the benefits of 'being there' at the work place, where some professional and social interactions take place. The weights assigned to these benefits and costs vary widely among individuals, depending on many factors, including personality traits.

We can distinguish between three types of decisions to work at home. The first involves using the home as a primary work base (see Christensen, 1988); there has been a long tradition of home-based work, added to by the opportunities now afforded to switch office location into the home, with only occasional visits to the head office (e.g. through the relocation of data entry functions to a home base). The second - which has attracted the attention of media and researchers (see Mokhtarian, 1991) - involves the relocation of some work activity into the home on a regular basis, perhaps involving tele-commuting two or three days per week. The third is a less formal arrangement, where an employee has the option to occasionally stay at home; for example, an academic who can work at either site.

In the latter case, we could assume that on a particular day, the individual assesses his or her utility of staying at home as greater than that of commuting, where the benefits and costs have short-term outcomes. However, the decision to work at home on a permanent basis, even if not full-time, must take into account a very different set of factors. It is the long term decisions which entail a significant change of living style, new forms of relationship with the employer, and with colleagues as well as with household members. Therefore, it is also very different from the short term decision to watch a film at home or elsewhere.

5.3.3 Buying goods and services from home

Increasingly, it is possible to purchase many goods and services from outside suppliers, without leaving the home. Sophisticated videotext systems enable people to obtain information services at home, perform transactions and shop from home. But also, simple technology like the telephone is used nowadays for ordering meals or almost anything to be delivered to the home. Snider and Ziporyn (1992) argue that new information systems will for the first time give consumers the 'perfect knowledge' that to date has only been available to theoretical 'economic man', and in the process may radically change shopping patterns and retail land uses.

In some instances home-based purchasing of goods and services may involve a clear substitution of an out-of-home activity by an in-home one (e.g ordering groceries by telephone, instead of making a personal visit), but in other cases buying in goods and services may substitute for an in-home activity (see section 5.3.4).

In a study of tele-shopping as an alternative to store-shopping, Koppelman, Salomon and Proussaloglou (1991) conclude that the decision to shop from home is probably related to personality; respondents in their sample could be grouped broadly into those who enjoyed the shopping experience and those who tolerated the activity - the latter represent an important target market for tele-shopping.

Some technological developments make it possible to extend the range of activities carried out remotely from home. For example, the newly installed KEYLINE system in the U.K. comprises an in-home terminal and a secure Smartcard read/write facility. With such a system, for the first time it is possible to place bets on horse races directly from home, and to carry out many other financial transactions that have hitherto required the presence of the person.

Three caveats need to be borne in mind, however. First, the development of a new technology does not automatically mean that it will be adopted and widely used; Arnold (1982) points to the failure of Prestel to significantly affect behaviour. Second, buying services from home does not imply an unambiguous directional impact on the transport system: to adopt tele-shopping may or may not lead to a net reduction in traffic, depending on the relative efficiencies of visit-and-collect versus home delivery services. Finally, there are constraints imposed on home deliveries by the difficulty of co-ordinating this with the presence of a household member at home to receive the delivery.

5.3.4 Domestic work

Domestic tasks are traditionally defined as maintenance activities carried out in the home (usually by household members), but this is changing in four respects:

(i) Some activities that used to be strictly domestic may be carried out by a service industry outside the home (eg ordering a take-away to be delivered and eaten in the house, rather than cooking at home), or the increasing trend to using child care services outside the home.

(ii) Other service industries travel to the home to carry out domestic activities on behalf of the household (eg cleaning of carpets and curtains, windows, etc).

(iii) Numerous technologies characterized as "time-saving" are used at home in order to increase the efficiency of domestic duties so that the individual will have more free time. Clearly there are other benefits too (less effort or hassle, no need to learn a particular skill), but time savings are an important feature.

(iv) There appears to be some change in the division of labour in households in developed countries (e.g. Gershuny and Robinson, 1988). Men seem to take an increasing part, in absolute and in relative terms, of the domestic responsibilities. To do so, they need to be at home. This also suggests that, correspondingly, women have somewhat greater flexibility which may affect the mix and location of their activities.

Questions have been raised, however, both as to the strength of these effects and their wider implications for activities and travel. Schor (1991), for example, has studied trends in time use in the U.S. over a twenty year period, and concludes that although there has been some small redistribution of domestic activities between women and men, the total has remained constant: "with all these labour-saving innovations, no labour has been saved; instead housework expanded to fill the available time." In other instances where there has been a real time saving, there is no clear evidence on how that time is now used - and whether it has increased in-home or out-of-home activity.

5.3.5 Assessment: the nature of in-home/out-of-home trade-offs

A variety of activities which have traditionally been undertaken outside the home can now be done at home. Conversely, the growth in service industries also provides some opportunities for transferring activities from inside to outside the home.

However, the substitutions between in-home and out-of-home activities involve more than a simple quantitative trade-off between activities in two locations. In-home and out-of-home activities are often very different in the **nature of experience** they provide. Commonly, an in-home activity is multi-faceted, with several activities occurring simultaneously; as a consequence, when completing an activity diary people often have difficulty in fully recording (and recalling) in-home activities without recourse to a system of primary and secondary activity codes. For out-of-home events, however, it is more common for activities to be sequential rather than simultaneous in nature.

On the other hand, out-of-home activities typically provide a richer experience: sights, sounds, smells, social contacts are more varied and intense than in the home. While classified as 'going to a movie', this activity is very different from watching the film at home, both in terms of the size of screen, experiencing the reactions of others in the audience, etc and in terms of various supplementary activities that may be carried out on the same outing, such as window shopping, drinking, etc. Rarely can the two alternatives be real substitutes, as they are likely to entail a different set of activity attributes, particularly in terms of the internal structure of the activity. Technologies facilitate different types and levels of substitution for out-of-home activities. Specifically, most in-home technologies fulfil only one type of purpose, unlike the richness and diversity of most out-of-home activities.

Note also that the various types of activities characterised in this section of the paper as being potentially substitutable are very different in terms of the **time frame** under which they take place. The decision to relocate work into the home may take some time to implement and implies a long-term commitment to a new mode of working; on the other hand, a decision to go shopping or telephone for goods delivery may be a realization of an impulse and implies no continuing commitment.

Finally, there is a significant difference in the **level of control** over the range of optional activities the individual has. Institutional and economic factors affect the supply of out-of-home alternatives, in terms of schedules and prices, more than in the case of in-home activities where the individual can exert more control.

5.4 Causal Factors

The factors which are hypothesized to affect the balance between in-home and out-of-home behaviour can be related to the conceptual framework outlined in Figures 1 and 2. We can view the home as providing a physical separation between the outside environment and the inside, and see behaviour patterns as the outcome of various forces acting on the individual.

Using as an analogy the work on migration, we can broadly distinguish those which 'push' outward from the home and those which attract ('pull') to the outside. There may be disagreement within the household as to which functions should be allowed to permeate the barrier, and under what conditions, thus possibly creating some tension, which in itself may be a push or pull factor. In this section, we consider some of these push and pull factors, and the counteracting factors which encourage the in-home activities.

5.4.1 Push forces

Migration studies cite, as common push factors, economic conditions, and social, political or religious persecution. This may broadly be equated to intra-household tensions and poor physical environment, but in addition we can cite another factor: informational deprivation.

5.4.1.1 Intra-household tensions

This may become a major push factor if some tensions are generated among the household members, and there are personality clashes. Teenagers, in particular, may feel the need to get away from the home environment, and tensions can arise after husbands retire and 'hang around' the home all day.

In addition, lack of privacy within a small or crowded home may act as a strong push factor. In some households, it is plausible to assume that there is severe competition for space and time resources: scheduling of the use of the bathroom in the morning, for example, may be an important issue (see Jones et al., 1983), as may decisions about which television programmes are selected. Such competition may be a source of tension among members that will generate a desire to spend some time outside the home environment, and perhaps find alternative facilities to use.

5.4.1.2 Physical conditions

There is some anecdotal evidence to suggest that where the home environment is a poor or uncomfortable one, people may seek to leave it and to spend time in outside environments that are more pleasant.

For example, it has been reported that in the U.K. some elderly people with free access to public transport may ride on it for long periods on inclement days to avoid a cold or damp home. In the USA, people from poor home environments may also be found hanging around shopping malls, keeping warm in winter and cool in summer.

5.4.1.3 Informational deprivation

The home environment acts as an information filter, constraining the flow into as well as out of the home. A number of channels can convey information to the home: media (printed and electronic), social contacts, information services (e.g., videotext), visual information directly observed from the home, and more. What typifies the penetration into the home are the channel capacities and the control options at the individual's disposal.

Each of these channels is characterized by the nature of information it can convey. For example, mass media provide information which is uni-directional, the content cannot be controlled, but the user has leverage over the choice of programme (from a given set) and over disconnecting the channel altogether. Information obtained from the mass media is also characterized by its internal structure: it is pre-processed by the providers who determine the sequence and perspective of the information, and the individual's leverage is only a binary choice of 'take it or leave it'.

The telephone, on the other hand, serves as an example of a communications channel on which the individual has much more control: the person has access to a very large number of individuals and information sources, and a telephone conversation is interactive and thus the individual has some influence on the content. Still, the telephone is considered by many as a route through which intruders can enter the home (sales persons, etc.); to counter this, answering machines, and more so, call waiting and caller identification, are now available in some countries and serve to block such intrusions.

Although there is a large quantity of information available in the typical modern western home - much more than any one individual can absorb - the richness and diversity of that data is limited to certain visual and audio images. The resulting limitation in the set of information stimuli can cause boredom. Boredom, according to Berlyne (1974) is generated when there is a "sensory deprivation", that is a flow of information which is not stimulating (repetitive, irrelevant) or when there is no flow of information altogether. Responses to boredom are either stress, or a quest for variety. Berlyne suggests that:

> "...there seems to be a moderate level of incoming information that human beings strive to maintain, taking corrective action when the information content of the environment exceeds it or falls short of it" (p. 39).

The desire to vary the information intake can be satisfied by taking part in activities in different physical environments outside the home.

5.4.2 Centripetal forces

The home environment also generates centripetal forces which encourage the individual to stay at home - or may encourage a return home if the person is completing an activity away from home.

Depending on the point at which a decision is taken, the home can present itself in two different ways: as the default, 'do nothing' situation, or as a competing attraction if the person is located outside the home. In the former situation, the decision to stay at home is actually a passive one - a state of inertia; once located at home, the decision to engage in an out-of-home activity involves some costs in terms of money, time and effort, which are largely avoided by staying at home. To go out requires an active choice, and making this choice can be expected to vary in frequency, in different periods of life.

For decisions made away from the home base, it may be more appropriate to view home as another competing centre in a destination choice decision, unless there are compelling personal (e.g. tired) or social (e.g. child care) reasons to return home.

5.4.3 Pull forces

In addition to factors which create centrifugal forces, there are many factors which attract people to activities outside the home. It is argued that the attraction to the outside is usually multifaceted, in the sense that for each instrumental function there are a number of other gratifications which the individual may benefit from, and which consequently affect his or her decision to exit the home.

In studying "why people go shopping?", Tauber (1972) has raised numerous hypotheses as to why people engage in shopping activities above and beyond the instrumental function of obtaining a particular good. These include:

* Role playing
* Physical activity
* Diversion
* Self-gratification
* Learning about trends
* Sensory stimulation
* Social experience outside the home
* Communications with others
* Status and authority
* Pleasure of bargaining.

The out-of-home environment facilitates an outlet for some functions which the home constrains. If an individual has the need to play divergent roles, for example, the set of possible roles which can be acted at home may be limited due to the presence of others, to whom the individual is committed in specific roles.

Possibly of greater importance is the need for sensory stimulation. Porteous (1985), for example, has suggested that odour is one type of non-visual stimulus which creates the "scape" in which people act; references to olfactory stimulus as an environmental attribute are often noted in the literature. Similarly, tactile sensation are to a large extent eliminated by in-home environments, as is the opportunity to experience shared feelings and perceptions in a crowd, and to absorb the general atmosphere of a place or a spectacle. The out-of-home activity can thus compensate for those stimuli which the physical setting of the home eliminates.

The desire for an interaction with the external, physical environment may also be driven by a need for **territoriality**. The study of territoriality in human behaviour has emphasized the importance of a protective and defensible space, which the individual can control (see Porteous, 1976; Altman and Chemers, 1980). The value of territoriality as a symbol of identity did not, it seems, attract much attention. We hypothesize the use of public spaces (see Goffman, 1971) as part of the individual's out-of-home activity, is a manifestation of the need to establish a territory with which he or she identifies and within which one feels "at-home".

5.4.4 Supply conditions

The option of performing activities at either the home or outside are obviously also dependent on supply-side factors (see Figure 2). Suppliers determine the availability of some of the options, as well as other relevant factors like location, prices and temporal availability. The characteristics, locations and opening hours of various activity facilities such as stores, cafes, and workplaces determine the extent to which the set of activity alternatives includes a range of out-of-home options. Similarly, the offer of the option to work at home as an alternative to a central workplace is determined by the particular employer.

Another dimension of the supply side involves the availability and level of service offered by different modes of transportation to the locations in which various activities can be performed. The lesser the availability or quality of the transportation services, the greater is the incentive to perform activities at home, or close to other destinations that have to be visited (e.g. work or educational establishments).

5.5 Areas for Research

A recent review of the state-of-the-art of activity analyses in relation to travel (see Jones, Koppelman and Orfeuil, 1990) has identified the interactions between in-home and out-of-home activities as one of the major research issues in this area, both as a component of an understanding of travel behaviour per se and as a means of identifying the likely indirect impacts on travel behaviour of new technologies in the home, workplace, etc.

Within the broad areas represented in Figure 2, a number of more specific issues can be identified for detailed research. Several of these are briefly discussed in this section.

5.5.1 Substitution

New developments across a wide range of technologies can lead both to activity substitution and locational substitution - or more usually a combination of the two (i.e. the activity changes both in its nature and its location). Various of the technological advances which have been offered to the domestic market provide opportunities to relocate certain activities which in the past where typically done outside to the home. These include: work, shopping and entertainment. Such a relocation into the home may also have space implications, for housing the equipment and supporting associated activities.

The most obvious examples are the television and the videocassette recorder (VCR) which offer in-home entertainment that in the past could only be acquired outside. Since the popularization of VCRs in the early 1980's there seems to have been a steady increase in their usage, combined with a decrease in attendances at cinemas in many countries. Similarly, the availability of live sports programmes on television has been associated with reductions in attendance at football and cricket matches in the U.K. For a general discussion of the impacts on households as consumers of communication and information technologies, see Silverstone (1991).

In a different sector of activity, microwave ovens have enabled a significant reduction in the time required for meal preparation and have thus reduced the potential demand for out-of-home dining by people who are "time poor" (see Nichols and Fox, 1983).

A new concept of work-at-home has emerged as a result of the opportunities offered by new information technologies (NIT) to perform white-collar work in locations remote from the traditional downtown office (see section 3.2). In some cases there is evidence that the use of computers in the home can lead to significant shifts in the time allocation patterns of households (see Vitalari et al., 1985).

These, and many other technologies, thus introduce the potential for a number of functions to be relocated into the home environment. Four main questions arise here in considering their likely impacts:

(i) Which technologies are now available or will become available in the foreseeable future?
(ii) What implications does their adoption have for housing design or residential location?
(iii) What will be the likely penetration of the technologies?
(iv) How will they be adopted and used and how will they affect household activity patterns, the balance spent in-home and out-of-home, and patterns of travel?

5.5.2 Potential transport system impacts

In many countries there are considerable efforts underway to influence - and if possible reduce - the demand for motorised travel and thereby to reduce the economic and social costs associated with congestion, pollution, energy consumption and traffic accidents. The relocation of activities into the home may have a positive effect in this direction. Advocates of the tele-commuting concept have long called for the implementation of such programmes, with the justification that they should produce potentially significant transport energy savings (see Nilles et al., 1976).

One problem that researchers have encountered in studying the scope for trip reduction is that current trip generation models do not take account of the availability of facilities inside and outside the home; most assume that trip rates are only affected by income, car ownership and household size - and in most cases they do not even take more general account of local accessibility levels. As a prerequisite to understanding the influence of new technologies and other products inside the home on levels of trip making, it becomes necessary to reformulate trip generation as a trade-off between in-home and out-of-home activities (see Jones, 1977).

The case for achieving significant transport benefits through telecommuting has yet to be proven, however. Research results so far are ambiguous as to whether telecommunications is a substitute for, a complement to, or a stimulus to travel (see Salomon, 1985). In addition, savings in travel costs and energy consumption might be off-set by increases in home lighting and heating or air conditioning.

In order to assess the potential impacts on the transport and energy systems of increasing the proportion of time spent on in-home activities, a better understanding is needed of the factors which affect the decision to substitute activities requiring access trips by work-at-home, shop-at-home, etc, together with a better awareness of how the home is used. In addition, rather than simply looking at energy savings in transport, a complete energy audit of the home/non-home environment is required.

In addition, research into travel impacts needs to take account of trips attracted to the home, as well as trips generated by the household: the former might increase as a direct result of the latter decreasing. In particular, through goods and services being delivered to the home, and through the need to service the growing number of technical items in the home. To examine these issues, we recommend an audit of travel to/from the home, possibly as one element of a broader household input/output analysis.

5.5.3 Motivations underlying travel

Rather than simply regarding travel as a disutility, there is a need to recognise travel as an activity in its own right, since there are indications that some trips are made with that objective in mind. Moreover, if we assume that individuals may derive positive utility from a certain amount of movement, and that such needs are largely satisfied today in the course of **necessary** travel (to work, shopping, etc.), then the question arises as to what will happen if the level of 'essential' travel is reduced substantially: will new types of trip emerge to fulfil this latent need?

If trips are only perceived as a cost, one should conclude that trip minimisation is desired and hence, the more that home-based alternatives are available, the less will be the demand for travel. However, if there is a positive utility for (some minimum level of) movement, then either new trips will be generated or the 'old' trip purposes will be maintained, even when to do so appears 'irrational', because any intrinsic need for travel is currently satisfied incidentally as part of essential travel.

There is relatively little information about trips made specifically for the purpose of travelling. This may be due partly to the ways in which trips are recorded and classified by the researcher; thus, it is possible that some travel will either go unreported altogether or, alternatively, be attributed to a trip purpose that is associated with it. For example, window shopping per se may be under-reported with such trips being classified as 'shopping' if a store was frequented in the course of the outing. Similarly, driving for recreation might not be recorded as travel. In addition, the consolidation into the home environment of activities which in the past were typified as either in-home or out-of-home may deprive individuals of a desired social/ temporal separation between roles they assume in different environments. There is some evidence of a utility to transition time between roles (the case of work and home roles may be the best example), which nowadays is satisfied by the necessary spatial separation (see Richter, 1984). If eliminated, individuals may either develop alternative mechanisms for creating a comfortable transition, or may feel deprived and suffer stress.

An examination of the interactions between the in-home and out-of-home activities may thus shed light on the basic underlying motivation for physical movement. It will enable researchers to evaluate the importance that individuals attribute to familiarity with the physical and social/cultural environment that is achieved through the direct (as opposed to mediated) interaction with that environment. It will also improve our understanding of trip making behaviour through a better specification of the utility function of individuals with regard to the costs and benefits of movement.

5.5.4 The housing market

Increased in-home activities may have a number of important implications for the housing market. First, if there is a significant substitution of activities into the home, the role of distance from major activity centres in determining household location may change. Individuals who have to drive to work only once or twice a week instead of daily may decide to trade-off environment/amenities for distance and relocate further away from their workplace (see Nilles, 1991). The implications of such a change are that there will be an increased demand for housing in more remote areas, but also that some of the social benefits and energy savings derived from the elimination of some trips will be lost due to the longer distances travelled on other days.

A second set of changes may be in the desired size and design of the living quarters themselves. With more functions (re)entering the home, there may be a growing demand for alternative designs which allocate more (and different) space configurations for work purposes, physical recreation etc. Time released from commuting might also stimulate greater interest in gardening and hence a demand for larger gardens. A recent study on the architecture of dwellings in the telematics' age has suggested ways in which the growing number of activities performed in the home could be integrated by means of alternative designs (see Caso, 1991).

5.5.5 Social and societal implications

In recent history, the role of the home was one of protecting the family and uniting it against the outside environment of paid labour and other functions. It was the environment within which the family institution and processes developed and prevailed. Individuals within the home usually play different roles then those they assume in the various realms of life outside, and there are still important gender differences: "A woman's place is in the home (or in the kitchen)" is a clear manifest of this division.

New claims suggesting that tele-commuting is an ideal solution for women who could participate in the paid labour force while maintaining their role in the home, follows the same tradition as it assumes that the household tasks need to be the responsibility of the woman.

On the other hand, introducing additional functions into the home may be alter the existing division of tasks. That may open new opportunities for individual members of the household, may change in intra-household relationships and power divisions, and may, of course, change the relationship between the home and other social institutions.

5.6 Conclusions

Traditionally, research into trip making, the use of the home, residential relocation and changes in service sectors (retailing, etc.) have been regarded as separate areas of study. Yet they are clearly interrelated - and increasingly so as the home environment broadens out from a domestic base to a nerve centre in a communications-rich world. Although the main focus in this paper has been on the spatial and activity perspectives, we emphasize that research should not take a narrow view, as the interactions are affected by and affect many different aspects of life, and should therefore be analyzed in a broad, multi-disciplinary perspective.

To do this successfully requires not only a conceptual reorientation, but also new methodological approaches to data collection and analysis; for example, while there are a number of time use studies, there has been much less measurement of how the various spaces in a house are used. Similarly, in the field of transport, we need to begin to address issues such as how much travelling people regard as necessary or fulfilling. The optional shifts that are taking place in the location of activities may serve as an opportunity to shed light on this question: if individuals generate additional trips to compensate for the extra time spent at home, the underlying need for trip-making behaviour may be revealed.

The type of research advocated in this paper, aside from being of intrinsic academic interest, has a number of important practical and policy implications. First, a study of in-home/out-of-home interactions provides a basis for improved forecasting of trip rates and their composition under changing social and technological conditions.

Second, either for reasons of congestion limitation or environmental enhancement, it is probable that restrictions may need to be placed on traffic levels in some areas at certain times. This raises questions concerning which vehicular trips are considered essential and should be given priority, and whether there are non-transport policies that can be adopted that would reduce the need for motorised travel. One aspect to consider here would be ways of making in-home participation feasible over a wider range of activities than at present - while recognising that to do so may release suppressed demand for personal travel and may increase the number of trips attracted to the home.

Third, policies designed to encourage a change in the balance between in-home and out-of-home activity participation may also have an important role to play in general energy conservation and the reduction of CO_2 emissions. However, as has been indicated in this paper, care needs to be taken to fully assess both the direct and secondary consequences of encouraging such a shift.

References

Ahrentzen, S., **Blurring Boundaries: Socio-Spatial Consequences of Working at Home,** Milwaukee University of Wisconsin-Milwaukee, School of Architecture and Urban Planning (mimeo), 1987.

Altman, I. and M. Chemers, **Culture and Environment**, Cambridge University Press, Cambridge, 1980.

Arnold, E., Information Technology in the Home: The Failure of Prestel, **Information Society for Richer, for Poorer** (N. Bjorn-Andersen, M. Earl, O. Holst and E. Mumford, eds.), North-Holland, Amsterdam, 1982, pp. 263-276.

Baer, W., Information Technology Comes Home, **Telecommunications Policy**, (March), 1985, pp. 3-22.

Berlyne, D., Information and Motivation, **Human Communications: Theoretical Explorations** (A. Silverstein, ed.), John Wiley and Sons, New York, 1974, pp. 19-45.

C.B.S., Central Bureau of Statistics. Statistical Abstracts of Israel, Jerusalem, 1990.

Carey, J., Consumer Adoption of new Telecommunications Services: Economic and Behavioral Components, **Telecommunications Use and Users** (P. Holmlov, ed.), 1989, pp. 73-84.

Caso, O., **Influences of Telematics on the Design of Dwellings**, Delft University, 1991.

Chamot, D., Blue-collar, White Collar: Homeworker Problems, **The New Era of Home-Based Work: Directions and Policies** (K. Christensen, ed.), Westview Press, Boulder Co., 1988, pp. 168-176.

Christensen, K.E., **The New Era of Home-Based Work: Directions and Policies**, Westview Press, London, 1988.

Ettema, J., Interactive Electronic Text in the US: Can Videotext Ever Go Home Again?, **Media Use in the Information Age: Emerging Patterns of Adoption and Consumer Use** (J. Salvaggio and B. Jennings, eds.), Lawrence Erlebaum, Hillside, New Jersey, 1987.

Gershuny, J. and J. Robinson, Historical Changes in the Household Division of Labor, **Demography**, 25(4), 1988, pp. 537-552.

Goffman, E., **Relations in Public**, Basic Books, New York, 1971.

Hall, D., **Telecommuting and Management of Work-home Boundaries**, 1989.

Jansen, A., Funshopping as a Geographical Notion, or: The Attraction of the Inner City of Amsterdam as a Shopping Area, **Tijdschrift voor Economische en Sociale Geografie**, 80, 3, 1989, pp. 171-183.

Jones, P.M., Travel as a Manifestation of Activity Choice: Trip Generation re-interpreted, **Urban Transportation Planning: Current Themes and Future Prospects** (P. Bonsall, Q. Dalvi and P. Hills, eds.), 1977, pp. 31-49.

Jones, P.M., M.C. Dix, M.I. Clarke and I.G. Heggie, **Understanding Travel Behaviour**, Gower, Aldershot, 1983.

Jones, P.M., F. Koppelman and J.P. Orfeuil, Activity analysis: State-of-the-art and Future Directions, **Developments in Dynamic and Activity-Based Approaches to Travel Analysis** (P.M. Jones, ed.), Avebury, 1990.

Koppelman, F., I. Salomon and K. Prossalouglou, Teleshopping or Going Shopping: A Choice Model, **Environment and Planning B**, 1991, vol. 18, pp. 473-489.

Miles, I., **Home Informatics: Information Technology and the Transformation of Everyday Life**, Frances Pinter, London, 1988.

Miles, I., **Information Horizons: The Long-Term Social Implications of New Information Technologies**, Elgar Publication, Aldershot, England, 1988.

Miles, I. and J. Gershuny, The Social Economics of Information Technology, **New Communication Technologies and the Public Interest** (M. Ferguson, ed.), Sage, London, 1986, pp. 18-36.

Mokhtarian, P.L., Telecommuting and Travel: State of the Practice, State of the Art, **Transportation** 18(4), 1991, pp. 319-342.

Nichols, S. and K. Fox, Buying Time and Saving Time: Strategies for Managing Household Production, **Journal of Consumer Research**, 10, 1983, pp. 197-208.

Nilles, J., Traffic Reductions by Telecommuting: A Status Report, **Transportation Research A**, 22A, 1988, pp. 301-317.

Nilles, J., Telecommuting and Urban Sprawl: Mitigator or Inciter?, **Transportation,** 18(4), 1991, pp. 411-432.

Nilles, J.M., F.R. Carlson, P. Gray and G.J. Hanneman, **The Telecommunication-Transportation Trade-Off: Options for Tomorrow**, John Wiley and Sons, New York, 1976.

Nowotny, H., The Information Society: Its Impacts on the Home, Local Community and Marginal Groups, **Information Society for Richer, for Poorer** (N. Bjorn-Andersen, M. Earl, O. Holst and E. Mumford, eds.), North-Holland, Amsterdam, 1982, pp. 97-113.

Porteous, D., Home: The Territorial Core, **Geographical Review**, 66, 1976, pp. 383-390.

Porteous, D., Smellscape, **Progress in Human Geography**, 1985, pp. 356-378.

Pratt, G. and S. Hanson, On the Links Between Home and Work: Family Household Strategies in a Buoyant Labor Market, **International Journal of Urban and Regional Studies**, 1991, pp. 55-74.

Richter, U., The Daily Transition Between Professional and Private Life, PhD Thesis, Boston University, 1984.

Robinson, J., Will the New Electronic Media Revolutionize our Daily Lives?, **Communications in the Twenty-First Century** (R. Haigh, G. Gerbner and R. Byrne, eds.), John Wiley and Sons, New York, 1981, pp. 60-68.

Salomon, I., Telecommunications and Travel: Substitution or Modified Behaviour?, **Journal of Transport Economics and Policy**, 19(3), 1985, pp. 219-235.

Schor, J.B., **The Overworked American; The Unexpected Decline of Leisure**, Basic Books, New York, 1991.

Silverstone, R., From Audience to Consumers: The Household and the Consumption of Communication and Information Technologies, **European Journal of Communications**, 6, 1991, pp. 135-154.

Snider, J. and T. Ziporyn, **Future Shop**, St Martin's Press, New York, 1992.

Tauber, E., Why do People Shop?, **Journal of Marketing**, 36, 1972, pp. 46-49.

Vitalari, N., A. Venkatesh and K. Gronhaug, Computing in the Home: Shifts in the Time Allocation Patterns of Households, **Communications of the ACM**, 28, 5, 1985, pp. 512-522.

CHAPTER 6

SPATIAL EFFECTS OF BORDERS: AN OVERVIEW OF TRADITIONAL AND NEW APPROACHES TO BORDER REGION DEVELOPMENT

Remigio Ratti and Shalom Reichman[1]

6.1 Introduction

Compared to the great Russian plains, Europe is a territory subdivided into small fragments, a space naturally divided into compartments presenting a segmented political force field on the West and on the Center.

In spite of such fragmentation Europe is a very densely populated territory, four times the world average if we exclude the Russian part, and very open to internal and external exchanges. This openness causes the border regions to face frequently recurring problems. However, they have never been the object of interest in the regional science literature (see Hansen, 1983).

There has been increased interest in the problems surrounding the development of the border areas in Europe since the introduction of the European Frame Convention on transborder cooperation of collectivities or territorial authorities (Conseil de l'Europe, Madrid, 21 May, 1980). This convention has also, on the one side, anticipated the objectives of the European Community for the year 1993, while, on the other side, the events in Eastern Europe have substantially automatically changed frontiers both politically and institutionally. An interesting question in this context, is whether borders, or border regions, are increasing in importance, or whether there is a tendency to decrease in importance. A partial answer is given in Figure 1, showing the situation in the late 1980s, and suggesting that in the wider Europe Scenario the actual number of border conflict zones might easily double, or close to ninety border regions in Europe itself, let alone in areas outside of Europe.

Border Regions Institutions in Western Europe

1 Nordkalotten (N,S,SF)
2 Mitt - Norden (N,S,SF)
3 Kjølen Gruppen Nordland - Västerbotten (N,S)
4 ARKO - (N,S)
5 Östfold - Nordliga Bohuslän (N,S)
6 Kvarken (S,F)
7 Skärgårdsprojektet (S,SF)
8 Öresund (DK,S)

---

1 The last mentioned author passed away in October 1992.

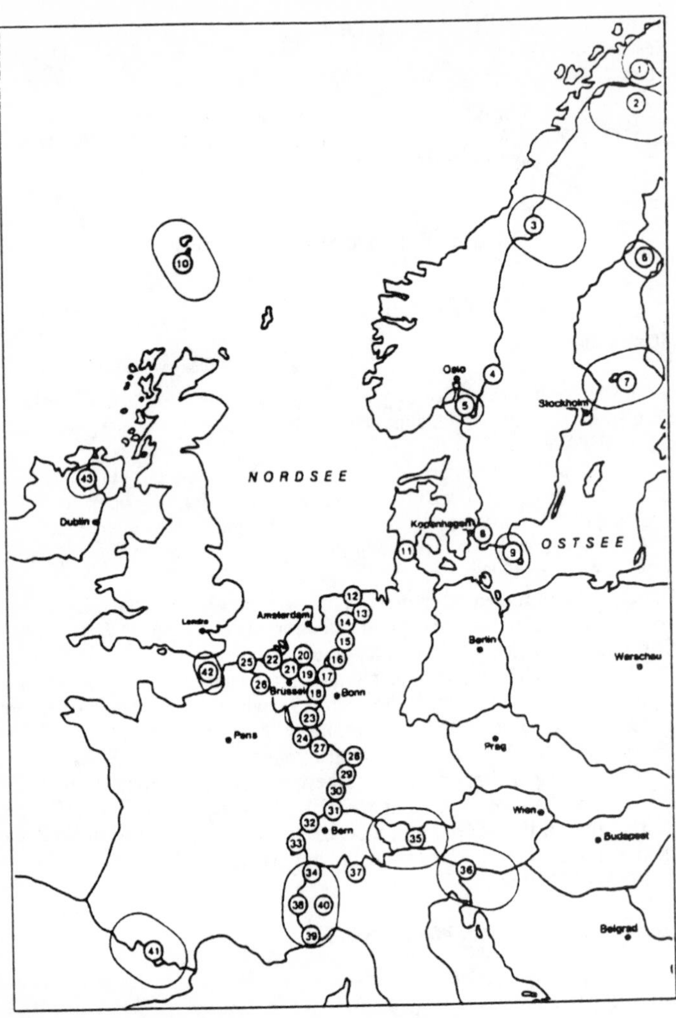

Figure 1 Map of border regions in Western Europe[2]

---

2 The map refers to the situation at the end of the 1980s. In the new European Scenario including Eastern Europe, the number of border institutions officialy constituted might easily reach the double of that number.

9 Bornholm - Sydoötra Skåne (DK,S)
10 Vestnorden (DK,FR)
11 Åbenrå - Flansburg (DK,D)
12 Europems - Dollart-Region (NL,D)
13 EUROREGIO (NL,D)
14 Regio Rhein - Waal (NL,D)
15 Europeuregio Rhein - Maas-Nord (NL,D)
16 Arbeitsgemeinschaft Kreis Heinsberg - Limburg (NL,D)
17 Arbeitsgemeinschaft Rodaland (NL,D)
18 Europeuroregio Rhein - Maas (NL,D,B)
19 Interlimburg Maasland (NL,B)
20 Weert - Noord-Limburg (NL,B)
21 Kemperland (NL,B)
22 BENEGO (NL,B)
23 Europäische Vereinigung fur Eifel und Ardennen (F,B,L,D)
24 Arlon - Longwy - Europesch (F,B,L)
25 Nord-Pas de Calais (F,B)
26 Lille - Roubaix - Tourcoing (F,B)
27 Saar - Lorraine - Luxembourg (D,F,L)
28 Regionalverband Mittlerer Oberrhein - Elsass (F,D)
29 Regionalverband Südlicher Oberrhein - Elsass (F,D)
30 Interessengemeinschaft Moyene Alsace - Breisgau - CIMAB (F,D)
31 Regio (F,CH,D)
32 Jura (F,CH)
33 Region Lac de Genève (F,CH)
34 Region Vallée d'Aosta - Haute-Savoie - Valais (F,CH)
35 Arbeitsgemeinschaft Alpenländer (ARGE Alp): Freistaat Bayern, Autonome Provinz Bozen - Südtirol, Kanton Graubünden, Region Lombardei, Land Salzburg, Land Tirol, Autonome Provinz Trient, Land Voralberg (D,A,I,CH)
36 Arbeitsgemeinschaft Alpen - Adria: Autonome Region Friaul - Julisch - Venetien, Autonome Region Trentino - Südtirol, Soz. Förd. Republik Kroatien, Land Kärnten, Land Oberösterreich, Soz. Förd. Republik Slowenien, Region Veveto, Land Steiermark (A,I,YU); Länder Salzburg und Bayern sind 'Beobachter'.
37 Ticino (CH,I)
38 Franco - Italiana delle Alpi (F,I)
39 Alpazur (F,I)
40 Arbeitsgemeinschaft der Kantone und Regionen der Westalpen: Schweizer Kantone Genf, Wallis und Waadt, Italienische Regionen Ligurie, Piedmont und Aosta-Tal, Franzosische Regionen Provence - Alpes - Côte d'Azur und Rhône Alpes (A,CH,I)
41 Konferenz der Pyrenäenregionen - Aragon, Katalonien, Navarra, Baskenland, Aquitaine, languedoc - Roussilon, Midi-Pyrénées, Fürstentum Andorra (E,F,AND)
42 La Manche - Dover - Calais (GB,F)
43 Ireland (GB,IRL)

Source: Europäische Charta der Grenz- und Grenzüberschreitenden Regionen, Arbeitsgemeinschaft Europäischen Grenzregionen.

This is an important process that implies great changes in many border regions and, in principle, the breaking down of barriers and obstacles which will create discontinuity or jumps in a normal process of communication and diffusion of people, goods, information or knowledge (see Nijkamp et al., 1990).

Whoever stops and ponders the phenomena will begin to evaluate the discriminating effect of these barriers, or frontier effects, that should be eliminated and, particularly, to evaluate the spatial effect of remaining institutional borders.

The need to resort to a theoretical framework of analysis is evident for the concept of 'frontier effect'. We will then discover that the existing reference literature is, apart from case studies, very poor in terms of theoretical spatial economic contributions (see Button and Rossera, 1990).

Above all, the very concept of frontiers appears in effect elusive, because barriers can be of a different kind: cultural, linguistic, institutional, physical, political-economic and social. Frontiers have also a polyvalent meaning: positive for the identity construction of single agents, groups or territorial identities; negative, when the border is perceived as a hostility factor. According to historical situations and contingencies a frontier can be a separating line, or, on the contrary, a contact area. We understand then how Europe could and should remove some of its boundaries, but there will never be a completely 'boundaryless' Europe.

Secondly, the study of the frontier effects means to identify and evaluate the modality, particularly in a spatial perspective, of those factors that influence, in a differential manner, the regional development and the normal process of spatial diffusion of a good whether it be physical or intangible. On the one hand, the theory - especially the one about localization - requires that these regions be generally dominated by conflicting relations (see House, 1980), that is, penalized in their development. On the other side, empirical observation shows that some of them are named among those that are the most developed (see Gaudard, 1971; Ratti, 1971; Hansen, 1983), and also present the chacteristics of the emerging peripheral regions (see Ratti and Di Stefano, 1986). Since then, it appeared necessary to go over the simple static vision in order to examine the development process bound to these regions.

Is the development of border regions comparable to the dynamics of the peripheral regions or, on the contrary, does it show specific characteristics? What happened to the traditional thesis of the development penalization of these regions? Under what development criteria will it be modified by the opening of the borders and by the integration of markets? In the following section we will attempt to answer some of these questions.

6.2 The Specific Nature of Frontier and Border Effects

6.2.1 The ambiguity of the frontier concept

The examination of the socio-economic literature (see Button and Rossera, 1990) has led us to distinguish between two different views or frameworks of analysis, as shown in Figure 2. 'Frontier' is an ambiguous concept (see Reichman, 1989), generally representing either a border as a region lying astride the boundary (a line representing the legal limit of a state), or referring to a concept of a marginal or peripheral zone. To every framework of analysis there is a corresponding specific prospective and also political objectives, diverse and complementary.

Thus, two diverse views can be distinguished (see Ratti, 1990):

- First, the traditional view, that is the one of the 'border area', defind as the territory immediately adjacent to a fixed frontier line (in most cases institutional) inside which the socio-economic effects due to the existence of a border are felt significantly (see Hansen, 1977).
- Second, the view of the 'frontier limit', according to which the border is seen less as a demarcation line but, rather as as external limit, which may be mobile over time. In economic terms the border is the place where the marginal costs are equal to the marginal prices (see Di Tella, 1982). Every opposition or disappearence of obstacles to the communication will have an influence, beyond the distance, on the diffusion processes of tangible or intangible goods.

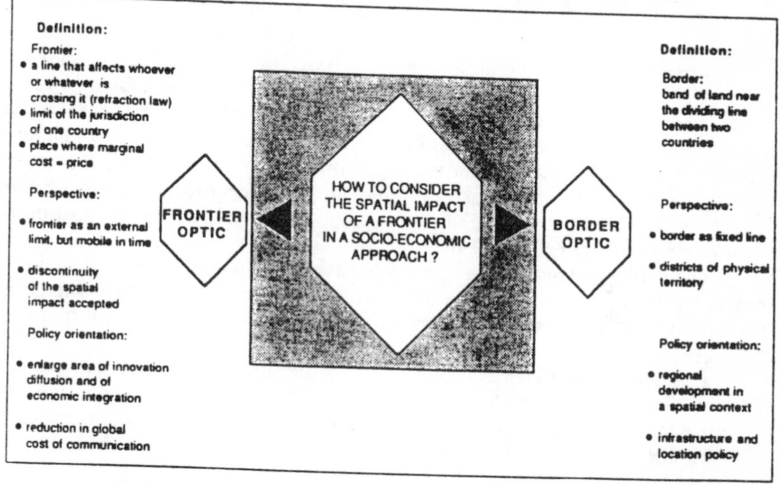

Figure 2 **Two different views and frameworks of analysis in order to evaluate the spatial effects of a frontier**

Source: Ratti, (1990)

In this contribution we limit our attention to the first approach trying to formulate a specific contribution to the theory of border regions' development; in fact, border regions are most affected by changes in the institutional border nowadays, and in this field there is a great need for theoretical improvement.

6.2.2 The duality of the boundary-border effect

After having discussed the ambiguity of the frontier concept and having chosen a border approach which is within an institutional framework of analysis, it is very important to consider the duality of the function of a frontier: as a dividing line or as a contact zone. Both these functions determine the specific nature of the development of border regions.

Let us begin by saying that the border can be taken into consideration as a separation factor, a demarcation line between different political-institutional systems. In this case, the border effect manifests itself in the following three functions (see Guichonnet and Raffestin, 1974):

(a) Legal function where the border line exactly delimits the territories subject to juridical standards and to the country rules.
(b) Control function where every crossing of the border lines is submitted, in principle, to state control.
(c) Fiscal function where the control function is accompanied by a perception of custom rights assuring the adaptation of the fiscal rights in force in the country of entry.

These functions are controlled by the central government which, at least in this instance, reduces the autonomy of the region to govern its own affairs. In fact, the concept of a border, seen as 'separation line', is essentially the fruit of some preoccupation with national politics. In the extreme, this justifies the peripheral and dependency character of the border region. In the sense of this definition, this operation consists of an evaluation, or even a cancellation, of some constituent characteristics of the region. Therefore, the term border area appears a more adequate description of territories marked by the 'border-line'.

The border can also be seen as a contact factor and, in this sense, should not be seen so much as a functional space but as an intermediary element between different societies and collectivities. By this definition it is convenient to talk about transborder regions.

This second approach concerns only the organisation of space and the global administration connected with the socio-cultural and identity factors, and is in clear contrast with the role of the strictly functional approach of the 'line-border demarcation'.

Finally, it is possible to show three main conclusions:

(a) The two notions of borders - namely line and contact - are often mixed up and their respective degrees of importance vary as a function of historical contingencies (for example, the notion of barrier-border has been historically bound - since the 18th century - to the construction of the nation states).
(b) The effects of one or the other concept determines specific and original consequences for the spatial organization of the border territories (for example, in the case of the establishment of a regional development process, the barrier-border is a penalizing one, while the contact-border provokes some original dynamics of development).
(c) The analysis and interpretation of the development dynamics of the border regions requires a multi-disciplinary and systematic approach.

It is evident then that the spatial-historical dimension of the economic and political-institutional elements (see Reichman, 1992) better explains the phenomena bound to the border. If we view the situation as analogous to that of an organisation facing a turbulent environment, then it stands to reason that it will seek ways of developing stategies to reduce uncertainty. It also allows us to characterize the border regions by distinguishing them from the other peripheral areas.

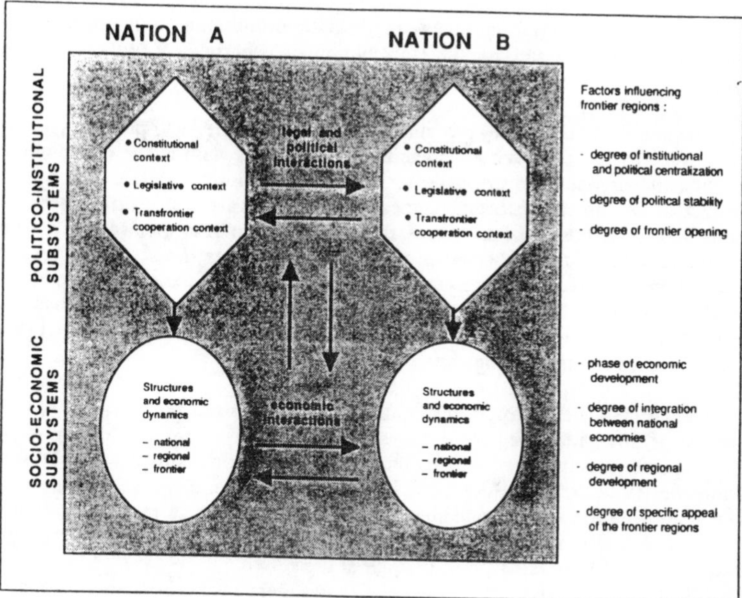

Figure 3 **The border regions and the interrelation framework of political and economic national subsystems**

Source: Ratti (1990)

For example, the development of the phenomenon of trashborder workers into Switzerland in the years 1960-1970, must be analyzed in the context of the Swiss legislation ruling the foreign workers, control and limitation of resident aliens since 1963, the relative liberalization of the border since 1966, and the theory of polarized growth (the case of Basel and Geneva) and the segmentation of the labour market (see the case of Jura and Ticino, Jeanneret, 1985; Ratti and Alii, 1981).

6.3 Elements of an Actual Theory of Border Region Development

In this section we will examine the traditional approach which considers the border regions as being economically penalized, and alternative analyses which are based on the theories of the international division of labour and revenue. Most of the emphasis remains either on a functional approach of the border 'demarcation line' giving more privileges to the national and international economy, or on a juridical-institutional approach aiming at inter-state and inter-regional cooperation.

6.3.1 The traditional hypothesis of the border region penalization

The inter-relation frame between political-institutional and socio-economic subsystems allows to appreciate the contribution of two classical authors on spatial analysis.

Christaller (1933) already recognizes the principle of the socio-political separation of the border as the third spatial organization system as well as the economic logic concerning the organization principles of markets and transportation. The border is recognized as an artificial distorting element of the market areas as central places which will not allow, in those regions where these effects manifest themselves, a limited economic development. The border is a factor that provokes the segmentation of the remote regions from the central places. The investment costs increase is tied to high risk of instability typical of the peripheral areas. In the border regions, the accumulation of these negative effects will inhibit the formation of central places having a high degree of complementarity and a strong capacity for development.

Loesch (1940) emphasizes the conflict existing between political and economic objectives for this type of region: to the economic priority order - efficiency, 'Kultur' (culture), power, continuity - corresponds a political priority order which is exactly reverse - continuity, power, 'Kultur', efficiency - (for example, the political issues or the custom taxes separate some complementary economic areas such that public contracts and military objectives introduce some real barriers). These barriers provoke a negative discriminating effect for this type of peripheral area.

It is true, even in the traditional localization theory, that the border also creates favourable effects. The case of border tax abolishment for the transportation sector (see Ratti, 1971; Spehl, 1982) and the emergence of the 'tariff factories' as a response to political protectonism, that is, making investments in foreign neighboring areas in order to more easily penetrate the market of the other country (see Peach, 1987). All these elements, together with the economic liberalization period, have since disappeared or have been modified by rationalization, economic integration and new technologies (see Ratti, 1988).

The earlier considerations are evidence of the weakness of the localization theory as having an essentially static character. Therefore, if the hypothesis of the penalizing effect is plausible, it does not really seem to be confirmed universally but only in fairly specific circumstances in relation to certain general factors of political and economic order. As for the negative effects in peripheral border-areas, the case of Alsace, unfairly treated for decades because of instability and political centralization (see Urban, 1971) and that of Ticino, penalized by the constitution of the Swiss Custom Union first, and then by the establishment of the Italian National State, are eloquent cases for this purpose.

To conclude, the existing literature on the matter at least allows us to affirm that the simple verification of the negative effects due to the border must not be retained as the 'theory of the border region development'. On the contrary, the development effect must be seen through the joint and dynamic action of the process of political and socio-economic order.

6.3.2 The development of the border regions from the point of view of the international division of labour

A more promising theoretical method of development, capable of interpreting the development process of the border regions, is based on more dynamic approaches of localization. It consists of considering these areas not only in their national space but also in the wider context of the emergence of the world economy (see Michalet, 1976), accounting for the spatial division of labour.

In present-day production and market conditions, it is the search for a differentiated revenue which drives the process leading to a territorial organization constituted by a hierarchical and spatial distribution of production segments, functionally and sectorally polyvalent (see Aydalot, 1986):"Les entreprises n'ont plus besoin de concentrer leurs activités en un point, dans une usine immense groupant toutes les activités et tous les types de main-d'oevre. Elles vont scinder l'ensemble de leurs activités en unités aussi homogènes que possible quant au travail qu'elles utilisent, et localiseront ces unités dans les lieux où le travail correspondant est disponible".

What then is the place of border regions in this process of organized dispersion of activities? Can some intrinsic characteristics in relation to other peripheral regions be defined? If yes, how could the consequences on their socio-economic development be appreciated?

In considerations on the spatial and international division of labour models, the border regions, when they really are open, present some attractive characteristics for the localization of specific segments of production activities for three main reasons:

- Economic order bound to a proximity effect, i.e., a border region, even though part of a national territory, is necessarily at the same time an area of separation and of contact. It therefore constitutes a tension space but, simultaneously, it anticipates, in some way, the other country. Eventual localization in this area whether in the national territory or in the contiguous foreign space can be very attractive, because it will profit from the proximity advantages, i.e. the presence in the area of economic operators from two or more political-institutional systems and from the benefits determined by the logic of spatial delocalization of activities;
- A social reason which is bound to the flexibility of the labour force availability. The border, because of its legal and control functions, very easily creates some discriminating conditions for the labour force as a function of the proper needs of the displaced production units - discriminations created by law or 'de facto' because of different motivations of the workmanship of the border labour force (see Doeringer and Priore, 1971);
- Cultural reasons which are bound to the permeability of the local societies. The border region can be considered to have greater permeability due to a series of circumstances - necessary practice of the adaptation spirit; frequent migratory phenomena; different values on identities and traditions. The behavioural analysis of the parties in question (see Spehl, 1982) and the perception of the transborder

reality (see Leimgruber, 1987) plays in fact a significant role in the border-effects manifestation.

If we consider the case of an open border, it is suggested that two types of border-related revenues are thus created (see Di Tella, 1982; Turner, 1921):

(a) A differential revenue which is determined, for example, by discrimination in the salaries between the areas divided by the border;
(b) A position rent which is determined by the effect of proximity that might create some specific comparative advantages.

These two types of revenue have some consequences which manifest themselves in an unequal way, both in 'sign' and intensity: the global effect can be of positive value, a null summation, or a negative value for the whole transborder region. The fragility and instability of the elements at the base of the revenues undoubtedly lead to a dynamic approach to these phenomena.

Let us try now to show whether these characteristics really introduce the border regions into the logic of the spatial organization process discribed above.

Numerous studies of this case seem to confirm the thesis of the potential attraction of certain border-areas for the localization of distributional activities inside the spatial hierarchy of production.

First, the significant effect of proximity on social-economic and cultural order has been demonstrated. This phenomena determines, for the regions located on both sides of the border, some privileged relations consisting of a level of investment and of exchange above the average (see Jeannerat, 1985: Swiss areas adjacent to Austria, Germany, France and Italy). The case of Swiss and German enterprises investments in Alsace (see Datar, 1974) correspond to a logic of minimization of production costs at the level of simple establishments.

The decisive revealing sign of the existence of a process of spatial and hierarchic division of labour is given by the verifiable results on the labour market. An empirical study covering all European border regions shows the existence of important differences in the remuneration level on one side of the border as opposed to the other side. This constitutes a favourable premise and a margin of manoeuvre for the creation, maintenance or development of the richest areas of production, segments strongly conditioned by labour costs (see Ricq, 1981). The dualism of the labour market, characterized by the strong presence of transborder workers, becomes then the thermometer of the attraction role of the border in the process of spatial diffusion of activities. This situation is also noted in studies concerning the transborder space between Mexico and the U.S.A. (see Hansen, 1981; Peach, 1987) and in the case of the transborder triangle area 'Alsace - Baden Württemberg - Basel', of the axis Swiss-French Jura as well as in the Ticino area (see Biucchi and Gaudard, 1981).

6.4 The Necessity for a New Theoretical Hypothesis Adapted to the Concept of 'Border Area of Contact'

In the current scenario of the construction of Europe, we sometimes hear of a 'Europe without borders' and a 'Europe of regions'. If one were to specify the actual objectives to be met, the first objective well indicates the attempt to eliminate some borders. The attempt of the European Community to introduce fundamental economic freedom will certainly reduce or eliminate the significance of border-line or separation barriers between states.

The second denomination is more global in its significance and also more complex. On one side, it aims to eliminate certain borders, but also leaves some room to some other limits of a geographic, social, cultural, structural and linguistic order. The difference between Europe at the end of the 20th Century with the Europe of the States will be synonymous not because of the suppression of the borders but because of the transition from the situation of a border which separates, to that of a border understood as a contact area.

It is important to emphasize the theoretical hypothesis by underlining not the effects of the barrier existence, but, on the contrary, the overcoming of these barriers and the construction of contact spaces allowing for inter-regional cooperation (see Ratti and Baggi, 1990; Ratti, 1989). For this purpose, we suggest two different approaches:

(a) First, with a micro-economic character which combines the study of the border with the analysis of the strategic behaviour of the economic actors of these regions. It is based on the industrial organization theory and on a network strategy.

(b) Second, with a meso-economic character which considers the role of the border in the determination of a supporting space, or even as a specific environment.

6.4.1 Overcoming the 'obstacle-border' by the operators' strategic behaviour

A border, whether institutional or of any other nature, is almost always characterized by a situation of uncertainty and growing complexity, often signifying imperfect information or lack of transparency. The profitable management of this uncertainly and supplementary transaction costs requires the necessary reference to the modern theory of industrial organization, particularly the strategy of horizontal integration.

(i) Postulates

- To both the 'firm' and the 'market', there exists an important form of organization and regulation of production: the cooperation between enterprises (see Richardson, 1972):"The dichotomy between firm and market, between direct and spontaneous coordination, is misleading; it ignores the institutional fact of interfirm cooperation and assumes away the distinct method of coordination that this can provide".
- The existence of 'uncertainty' requires new functions, particularly of coordination (see Camagni, 1991):"The presence of inescapable static and dynamic uncertainty in the real world implies the presence of extra costs and therefore new functions to cope with these costs and new 'operators or institutions' organizing these functions and shaping factual behaviour".
- The concept of 'transaction cost' constitutes the discriminating instrument between the functions assumed by the firm, the market or the cooperation (see

Coase, 1937):"A firm will expand until the cost of organizing an extra-transaction within the firm becomes equal to the cost of carrying out the same transaction by means of an exchange on the open market or the cost of organizing within another firm".

(ii) Thesis

The existence of market distortions and transaction costs constrains the enterprise to adopt two types of strategic behaviour:

- vertical integration, following the classical argument (see Williamson, 1975, 1985, 1986);
- horizontal integration, as an intermediary organization form, more flexible and based upon a logic of dialogue (see Porter, 1980, 1986), particularly attractive for the SME (Small and Medium Enterprises) searching for 'synergies' (see Kamann and Strijker, 1991).

There is a good probability that these intermediary forms of cooperation will be territory dependent, because of the need to perform in accordance with a common code of behaviour (see Christensen, 1988):"The distance of dialogue is restricted by the need of common code and the need of face-to-face contacts ..... This need for proximity is based on the assumption that common code is embedded in a contextual macroframe characterized by common language, law, value, social background and joint ability of orientation".

(iii) Corollaries

The existence of a 'border' or any other form of 'barrier to communication' constitutes immediately a determinant factor of uncertainty and costs of transaction. The study of these 'borders' or 'barriers' becomes then a crucial element in the constitution and dynamic explanation of an intermediary organization of the 'reseau (network)' type (see Figure 4).

- The degree of integration of a firm, constituted by the agreement with other enterprisies (from the simple licence agreement, to the joint venture of a branch) is a function of the transaction costs or the market access costs (CT-CT or CT'-CT'), or of the control costs of the developed interfirm organization (CC-CC or CC'-CC') and also of a preference curve to the integration, corresponding to the demand curve (D-D or D'-D').
- The transaction costs are an exogenous constraining given phenomenon. Below a certain level (CT'-CT'), the firm will be interested in further developing its internal organization. Beyond that point, an inter-enterprise cooperation would constitute a less expensive option in relation to the market solution.
- The control costs are represented by a growing function of the 'integration quantity'. The points E1 and E2 are situations where there are equivalents between the possibility of recurring to the market and that of organizing certain functions of production with other enterprises.

(a) The optium is established by considering the demand curve, that is, the preference curve of the integration. Point E3 is lower than E1, because it is possible to account for a certain fear due to the risks of all external cooperation formulas.

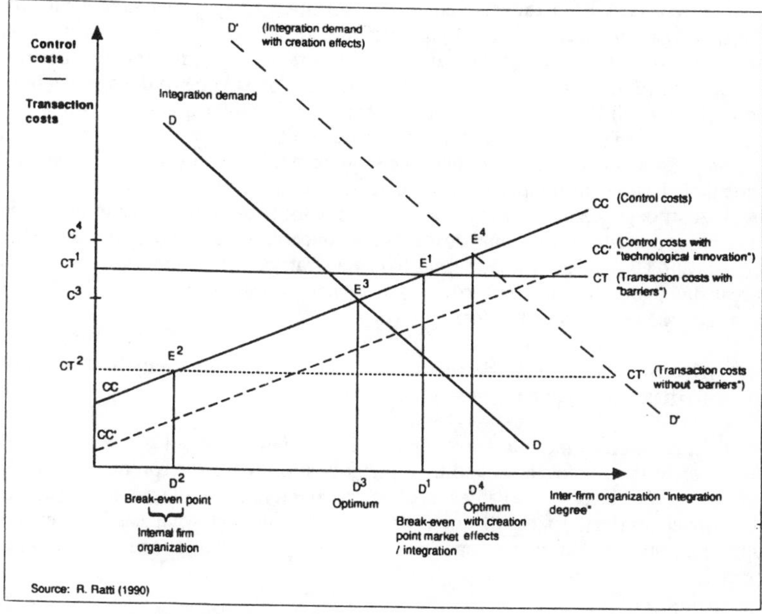

Figure 4 The degrees of integration of a firm (transaction costs, control costs and preference to the integration)

(b) The presence of a border barrier signifies a line of high transaction costs (CT'-CT'). It will then allow some intermediary solutions with an integration as high as the market distortion. All 'uncertainty' reductions due to the barrier-border would approach market solutions. This would indicate that the cooperation solutions are not necessarily stable or better.

(c) The opportunity of the firm to take advantage of a planned solution with other enterprises consists in the lowering of the curve CC-CC toward CC'-CC', by technological innovation and management. This shows the innovative character of the network, but does not necessarily guarantee that it will be advantageous to the firm in absolute terms.

(d) The above reasoning has been conducted in terms of minimized costs. To the objection that the resilient integration requires also a creation effect, it is possible in this case to reply that the preference curve can be displaced upward (from D-D to D'-D'). It will also determine an optimum (E4) which will even be above the transaction costs, having as a consequence a particularly high degree of integration.

Finally, even supposing that the trends of some transaction costs are reduced following the 'Europe without borders'-postulates, the relevance and the continuity of an organization in a network depends on its capacity to innovate, both in terms of minimizing control costs and in terms of value creation.

In conclusion, in the new context of an open border, the theoretical analysis advocates that the economic development of the border areas will not be determined by the political-institutional differential and therefore by the differentiated position of profits, positive or negative, due to the effect of belonging to one or the other nation, but more likely, by the compared real advantages of both border areas. The 'open border' implies the passage from the concept of border areas economy to that of transborder economy. This situation can imply some quick and fundamental adjustments. The strategic behaviour of the partners is particularly crucial.

A strategy in terms of a cooperation network is the most efficient approach for overcoming persistent or residual obstacles and 'uncertainty' situations typical of a border context. But, all this needs to be supported by a strategy of functional synergies, capable of realizing themselves at a level covering the whole transborder area in a timely manner as in the case of the filter border.

6.4.2 Overcoming the 'obstacle-border' by a functional space analysis of the regional parties: the supporting space

In addition to the micro-economic point of view, analyzed through the strategic behaviour of the parties, a second theoretical possibility for interpreting the border in its function, particularly as a contact area, is presented in terms of spatial anaysis, i.e. the study of the strategic spaces of enterprises and, particularly, what has been called the supporting space, that is the ensemble of the factor frames and of the relations 'preceding the market'.

(i) Postulates

The 'strategic' or 'life' spaces of an enterprise are determined by three functional spaces (see Ratti, 1971; Ratti and D'ambrogio, 1988; Ratti, 1989):

(a) The 'production space' of the firm is determined by the spatial division of the work following the model of the segmentation theory. An enterprise buying outside will define and delocalize its production, following the technological, economic and socio-cultural characteristics specific to each segment and to each production region.

(b) The 'market space' is determined by the relation the enterprise maintains with its different markets. These spatial relations are characterized by the number, intensity, structural characteristics, and by the evolutionary process of these markets relative to their environment.

This definition, in spatial-functional terms of supply and demand, already makes up significant progress in the dynamic approach of the enterprise development. However, it still seems insufficient to deal with the interior and exterior strategic aspects of the enterprise. It is then proposed to define a third functional space of enterprise.

(c) The 'supporting space' describes three types of non-marketing relations:

- The qualified or privileged relations at the organizational level of the production factors (capital origin, information source, technological ability, particular ties at the human capital level, etc.);
- The strategic relations of the enterprise with its partners, suppliers or clients (privileged information exchange, cooperation, partnership, alliance, partial integration, etc.);
- The strategic relations with the territorial environment parties (public institutions, private or semi-public associations, etc.).

It is possible to represent in Figure 5 the characteristic traits of the spatial-functional relations of an enterprise following the traditional non-spatial model. Following this model the strategic space of the enterprise is defined.

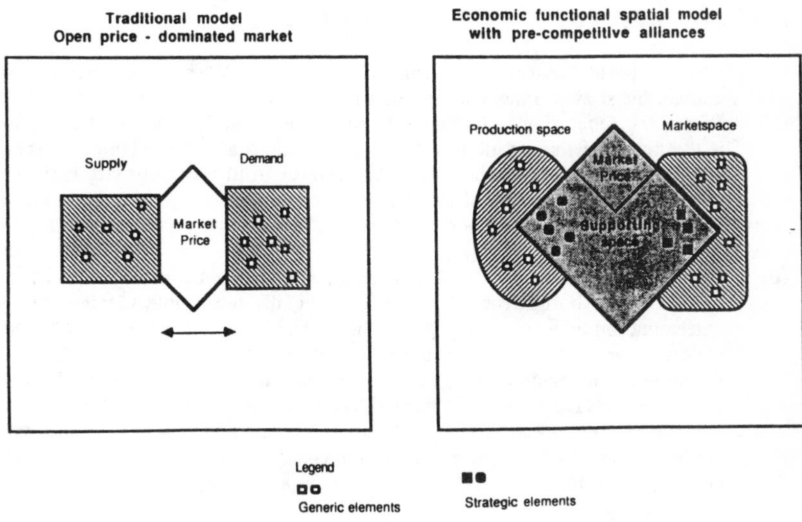

Figure 5 The economic-functional strategic spaces of a firm
Source: IRE/Ratti (1991)

(ii) **Thesis**

(a) Among the three functional spaces of the enterprise, the supporting space appears to be particularly crucial to the strategic orientation of the enterprise. Specifically it enables a direct consideration of the so-called factor frames and also some important relations of a pre-competitive character.

(b) The aggregation of functional spaces of the different enterprises can, with a certain possibility (see Christensen, 1988), give way to some spatial functional relations. Territorially, in terms of polarized space or of functional space 'force fields', the supporting space dynamics pushes the enterprises to look for common interests and to cooperate with the territorial institutions for the creation of a favourable environment.

(c) This relative coincidence between a strong node of functional spaces and territorial spaces allows 'local synergies'. This is defined as the result of a territorial materialization of an ensemble of functional relations structured in terms of a pole or force field. This logic leads to other notions applied in recent regional literature: 'local industrial network', 'localized ecosystem', 'industrial district', 'localized industrial system' and, finally, towards the notion of 'milieu' developed by GREMI (1985, 1988).

(iii) Corollaries

(a) The two border characteristics (barrier or contact) influence in a determinant manner the strategy spaces of the enterprises, particularly their supporting spaces.

(b) Where the separation factors are dominant, the possibility that the border area is the origin of the creation of a real supporting space is insignificant. This is confirmed by the Jura chain. Often, the existence of this type of space is strongly influenced by the politics of the nation states and the entry port. The eventual synergy effects have a temporary and unilateral character, with the exclusion of 'regional' effects.

(c) Where the contact factors (effects of economic, social and cultural proximity) are dominant, the border can constitute a potentially favourable element for the determination of a supporting space. The probability of synergies appearing at a regional level will be stronger, and essentially dependent on the strategic determination of the regional parties. History shows that each town or port, where the localization is favourable to exchanges, has developed a real 'supporting' strategy (custom tax free towns, duty free fairs, etc.). A recent and very pertinent example in the framework of the Europe of Regions context is the regio Basilensis created about thirty years ago.

To conclude, it becomes evident that with the economic and political necessity tied to the creation of a real space of a free European market the 'open border' implies the passage from the concept of border areas economy to that of transborder economy. This situation can imply some quick and fundamental adjustments. The strategic behaviour of the partners is particularly crucial. A strategy in terms of a cooperation network is the most efficient approach for overcoming obstacles and 'uncertaintly' situations typical of a border context. But all this needs to be supported by a strategy of functional synergies, capable of realizing themselves at a level covering the whole transborder area in a timely manner as in the case of the filter-border. The border in its contact functions therefore needs to be pursued positively as a pre-condition to the opening.

6.5 Conclusions: an Overview of Different Approaches and Further Research

6.5.1 The border area view: value and limits

The border view (in contrast to the frontier approach, see Section 6.2) is perhaps the more traditional, and more often found in arguments of empirical studies on frontier effects. As indicated in the English dictionary, the word 'border' means those territories immediately close to the dividing line between two or more countries.

The perspective is that of a border territorially defined by a fixed line. This given boundary line is the starting point for the analysis of the territory close by to it. In areas close to the border line we will verify a series of effects directly connected with the barrier in which the institutional border between two countries is the responsible factor. It is a narrow and rather empirical definition of the concept of the border area as treated by Hansen (1977):"This relates to that part of a natural territory in which economic and social life is directly and significantly influenced by the proximity of an international frontier. We thus consider here only open or potentially open regions, excluding regions with a closed natural border situation, like, for example, some parts of the Alps". Concerning the area under consideration, there exist two concepts: the **border area** which extends along the boundaries on the national territory and is therefore an expression of the national **centripetal** idea; the **transborder area** which extends across the political boundary and represents the **centrifugal** forces (which characterizes the free economy). Yet, even this approach, apparently simple, immediately presents some difficulties: **is the border effect exhausting itself in the area territorially adjacent to the border?** Evidently not. House (1981), for example, already distinguishes a second territory, further away, which he calls 'regional intermediate', meaning the intermediate area between the border area (coinciding roughly with the activity area of the 'commuters') and the national centers. It derives a typology of relations between national centers, provincial centers and bordering areas supporting an input-output model of transbordering flows.

6.5.2 Four theoretical approaches to the study of the spatial impacts of the frontier-border

From the viewpoint of 'border region' then, it is possible to relate four types of approach to the territory immediately close to the dividing line between two or more countries which, directly or indirectly, can be found or derived from the regional science literature (cf. Figure 6).

A first economic approach is that of 'functional' type (see Guichonnet and Raffestin, 1974). Moreover, in the case study concerning the regional development of a border area (see Biucchi and Gaudard, 1981) one can find, even though it is not always explicity evident, an attempt at measuring the functions of a frontier (see Ratti, 1988): one will ascertain real and true flow interruptions (barrier paradigm); in other cases discriminating effects (positive or negative) will be evident and will lead to the phenomena of differential incomes (manifested, for example, by smuggling), while, in other cases, one can directly ascertain some polarizing effects (localization at the border permitting a break of bulk).

Economic activities in border areas are facing a number of institutional barriers which may be translated into a higher probability of market failure (lack of information), bounded rationality and greater uncertainty. As a result, border areas are facing a number of functional effects, which have been classified into three types (see Ratti, 1990):

- **Frontier effects**, consisting in stopping or strongly penalizing movements of persons, goods and capitals (see Christaller; Loesch) while on the other hand focusing on the 'principle of separation' which has been promoted by Hansen;
- **Filtering effects**, related to the distortion in the direction and intensity of flows implied by the existence of a frontier. This evokes the important concept of differential rent. In other words, the economy of border regions can create such income situations, positive or negative, for one or the other side of the border, in which the total effect - and this is very important - is not necessarily **a zero sum**;
- **Polarizing effects**, referring to the function of contact between two or more political-institutional systems or socio-economic subsystems. In this context, the economic development of the bordering regions will no longer be determined by the political-institutional differential (and therefore the position rent, positive and negative, due to the effect of belonging to this or that country), but, eventually, by the comparative advantages of the **combination** of the two areas, on both sides of the border. In other terms, the 'open border' implies (see Ratti and Baggi, 1990) the bypassing of the economic concept of the bordering areas (see Hansen, 1983) to proceed to that of **transbordering economies** (see Section 6.4).

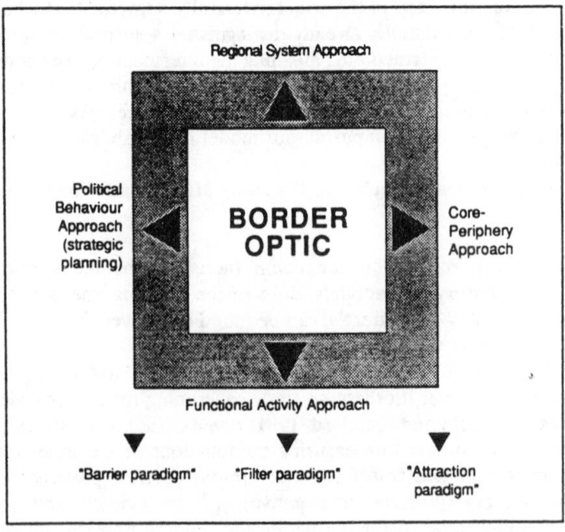

Figure 6 Spatial impact of transport and communication barriers: theoretical approaches in the 'border optic'

Source: Ratti (1990)

The second approach for evaluating the development of the border area is that referring to the theoretical interpretation key of the type 'core-periphery' (see Friedmann and Weaver, 1979; Giaoutzi, 1991). In fact, in most cases (and almost by definition) the border areas are not only institutional peripheries but also peripheries in an economic sense (see Giaoutzi and Stratigea, 1989). Yet, in a world of increasingly complex interrelationships between areas, the dualistic reference to a unigue center and to periphery, generally appears as a limitation, so that with this approach it seems preferable, particularly because of the dynamic aspects, to use a framework of analysis that uses an explicit reference to a systemic type of approach (see Dauphiné, 1979).

By this third approach the changing form of regional development can be interpreted as a spatial response to changes of a dynamic, but contradictory, economic system (see Stillwell, 1991). Thus, political disarticulation, like borders, could be identified as specific elements of a regional restructuring process which show why there are instabilities in patterns of regional economic development; for example, the studies on the evolution of territorial organization of the Canton Ticino emphasized how in only one century, or even more surprisingly, in a few decades, this area could evolve (see Ratti and Di Stefano, 1986) from a situation of a double peripheral area with respect to the North of the Alps and to Italy, to a space position of intermediation and, even more, to a situation of an emerging open space. Particularly, the systemic type of approach has the great advantage of overturning the emphasis from the discovery aspect of the border to that of a contact area, where the transborder relationships can arise from the encounter of diverse structures.

At last, geographers of perception have used an interpretation key which recently has demonstrated its usefulness as a reference to a strategic planning approach (see Faludi, 1986). If the border really exists, it will influence the individual subjective perception of the economic agents and, particularly, the strategic behaviour of the latter will be influenced (see Covin and Slevin, 1989).

In the economic literature the response to a host of institutional barriers is given in terms of a greater emphasis on economic organization; by vertical integration of the hierarchy (see Williamson, 1975), by intermediate forms of coordination and alliances (see Camagni, 1991), and by the elaboration of common codes of conduct in border regions (see Christensen, 1988).

In the political geography literature, the notion most relevant to our discussion would be that of territoriality, which would reveal itself in the behaviour of the different actors living in a border region. In this case, it is suggested that there exists a specific territoriality in frontier regions. Indeed, a list of indicators for coping behaviour with barriers and boundary situations can be drawn (see Reichman, 1989), based as they are on the perceptions and practice of strategic planning.

More recently, the social boundaries of organization have been perceived as acting as sieves, not shells, determining which flows from the environment to admit, and what elements are to be rejected. This calls for two alternative strategies to be adopted: **buffering strategies**, whose main goal is to protect the organization and reduce uncertainties; **bridging strategies**, particularly within a non-zero-sum view of power (see Scott, 1987). Finally, an analogy can be drawn from concepts derived in the field of organizations to that of spatial boundaries, including that of open and less-than-open political boundaries. This new theme is increasingly encountered in the current literature which emphasises transborder cooperation (see Reichman, 1992).

Acknowledgement

The authors wish to thank the members of the NECTAR subgroup on Border Areas Strategic Studies (BASS) for their comments.

References

Aydalot, Ph., Les Technologies Nouvelles et les Formes Actuelles de la Division spatiale du Travail, **Dossier du Centre Economie, Espace, Environment**, 47, Paris, 1986, pp.1-16.

Biucchi, B.M. and G. Gaudard (eds.), **Régions Frontalières**, Ed. Georgi, St.-Saphorin, 1981.

Button, K. and F. Rossera, Barriers to Communication, a Literature Review, **The Annals of Regional Science**, 24 (4), 1990, pp.337-357.

Camagni, R. (ed.), **Innovation Networks**, Belhaven Press, London and New York, 1991.

Christaller, W., **Die Zentrale Orte in Süddeutschland**, Wissenschaftliche Buchgesellschaft, Darmstadt, FRG, (reprinted 1980), 1933.

Christensen, P.R., **Enterprise Flexibility and Regional Networks**, paper presented at the RSA Annual Congress, Athens, 1988.

Coase, R.H., The Nature of Firm, **Economica**, vol. 4, 1937, pp.33-47.

Covin, J.G. and D.P. Slevin, Strategic Management of Small Firms in Hostile and Benign Environments, **Strategic Management Journal**, 10 (1), 1989, pp.75-87.

DATAR, **Investissements Étrangers et Aménagement du Territoire: Livre Blanc**, Datar, Paris, 1974.

Dauphiné, A., **Espace, Région et Système**, Economica, Paris, 1979.

Di Tella, G., The Economics of the Frontier, **Economics in the Long View** (C.P. Kindleberger and G. Di Tella, eds.), Macmillan, London, 1982, pp.99-116.

Doeringer, P.B. and M.J. Piore, **Internal Labor Markets and Manpower Analysis**, D.C. Heath, Lexington, 1971.

Faludi, A., Toward a Theory of Strategic Planning, **Netherlands Journal of Housing and Evironmental Research**, 3, 1986, pp.253-268.

Friedmann, J. and C. Weaver, **Territory and Function**, Edward Arnold, London, 1979.

Gaudard, G., Le Problème des Régions-frontières Suisses, **Cahiers de l'ISEA**, Paris, 1971.

Giaoutzi, M. and A. Stratigea, The Impact of New Information Technologies on Spatial Inequalities, **Regional Science-Retrospect and Prospect** (D. Boyce, P. Nijkamp and D. Shefer, eds.), Springer Verlag, Berlin, 1991, pp.240-257.

Guichonnet, P. and C. Raffestin, **Géographie des Frontières**, Presses Universitaires de France, Paris, 1974.

Hansen, N.M., Border Regions: A Critique of Spatial Theory and a European Case Study, **Annals of Regional Science**, 11, 1977, pp.1-14.

Hansen, N.M., Mexico's Border Industry and the International Division of Labor: Abstracts, **Annals of Regional Science**, 15, 1981, pp.255-270.

Hansen, N.M., International Cooperation in Border Regions; An Overview and Research agenda, **International Regional Science Review**, 8 (3), 1983, pp.255-270.

House, J.W., The Frontier Zone, a Conceptual Problem for Policy Makers, **International Regional Science Review**, 1 (4), 1980, pp.456-477.

House, J.W., Frontier Studies: An Applied Approach, **Political Studies from Spatial Perspectives** (A. Burnett and P. Taylor, eds.), John Wiley, Chichester, 1981, pp.74-94.

Jeanneret, Ph., **Régions et Frontières Internationales**, EDES, Neuchâtel, 1985.

Kamann, D. and D. Strijker, The Network Approach: Concepts and Applications, **Innovation Networks: Spatial Perspective** (R. Camagni, ed.), Belhaven Press, London and New York, 1991, pp.101-116.

Leimgruber, W., **Il Confine e la Gente**, Lativa, Varese, 1987.

Loesch, A., **Die Räumliche Ordnung der Wirtschaft**, G. Fischer, Jena, 1940.

Michalet, Ch.A., **Le Capitalisme Mondial**, Presses Universitaires de France, Paris 1976.

Nijkamp, P., P. Rietveld and I. Salomon, Barriers in Spatial Interactions and Communications, a Conceptual Exploration, **Annals of Regional Science**, 24 (4), 1990, pp.237-252.

Peach, J.Z., U.S.-Mexican Border Workers: A Review of Selected Issues and Recent Research, **Cross-Border Relations: European and North American Perspectives** (S. Ercmann, ed.), Schulthess Polygraphischer Verlag, Zürich, 1987, pp.54-67.

Porter, M.E., **Competitive Strategy: Techniques for Analyzing Industries and Competitors**, Free Press, New York, 1980.

Porter, M.E., **Competition in Global Industries**, Harvard Business School Press, Boston, 1986.

Ratti, R., **I Traffici Internazionali di Transito e la Regione di Chiasso**, Editions Universitaires, Fribourg, 1971.

Ratti, R., Development Theory, Technological Change and Europe's Frontier Region, **High Technology Industry and Innovative Environments: The European Experience** (Ph. Aydalot and D. Keeble, eds.), Routledge, London and New York, 1988, pp.120-134.

Ratti, R., Economia di Frontiera: l'Evoluzione di un Concretto, Barriera Filtro o Luogo d'Incontro?, **Insieme Cultura**, Como, 12, 1989, pp.37-40.

Ratti, R., The Study of the Spatial Effects of the Borders: An Overview of Different Approaches, **NETCOM**, 4 (1), 1990, pp.37-50.

Ratti, R. and Alii, Régions Frontières, **Problèmes Régionaux** (B.Biucchi and G.Gaudard, ed.), Berne, Ed. Georgi, St.-Saphorin, 1981, pp.101-124.

Ratti, R. and A. Di Stefano, L'innovation Technologique au Tessin, **Innovative Environments in Europe** (Ph. Aydalot, ed.), GEMRI, Paris, 1986, pp.160-174.

Ratti, R. and F.D. 'Ambrogio, Un Essai d'Analyse Fonctionelle et Territoire de l'Industrie Innovatrice au Tessin, Colloque GREMI, Ascona, 1988.

Ratti, R. and M. Baggi, Strategies to Overcome Barriers: Theoretical Elements and Empirical Evidence, Paper Workshop NECTAR, Lund, 1990.

Reichman, S., Barriers and Strategic Planning - A Tentative Research Formulation, Paper presented at NECTAR Meeting, Zürich, 1989.

Reichman, S., Barriers and Strategic Planning: Spatial and Institutional Formulations, **Theory and Strategy of Border Areas Development** (R. Ratti, and S. Reichman, eds.), Bellinzona, 1992 (forthcoming).

Richardson, G.A., The Organization of Industry, **The Economic Journal**, 82, 1972, pp.883-896.

Ricq, Ch., **Les Travailleurs Frontaliers en Europe: Essai de Politique Sociale et Régionale**, Ed. Anthropos, Paris, 1981.

Scott, W.R., **Organizations: Rational, Natural and Open Systems**, Prentice-Hall, Englewood Cliffs, 2nd edition, 1987.

Spehl, H., Wirkungen der Nationalen Grenze auf Betriebe in Peripheren Regionen - Dargestellt am Beispiel der Saar-Lor-Lux-Raumes, University of Trier, 1982.

Stillwell, F., Regional Economic Development: An Analytical Framework, **Revue d'Economie Régionale et Urbaine**, 1, 1991, pp.107-115.

Turner, F.J., **The Frontier in American History**, New York, 1921.

Urban, S., L'Intégration Économique Européenne et l'Évolution Régionale de Part et d'Autre Rhin, **Economie et Société**, 5, 1971, pp.603-635.

Williamson, O.E., **Markets and Hierarchies, Analysis and Antitrust Implications**, Free Press, New York; Macmillan Publ., London, 1975.

Williamson, O.E., **Economic Institutions of Capitalism: Firm, Market, Regional Contracting**, Free Press, New York; Macmillan Publ., London, 1985.

Williamson, O.E., **Economic Organization: Firms, Market and Policy Control**, Wheatsheaf Books, Brighton, 1986.

PART B

IMPACTS OF INFORMATICS AND LOGISTICS

CHAPTER 7

INFORMATION AND COMMUTERS BEHAVIOUR: A COMPARATIVE ANALYSIS

Eli Stern, Einar Holm and Martin van Maarseveen

7.1 Introduction

Due to rapid technological developments and growing urgency for a more efficient use of existing infrastructure, Road Transport Informatics (RTI) receives increasing attention from transportation planners. Most studies on RTI potential impacts concentrate either on electronic in-vehicle information systems (see Al-Deek et al., 1988; May, 1989), or on travellers responses and transportation systems reactions (see Garrison and Deakin, 1988; Coe, 1989; Stergiou and Stathopoulos, 1989; Zumkeller, 1991).

Early works attempting to assess potential system impacts, concentrated mainly on choice of departure time (see Abkowitz, 1981). Later studies included also route choice information (see Abu-Eisheh and Mannering, 1987; Mannering, 1989). The effect of information, mainly referred to self-experience, was studied through aggregate types of simulation (see Mahmassani and Tong, 1986; Tong et al., 1987). Apart from very few efforts to use microsimulation for studying network impacts (see Stern and Sinuani, 1989; Alfa, 1989), the various studies used a macro approach with relatively simple network structures (see Mahmassani et al, 1986; Mahmassani and Harman, 1988; Mahmassani, 1989). Combining the micro-simulation approach (see Clarke and Holm, 1987) with personal attributes concerning the use of information, the present authors examine potential impacts of road transport information on the performance of transport systems, especially in terms of congestion. They estimate the possible effects of information presented to commuting drivers (by conventional means like media and roadside information) on network performance. Due to the universal nature of congestion, the study is based on behavioural data collected by three identical questionnaires in Sweden and Israel. The international comparative nature of the study is also aimed to identify differences in both travellers needs and responses to road traffic information between countries.

The present paper reports, however, only on the pre-simulation phase of the above mentioned comparative study. It is a two-stage phase which (a) identifies discriminating factors between commuters who change and commuters who do not change their travel behaviour due to information, and (b) uses the identified factors in a causal model to estimate the effect of information on commuting drivers' route choice. It thus examines only selected behavioural aspects of the drivers, aspects which will later be used through micro-simulation to estimate overall network performance.

7.2 Theoretical Foundation

Among the questions, which arise as the transport environment becomes more information-rich, is the one concerns with the determinants of information use by individual commuters. Apart from factors related directly to the information itself like when, how and where it is provided (see e.g. Polak and Jones, 1991), personal and environmental factors seem to determine whether commuters will use given traffic information. These factors have been partially discussed in the wider spatio-behavioural context dealing with travel behaviour.

The man-environment interface paradigm (see Golledge and Stimson, 1987) considers travel behaviour to result from the following series: (a) an objective situation, (b) a subjective situation, (c) personal perceptions, and (d) personal decisions, in the way presented in Figure 1A. Travel behaviour is influenced, accordingly, by four groups of factors, at both the objective and the subjective levels:

1. **The physical environment**; including the network infrastructure which determines, for example, travel possibilities and their characteristics.
2. **The socio-demographic environment**; including the household characteristics like modes of transport chosen, age, and the like. These attributes will affect the cognition and perception of travel opportunities as may also impose constraints on travel (see Bovy and Stern, 1990).
3. **The normative environment**; including the set of norms, values and concepts derived from society and, in particular, from the immediate surrounding of the traveler.
4. **The personal environment**; comprising of the personality of the decision-maker, which may cause the three factors mentioned above, together forming the objective situation, to be observed subjectively, and the information derived therefrom to be converted into a decision.

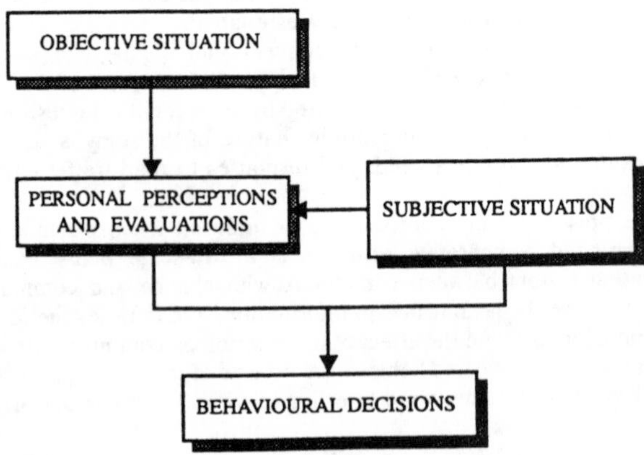

Figure 1A. The men-environment interface paradigm. Basic structure

The decision studied in the present paper concerns with a change in travel behaviour of commuters due to information. A change in travel behaviour refers to modal change, route change, and change in departure time, each of which may be practiced by the driving commuter in order to avoide morning congestion. It is assumed that each one of these behavioural changes could be influenced by the factors presented above in the way presented in Figure 1B. Accordingly, we use these factors to discriminate between those who change and those who do not change their travel behaviour as traffic information becomes available.

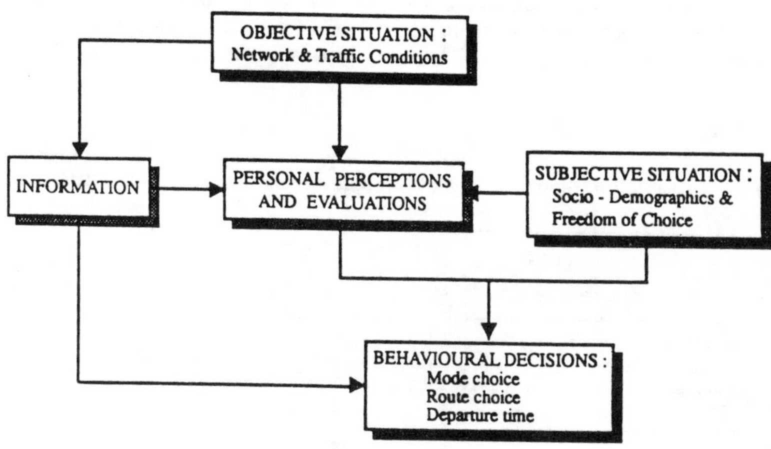

Figure 1B. Information-wise expanded structure

7.3 Empirical Framework

Several methods and designs have been used by public agencies and research institutions for administrating surveys on motorists behaviour. There is a wide diversity among these methods as presented by Spyridakis et al. (1991) and Haselkorn et al. (1990). The off-ramps solicitation method was found most accurate in both response proximity and sample frame. The data needed for microsimulation had, however, to be based on a limited number of origin points (see Stern et al., 1990) and therefore, instead of an off-ramps method our questionnaire was distributed in selected business locations.

Locations were determined according to the geographical pattern of morning congestion, assuring that sampled employees would experience congestion on their way to work.

In each location 1-3 firms were selected, each of which with a high proportion of car owning employees, flexibility of working hours for part of the staff, and access to public transportation. Two identical questionnaires were distributed to both male and female employees in Tel Aviv, Israel (3 business locations), and Gothenburg, Sweden (one business location). Sample sizes were 109 and 189, respectively.

7.4 Comparing Behavioural Changes

Survey results show that, on average, two thirds of commuters will change their travel behaviour upon receiving traffic information (Table 1). The larger response to information was found in Sweden (67.9%) and the smaller response in Israel (62.4%).

Table 1 Driver's behavioural change (% of total drivers) by type and country

	COUNTRY		
BEHAVIOURAL CHANGE	Sweden	Israel	Total
Change of route	47.5	34.7	42.8
Change of mode	4.2	5.9	4.8
Change of departure time	16.2	21.8	18.3
Total	67.9	62.4	65.9
No change	32.1	37.6	34.1

As observed, about 43 percent (on average) of the total drivers would change their habitual route upon receiving information about anticipated traffic problems. Only few drivers (less than 5 percent, on average) would change their mode, and about 18 percent would change their departure time. Changing route and departure time depends, to a large extent, on commuters' freedom of choice. Evidently, (Table 2), as the freedom to come to work either early or late is larger among the sampled commuters in Israel than among those sampled in Sweden, the prcentage of changing departure time is accordingly higher. A similar pattern is observed with regard to changing travel route; its probability is higher in Sweden as well as the availability of route alternatives. These observations encourage the inclusion of 'freedom of choice' as a discriminating factor of behavioural change.

Table 2 Commuters freedom of choice (in %)

Country	Type of choice: Time flexibility		Route alternatives	
	Yes	No	Yes	No
Sweden	34.4	65.6	53.7	46.3
Israel	43.2	56.8	47.0	53.0

7.5 Discriminating Behavioural Changes

The variables considered for inclusion in the discriminating analysis are all related to the factors presented earlier. The factors and their related variables are shown in Table 3. The justification for selecting these particular variables for each factor is based on proven relationships found in modelling route choice (see Bovy and Stern, 1990; Lotan and Koutsopoulos, 1992; Byrne, 1979), mode choice (see Ben-Akiva and Lerman, 1985), and choice of departure time (see Abkowitz, 1981; Hendrickson and Plank, 1984).

Table 3 Factors and corresponding discriminant variables

FACTOR	VARIABLE
A. Information	1. Exposure 2. Source 3. Content
B. Perceived Congestion	4. Value for urban roads 5. Value for motorways 6. Total delay time
C. Freedom of Choice	7. Route alternatives 8. Time flexibility 9. Car constraint
D. Location	10. Distance to work (length/duration)
E. Socio-Demographics	11. Age 12. Gender 13. Profession

A linear discriminant analysis was applied to distinguish between those who change and those who do not change behaviour due to information, and to find the variables which contribute most to this separation. Tables 4 and ummarize the results of the analyses for Israel and Sweden. The discriminant function for Israel is comprised primarily of five variables which enabled to classify correctly 79.2 percent of the 'grouped' cases. Three of the five discriminating variables in Israel relate to the information factor including, in a declining order of relative contribution, content of, exposure to, and source of information. Perceived congestion also highly contributes to dicriminate behavioural changes in Israel, but the most important contributing variable is the freedom to change routes.

The discriminant function for Sweden is comprised primarily of seven variables (Table 5) which enabled to classify correctly 98.2 percent of the 'grouped' cases. The role of information in Sweden is smaller than in Israel, while the subjective evaluation of congestion has the major role in discriminating travel behavioural change. Other affective variables are those related to freedom of choice (both of route and mode), location, and age.

The larger role of perceived congestion in discriminating travel behavioural changes in Sweden, can be attributed to the higher sensitivity of the Swedes to congestion. While the Israelies would perceive an urban road to be congested when driving speed drops to 25 km/h, the Swedes would perceive it likwise when driving speed reaches 32 km/h (Table 6). Even a higher sensitivity exists when motorways are concerned. Driving speed of about 65 km/h would already make a motorway seem congested

Table 4 Summarized results of the Discriminant Analysis for Israel

Variable	Group Means		Significance level (F-test)	Wilk's Lambda (A)	Standardized discriminant function coefficient
	Group 1 (change in behaviour)	Group 2 (no change in behaviour)			
1. Exposure to Information (daily frequency)	3.40	2.03	.0000	.274	.386
2. Source of Information (importance rank)	.500	.350	.0000	.354	.343
3. Content of Information (import. of behav instructions)	.308	.100	.0000	.331	.710
5. Perceived Congestion (on motorways)	52.1	48.8	.0000	.380	.682
7. Route alternatives (est. possibil.	49.2	25.7	.0000	.562	.761

(A) - All Wilk's Lambdas are statistically significant at the .0001 level.

Table 5 Summarized results of the Discriminant Analysis for Sweden.

Variable	Group Means		Significance level (F-test)	Wilk's Lambda (A)	Standardized discriminant function coefficient
	Group 1 (change in behaviour)	Group 2 (no change in behaviour)			
1. Exposure to information (daily frequency	2.70	3.25	.0001	.496	.332
4. Perceived congestion (on urban roads)	60.0	32.8	.0065	.825	.782
5. Perceived congestion (on motorways)	62.3	32.2	.0005	.671	.765
7. Route alternatives (est. possibil.)	53.2	20.3	.0002	.454	.330
9. Car constraint (availability)	4.8	5.3	.0002	.591	.625
10. Distance to work (in minutes)	18.2	7.5	.0001	.518	.365
11. Age (years)	30.0	39.0	.0002	.477	.353

(A) - All Wilk's Lambdas are statistically significant at the .0001 level.

in the eyes of the Swedes in comparison to 52 km/h in the eyes of the Israelies. These differences may also explain the higher dependency of the Israelies on information. The Swedes are influenced only by the amount of exposure to information, while it takes more for the Israelies to change their travel behaviour. It is not only the instructions to change behaviour which matter to the Israelies, but also the reliability of the information source. In this case, the radio is considered an an affective instruction mean.

Table 6 Levels of perceived congestion.

Country	Perceived Congestion (Km/h)	
	Urban roads	Motorways
Sweden	31.8	65.3
Israel	25.0	52.0

The group means of the discriminant variables provide more information about the profiles of the two separated groups. Evidently, in both countries, commuters who change their travel behaviour are more exposed to information, are more sensitive to congestion, and have more freedom of choice. In Sweden they are also younger and live relatively further from their workplace. The distance to the workplace may have two effects. As the distance increases, the traveller may have more route alternatives and, therefore, a higher freedom choice. At the same time, however, the larger distance, or trip duration, may force the commuter to change behaviour due to a possible larger delay.

Table 7 Characteristics of Israeli traveller types according to travel behavioural change (A)

Characteristics (Group mean value)	Type of travel behavioural change Route	Mode	Departure time
Experience (# of weekly driving days)	4.7	4.0	5.0
Fixed arrival time (%)	43.7	100.0	55.6
Route alternatives (1-100 scale)	54.4	40.0	38.8
Exposure to information (1-4 frequency scale)	1.7	3.0	2.6
Content of information (importance of behav. instructions)	.81	.00	.89
Source of information (importance of radio)	.25	1.00	.33
Age (years)	44.7	(B)	33.3

(A) - predictability 61.9%
(B) - missing data

Since not all anticipated discriminating variables appeared significant cant in the two-group separation, we further investigated the profiles of the commuters. Based on a three-group discriminant analysis, Tables 7 and 8 present only the significant ($p < .001$) characteristics of the three types of travel behavioural change namely, change of route, change of mode, and change of departure time.

Commuters who have changed mode due to anticipated congestion formed the smallest group in both countries. The only meaningful attribute in comparison to other groups, and only in Sweden, was age. Apparantly, the average age of those Swedes who left their car at home and used public transportation has been 57. Among the Israelies, those who changed mode were all commuters with no freedom of arrival time.

Commuters who have changed route due to anticipated congestion in both countries are travellers sensitive to congestion, with relatively more freedom of route choice, comprising of more male than female drivers. Those who have changed departure time usually live further away from their workplace, they have a fixed arrival time, and are (on average) younger people. The Israelies among them also have more daily, first hand, experience with congestion, as they drive more frequently to work than their Swedish counterparts.

Table 8 Characteristics of Swedish traveller types according to travel behavioural change (A)

Characteristics (Group mean value)	Type of travel behavioural change		
	Route	Mode	Departure time
Distance to work (min.)	20.8	10.0	24.3
Fixed arrival time (%)	33.3	00.0	85.7
Perceived congestion:			
-on urban roads (Km/hr)	36.0	20.0	26.4
-on motorways (Km/hr)	66.7	50.0	57.9
Route alternatives (1-10 scale)	68.0	4.0	52.9
Exposure to information (1-4 frequency scale)	2.3	1.0	2.4
Age (years)	43.2	57.0	39.7
Gender (% male in group)	73.3	N.S	71.4

(A) - predictability 47.5%
N.S - not significant.

7.6 Information and Route Choice

As presented previously (Table 2), change of route is the most frequent response to traffic messages in congested situations. Proper information on optimal available routes can greatly improve the performance of the traffic system, but complete information can also lead to a reduced performance (see Brocken and Van der Vlist, 1991) up to a full cahos in the system. Therefore, the determinants of travel behavioural change are used in a causal model to estimate the effect of information on commuters route choice. Information, however, is only one of four factors hypothesized to have a direct effect on the probability of route change (Figure 1). Unlike other factors, information is assumed to have also an indirect effect on route change through its effect on percieved congestion. The latter, is affected also by personal experience (see Tong et al., 1987), socio-demographics, and the individuals' freedom of choice.

These four direct and two indirect factors shown in Figure 2, are comprising of thirteen variables. Based on the results of the discriminant analyses, their hypothesized interrelationships are listed in Table 9.

As the general model (schematized in Fig. 2) is based on a casual structure, the hypothesized effects are examined through path analysis. All of the hypothesized direct and indirect casual linkages are embodied in the following five equations presented in standard notation:

{X8}{X1,X2,X3,X13} [1]
{X9,X10,X11}{X1,X2,X3,X4,X5,X7,X12} [2-4]
{X14}{X1,X2,X3,X4,X5,X6,X7,X8,X9,X10,X11} [5]

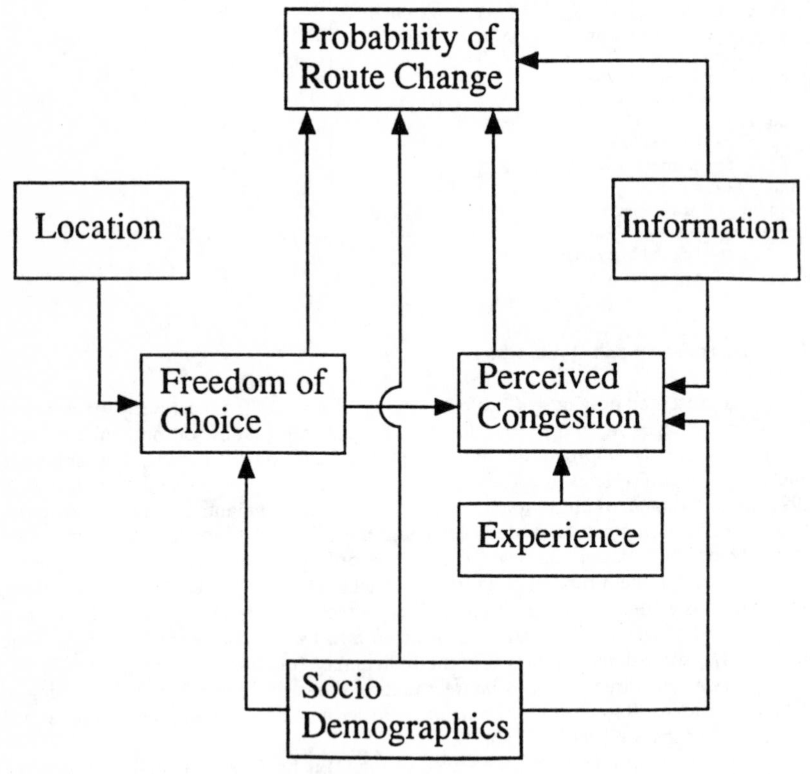

Figure 2. A general model of route change probability in congested situations

Table 9 Hypothesized causal effects (A)

DEPENDENT VARIABLES (X)	DEPENDENT VARIABLES			
	Route Change(B) (X14)	Perceived Congestion(C)		Freedom of Choice(C) Route
		Urban	Motorways	
Socio-demographics:				
1. Age -	(1)-	(12)-	(19)m	(26)m
2. Gender -	(2)+	(13)+	(20)+	(27)+
3. Profession -	(3)m	(14)m	(21)m	(28)m
Information:				
4. Exposure at home -	(4)+	(15)+	(22)+	
5. Exposure in car -	(5)+	(16)+	(23)+	
6. Road signs -	(6)+			
Freedom of Choice:				
7. Time flexibility -	(7)+	(17)+	(24)+	
8. Route alternatives -	(8)+			
Perceived congestion:				
9. Urban roads -	(9)+			
10. Motorways -	(10)+			
11. Total delay -	(11)-			
12. Experience-		(18)m	(25)m	
13. Location-				(29)+

(A) - Hypotheses numbered in parentheses. The sign indicates the direction of relationship, with "m" indicating mixed effects.
(B) - Direct effect.
(C) - Indirect effect.

An OLS regression was used to solve equations 1 through 5 in succession. The final results are presented in Tables 10. The data supported only part of the hypothesized effects on the probability of route change. Indirect effects are shown only if the respective mediating variable affects the probability of route change.

Among the 13 explanatory variables, the freedom of route choice and the perceived congestion on urban roads were found most affective attributes in Israel and Sweden respectively. Thus, the perceived environment, both in terms of opportunities (alternative routes) and constraints (limited travel speed) is the main factor in explaining the individual probability to change route when congestion is anticipated. As the perceived environment is a mental image of an objective environment (Stern and Krakover, 1992), variations in infrastructure and spatial organization explains the differences in the mix of explanatory variables between Sweden and Israel.

Table 10 Decomposition of total bivariate effects (A)

PROBABILITY OF ROUTE CHANGE (X14)	EFFECTS Direct	Indirect
Exposure to information (X4)		
- Israel	.091	-
- Sweden	.384	-
Information source (X6)		
- Israel	.180	-
- Sweden	-	-
Route alternatives (X8)		
- Israel	.642	-
- Sweden	.331	-
Perceived urban congestion (X9)		
- Israel		-
- Sweden	.48	-
Location (distance to work- X13)		
- Israel		-
- Sweden		.085

(A) - Only effects with p<.005.

7.7 Summary and Conclusions

The present study, being part of an on-going broader research, examines and compares the factors discriminating between commuters who change their travel behaviour due to anticipated congestion in Sweden and Israel. It further estimates and compares the effect of information on drivers route choice in these two countries. The comparison is aimed to examine the commonalities in the universal problem of congestion.

Cross country results show that two thirds of morning commuters are likely to change their travel behaviour when notified about anticipated congestion. The most frequent reaction is the change of route. Differences between countries show the important role of the information environment and the objective environment upon travel behavioural patterns.

In general, the results imply that commuters who are less sensitive to congestion (have lower perceived thresholds of travel speed) are likely to be more affected by the source and the content of the provided information. To be more affective, the contents should include behavioural instructions and not only informative announcements. Source of information should also be considered as reliable by the public. First-hand information like road signs, for example, are playing a major role in route change decisions. As sensitivity to congestion increases (commuters with higher perceived thresholds of travel speed), exposure to information becomes more important.

Sensitivity to congestion is believed (and partially supported by the literature) to depend on the objective environment in each place. The present study shows that both the opportunities (see a high degree of network connectivity) and the constraints (actual travel speed) provided by each of the examined environments affect the sensitivity to congestion. The latter thus depends on the kevek of service of actual networks. The higher the level, the higher is the individual's sensitivity to congestion.

From a practical point of view, high exposure to information on congestion should be practiced in countries with a well developed road infrastructure, and more instruction-type information should be broadcasted in countries with less developed networks.

From a research-experimental point of view, micro-simulation aimed to estimate the effect of information on network performance should therefore eliminate the idiosyncracity of local networks and be based on a controlable, although artificial, network.

References

Abkowitz, D.M., An Analysis of the Commuter Departure Time Decision, **Transportation**, Vol. 10, 1981, pp.283-297.

Abu-Eisheh, A.S. and L.F. Mannering, Discrete/Continuous Analysis of Commuters' Route and Departure Time Choices, **Transportation Research Record**, 1138, 1987, pp.27-34.

Al-Deek, H., M. Martello and D.A. May, **Potential Benefits of In-Vehicle Information Systems in a Real Life Freeway Corridor under Recuring and Incident-Induced Congestion**, Institute of Transportation Studies, Research Report 88-2, University of California, Berkeley, 1988.

Alfa, S.A. , Departure Rate and Route Assignment of Commuter Traffic During Peak Period, **Transportation Research**, Vol. 23B (5), 1989, pp.337-344.

Ben-Akiva, M. and S.R. Lerman, **Discrete Choice Analysis: Theory and Applications to Predict Travel Demand**, MIT Press, Cambridge, 1985.

Bovy, P.H.L. and E. Stern, **Route Choice: Wayfinding in Transport Networks**, Kluwer Academic Publishers, Dordrecht, 1990.

Brocken, G.M. and J.M. van der Vlist, **Traffic Control with Variable Message Signs**, Ministry of Traffic and Public Works, Rotterdam, 1991.

Byrne, W.D., **Route Choice Factors - Literature Review**, Cambridge Systematics, Cambridge (Mass.), 1979.

Clarke, M. and E. Holm, Microsimulation Methods in Spatial Analysis and Planning, **Geografiska Annaler**, Vol. 69B (2), 1987, pp.145-164.

Coe, G.A., **Driver Response to Teletext Monitors at Service Areas on the M1 Motorway**, TRRL Research Report 232, Crowthorne, 1989.

Garrison, W.L. and E.A. Deakin, Travel, Work, and Telecommunication: A Long View of the Electronic Revolution and its Potential Impacts, **Transportation Research**, Vol. 22A (4), 1988, pp.239-245.

Golledge, R.G. and R.J. Stimson, **Analytical Behavioural Geography**, Croom Helm, New York, 1987.

Haselkorn, M., W. Barfield, J. Spyridakis, and L. Conquest, **Improving Motorist Information Systems**, Final Report, Washington State Department of Transportation, 1990.

Hendrickson, C. and E. Plank, The Flexibility of Departure Time for Work Trips, **Transportation Research**, 18A(1), pp.25-36, 1984.

Lotan, T. and H.N. Koutsopoulos, Fuzzy Control and Approximate Reasoning Models for Route Choice in the Presence of Information, Paper presented at the 71st Annual TRB Meeting, Washington D.C., 1992.

Mahmassani, S.H., Dynamic Models of Commuter Behavior: Experimental Investigation and Application to the Analysis of Planned Disruptions, Paper presented at the International Conference on Dynamic Travel Behavior Analysis, Kyoto University, Japan, 1989.

Mahmassani, S.H. and R. Herman, Interactive Experiments for the Study of Tripmaker Behaviour Dynamics in Congested Commuting Systems, Paper presented at the Oxford Conference on Travel Behaviour, Oxford, 1988.

Mahmassani, S.H. and C.C. Tong, Availability of Information and Dynamics of Departure Time Choice: Experimental Investigation, **Transportation Research Board**, 1085, 1986, pp.33-49.

Mahmassani, S.H., Gang-Len Chang, and R. Herman, Individual Decisions and Collective Effects in a Simulated Traffic System, **Transportation Science**, Vol. 20 (4), 1986, pp.258-271.

Mannering, L.F., Poisson Analysis of Commuter Flexibility in Changing Routes and Departure Times, **Transportation Research**, Vol. 23B (1), 1989, pp.53-60.

May, D.A., **The Highway Congestion Problem and the Role of In-Vehicle Information Systems**, Institute of Transportation Studies, Research Report 89-8, University of California, Berkeley, 1989.

Polak, J. and P. Jones, In-Home Information Systems: An Exploration of Travellers' Needs and Responses, Paper Presented to the 23rd Annual UTSG Conference, University of Nottingham, 1991.

Stergiou, B. and A. Stathopoulos, Traffic Models and Road Transport Informatics (RTI) Systems, **Traffic Engineering and Control**, 104,1984, pp.580-586.

Stern, E. and S. Krakover, The Formation of a Composite Urban Image, **Geographical Analysis**, 1992, forthcoming.

Stern, E., E. Holm, and M. van Maarseveen, **Choice Behaviour in Congested Situations: The Effects of Information**, Twinning Grant Report submitted to NECTAR, ESF, September, 1990.

Stern, E. and Z. Sinuani, A Behavioural-Based Simulation Model for Urban Evacuation, **Papers of the Regional Science Association**, Vol. 66, 1989, pp.87-103.

Tong, C.C., S.H. Mahmassani and Gang-Len Chang, Travel Time Prediction and Information Availability in Commuter Behavior Dynamics, **Transportation Research Record**, No. 1138, 1987, pp.1-7.

Zumkeller, D., RTI in an European Artificial City, **Proceedings of the PTRC 19th Annual Meeting**, University of Essex, U.K., 1991, pp.23-37.

CHAPTER 8

ROAD TRANSPORT INFORMATICS (RTI) AND DRIVERS' BEHAVIOR

Stavroula Kokkota

8.1 Introduction

In recent years most of the world's cities are facing serious urban transport problems mainly caused by the increasing use of motorcars. The environmental, economic and social implications of these problems are at the core of interest of both public and private decision-makers.

The most prevailing aspects appear to be the increased rate of automobile accidents resulting in approximately 150,000-200,000 human beings killed in accidents every year, a number which corresponds to the population of a medium-sized city; traffic congestion causing considerable time delays; increasing air and noise pollution levels; decreasing efficiency of public transport systems.

Such problems appear in almost all industrialised nations of both the East and the West as well as in an increasing number of developing countries, exerting thus a considerable influence on the quality of urban life. So far policies adopted to combat this can be classified along four directions:

- Changes in the rules of the game (e.g. changes in peak hours by staggering working hours, limits in fuel consumption, pedestrianization schemes etc.);
- Improvements in existing public transportation systems;
- New technological options; and finally
- Evaluation of certain combinations of new technological options and improvements in the existing transportation systems.

Recent developments in Road Transport Informatics (RTI) provide a rather promising -policy wise rather unexplored- framework for indulging in new solutions in facing the problems of urban decline and environmental deterioration.

The scope of this paper will be to assess the likely impact of new technologies on specific aspects of human behaviour as it relates to the improvement of the traffic environment. As a supporting framework we will use the work undertaken in the context of different projects with similar and complementary objectives (the DRIVE and NECTAR network) drawing mainly from the results of the EURONETT project.

The patterns of behaviour explored focus upon the impact of the RTI in the context of route and parking guidance by means of changeable route signs, as well as route guidance by means of on-board driver displays.

8.2 Literature Review

8.2.1 Trip-maker behaviour dynamics in congested systems

The trip-maker behaviour dynamics is of fundamental importance to the study of peak-period traffic congestion and to the analysis of traffic control as well as to the broader demand side for congestion relief measures, such as pricing, ride-sharing incentives, flexitime, and others.

The dynamics of trip-maker decisions are highly complex in nature. This stems first from the fact that the consequences experienced by an individual trip-maker as a result of a personal decision depend on the decisions of a large number of other trip-makers; and second that the interactions which determine these decisions take place in the traffic system and are highly nonlinear. A further difficulty for the average traveller is that of obtaining information and real world data on the actual behaviour of decision-makers.

Statistical analysis (see Mahmasani, Herman, 1988) of data based on observation shows that:

- Route switching decisions are not taken independently from departure time switching decisions.
- More users switch departure time (DT) than route (R).
- If a user switches only one decision, it is more likely to be DT.
- If a user switches route, he frequently switches DT as well.

Switching of activity may take place, if greater information is available, and steady state equilibria are approached in longer times. More distant sectors experience longer travel times and greater switching activity (locational choices),and therefore greater cost. If full information is available to all users, then more switching of activity occurs than in (no information) cases where no information is available.

In the case of two groups, one with full information and the other with no information, then the first is better off in terms of switching activity, travel time, and average schedule delay. This finding has important implications in practice, since it contributes to the effectiveness of advanced on-board information systems for traffic management. Even when only a limited number of users have equipped themselves with such systems, benefits can be expected for these individuals and possibly for the system as a whole. However, there are obvious issues of equity associated with such a scenario. On the other hand, when all users have access to the same amount of information, the effectiveness of this information may be jeopardised. It appears that the threshold beyond which the informational advantage may be diluted, lays somewhere in between. As a result an important planning question can be that of the strategy for providing information, namely, what kind of information should be given to which users.

8.2.2 Factors influencing route choice decisions

It can be argued that the individual trip-maker does not necessarily base his route choice decisions on the shortest time, speed, or distance path for a number of reasons such as: he is unable to compare alternative available routes; he is accustomed to a certain familiar route (see Wachs, 1967); he is unwilling to change his habits even for a shorter time, speed, or distance alternative. Thus, once a certain behaviour becomes habitual, the individual no longer systematically acquires information about substitutes while almost systematically he excludes any information which is considered irrelevant to his current choice (see Outram, 1976). On the other hand it was found that infrequent travellers have at least some knowledge of alternative routes which makes them choose the most familiar and well signposted options (see Heggie, 1978). Furthermore, the attitude of the driver toward time, speed, or distance, can be influenced by other route attributes such as pleasant-unpleasant driving environment, convenience, or driving efforts involved with a certain network configuration.

Several route-choice studies have already shown that other factors like type of trip or individual differences have a significant influence on the driver's choice process (see Wachs, 1967; Hensher, 1977; Robertson and Kennedy, 1979). Results show, for example, that the use of objective performance data in urban transportation planning models need to be questioned, as actual time and cost seldom reflect the subjective images of the trip-makers (see O'Farrel and Markham, 1974).

Three major factors have been developed to account for the choice of patterns drivers make among alternative routes; namely time savings, direct and indirect operating cost saving, and comfort and convenience saving.

In general, travel time savings have been the dominant criterion when using alternative facilities, with the best predictor being the travel time ratio. In several studies a driver appears to choose routes which provide significant time savings, even though he may actually have to drive a greater distance.

The car driver appears to be in a weak position when relating operating costs to the choice a passenger may make. Either drivers do not evaluate operating cost differences or these differences are insignificant. Relative to the total costs of a trip, it may well be that operating cost differences among alternative routes are quite trivial for the passenger car driver.

In addition to these physical measurements, the purely subjective concept of comfort and convenience has been developed. This has generally been described qualitatively as the ease of driving or freedom of movement. Although the research on the whole problem of following alternatives routes has described how traffic behaves, little research has been carried out on drivers' perception of the alternative routes available to them.

Considering the problem of selection of alternative routes, it seems reasonable to assume that the choice will be based on what the driver has learned about the alternatives. Either directly or indirectly a driver must develop some stable evaluations; that is, he must have some predefined views toward the routes or his choices would be random. These views can be the attitudes an individual holds toward some object or process. If route choice is rational, then a direct measure of a driver's evaluation should be his attitudes toward the alternatives. By determining the intensity of these attitudes toward a pair of alternative routes, it should be possible to determine how they relate to the characteristics of the routes and the choices drivers make toward them.

To achieve these objectives, however, it is necessary to determine first whether there is a constant set of attitudes toward routes of different character. Second, it is necessary to determine whether these attitudes depend on the characteristics of the drivers which are relatively permanent, or on the characteristics of a particular trip which would lead to highly variable attitudes.

The results of a study by Stern (1988) indicated that time-related utility is not the only factor which determines the driver's route choice decision. The effort involved in driving is another factor taken into consideration in such decisions. Besides factors which derive from activity scheduling decisions that may be included in a trip chain, such as possibilities of secondary on-route stops have a bearing on route choice. Moreover, the effects of each of these factors on route-choice are dependent upon each other.

These findings suggest that a time-based model is not sufficient to describe route choice behaviour. A better model should include the effect of driving efforts (both psychological and physical) and its interaction with time. The psycho-physical functions of driving efforts and their interaction with travel time are not yet known.

Factors which also influence the route choice decisions and maximising the importance of the shortest path are habits, environmental preferences, subjective evaluations and beliefs. In addition, the socioeconomic characteristics of the user can be used as a good indicator of the user's route choice decision.

8.2.3 Impact of information on route choice decisions

The Wardrop user equilibrium proposition states that travellers choose the fastest available route and always choose the same route on repeated trips. However, travellers are not always capable of choosing the fastest route, and if travel time is uncertain, they may acquire information on the day of travel that helps them to select a better route.

Under the Wardrop assumption the transportation practice is primarily concerned with one type of behavioural question; do travellers choose routes which are optimal for the transportation system as a whole? For example, research has shown that in the absence of tolls, motorists do not select routes which minimise the combined travel time of all drivers. Subsequently, a number of remedies have been proposed, including congestion fees, ramp-metering, and closing road links.

Traveller route choice has been studied primarily within the context of traffic assignment theory. Several authors have sought to verify Wardrop's paper. Adaptive route choice can arguably give better prediction results. Whenever the traveller is able to learn information en-route or on the day of travel, adaptive route choice can reduce travel time over fixed route choice. This type of information has value; by incorporating it into an adaptive decision rule, travel time can be reduced. Other types of information, real-time and non real-time have value as well. For any given piece of information, an ideal decision rule may be formulated to minimise travel time. However, actual travellers do not always choose ideal routes. Actual travel time depends on their understanding of available information (and/or skills in using the information) as well as the ideal travel time.

Potentially, actual travel time may be improved either by making more information available or by making existing information more understandable. A comparison of ideal travel time to actual travel time for different types of information can provide insight into the effectiveness of the two approaches.

8.3 What is RTI?

The Road Transport Informatics (RTI) originated from the need for an "Integrated Road Transport Environment", as has been envisaged by the EC Programme

DRIVE (see EURONETT project) in its effort to face the capacity problems of road networks emerging in most European Regions.

In assistance to the physical expansions and large investments which have been undertaken at all levels for the solution of the various transport network problems, comes the use of User Information systems and New Information Technology in general which aims towards better management schemes of the network capacity both at the micro and macro level.

Information systems can be further distinguished in to those affecting the preparation of a trip (trip planning function) and those providing information while driving (e.g. electronic route guidance, on board navigation systems, radio data systems, and roadside displays - variable message signs).

A rough description of the main RTI technologies will be presented in the following part of this chapter drawing upon the description of RTI technologies used in the context of the EURONETT project (see chapter 4).

Pre-trip information as envisaged will be provided to users at their home, at their work-place, or at selected roadside sites. It will involve various technological options such as telephone services, teletext services broadcast over television channels, and videotext facilities with direct links to central computers. Pre-trip information services were expected to help drivers plan their routes and departure times. The technological capability exists to provide both route and traffic information.

Variable Message Signs (VMS) are used in most countries to set speed limits and to advise drivers of conditions on the road ahead. They would be used to provide information of hazards and recommended speeds, divert traffic, control access to motorways, and generally modify driver behaviour. However the amount of information that can be given is very limited. It is evident that with this kind of collective guidance systems destinations can be described in very broad terms. Nevertheless, as motorists prefer to receive information about traffic conditions before they enter a specific road and at locations where decisions can easily be made in selecting alternate routes, it is usually possible to find appropriate locations where a sign displaying general information will reach the majority of affected drivers

On-board navigation systems would provide the motorist with information on his current location and how this relates to his starting point and destination. There are three main types of on-board navigation systems which could be used by motorists: simple directional aids, location displays, and self-contained route guidance aids. Most such systems comprise an "electronic map" carried in the vehicle which can be combined with a navigation system to enable drivers to keep track of their position in the network (radio trilateration, map-matching, or dead reckoning).

The radio data system-traffic message channel (RDS-TMC) transmits coded information which is broadcast inaudibly and superimposed on normal radio signals. These systems achieve targeting of information ensuring relevance to motorist's locality. One possible option would be to integrate RDS with navigation systems to provide updated (real time) information of link times which are used to calculate minimum paths.

Electronic route guidance systems (ERGS), in contrast to all previously discussed systems achieve selectivity of information given to the driver. They require an extensive roadside infrastructure and units in vehicles to enable drivers to receive guidance at instrumented junctions. Advanced implementations of ERGS would permit the driver to select the type of information he receives. The ultimate system could combine route control and dynamic signal control.

8.4 Description of Projects

The argument carried through this paper has been based mainly upon the results of a number of projects supported by different organisations. We now present a brief resumé of these projects.

8.4.1 EURONETT

EURONETT (Evaluating User Responses On New European Transport Technologies) is a project sponsored by EEC in the framework of **DRIVE** Programme. Euronett's aims are:

(i) To evaluate the changes in user behaviour in response to a number of possible European RTI scenarios,
(ii) To assess the potential short and long term impact of RTI technology on European society, land use patterns and the European transport industry,
(iii) To produce a collection of methods and models for assessing and predicting the effects of RTI-based policy initiatives on travel behaviour and on European society at large.

In order to achieve its objectives, a number of cross-national experiments were conducted to assess how RTI-based technologies will influence various aspects of travel behaviour. Athens (GR) and Birmingham (UK) were the selected case study areas, and the survey work followed almost the same guidelines in both countries.

8.4.2 The NECTAR route choice project

The ESF project "Choice Behaviour" in congested situations: The effects of information is an international comparative study which examines the potential impacts of road transport information on the performance of transport systems, especially in cases of congestion.

A survey will be mounted in several member countries in order to explore differences in response to RTI technologies in the various countries. The interviews take place at the respondents' workplace.

The results of this survey will be tested in an experimental network so allowing control of the freedom of people's choice within it.

The simulation model is operational and is to be adjusted for the needs of this project. The scope of the project is as follows:

- Draft conceptual model
- Information needs
- Survey
- Experimental networks

8.4.3 The DARTS project

DARTS (Development of Advanced Road Transport Strategies), is a project sponsored by the Dutch government. The team working on the project consists of participants from the Institute of Spatial Organisation (INRO); of the Netherlands Organisation for Applied Scientific Research (TNO) and the Department of Public Administration, Faculty of Civil Engineering of the University of Twente.

The project consists of several projects the main goal being to examine the various attributes of the network which are influenced by the RTI systems in order finally to apply a cost benefit analysis of the RTI systems and the traditional ways of solving urban traffic problems (e.g. improving the infrastructure) The objectives of DARTS briefly are the following:

- To control traffic demand in peak hours.
- To evaluate the construction of new roads.
- To increase the efficiency of the present system by using new technologies.
- To evaluate the different types of investment.

8.5 Implications of RTI on Users' Decision Process

A first evaluation of travellers' change in behaviour in the context of a number of possible RTI scenarios gives the following patterns, which are considered pertinent for predicting the possible effects of RTI-based policy initiatives on travel behaviour throughout European society.

Six major types of behavioral response were examined:

- The decision to make or not make trips.
- The choice and use of different travel modes.
- The choice of time in various types of trips.
- The choice of destinations.
- The choice of route.
- The decision to consolidate or reschedule trip sequences.

8.6 RTI implications on Drivers' Travel Decisions

Another project which deals thoroughly with the impact of RTI on drivers' travel decisions is the EURONETT project.

Traffic conditions and the resulting congestion in most cities depend upon the ability of road networks to meet the traffic flows resulting from the travel requirements of drivers. The occurrence of incidents overtax road systems to the extent that the system cannot effectively control the demand. If the traffic demand could be redistributed in time and in space, improvements in the level of service could be realised. This requires some type of a real-time information system that allows the driver to intelligently choose a suitable route from the alternatives available to him.

The Integrated Road Transport Environment envisaged by DRIVE Programme was also examined in the EURONETT project, in a sequence of distinctive technological options, or scenarios. These options were distinguished as those which directly affect demand (information systems) and to those that affect supply (traffic control systems and car restraint measures).

One of the most important items that must be determined during the development of any new system is the present and potential need for its services. There must be a personal need associated with a traffic information system if the driver is to respond in the desired manner in any voluntary operational environment.

Information systems are further distinguished as those affecting the preparation of the trip (trip planning function) and those providing information while driving (electronic route guidance, on-board navigation systems, radio data systems, and roadside displays-variable message signs).

A real-time information system must be designated to allow the driver to make effective decisions regarding route selection based on the information presented to him.

One of the possible reasons a driver information system may not produce the desired operational results is that motorists are being asked to do something that, for some reason, they strongly object to doing so. Hence, in the design of a real-time information system, it is important to determine at certain points along their routes the drivers' potential responses to specific traffic conditions.

We now present summaries of the most important features of each scenario which have been assessed in the qualitative work of the EURONETT project, and additionally a rough description of the main RTI technologies. The EURONETT project consisted of two phases; the qualitative and quantitative phase. By March 1992 the qualitative phase of the project had almost been completed while the quantitative phase was still at the stage of design. The former was divided also into two phases. During the first phase the aim was to explore the levels of interest in likely RTI-based initiatives. A number of group discussions among different social groups and a number of in-depth interviews with individuals representing groups of innovators were carried out. The second phase of the exploratory qualitative work involved household interviews. These were undertaken among households of different stages in life-cycle and income groups. The aim of this phase was to obtain more detailed behavioral responses of households to RTI initiatives unlike the more general responses to RTI technologies obtained in the earlier phase.

8.6.1 Group discussions

The purpose of a group discussion is to allow a dialogue to take place between the respondents with views and topics arising spontaneously.

A topic guide was used by the interviewer throughout the discussion. The topic guide was made up of a list of general areas to be covered in each group discussion. The eventual list of questions asked was not necessarily of the same order as those specified in the topic guide and also tended to be more extensive. The questioning by the interviewer throughout the group discussions was always open-ended to allow the respondents to select the manner of their response. The phrasing of the questions was such that it did not allow for any preconceptions, expectations and personal opinions of the interviewer.

The interviews were structured into two distinct parts; an introductory discussion covering background information about the respondents and a second one which focused on responses to RTI technologies, the perceptions, feelings and manner of thinking of transport system users about the technologies. Throughout the second part of the group discussion, relevant stimulus materials were shown to respondents to help provide a clear explanation of each scenario.

Some of the findings of the group discussions among private car users were grouped for both countries, for the different information scenarios.
Respondents participating in different groups gave several common responses:

- A lot of questions arose about the technologies presented.
- It was maintained that if everybody had information for alternative routes, it is most probable that the majority will follow the "affected" route (chicken-egg dilemma).
- **Variable Message Signs information** seemed to be acceptable and useful by most respondents, only if it was about incidents or for use in the inter-urban network.
- **Radio Data Systems (RDS) - Traffic Message Channel (TMC):** The system was well accepted by the majority of the respondents in all groups, especially lorry drivers. RDS was considered useful if it could provide information about inter-urban trips.
- **In-home Information Systems:** It appears that respondents would not buy any system providing only transport information. On the contrary, they considered it useful only if it could also give general information. Some of them found it difficult to operate such a facility (e.g. Minitel) for their every day journey needs.
- **On-board Navigation Systems:** It seemed useful to those who, due to the nature of their job, had to make several daily trips to unknown destinations, but not to those who used specific routes for their customary trips. Lorry drivers - as they use specific routes - did not find the navigation equipment useful. Some respondents considered also the cost issue.
- **Electronic Route Guidance Systems (ERGS):** The majority of respondents found ERGS very useful, almost unbelievably ideal. A reduction of anxiety caused by traffic congestion was often mentioned as the main benefit of the system. There were many doubts about the actual implementation of the system, as well as questions and concerns about the type of suggested alternatives routes. Lorry drivers found ERGS quite useful.

8.6.2 Home interviews

Home interviews allow for the collection of more detailed information about the characteristics and background of an individual. Additionally the emphasis in the household interviews was to focus on possible changes to actual trip patterns. This is in contrast to the more general responses to the RTI technologies which were obtained by the EURONETT group discussions described previously.

Prior to the interviews, questionnaires and diary sheets were given to the respondents for obtaining person and household information. The diaries were required for recording two days of travel including at least one trip into the city centre. Household interviews were divided into two parts.

Both parts were based on a topic guide with a list of areas to be covered. In part one, the respondents' current travel and activity patterns were discussed, including aspects of personality related to travel perceptions. In part two, respondents' responses modifying EURONETT scenarios were obtained. For this part of the interview the discussion was focused on specific preselected journeys which had been recorded by the respondents in their travel diaries. The aim of this part was to assess specific changes in travel behaviour and how RTI might affect these changes.

This phase indicated the following:

- Dynamic information was found more likely to influence travel behaviour than static information, which was perceived by individuals as comparable to their present main source of information-driving experience. The majority of them would prefer a "perfect" RTI-equipped environment which could provide them with either dynamic pre-trip or en-route information.
- Several respondents expressed a clear preference for in-car information, when this option was presented. On the other hand, some of them did not seem to be interested in getting pre-trip information for their every-day trip, especially if they had to get up earlier in the morning. Most of them would like to have updated information about incidents in their every-day trip.
- Information about traffic conditions was preferred for irregular and inter-urban trips.
- The criteria for using the RTI information are reliability of the information, cost and ease of use. Almost all respondents said that they would firstly test the transmitted information and then if this information was judged reliable, adopt it.

Some possible changes to motorists' travel choices, in response to the availability of static or dynamic information, are listed below:

- **Route choice** was strongly related to information availability as far as non-work trips were concerned.
- **Departure time choice** was found to be less affected by information availability, the opposite happened where there were no possible route alternatives.
- **Trip sequencing** was likely to be affected by information availability; so was trip suppression, in some special cases, too.

The EURONETT project through the qualitative surveys, aimed to investigate the impact of RTI on travellers behaviour. The work was based on the presentation of specific technologies to the traveller. Group discussions and in-depth interviews based on the above approach have shown that the presentation of RTI-scenarios had to be reconsidered in the context of the future survey work and to emphasise the kinds of information provided to the respondents. This leads to a modified classification along the following lines:

- Pre-trip information
- During-trip information

Pre-trip information is likely to have the greatest overall impact on travel behaviour, since it is the point that the travel decision is taken and it is sometimes possible to influence most attributes of the journey, including timing, route, mode, destination and whether to make the trip at all.

8.6.3 Attitudes towards pre-trip information systems

Qualitative surveys have shown that technology such as minitel or teletext, providing information prior to a trip seems to be useful to travellers but that they would not be keen to buy them for that function only.

A general remark was that prior to trip information will be useful for longer journeys (particularly motorway driving) rather than every-day trips where travellers were familiar with traffic conditions. This will be reversed if the pre-trip information provided through new technological systems is reliable and dynamic.

On the other hand pre-trip information for public transport users will increase the reliability and convenience of the public transport service. It was then evident that under these circumstances non public transport users would be willing to change mode.

8.6.4 Traveller responses to pre-trip information systems

From the qualitative survey the provision of dynamic pre-trip information identified the following responses to traveller attributes.

- **Decision to make or not to make the trip.** There were very few instances of respondents actually choosing to postpone or cancel their trip in response to dynamic or real-time information compared to static information.
- **The choice and use of different modes.** Pre-trip public transport service information would increase the use of public transport by non-users as an alternative mode.
- **The choice of when to make a trip-departure time.** Dynamic or real time information has a greater impact on decisions to alter departure time than static information. Knowledge of traffic conditions reduces uncertainty for the traveller and enables him to change departure time or not, and in what range, in order to achieve a preferable arrival time.
- **The choice of route.** Accurate and reliable dynamic information given through new technological systems to motorists will always make them change their route to avoid congestion.
- **The decision to consolidate or reschedule trip sequences.** For discretionary trips and when feasible for work trips, information seems to have an effect on the trip sequences.

8.6.5 The choice of destination

The qualitative surveys did not clearly imply that information will have an impact on motorists so as to change the destination of their trip. However, for shopping and recreation trips there is evidence that the change of destination is possible.

As shown in the results of the qualitative work, summarised above, pre-trip information has the potential to influence many attributes of a journey, including the timing of a trip, route choice, mode, destination and the decision of whether or not to make the trip at all. In order to focus the research on the impacts of the pre-trip make the trip at all. In order to focus the research on the impacts of the pre-trip information on traveller behaviour it was decided to limit the sample to car drivers visiting the city centre. The methodology of Stated Preference was used to examine the effects of information available in-home and at the non-home destination on travellers.

Two distinct SP exercises were designed for the trips from and to home. These were as follows:

- From X to Home: this exercise looked at the effects of information on time of departure and route choice given that mode, destination and travel/not travel, are predetermined by this stage of the trip.
- Home to X: this exercise looked at the effect of information on time of departure, mode, destination and travel/not travel given that route choice is predetermined as the shortest route only.

8.6.6 X-to-Home exercise findings

In most of the cases respondents had a choice of an alternative route for the journey to home. In some cases respondents gave less travel time on the alternative than the one on the current route they were willing to use. This was an indication that travel time is not the only factor affecting route choice. Other factors like safety, comfort, convenience, stress etc. were recorded.

Travel time seemed to be the first criterion in the chosen order of ranking. Respondents were willing to leave even half an hour later or earlier than the one planned, rather than make a longer trip.

For non-work trips and especially for shopping trips later departure times were employed if they led to shorter travel times. In some interviews parking costs were a factor that could influence the shift in departure time. Staying longer in town to avoid traffic could mean incurring an additional parking charge, and in such cases the respondent was not willing to delay his departure.

8.6.7 Home-to-X exercise findings

This exercise was more interesting and exciting for the respondents. They found it easy to comprehend and they did not question the realism of the simulated information of travel time provided.

If reliable and accurate information about traffic conditions is provided by the RTI technology it was observed that travellers were willing to change destination (i.e. shopping trips). If travel time was exceptionally long, suppression of trips was recorded in some cases.

Some of the respondents were taken to receive information about Public Transport. Parking conditions are discouraging for the private car user, especially in city centres. Instead of giving an estimate of door-to-door travel time by Public Transport it was decided, for the main interviews, to give the suggested departure time, in order to minimise waiting time or ensure arrival at a destination by a given time.

Some respondents who contemplated switching from car to bus, on the basis of the information given, were also keen to know what the attributes of the return journey home were likely to be.

If information for parking availability is supplied, the respondent is willing to adjust his departure time.

Once the respondent had become used to the way information was supplied he asked more and more questions of the system. The number of different pieces of information requested varied from iteration to iteration; generally, if the reported travel time was considered to be "good" then little searching was carried out; where travel times were "bad", the amount of searching was much greater, and involved both different departure times and different modes. In most interviews, the number of "days" examined was around four or five.

The order of ranking was made, on average, with a trade-off between travel time and departure time shift.

8.7 **Conclusions**

Highlights of the conclusions obtained by the EURONETT survey work are listed below.

Of the two major decision parameters, departure time is clearly dominant over route choice. This statement remains valid for both Birmingham and Athens respondents. A remarkable variability in travel times over current and alternative routes in the Athens survey was noticed which was not present with equal propensity in Birmingham. This observation implies greater and sustained variations in traffic flows in the Athens case. It thus leads to low predictability and forces users to make frequent experimentations.

The influence of parking conditions on departure time and route choice needs further analysis. Preliminary studies show insignificant or marginal effects.

Trade-off conjoint measurements between departure time and travel time and subsequent computation of aggregate preferences indicate no significant differences between Athens and Birmingham.

The early departure/early arrival shows maximum aggregate utility and sort out as the first preference policy.

Finally, travellers in both Athens and Birmingham would change their habits when provided with information. Identifying their first choice as being earlier departure/shorter travel time with a consequence of arriving earlier, or later departure/shorter travel time even if this results in a later arrival at home, show clearly their intention to travel shorter times and to trade-off these choices with a shift to departure or arrival times.

Acknowledgements

Initially I would like to thank the ESF Organisation for giving me the opportunity to participate in NECTAR Network in the framework of this fellowship and Prof. Ambakoumkin for supporting me. I would also like to thank Dr. M.van Maarseveen for his kind hospitality at the University of Twente and his contribution to this paper and Prof. A.Stathopoulos and Ms V.Psaraki for providing me with the information about the EURONETT project. Finally I would like to thank Professor Maria Giaoutzi for revising this paper.

References

Boyce, D., Route Guidance Systems for Managing Urban Transportation Networks: Review and Prospects, 10th Italian Regional Science Conference, Rome, Italy, 1989.

Heggie, I.G., Behavioral Dimensions of Travel Choice, **Determinates of Travel Choice** (D.A. Hensher, and Q.Dalvi, eds.), Saxon House, 1978.

Kenny, F., L.Pickup, V.Psaraki, S.Kokkota, C.Petrakis and G.Argyrakos, Results of the Qualitative Surveys, EURONETT Deliverable 9, Transport Studies Unit, University of Oxford, 1990.

Mahmasani, H. and R.Herman, Interactive Experiments for the Study of Tripmaker Dynamics in Congested Commuting Systems, **Transp. Res.**, Vol. 17A, No. 3, 1988.

O'Farrell, N.P. and J.Markham, Commuter Perceptions of Public Transport Work Journey, **Environment and Planning A**, Vol. 6, 1974.

Outram, E.V., Route Choice, Mathematical Advisory Unity Note No. 256, Department of Environment, London, 1976.

Polak, J.W., P.M.Jones, F.Kenny and V.Psaraki, Development of a Pre-trip Information Simulation Exercise, EURONETT Deliverable 11, Transport Studies Unit, Oxford University, 1990.

Psaraki, V. and A.Stathopoulos, Assessing the Responses of Travellers in Athens and Birmingham Out-of-home Pre-trip Information, EURONETT Deliverable 26, Transport Studies Unit, Oxford University, 1991.

Robertson, I.D. and J.V.Kennedy, The Choice of Route, Mode, Origin and Destination by Calculation and Simulation, TRRL Laboratory Report 877, Crowthorne, 1979.

Simon, H., A Behavioral Model of Rational Choice, **Quarterly Journal of Economics**, Vol. 69, 1955.

Stathopoulos, A., G.Kanellaidis and V.Psaraki, Road Transport Informatics and Behaviour Dynamics, 6th International Conference on Travel Behaviour, Quebec, Canada, 1991.

Stern, E. and P.H.L.Bovy, Theory and Models of Route Choice Behaviour, Research Institute of Urban Planning and Architecture (OSPA), 1989.

Stern, E., E.Holm and M. van Maarseveen, Choice Behaviour in Congested Situations: The effects of Information, Report on Research Structure Formulated with NECTAR Twinning Grant, 1990.

Stern, E., J.Tzelgov and A.Henik, Driving Efforts and Urban Route Choice, The Logistics and Transportation Review, Vol. 19, No1, 1988.

Wachs, M., Relationships Between Drivers' Attitudes Toward Alternate Routes and Driver and Route Characteristics, Highway Research Record, No. 197, 1967.

CHAPTER 9

PRODUCT CHANNEL LOGISTICS AND LOGISTIC PLATFORMS

Ben J.P. Janssen

9.1 Introduction

According to Andersson (1986) we have entered a structural transition of global dimensions, which might be described as the Fourth Logistical Revolution. Such discontinuities and structural economic changes prompt for new concepts and tools. Much is and has been written about logistics, but there is not much 'reflection'. The development of a concept "proceeds the development of organisations" (Tixier et al., 1983, VIII). In this paper recent developments in logistics and transport are examined within the framework of Product Channel Logistics (PCL), originally proposed by Anderson (1989). PCL can be defined as the cross-functional formation, organization and control of all logistical activities needed to bring a product to its customer. Its aim is to maximize overall logistical efficiency in pipelines or networks, rather than individually managing these activities. So far, only a few companies have succeeded in making the transition to PCL. It is, nevertheless, expected that this type of logistic management will give many companies a significant competitive edge and that companies therefore strive to achieve this type of logistics.

The first section of this chapter outlines the main features of PCL and shows how its adoption can yield competitive advantages. It also considers how it is inducing changes in the physical structure of logistical systems and, in particular, transport networks. In the second part the results of research into the networks are presented to illustrate the effects of PCL on 'logistic platforms' (in French, 'plateformes de logistique').

The term logistic platform is used to denote the material, technical and organizational terminalling and switching points in logistical channels. A logistic channel is understood as the means through which the transport of goods from initial supplier or shipper to final user or buyer is organized.

9.2 Product Channel Logistics

9.2.1 Product channel logistics: a conceptual framework

During the last decade, the concept of integrated logistics has become a dominant element in discussions about material flows in and between firms. This involves establishing where, when and how activities should take place to ensure the optimal flow of goods. All aspects of logistics have to be taken into account, regardless of whether they are occurring within the realm of one company or in a network situation comprising several companies. Firms are using integrated logistics to help achieve a good positioning within highly competitive market niches. They are trying simultaneously to increase logistics productivity and to raise standards of customer service and market responsiveness.

To achieve this goal, a management strategy is needed that defines operations from a cross-functional perspective and recognises the importance of upstream, downstream and diagonal co-ordination within logistic networks. Following Anderson (1989) we will call this approach Product Channel Management. It aims to maximize overall channel profitability, rather than managing production, supply or distribution activities individually. For the successful implementation of product channel management organizational structures and logistical information systems must be transformed. Anderson calls this 'the next revolution in logistics' (see Anderson, 1989). It requires the formation of networks of inter-related decision - making in which the contributions of all activities are evaluated against channel-wide objectives.

'Product logistics' and 'transport logistics' are key elements in this newly emerging approach to logistics management (see Janssen and Machielse, 1987; Ruijgrok, 1991). Product logistics has as its focal point the individual product moving through along a logistic chain. Along this chain a range of activities is performed which add value and tailor the product to consumer needs. This concept of a 'logistic chain' closely resembles the idea of 'value chain' advanced by Porter (1985). Both concepts highlight the interrelationships between value-adding activities. As Porter observes: "A firm is more than the sum of its activities ... Competitive advantage grows out of the ways firms or companies organize and perform the totality of discrete activities" (see Porter, 1990).

Transport logistics refers to the efforts of transport firms to optimize the utilization of their equipment and networks while maintaining the required level of service. This type of logistics and product logistics operate in a similar way but their objectives differ (see Colin and Fiore, 1986). In product logistics, emphasis is placed on meeting the varying needs of consumers at the end of the channel. In transport logistics, the main objective is to consolidate the flows of different products in a way that maximises the efficiency of the transport system within service level constraints. It effectively integrates separate logistics chains into a single transport network. This network is a physical entity consisting of nodes and linkages.

The key difference between traditional approaches to logistics and channel logistics is the shift away from managing assets (such as warehouses, trucks, inventories) towards managing processes (such as product systems, transport systems, product flows and information flows). Product channel logistics redefines the nature of the linkage between a firm and its suppliers and distributors. It demands upgrading of intra-company and above all new inter-company transport and information systems. Instead of seeing inbound and outbound traffic as 'just transportation' provided at minimum cost, transport is a critical factor for effective product channel and value system management. In addition to the customers, supply and distribution and hence the transportation companies are the chain's critical linkages. "A company, its suppliers, and its channels can all benefit from better recognition and exploitation of such linkages" (see Porter, 1990).

Competitive advantage is created by improvements in technology but also by better ways or methods of doing things; economies of joint production (economies of scope), new approaches to marketing, and last but not least, new forms of transport and distribution like the rise of the 'integrator' and the 'a-modal' carrier (see Colin, 1986) and the formation of 'hubs and spokes' networks in international transport and distribution.

By exploiting new communications and information technologies, firms are able to re-arrange activities in physical space in such a way that the time involved in production and distribution is drastically reduced. The development of new types of transport and distribution services, such as those provided by 'integrators', 'a-modal' carriers, and the creation of 'hub and spoke' networks have facilitated this geographical restructuring of logistic systems.

9.2.2 **Product channel logistics and transport**

An essential principle of PCL is the requirement that an agency is responsible for the overall monitoring and control of the logistic system. This role is increasingly being assumed by transport firms. Their professional interest is shifting from merely providing transport capacity to organising an integrated, reliable and market-oriented logistic service. Transport firms are being evaluated less on the basis of cost and much more with respect to quality criteria, such as flexibility, controllability, speed and reliability (see De Leijer et al., 1992).

The transportation link is vital in Product Channel Logistics. It accounts for approximately 45 percent of all logistics costs and physically links all elements of the chain. It offers one of the greatest opportunities for improved resource utilisation and service improvement. Transport and distribution, integrated and coordinated from a channel perspective, can improve delivery speed and reliability as well as reduce in-transit inventory. Furthermore, within these channels, the added value takes on new forms, including EDI for tracking shipments and transferring documents, intermodalism and just-in-time transport. With the rise of channel logistics, one can witness in Western Europe the design and operation of the physical, managerial and information systems needed for the upstream and downstream coordination of material flows.

The use of "one-stop-shopping/shipping" whereby 'third party' (logistic services company) assumes control over product shipments from vendors, is a direct response to the need to improve the quality of transport and logistical performance. It is exactly for this reason that international operating companies like DEC, Philips, Unilever, General Motors, Volvo and Rank Xerox are prominent users of contract logistics: the use of outside transport and logistic services companies to perform all or part of a company's inbound and outbound transport functions. In fact, in Europe we can observe a trend of transport companies offering new kinds of services. Relationships between shippers and carriers are being altered with the creation of shipper-carrier relationships and core carriers. These changes are affecting the institutional status of carriers including their financial stability, industry concentration, ease of entry and fleet planning. Multimodal transport companies providing pickup, line haul and delivery service using a variety of transport modes, are becoming more common place.

Carriers are altering their operating strategies in response to the changing demands of customers. Examples of the new operating demands are:

- providing adequate information and information systems;
- on-line information processing;
- guaranteed service levels which means high reliability;
- flexibility in volume, places, trips and time;
- rate discounting and cost reducing;
- freight consolidation and
- high international penetration ability.

Road transport companies, in turn, are demanding greater reliability from their transportation equipment and services, and are placing far greater importance on current and continuous information on the location and status of their equipment and on the operating conditions of the transportation system. There is a strong pressure to reduce the cost of transportation and at the same time to increase speed, service and reliability. These improvements are to be reached through:

- increasing the rapidity in loading and unloading;
- enlarging the capacity of vehicles;
- unification of parallel stream of goods (consolidation);
- improving the routing;
- specialization of transport units;
- creating safe and less energy consuming vehicles, and
- changing the truck from a 'working tool' to a 'sophisticated tool'.

The need of planning and control in transport companies increases. Also the possibilities of planning and control increase, caused by technological development. Roughly the following strategies towards better control and planning (i.e. towards more efficiency and logistic effectiveness) can be observed (see Janssen, 1990; Janssen and Wang,1991):

(a) Integration between shipping and transport company. The latter will serve as logistic services company for the former. These companies are developing into a new type of 'intermediary'. Their function is to provide industrial and trade companies with the logistic know-how and to arrange the procurement and distribution networks that fit best to their clients' different product market demands. The specific ability of the 'new intermediary' is to provide value adding services by enabling a better market positioning of the different products. Often the actual transport is being contracted out to other transport companies. The Dutch have coined the word 'co-shippership' for this form of integration. Often this type of strategy is combined with one of the strategies discussed hereafter.

(b) Enlarging scale by the transport companies through integration between transport companies through integration between transport companies and agents that act as forwarders. One aim is to complement the existing logistics services and/orgeographic coverage. Another aim is to create multi-modal transport companies in so called a-modal companies having all transport techniques through which they can offer door-to-door services (the 'one-stop-shopping' solutions for logistic activities of shippers). Their specific ability is to provide a general level of service of physical distribution while dealing with different flows of goods and using different modalities of transport.

(c) Specialization into distinctively highly specialized logistic services provided for particular product-market niches. Many medium sized companies are pursuing this strategy of specialization into specific niches of the transport market. Highly distinctive and dedicated transport, warehousing and other logistical services are provided by these companies.

(d) Scale enlarging of transport companies by taking over of similar or nearly similar foreign transport companies in order to reach a more than national (and pan-European) coverage and scale economies.

These four ways of restructuring of transport companies lead to changes in the way (inter)national transport is being carried out. The building of networks - transport and logistic networks - is essential for all strategies.

According to their strategic choices transport companies or logistic services provides adjust their logistic systems, and hence their usage of networks and logistic platforms (see Janssen and Fiore, 1990). Their strategies can be described by the following dimensions:

- the logistic functions or skills deployed;
- geographic orientation of the transport company.

The functions refer to the scope of the logistic services, ranging from common and generic transport and logistic services to customized, potential services which have a high value added for the customers. The geographic orientation indicates the scale on which the company is active, distinguished into regional, national, European and world-wide (see Figure 1).

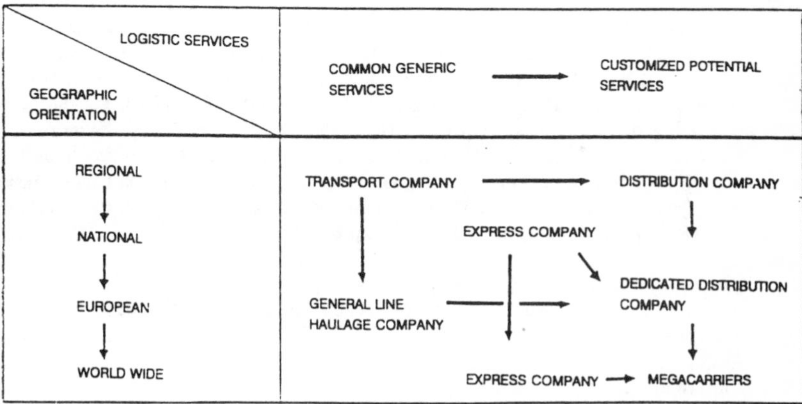

Figure 1 Strategic options for transport and logistic services companies

9.3 Logistic Systems and Logistic Platforms

9.3.1 Existing network systems

The processes of cross-functional re-definition of the logistical operations by individual companies lead to the formation of integrated international transport and logistic networks. A transport network consists of all elements which a transport economy possesses to arrange the transport of goods for shippers. It is a geographically extended system transporting goods from one point to another and it is used by many shippers. Normally for a transport company the emphasis lies on the combination of the economies of the transport of many and different goods and the organization of these heterogeneous transport demands into one and the same transport network. For the 90's more than just transport networks are needed. For a good logistic performance logistic networks are necessary, consisting both of transport networks and communication networks. And besides this, dedicated distribution and value adding capacities have to be provided. A logistic network consists of all transport and other value adding logistic activities necessary to perform inbound and outbound transport functions of specific products for one specific client. It may be a geographically extended transport system. In these networks the different nodes of consolidation and deconsolidation are more and more hierarchically positioned.

The networks are rationalized in order to meet business marketing (efficiency) and customer requirements (effectivity). In this formation 'logistic platforms' (platforms or terminals in both transport and logistic networks) are becoming both the 'material platforms' for the consolidation and de-consolidation of flows of goods. At the same time they become also the 'platforms' in the data flow networks in integrated logistic networks.

An important criterion for the positioning of distribution centres has always been the geographical coverage. But transportation is not anymore simply the mastering of space. It is more and more aimed at the control of space and the insertion of the real time dimension into the production processes (see Colin and Fiore, 1986). Therefore, for the positioning of distribution centres, it is not just spatial proximity anymore; it is "closeness in lead time" (see Wandel and Hellberg, 1987), i.e. the positioning in and the formation of distribution networks which guarantee high levels of control, reliability and customers service. How far the sphere of influence of a logistic platform stretches, depends on the types of goods handled and the positioning of the platform in the logistic chains.

If we look at the present tendencies in Europe in transport and distribution, the following overall four-layered picture emerges, each type of distribution or logistic centre having its own typical geographical coverage (see also Janssen and Oldenburger, 1991):

- international main logistic centre or international main port;
- international logistic centre;
- international transportation and distribution centre;
- regional transportation and distribution centre.

International main logistic centres

At the top of the newly emerging hierarchical logistic landscape are the platforms we have called international main logistic centres. It may be obvious that these central platforms are located at the main economic development and transport-axes in Europe, such as the regions of Hamburg, Amsterdam/Rotterdam/Antwerp and Dortmund/Essen/Duisburg/Cologne, the Rhine/Rhone development axis, the Paris/Ile de France region, the Lyon region, the Marseille region, the Milano region and the Barcelona region.

These international main logistic centres have the following characteristics (see Janssen and Ter Brugge, 1990):

(a) The availability of technically advanced combined loading and unloading facilities for rail and road transport, and if possible intermodal facilities for road/rail and water transport. On the various logistic platforms different flows of goods, hitherto treated separately, might be mixed into shipments with the same logistic characteristics (lead-time, handling, transport mode, etc.);
(b) The presence of sophisticated information exchange facilities, especially for EDI and other forms of telematics. For logistic services companies as well as for intermodal carriers it is necessary to be able to link on real time basis the different hubs in Europe in order to guarantee the required levels of quality and reliability;
(c) The capacity and space to handle and store large quantities of different types of goods for different customers according to different quality levels. The capacity to mix goods of different customers and the use of intermodal transport rely heavily on the availability of entrepots which can store different types of goods (express, just-in-time, highly perishable, etc.);
(d) The availability of vacant space which can directly be used as logistic platforms and/or sold to private or public investors; and last but not least
(e) The (immediate) availability of all different kinds of logistic and other producer services.

In the case of the Netherlands, it is clear that the Rotterdam region functions as such an international main logistic centre. But also the Amsterdam region, especially because of its international airport and its international harbour functions, can be designated an international main logistic role.

International logistic centres

The second tier of the hierarchy consists of the international logistic centres; locations which function as logistic platforms for the consolidation and deconsolidation of nearly all types of goods in various international logistic networks. In the Netherlands up till now only Venlo can be characterized as an international logistic centre. More than others it is preferred as 'hub' by internationally operating transportation companies. The dominant mode of transport is truck, but these types of modes are also accessible by rail and combined rail/road transport.

International transportation and distribution centres

The third category of logistic platforms have been labelled by us international transportation and distribution centres. Explicitly we have used here the term transportation and distribution centre, since these logistic platforms function primarily as the favoured locations for the transfer, transshipment, storage and/or distribution activities of internationally operating carriers (transportation firms and 'logistic service companies') and shippers (manufacturing, wholesaling and retailing companies). These centres function as important platforms in their transportation and logistic networks.

As is the case with the international logistic centres, the dominant mode of transport (and hence accessibility) is truck. But many of these centres are also linked to another mode of transport, be it rail or water.

In the Netherlands, of particular importance in this respect are the regions of Rotterdam/Rijnmond, Amsterdam/Schiphol and Venlo, but also the regions Arnhem/Nijmegen, Tilburg/Breda and Enschede/Hengelo. The latter three are border regions located on important international transport-axes to and from the mainports of the Netherlands.

Regional transportation and distribution centres

The fourth category is that of the so-called regional transportation and distribution centres, being spatial clusters of transportation firms located at junctions and other platforms in infrastructural networks and/or platforms for the distribution of goods within a range of approximately 50 km. In the latter case, predominant location factors are the size of the market (population) and the degree of competition for space.

This newly emerging hierarchy of distribution centres reflects the change in the logistics systems whereby the accessibility of markets is no longer only conceived in terms of physical proximity or distances to be covered, but also in terms of proximity in lead-time and reliability, i.e., the capacity to handle given quantities and flows of goods by means of certain modes of transport within given time schedules according to given quality levels. This means that those transport nodes which have the logistic capacity (and operators) to handle the international transportation flows, to handle the different commodities according to very specific quality requirements, to store, to mix and to consolidate goods, and to be a highly reliable intermodal logistic platform which can deal with the necessary information (EDI), are the ones which will be central nodal points. Distribution centres are located where the needed quantities of goods can be delivered as many times as necessary (daily, weekly, fortnightly, etc.), with the highest customer service levels and the shortest total-lead-time against the lowest costs as possible. This means that the optimal form of the distribution network is influenced by the structure of the market and product characteristics such as value and shape.

Each of the four types of logistic platforms is in fact an addition of a multiplicity of nodes in different logistic channels. It may involve nodes in networks of producing companies, being closed logistic systems which are not open for use by any other logistic actor and which are part of multi-layered, strictly hierarchically ordered privately organized networks consisting of international distribution centres, national distribution centres and regional distribution centres. It may be operated by the producing companies themselves but also by dedicated third logistic parties. Logistic platforms are also the locations of the operations of logistic services company, operating in specific market niches of the transportation market and serving a variety of customers all over Europe.

Logistic platforms are also nodes in networks linking producers/vendors of products and the final points of sales/ the final destinations. These links are differently organized, according to the volume of flows involved, the appropriate levels of customers service, the capital-intensity of the goods, etc. Sometimes distribution takes place directly from producer to customer, without any transshipment, just using one mode of transport. In another situation storage near to the various points of sale (retailers) is needed. Different modes of transport may be involved and the transport within the networks may be both consolidated transport and distributive transport, involving Full Truck Loads (FTL) as well as Less than Truck Loads (LTL). In one logistic network the transport can be phased using three or more consolidation and distribution centers, while another network uses only local and urban distribution centers located adjacent to the consumers. The overall picture is one of different logistic patterns and different physical distribution networks meeting different logistic requirements (see Figure 2).

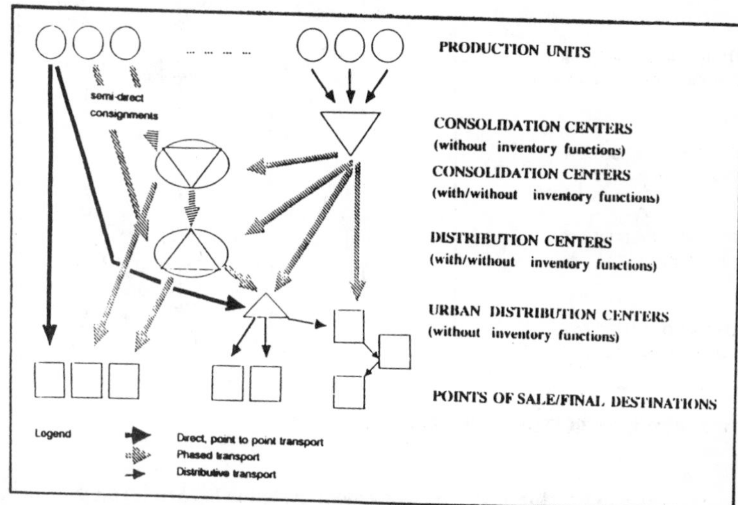

Figure 2 Different logistic networks and centers

Adapted from Colin (1983,p. 55)

9.3.2 A typology of logistic networks and logistic platforms

The following five basic types of logistic (distribution) networks can be distinguished:

- direct distribution from units of production (UP) to points of sale (POS) (type **A**);
- distribution from UP to local/city distribution centres (CDC),proximate to urban centres and POS (type **B**);
- distribution from UP to regional distribution centres (RDC), from there to CDC and from there to POS (type **C**);
- distribution from UP to national distribution centres (NDC), from there to RDC, to UDC and finally to POS (type **D**);
- distribution from UP to NDC, from there to UDC and from there to POS (type **E**).

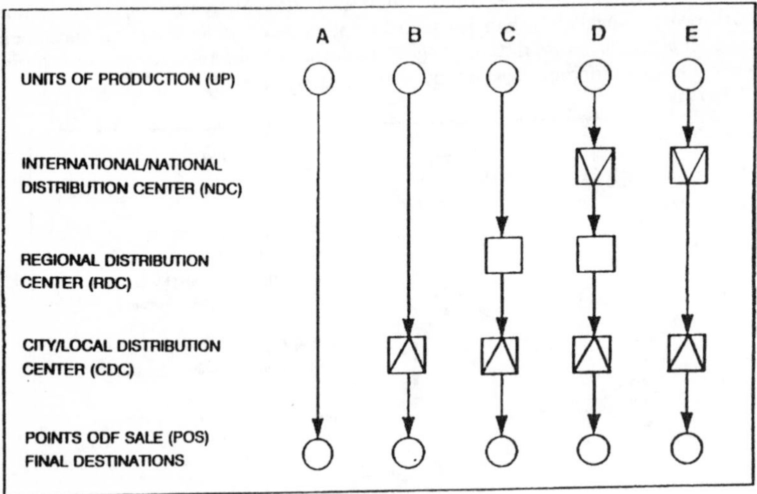

Figure 3 Five types of logistic distribution channels

According to the criteria of length of vendor-customer lead-times on the one hand and size or volume of consignments on the other, four typical situations of physical distribution of goods can be distinguished (see also Figure 4):

(I) distribution of small consignments within very tight lead-times. In order ensure economically sound distribution, there is the need to regroup the consignments. Due to the short lead-times this regrouping must be done as near to the points of sale as possible, i.e., in the city distribution centres. The type of distribution network involved is B.

(II) distribution of larger consignments/quantities within short lead-times. Regrouping of the different consignments can be done here easier because of the larger size of the individual consignment. But the localization of these places of regrouping determines the type of distribution network involved. If the consolidation takes place at the units of production, distribution takes place along distribution network type A. If the consignments are made up of deliveries from different production units at different places, on can either choose for direct delivery from this national distribution centre or via an urban distribution centre (type E).

lead-time / volume	short	long
small	• heterogeneous markets characterized by specific lead times → (economic) necessity of consolidation of goods in distribution centers near points of sale (B)	• heterogeneous markets and economic necessity of consolidation of flows → groupage in (inter)national distribution centres (D) → groupage in regional (and sometimes national) distribution centres (C)
big	• homogeneous and concentrated markets → direct supply and distribution (A) → consolidation in (inter)national centres (E)	• concentrated markets with low competition → direct supply and distribution (A)

Figure 4 A typology of product channel logistics networks

Adapted from Fiore (1990).

(III) distribution of small quantities within relatively long lead-times. In these cases there is a strong economic necessity to consolidate. For slow-movers this consolidation can be best done at national distribution centres. The type of distribution network will then be of type **D**. For a product with a relatively faster turn-over, this re-grouping is to take place at regional distribution centres and the distribution networks are of type **C**.

(IV) distribution of large quantities within relatively long lead-times. This is the most simple situation and holds for a market that is relatively concentrated and where there is little competition between the vendors. The type of distribution network is **A**.

The above classes lead to the typology of product channel logistics networks, being combinations of goods flows, transport and logistic networks, sketched in Figure 4.

9.4 Concluding Remarks

Due to business' strategies the complex interrelationships between product logistics and transport logistics are changing. More and more firms are using logistics as one of their competitive edges in gaining highly competitive market niches. Overall logistic channel effectivity and profitability are important and therefore logistic networks are formed in which this channel management is to be achieved. We have called this strategy product channel logistics. Although it is as yet in most cases a concept, in the practices of many, predominantly internationally operating firms one can already witness the realisation of this concept in the form of new ways of organizing economic activities in time and space. The spatial structure of economic activities (i.e. the infrastructural and organizational networks for production and distribution) are gradually being altered. In many economic and geographical studies these spatial aspects of logistics have been treated as 'externalities'. It seems to us that Product Channel Logistics bears practical witness to the fact that time-space dimensions cannot be treated (anymore) as external conditions. They have to be viewed as direct elements of the production, transaction and distribution processes themselves. Transport costs and hence logistics cost are no longer just costs of the annihilation of space and the cost of dead time. They are the cost incurred in the process of defining networks and the positioning of nodes in these networks in terms of 'closeness in lead-time'; i.e., the logistic capability and reliability to organize flows of goods and information.

Acknowledgement

This chapter presents findings from a research project undertaken by the author as part of a broader project on the relationships between logistics and spatial development. Other relevant publications are Janssen and Fiore (1990), Janssen (1991) and Janssen and Oldenburger (1991). The research for this project has been supported by the European Science Foundation (NECTAR Research Fellowship), the Institute of Spatial Organization INRO-TNO and NEA Transport Research and Training in the Netherlands. Last but not least the project has been made feasible by the hospitality of staff of the Centre de Récherche d'Economie des Transports of the University of Aix, Marseille (Daniel l'Huillier, Jacques Colin, Claude Fiore, Nathalie Fabbe-Costes and Daniel Boudoin). I would like to thank Jacques Colin, Claude Fiore, Michel Savy, Cees Ruijgrok and Alan McKinnon for their valuable comments on earlier versions of this paper.

References

Andersson, A., The Four Logistical Revolutions, **Papers of the Regional Science Association**, vol. 59, 1986, pp 1-13.

Anderson, D., **International Logistics, Meeting the Challenges of Global Distribution Channels**, Temple, Barker & Sloane Inc., Lexington, Massachusetts, 1987.

Anderson, D., **Product Channel Management, the Next Revolution in Logistics?** Temple, Barker & Sloane Inc., Lexington, Massachusetts, 1989.

Colin, J., Logistique et Plateformes Régionales de Fret, **Transports**, Fevrier, no. 28, 1983, pp. 53-63.

Colin, J., **Le Rôle des Chargeurs et des Transporteurs dans la Logistique, le Cas de la France**, Rapport Introductif á la 76eme Table Ronde organisée par la ECMT 29-30 avril 1987, ECMT, Paris, 1987, pp. 5-53.

Colin, J. and C. Fiore, La Logistique, Clé de l'Introduction du Temps Réel dans la Production, **Transports & Communications**, no. 6., Université de Marseille II, Marseille, 1986.

Colin, J. and G. Paché, **La Logistique de Distribution**, Chotard et Associés Editeurs, Paris, 1988.

Fiore, c., **La Logistique en Europe, une Nouvelle Strategie-Client**, Les Editions d'Organisation, Paris, 1990

Janssen, B., **Transport, Distributie en Logistiek in Gelderland**, INRO-TNO, Delft, 1990.

Janssen, B., Product Channel Logistics, Networks and a Changing Spatial Organization, Conceptual Issues and Empirical Results, a Tentative Picture of the Logistic Landscape of the Netherlands, **Flux Logistiques et Organisation du Territiore** (M. Savy and P. Veltz, eds.), DATAR Programme de Récherche Prospective, Groupe no. 2, Certes-ENPC, Juillet, 1991, Paris, pp. 15-51.

Janssen, B. and R. ter Brugge, **Logistiek in Amsterdam, een Verkenning van de Logistieke Ontwikkelingen in Industrie, Transport en Groothandel in de Regio Amsterdam**, INRO-TNO, Delft, 1990.

Janssen, B. and C. Fiore, **Logistique et Evolution des Réseaux de Transport dans le Perspective de 1993**, Paper Presented at the A.S.R.L.D.F. Colloque "Mondialisation de l'Economie et Dévelopment des Territoires", Lyon, 1990 (mimeo).

Janssen, B. and A. Oldenburger, Product Channel Logistics and City Distribution Centres: the Case of The Netherlands, **Proceedings of the Japanese Ministry of Construction and OECD/Road Transport Research Programme**, Seminar on "Future Road Transport Systems and Infrastructure in Urban Areas", Tokyo, Japan, IRRD no. 846083, 1991, pp 289-302.

Janssen, B. and W. Wang, Logistic Strategies in The Netherlands, from European Gateway to European Distribution Centre?, **National Logistic Systems** (P. Dimitrov), Collaborative papers CP-91-06, June, Institute for Applied Systems Analysis, Laxenburg, Austria, 1991, pp. 212-157.

De Leijer, H., B. Janssen and C. Ruijgrok, **Loper; an Instrument to Measure the Logistical Performance of Logistic Service Organisations**, Paper Presented at the 6th World Conference on Transport Research, June 29-July 3, Lyon, 1992.

Porter, M., **Competitive Advantage**, The Free Press, New York, 1985.

Porter, M., **The Competitive Advantage of Nations**, MacMillan, London, 1990.

Ruijgrok, C., **Logistics and Transport, The Case of The Netherlands**, Contribution to the International Symposium on Advanced Logistics, Yokohoma International Conference Centre, 1991 (mimeo).

Tixier, D., H. Mathe, and J. Colin, **La Logistique au Service de l'Entreprise**, Paris, 1983.

Wandel, S. and R. Hellberg, **Transport Consequences of New Logistics Technologies**, Paper Second World Congress of Production and Inventory Control, Geneva, IIASA Working Paper, WP-88, Laxenburg, Austria, 1987.

PART C

EUROPEAN TRANSPORT POLICY ISSUES

CHAPTER 10

EUROPEAN TRANSPORT INFRASTRUCTURE AND NETWORKS: CURRENT POLICIES AND TRENDS

Bernard Gérardin and José Viégas

10.1 Diagnosis of the Present Situation

The present situation in European transport infrastructure cannot be characterised with a single statement. There are many complaints that the European infrastructure is not adequately fulfilling its role, and that policies should change in order to achieve an improvement.

There are in any case two major aspects that can immediately be identified by simple observation: accessibility levels to the peripheral regions in Europe (and within these regions) are poor, and congestion levels in the central parts of Europe have reached a level of intensity that is difficult to accept.

It is these two clearly visible problems that have often been addressed in political debates, but it must be understood that, while these very clear symptoms, there are underlying factors explaining their existence, so that efficient solutions must be based on adequate correction of those factors.

One of the key factors explaining the present situation is that transport networks have always been planned and decided on a national basis, thus reflecting not only the individual interests of each of the countries, but also their individual financial capability to invest and maintain those infrastructures.

This has created not only large differences in the level of provision of those infrastructures, but also other effects of bad tuning between adjacent networks on two sides of the same border; sometimes we observe even an entire or partial physical incompatibility of infrastructures (most visible on railways), and sometimes we witness merely the fact that each country has been planning the capacity of its transport networks for the traffic generated within its borders, while nobody took into account transit traffic, which plays a strong role in some of the most congested regions in central Europe.

Even after the weaknesses of this "nationalistic" approach have been recognised, and some formal bilateral or multilateral cooperation and negotiation procedures have been introduced, it is a fact that infrastructural decisions have a strong political component and are often the subject of tough negotiations with local interests. Thus, even if the problems of future incompatibility are avoided by bilateral or multilateral negotiation processes, there is still a national logic that prevails in the definition of the configuration and topology of the networks.

A European perspective, which is even more demanding than what can be achieved through bilateral or multilateral cooperation, has not yet been (completely) developed, and will probably only start to take shape during the discussion on Trans-European

Networks, which have recently begun. This diagnosis of the present situation does not mean that we under-evaluate the role of international bodies, such as the ECMT or the EC, but that we draw attention here to the dominant position of nationalistic approaches in Western Europe.

Peripheral regions in the European Community naturally suffer from the distance factor to the rest of their partners, and this can never be totally overcome, no matter how much improvement there is in the infrastructure. But there have also been significantly lower levels in the provision of transport in these regions, not only in quality, but also in quantity.

In these regions (notably Portugal, Ireland, Greece and parts of Spain) there has been a poor network supply, not only for the connections with the rest of Europe, but also for internal connections. Under these conditions, any industry requiring a local market or significant dimensions of manpower had to locate close to the main cities, which has led to highly concentrated population patterns.

As for the location of export-based industries, it must be recognised that only those industries based on maritime transport or on non-European markets could have chosen any of these regions: apart from the distance by land to the major European markets, there were either long distances to cover through poorly served regions (in the cases of Portugal, Greece and parts of Spain), or the additional cost of two transport interruptions for sea crossings (in the case of Ireland).

Without the wealth created by export-based industries, these regions have not had the capacity to invest in the improvement of their transport networks, thus increasing the gap with the richer nations of central Europe. Only in recent years this gap has possibly diminished, because of the improvements in peripheral networks (as a result of participation of the EC structural funds) and of the growing congestion in the central regions of Europe.

At the same time, congestion in the core area of Western Europe is growing stronger, especially since 1985. This situation is the result of three additive components:

(1) A high density population and a high concentration of economic activities in those regions.

(2) North-South traffic crosses this area through a limited number of congested corridors.

(3) A rapid and recent development of East-West flows related to the political and economic evolution in central and Eastern Europe. The quality of transport infrastructures is generally high; there are in this core area a significant number of international airports, a high density of highways and many railway services, but the development of traffic and congestion frequently disrupts transport systems and generates more and more bottlenecks.

The available capacity is no longer sufficient to keep the traffic flowing during the peak periods. Building of new infrastructures has to face increasing difficulties related to:

- lack of available space
- high price of land
- increasing consciousness of environmental questions.

Therefore, the core area of Western Europe seems to be privileged in terms of transport infrastructures but the real situation is not so satisfactory.

More generally speaking, in both the periphery and the core area of Europe, we can observe delays in the effective implementation of a European infrastructural network policy.

The European transport policy is a key element of the European Community Policy, the importance of which was recognised in the Treaty of Rome in 1957 and was pointed out as one of the major priorities from the beginning.

The implementation of the European Transport Policy continues to meet major difficulties, some of which are due to technical questions, but most are related to political reservations.

In 1985 the European Parliament asked the European Court of Justice to officially recognise the lack of a real European Transport Policy due to the inefficiency of the European Council of ministers. There is no mention of the transport policy in the Single Act.

This situation partly explains the delays in the process of adapting infrastructure to changing European demand patterns. The questions concerning the financing of European infrastructure networks are strongly related to the institutional ones.

Most of the national governments decided during the seventies and eighties to strictly control their national budgets, while the EC budget directly assigned to transport infrastructure investments remained very limited. The long term loans provided by the European Investment Bank have dramatically increased but they support individual projects submitted separately by private and public promoters in each of the EC countries. They are not yet directly related to a European infrastructure network masterplan. So, purely private solutions or mixed public/private solutions were presented as a solution to try to solve this key issue. This implies an increasing contribution by the users to permit a minimum of profitability for the capital invested during a long-term period.

Private investments need to be boosted in a clear institutional framework; this is particularly true for transport infrastructural projects.

Lack of adequate financing delays the implementation of a high priority investment and this cannot be solved only by academic studies or ambitious but realistic masterplans. We would like to point out the fact that the question is not a technical one, but mainly a political one.

The pragmatic approach chosen by the promoters of the European Community in the early fifties is certainly the most efficient way to succeed. The creation of a European Investment Fund could contribute towards improving the existing situation.

10.2 Missing Elements and Bottlenecks

From the elements presented above, we can conclude that several aspects of the procedures for planning, implementation and management of transport infrastructures must be improved in order to achieve a higher level of efficiency in their contribution to the quality of life in Europe.

Before planning new infrastructures, it is absolutely necessary to have a clear and realistic view of the present situation.

International transport within the European Community is still a limited part of the total traffic for both passenger and freight transport, which is the reason why frontier effects are so evident, especially for railway services; the level and quality of services are therefore very poor because of the very low level of demand. How can we escape from this vicious circle? That is the question to be resolved when talking about a European integration of transport networks.

The question is how to integrate in a coherent single European transport infrastructure network, twelve largely independent national transport networks. This is clearly a challenge. Except for some corridors, most of the international relations offer a very limited reserve capacity; there are many missing links in the existing networks (see Maggi et al., 1992).

If we consider the principle of subsidiarity, the main responsibility of the European institutions is to contribute to the improvement of the existing situation. This requires a long-term view. In a short or medium-term perspective, the level of traffic remains too low to justify significant and profitable investment.

With the perspective of the implementation of the single European market and the economic and political European integration, it is reasonable to assume that demand will increase dramatically and that international relations will therefore have to be improved in due time, but that is a risky undertaking for private investors. They can only accept this risk when the net present value and the internal rate of returns of the project are reasonably high. For most of the project, therefore, purely private investment seems to be unrealistic.

Because subsidiarity does not automatically mean subsidies, it is necessary and urgent to envisage mixed solutions in order to develop synergy between private and public interests.

The tradition of isolation in the planning and operation of transport networks does not only apply in the geographical dimension, as was stated above. This isolation is also real in the technological dimension, that is, networks of different modes are generally conceived and operated in isolation from each other.

The reasons for this generalised practice are to be found in the organisation of public administrations in which there are too often artificial barriers between the different agencies or bodies responsible for them. To resolve this weakness is probably harder than to develop a better geographical coherence of the European networks.

Connection and real compatibility between networks of different modes is a very complex subject, in which several types of compatibility are engaged, and physical adjacency is far from being sufficient.

Another critical issue is the growing awareness of the need for environmental preservation. Protection of the environment is of crucial importance in the highly industrialised European Community and, conceivably, is causing growing public concern. Transport infrastructures are increasingly regarded as one of the major sources (and social) causes of environmental pollution both during the implementation and the operation periods and therefore, the development of new European infrastructure networks will have to cope with this critical issue.

This is not only a technical question. The application of the EC directive 85/337 requires for most of the new infrastructures a formal environmental impact assessment (EIA). A key element in such a procedure is the opportunity given to the public concerned to express an opinion before the project is initiated.

The detailed arrangements for such information and consultation is determined by each member state and the information and opinions gathered must be taken into consideration in the development consent procedure.

Running parallel to this steady movement towards a growing weight of environmental concerns in decisions about transport investments, is a sometimes passionate debate about regulation or deregulation in the transport sector, and its importance for the improvement of quality in this sector.

The typical position of public authorities in Western European countries at the beginning of the eighties, reached after some decades of growing intervention, was based on the production of very rigid administrative rules about access to the profession and the market, often accompanied by direct involvement in transport production through publicly owned enterprises enjoying a monopoly in their markets.

This picture was strongly shaken in the early eighties by very radical deregulation ideas, according to which the role of the State could be reduced to simple definition of technical rules ensuring minimum levels of safety. The argument for this position was that the preceding system was too wasteful, and the market would be the best regulator of the services that should (could) be provided, and at what price.

After the heat of the first years of debate has passed, and the results of the extreme positions adopted in some cases have become apparent, it is probably accepted by most people that both extreme models have too many weak points, the former one (total regulation) on the side of inefficiencies, the latter (total deregulation) on the side of asymmetries of service levels to different segments of the population and territory.

The debate and experience have certainly been very helpful in reminding us all that competition is a strong inducer of efficiency, but they have also shown that there may be several forms of competition, both on-street and off-street. But we have also learned that the intervention of the State is a very convenient measure in defence of the general public interest, through the definition of a framework of general rules and quality requirements to ensure the citizen's greater ease of combination of transport services of different providers and, of course, security and safety.

Thus, we see that the debate must no longer be between regulation and deregulation, but among different levels and styles of regulation, under the commonly accepted framework of the search for efficiency, safety and guarantee of access for the different segments of the population.

10.3 Some Guiding Principles for the Future

In this section we present some principles we believe should be followed in the future stages of development of transport networks in Europe if we want them to be an efficient support to the quality of life and not a source of discontent and complaints.

Some of these principles have been known and accepted in general terms, but there has not yet been any adaptation of them by the deciding bodies to ensure that they are naturally followed. Thus, the recommendation of those principles must be understood as including the corresponding forms of reorganisation of public administrations.

It must be ensured that the layout and capacity of all transport infrastructure networks are decided on the basis of anticipated perspectives of the future states of the regions they are supposed to serve. This means that regional policy must be developed with an explicit consideration of this aspect, in order to guarantee a proper balance between demand and supply of transport capacity, and also the availability of an adequate level of funding to have the infrastructures ready at the time they are needed.

For this policy integration to occur successfully, European institutions have to play a very important role; not only do they have a strong voice in the coordination of the regional policies, assuming a significant part of the investment needs, but also can they be the natural conveyors of information about influences in one region of the policies developed for another region, no matter whether the latter is situated in the same country.

The second type of integration needed is within the transport sector, and seeks to take the highest benefit from the individual attributes of each of the modes to obtain the best global efficiency. Even at the European level, most of the transport infrastructure problems are dealt with on a purely unimodal basis, and solutions are sought that respect that invisible modal boundary.

At a time when Trans-European Transport Networks are being planned, it is essential that we understand that a coherent coordination between the networks of the various modes is crucial, to ensure not only freedom of choice for the users, but also the best global efficiency and resilience of the transport system. This is another principle with which all agree in theory, but soon gets forgotten when each person goes back to work in the office. A possible solution would be the appointment of a specific group of officials (probably a small division) with their only assignment to ensure the identification and implementation of synergies between the networks of different modes. They would be present at the mode-specific procedures, as a "representation" of all other modes, and would try to ensure implementation of a globally efficient, multi-modal system with efficient interchanges.

Another key guiding principle is transparency, to be able to clarify the relationship between cost of infrastructure and user charges; this does not mean that there would be a direct relationship between marginal cost and user charges. Due to economic externalisation and more generally to environmental and social costs, too narrow an economic perspective is not relevant, but whatever the methodology and criteria used to evaluate the efficiency of the individual projects and networks, in such a complex decision-making process transparency is required.

Modernisation and building of new networks in Europe will require investments on a massive scale (especially in Central and Eastern Europe). User charges will increase and will therefore contribute on a larger scale to the financing of networks but they cannot, of course, assume the whole burden. Due to national budgetary constraints therefore, the private sector will have to play a larger role in this area. There is a need for financial innovation to combine private investor criteria and public utility requirements. When using a mixture of private and public funding the positive or negative externalisation of a given investment will have to be clearly recognised and not only the internal profitability of the project.

The other key issue is the analysis of risks. Private sector involvement in the financing of a project not fully secured by a public body means that the private sector therefore assumes a partial share of the risk. Private investors depend on public licences and on the result of a very complex and long public planning process.

Transport infrastructure projects involve specific features:

- long planning and construction period
- lengthy lifespan after construction

Long time scales involve increased levels of risk and therefore the risk profile of a project can be significantly improved if private investors and governmental agencies cooperate efficiently within the framework of a clear and well managed planning process.

Financial risks related to changes in foreign exchange parity and in interest and inflation rates can be reduced by the development of the integrated European Capital Market and the use of a single currency: the European Currency Unit ECU.

For many years, the European Investment Bank has played a key role in that field, offering long term loans in ECU's to promoters at better conditions on the market. The excellent credit rating AAA is the result of an efficient combination between public and private requirement (public shareholders and international capital market). So many of the problems specific to international transport infrastructure networks could be solved in such a way.

The last guiding principle which we believe should help the development of transport networks in Europe is the necessity to increase the role of regions in the decision-making process.

Regions represent the decentralised power that can respond to human aspirations, either social, cultural or economic. With its capacity of dialogue and collaboration it can contribute efficiently to a better synergy between transport and regional development.

10.4 Conclusions

The above perspective of various aspects of the situation and trends on the European transport infrastructure system allows us to draw some conclusions.

The first one is that most regions in Europe consider their transport infrastructure as an area of priority on the political agenda, even if they do so for different reasons. As we can see, for some it is the problem of modernisation and provision, for others it is the problem of lack of capacity. On a more global scale, there is also the problem of interlinkage of national networks, especially the railways. To a large extent due to the direct pressure from the population, environmental concerns have been gaining weight in the decision processes.

In order to solve these problems, political initiatives have been taken in many directions:

- European Community Structural Funds have had a dominant application in transport infrastructures, thus helping to improve the accessibility levels of the less developed regions in the Community;
- New regulatory regimes for various modes and types of transport have been experimented in a variety of ways, searching for increased efficiency in the use of existing infrastructures;
- New financial schemes have been set up, with growing involvement of private capital, in an attempt to shorten the time needed between identification of the need for a new segment of infrastructure and the commencement of operation;
- New procedures have been developed for the approval of construction of infrastructures, including Environmental Impact Assessments and consultation of citizens.

The completion of the Internal Market in 1993 and the implementation of the Treaty of Maastricht will increase the current pressure in this domain: not only will it definitely raise the intensity of transport in Europe (thus increasing congestion levels), but it will also raise the relative significance of transport costs in the balance of competitiveness. The concept of Trans-European Networks is a first unified answer to this challenge, but the main difficulties will come through its implementation.

Underlying all these difficulties is an apparent conflict of interest between the development process of modern society, based on an ever increasing mobility of people and goods, and the desire to keep a stable and livable environment in our regions and on the planet as a whole.

We will have to manage the transport system through the next decades bearing in mind these two goals. Some of the economic and political measures will need a unified approach at a European (or even global) level, in order to avoid strong distortions between competing regions or countries, but in the end the construction of transport infrastructure has always a strong local and regional impact.

Acknowledgement

This paper builds on the work of the NECTAR working group on "Infrastructure and Networks in Transport Policy Analysis" and covers work conducted between 1988 and 1992.

References

Gérardin, B., Financing the High Speed European Rail Network, Paper European Transport and Planning, 17th Summer Annual Meeting, Brighton, PTRC, September 1989.

Gérardin, B., The Necessity of an Integrated Approach for Transport Infrastructures in Europe, Mid 90's Europe Key Issues and the Prospects for Business, Report to Kent Economic Development Board, Rochester, October, 1989.

Gérardin, B., Investissements Publics et Privés dans le Secteur des Transports, Table Ronde, ECMT, Paris, May 1990.

Gérardin, B., Transport Infrastructure Networks in Europe, Deregulation of Transport and European Integration, Paper European Transport Planning Colloquium, Brussels, March 1990.

Gérardin, B., Missing Networks in Europe, A Case Study: The European Rapid Train Network, in: **Missing Networks in Europe**, Study Prepared for the Round Table of European Industrialists, Brussels, November 1990.

Maggi, R., I. Masser and P. Nijkamp, Missing Networks in Europe, **Transport Reviews**, vol. 12, no. 4, 1992, pp. 311-321.

Viégas, J., Long-term Issues in the Development of a European Higher Speed Railway Network, CESUR, Instituto Superior Technico and CISED, CRL, Lisbon, 1990.

CHAPTER 11

TRANSPORT, COMMUNICATIONS AND TECHNICAL CHANGE IN EUROPE: FUTURE ISSUES AND POLICY IMPLICATIONS

George A. Giannopoulos and Sten Wandel

11.1 **Introduction**

Transport originated in the realm of engineering but has today become such a complex organisation that research and development have to involve many other disciplines, e.g. economics, management, computer science, behavioural science, geography and policy sciences. As pointed out by Frybourg in his paper "The Imaginary in the World of Transport" (see Frybourg, 1991), the engineer's dream has always been to eliminate friction between moving parts, the myth of the magic carpet. With magnetic suspension and linear drive he is not far from realising his ambition. What is now needed is to achieve the right economic conditions for these new techniques to become competitive.

In other words, whatever the progress of engineering, i.e. the transport equipment industry, such equipment must be integrated into the technical and organisationaal system of the transport mode concerned and its market. The technical system assumes that vehicles, infrastructure and operating techniques will evolve in harmony, as was the case for the TGV in France.

The existence of a transport market in the true sense of the term is all the more essential, given the diversity of demand of travellers, depending on income, trip purpose, and physical and geographical conditions, and of goods, depending on their nature, destination, shipment size, frequency, reliability and speed of delivery; only a genuine market combining a diversity of products and tariffs can meet this multiplicity of needs. It is clear that the transport sector, which had been over-administered, needed to be given greater freedom, and that true cost efficiency, which is incompatible with mandatory price structures and market entry restrictions, had to be restored.

These major technical and commercial systems will call for all the resources of science and organisational and information technologies. Complexity needs to be overcome and this will require the creativity of the communications industry which is investing primarily, if not solely, in the non-material and which has the ability to transmit the right messages to the manufacturing industry on the basis of an almost instantaneous knowledge of demand. These integrated service enterprises are set to be the prime users of the future service-integrated digital networks of the telecommunications industry and the value-added networks. These will be able to integrate the whole process from production to distribution and thereby fulfil a logistic role which is nothing else than the provision of value-added transport. As Frybourg puts it (see Frybourg, 1991) "Transport has moved from integers - the wheels - via the irrational numbers - the commercial transactions - to the complex numbers - computerised systems. It has hence become permeable to innovations of all kinds that Jules Vernes could scarcely have conceived of, fascinated as he was by the science of movement".

It is evident that within the above context, transport in the Europe of the future will not be comprised of engineering or just infrastructure provision, etc. It will rather have to be looked upon as an interplay of a number of influencing factors, and most importantly:

- the technology available for the construction and operation of vehicles and infrastructure
- the development of the demand for transport services
- the mechanisms of interaction that will allow for the satisfaction of that demand, and
- the various constraining factors, mainly those referring to the quality of life and the environment.

In the following we will try to give a concise picture of the state and status of these factors as we approach the 21st century, with particular emphasis on the policy issues which become necessary in order to bring about an anticipated better future for road transport in Europe.

11.2 The Technology Prospects

11.2.1 Private road transport

11.2.1.1 Trends in automobile technology

During the last decade several techniqual problems related to the automobile were solved and new technological fields were developed to solve these problems. Together with the introduction of chemistry-based technology, such as catalysts for exhausts, great advances were also made in engine combustion and the electronic and mechatronic systems for controlling combustion. As a result, automobiles, exhibited higher reliability with superior performance and lower fuel consumption. The increased demand for the technology providing this high performance has in turn stimulated the development of new technologies in the chassis and drive-related systems, such as electronically controlled suspension, four-wheel steering, constant four-wheel drive, and antilocking brakes. Optimum control systems using electronic technology have also been adopted for these components, besides the technology providing high engine performance. Furthermore, the industry has begun to accelerate the introduction of telematics and communications techniques, the development of new materials, and the utilization of computer-controlled mechanisms.

As explained in Giannopoulos (1991), the trends in automobile technology for the next decade and beyond can be summarized as follows:

1. Vehicle control and systems to secure driving functions, safety, and better overall control.
2. Communications technology with the infrastructure.
3. New materials of construction such as fiber reinforced plastics or fiber reinforced metal.

4. Use of next-generation computers for car design.
5. Use of biotechnology methods and techniques in order to detect obstacles and reduce movement resistance.
6. More environment friendly vehicles.
7. Use of new energy sources (see next section).
8. Automobiles designed for the "individual" and not the "many".

11.2.1.2 **Clean fuel, new engine systems**

In the coming three to four decades the world will have to discontinue the use of crude oil as a primary energy for transportation fuels. This event will undoubtedly be dramatic if a substitute supply is not planned well in advance. It also provides mankind with an opportunity to redesign the complete energy supply and conversion chain from mining, refining, to the combustion in the vehicle engines in such a way that it can meet the global ecological criteria. Indeed, the issue of ecological friendly transport is more urgent than to find a substitute for oil. The broader environmentel considerations will be covered in Section 11.5 below.

The change in primary energy usage is one of the most slow moving changes to be observed in our society. New attitudes and lifestyles also change over long periods in time. The environmental issue is a "century question" similar to what industrial growth/liberalism and equality/socialism have proved to be. The issue of clean engines has now reached a level of concern that has made us start with the removal of some obviously harmful substances and bi-products of our civilized life. It can later lead to global mind changes, new scientific patterns and engineering tools that enable us to create our new support systems to be ecological by design. This can then result in a completely new ecological lifestyle, different living and working patterns and with new means for transport, communication and mobility.

It is therefore imperative that a new clean fuel/engine system should be designed to meet the ecological criteria. Currently research programmes in Eureka programme of the EEC can provide a number of technical, economic, organizational tools that can help manage the long-range fuel/engine issue (see also Sviden, 1991).

11.2.1.3 **Travel and transport demand management**

The management of demand includes a number of functions and measures that are needed to preserve the capacity and operation of the infrastructure networks from unlimited and uncontrolled increases in traffic. With correct action at this level, three main objectives can be achieved.

a. move the travel demand to more suitable modes,
b. obtain a better distribution of traffic both in time (modifying departure times) and in space (influencing route choice), and
c. achieve a better balance between transport and other activities, e.g. communications, spatial organisation and land use.

Our impression is that demand management actions are probably due in the near future, and they need an early agreement at the European level, not only on the applied principles, but also in standard technologies for communications. Also the operation will need proper integration with the other emerging systems.

There has to be early agreement on this, if some concerted action is to take place. For example, the technologies for road pricing - and the principles of it - have been discussed for several years now, but agreement on common standards and implementation is far from being reached.

11.2.1.4 **Travel and traffic information**

In this area many technological breakthoughs can be observed, some of which are now at the point of general application in Europe.

According to a classification established earlier by project COST 30 and the OECD (see COST, 1985; OECD, 1987, 1988), the following are to be expected.

Class 0 - Autonomous navigation aids. These are wholly self contained in-vehicle systems that help the driver to locate his position on the road network and to navigate to his destination. They do not need a communication link but could be enhanced by the use of one or more of those described below.

Class 1 - Area broadcasting systems. These are usually radio broadcasting systems, and are used to communicate traffic information to drivers over a wide area.

Class 2 - Local roadside transmitter systems. These also broadcast traffic information, but usually only within the area immediately surrounding a road junction, or similar points.

Class 3 - Mobile radio systems. These provide two-way radio communication over a wide area between drivers in their vehicles and a control centre.

Class 4 - Local roadside transceiver systems. These also provide two-way communication between drivers in their vehicles and a control center, but usually only on the approaches to a road junction.

Concerning the travel and traffic information technologies, the important issues are that of data collection, forecasting models, and coordinated database networks. The latter is considered to be the most important.

11.2.1.5 **Driver assistance and cooperative driving**

The main technologies included in the area of driver assistance and cooperative driving are those linked with Intelligent Cruise Control (ICC), Interactive Route Guidance, (IRG), Co-operative Detection and Ranging (CODAR) and the Unified Shortrange Communication Link (USC). They are all aimed at providing the vehicle and the driver with the necessary information for safe and more efficient driving under all conditions.

For driver assistance and cooperative driving systems and their major functions of ICC, CODAR and IRG, an early implementation requires technology for detection and range finding. Such implementation however, can only be envisaged for IRG and only for dense urban road networks.

11.2.2 **Freight transport**

Regarding freight transport, from the many applications that modern informatics have on freight transport operation, there are some that can be distinguished as discrete and independent systems for which existing technology - or research and development now going on - can make a commercial application in the near or medium-term future a real possibility. In a recent survey of 215 freight forwarding companies, transport operators, and shippers of goods from 15 European countries, conducted within the framework of 2 DRIVE research projects (EUROFRET and FLEET) in early 1989, the following preferences were shown (EUROFRET, 1991).

a. Freight Management and Logistics

1. Electronic Data Interchange (EDI) networks (standardised, European-wide) for order processing, paperless invoicing, order capture, cost calculations, communication with authorities, communication with forwarders and shippers, etc.
2. On-line tracking of shipments.
3. Order capture, finding return loads.
4. Paperless invoicing and automatic notification of shipment arrival times.

b. Fleet Management

1. Automatic fleet monitoring.
2. "On-line" route planning (diversions for new orders).
3. Route planning (routing and scheduling) based on actual road and weather data.
4. Route planning for dangerous goods and special cargoes.

c. Vehicle / Drive Management

1. Automatic vehicle positioning.
2. Automatic vehicle navigation and route guidance.
3. Electronic shipment orders and instructions
4. On-board telefax for document exchange and/or telephone for voice communication.

Furthermore, the survey showed a key division in telematics use which influences the acceptance of systems by freight operator companies. When the system performs a task of "data-transmission" (e.g. sales order processing, despatched goods invoicing, etc), it is likely to have ready acceptance. By contrast, when the "decision-making" systems are regarded as more external by companies, most had little interest in using them (e.g. interactive route guidance, depot location, and vehicle routing and scheduling).

As a general rule, it is the larger companies that are more willing to invest in new informatics and telematics applications. A fleet of 10 vehicles appears to represent a threshold for telematics applications. Below about 10 vehicles, the operator requirement for telematics is restricted to general management applications such as accounting. For larger fleets the applications will be more specifically related to freight transport and its associated activities.

11.3 The Demand for Transport

11.3.1 Introduction

Certainly the driving force for all transport innovations is the demand for the movement of people and goods. This demand changes in both its nature and its magnitude, and the ongoing transformations of the European reality are expected to have a profound impact on this demand. To mention the most profound of these changes we foresee:

- the application of the Single European Act as of the end of 1992 and the related changes in the 12-member EEC market place,
- the Creation of the European Economic Space with the inclusion of the 7 EFTA countries in the EEC's economic space,
- the economic transformations and stronger linkage to EEC taking place in the former Eastern European countries,
- the economic development and the related changes in leisure and working times, and
- the advent of new telematics applications in all sectors of society and especially the so-called Integrated Road Transport Environment.

It is not the purpose of this paper to make detailed forecasts for future demand levels, but rather to point out trends and policy implications regarding demand management and necessary actions.

11.3.2 The demand for passenger transport

Urban and inter-urban passenger movement is expected to increase both for business and pleasure (tourism).

Business travel by air or road is expected to increase at least twofold within the next ten years creating obvious needs for infrastructure in airports and roads. Urban travel for all purposes is also going to increase, setting the pace for more public transport demand and new information technology applications, such as road pricing, in order to ensure full utilisation of the existing capacity at all times and at all links of the network.

A new and potentially "explosive" element in European passenger movement will be tourism. As Biéber and Potier (1991) point out:

- An overall perspective of growth is generally expected for tourism in the context of post-industrial societies. "Democratization" of hoiidays is still in progress in many countries, particularly in the South of Europe. Transport progress allows more frequent departures, by all modes. Leisure orientations of important groups (young people, pensioners, singles without children, etc) are reinforcing this diagnostic of growth.
- Congestion created by touristic concentrations will be an increasingly important matter of concern. The littoral zones are, in particular, areas where new transport investments already are critical.
- The ability to build high speed railways and new freeways is likely to become an increasing source of intense local conflict. In some areas the drastic regulation of

tourism might be the result of a lack of new transport facilities.

- Proximity tourism, with its overwhelming motor-car orientation, appears as the most promising perspective in order to reconcile growth and equity in this field of activity.
- Long distance tourism will of course remain in the realm of air transport. Costs of air transport evolution is a praticularly difficult topic to forecast. Concentration, deregulation and streamlining of old fashioned services are favourable to a decrease in costs. Long-term energy scarcity, relative decline of business traffic, congestion of airports can on the other hand increase the costs of air transport. But, associated with long-lasting political unrest in third world countries, a rather positive balance seems possible for Europe bound long distance tourism.

A final, but no less important, point that will affect the demand for passenger transport has to be made here about the mobility of rural populations (see Eskelinen, 1991).

On the whole, the socio-economic and spatial development of rural regions in Western Europe is to a lesser degree based on areal economic activities; land as a factor of production has decreased in importance. Contrastingly, the role of the countryside as a compensation area of urbanised society has become more prominent. It provides milieux for housing, leisure and tourism and is utilised as a reserve of natural and cultural landscape. Consequently, the role of space as the basic resource of rural areas is accentuated. Competition for this resource intensifies in most accessible regions, whereas there is a surplus of it in most remote areas.

From the perspective of rural areas, trends in production structure, organisations and technology have both positive and negative implications. New organisational modes might contribute to decentralisation of decision-making from centres of markets and administration, some growth industries are locationally rather footloose and they are not tied to urban agglomerations. In contrast, face-to-face contacts and utilisation of special services, which are more easily accessible in urban surroundings, play an increasingly important role in modern economic activities.

At a closer glance, even genuine rural areas in Western Europe are internally differentiated to the extent that it is a highly questionable practice to analyse them in terms of averages. This variation concerns both current structural characteristics and ongoing processes - and naturally, the problems of development and the strategies needed in alleviating them as well. With regard to the potential role of network infrastructure, for instance, this differentiation is evident in the comparison of the southern most and northern most rural regions in Western Europe. The former are still characterised by the rural exodus syndrome and deficiencies in the provision of basic services. In contrast, the very thinly populated regions in the north are fairly well equipped with up-to-date infrastructure networks, but they face the intricate problem of how their small and scattered centres could develop into dynamic nodes in a modern international economy. As a consequence, the need to adjust strategies according to local circumstances is obvious, both in the provision of services and in the restructuring of economic activities.

This creates a potential conflict with the ongoing developments in infrastructure policies. They are, to an increasing degree, based on the priorities of the urbanised society as seen from an international perspective, and carried out in a more homogeneous institutional setting. The resulting emphasis on demand and competition is difficult to bring into accord with the requirements of rural or peripherial regions. Although advances in network infrastructure technologies offer some new options, their contribution to the development of rural areas will not be realised without measures to stimulate the demand for new services in rural or peripherial contexts and without policies to ensure the supply of services ahead of demand.

11.3.3 The demand for freight transport

Freight transport demand is also expected to increase (by as much as 2% per year for some modes) and at the same time to transform in nature. Wandel and Ruijgrok (1992) analyse this transformation to advanced product logistics, and how the freight sector is likely to respond to it, with advanced transport logistics that takes the environmental and infrastructure constraints into account.

The increasing global integration of production systems and regional specialisation result in longer shipments, which increases demand in tonkm, even if the amount of ton to be moved is fairly constant in most countries.

Except for "between plant" transport in those sectors where the sizes of plants increases, the new logistics patterns result in smaller shipment sizes and higher frequencies. In order to keep the costs down and to avoid an unnecessary increase in the number of trucks on the road, shipments will have to be consolidated even more. Consolidation without losing speed and precision in delivery, compared to unconsolidated dedicated distribution. It demands sophisticated EDI communication among all parties along and between logistics chains, on line tracking of the parcels and not just tracing the paper flows, e.g. freight bills, corrective actions and preferable communication with the driver. A radical advancement of hub automation, with automatic loading/unloading sorting, storage, retrieval, picking, and packing, could considerably improve load factors and reduce traffic.

As was reported in the EEC DRIVE project EUROFRET (1991), tailor made transport is expected to triple up to the year 2010, while express services are expected to increase by 50%, all calculated in market shares. The FTL market however, will lose half of its current market share. This is a result of the above described new logistics patterns.

The transport industry is responding to these new type of demand by a re-organisation of their production systems and by offering new transport services, e.g. hub-and-spoke systems, third party logistics, reliable combined transport and urban consolidation terminals.

11.4 The Mechanisms of Interaction

11.4.1 Transport and communications interaction

This notion refers to the "mechanisms" that will interact in order to result in a (natural or forced) equilibrium between the demand for transport and the provision of communication infrastructure.

The idea of communications and transport as the carriers of new industrial and spatial forms is of course not new. Many commentators have drawn attention to the historical association between advances in transport and/or communications technologies and changes in the nature of society, changes in the way the economy is organised, and changes in spatial structure and organisation. In one sense, the very existence of the city can be understood as the spatial response to the severe limitations upon the movement of people, goods, and information which prevailed before, and during the early stages of, the industrial era.

Capello and Gillespie (1991) examine three different configurations of possible industrial and spatial systems, their impact on traffic and transport flows, and the corresponding policy priorities that emerge from these scenarios.

Of the three scenarios the most likely appears to be what they described as the "integrated networks" scenario. This scenario has clear implications for the development of transport and communications infrastructures. Not only is this industrial and spatial scenario built on the assumption that long distance, reliable transport and communications networks are implemented, but it rests on the idea that these networks have to be "integrated networks", both geographically and technologically speaking. The integration of these networks permits the development of the industrial and spatial system outlined above, for a "quasi-vertically integrated" form of organisation requires both an advanced communications infrastructure and a highly reliable complementary transport system.

Some clear policy recommendations for the transport and communications infrastructure can be drawn, on the assumption that the "integrated networks" scenario is the one most likely to be represented in Europe "2010". Long distance movements of people, freight and information seem likely to increase in importance as national territorial systems dissolve, and in consequence the emphasis in infrastructure provision needs to shift towards advanced international transport and communications networks. Physical discontinuities in both transport and communication networks have to be avoided if the new industrial and spatial system in Europe is to be effectively supported.

The transport and communication infrastructure requirements are well beyond the geographical and technological integration of networks. The Capello and Gillespie "integrated networks" scenario rests on the assumption that a complete integration between transport and communication networks exists. A final consideration concerns the need for integrated transport and communication systems to be developed in conjuction with broader spatial (urban and regional) planning. Only in this way will transport and communication networks be developed on the basis of the real needs and necessities of the newly emerging industrial and spatial system. This assumption refers to the idea that transport and communication technologies in themseves are not sufficient forces for generating indigenous local economic development. On the contrary, they have to be thought of as strategic instruments to be exploited with reference to broader spatial economic planning. In this way, supply-driven transport and communications projects with little or no connection to real demand requirements and needs can be avoided, and the future development of these leading technological infrastructures can be conceived rather in terms of their contribution to the creation of an integrated economy for "Europe 2020".

With respect to this issue, a group of international experts has developed a project on "Missing Networks in Europe" for the European Round Table of Industrialists, primarily concerned with identifying the discontinuities which exist in international networks, both in transport and communications. Transport networks could perform much better if missing networks were addressed, at five different levels (Nijkamp et al., 1990):

- hardware (physical infrastructure)
- software (logistics and information)
- orgware (institutional and organisational setting)
- ecoware (environmental and safety effects)
- finware (financing and economic viability)

The "missing networks" becomes more crucial once a spatial and industrial system is envisaged in which economic transactions are developed primarily at an international scale and where synergies among firms take place globally.

11.4.2 Transport and changes in spatial structure, industrial production and information disemination

These "mechanisms" are to be found in the interplay between spatial structure and organisation that generates transport demand and the available infrastructure in its broad sense including transport organisation, communication etc.

Changes in economic and social organisation are occurring in Europe which are associated with a variety of new forms of spatial organisation. These new forms of spatial organisation encompass a range of scales, from the European states and their constituent regions, to changes taking place within metropolitan regions which are affecting the relationships between central cities, their suburbs and their broader hinterlands. These changes have significant implications for the future demand for transportation, both of goods and of people.

Gillespie (1991) states that the last decade has witnessed considerable experimentation in the organistation of production activities. Shifts in the nature and volatility of markets have necessitated the development of intra-and inter-organisational forms which have enabled companies to respond quickly and flexibly to changes in the level and nature of demand. According to some, these responses are of sufficient importance to be indicative of a new "paradigm" of industrial organisation, termed by some as 'post-Fordism' and by others as 'flexible specialisation'.

The emergence of so-called 'scope economies' alongside scale economies in a number of industries, the diffusion of re-programmable production technologies, and the decentralization of decision-making that is needed to 'get closer' to markets, have together resulted in powerful pressures for decentralised systems of production organization. Such systems involve the increased use of sub-contracting and the emergence of new forms of co-operation between legally separate companies. Perhaps the most widely discussed aspect of this new organisational paradigm is the **'just-in-time'** production systems first introduced by Japanese companies, but now finding widespread application and development in the European context.

There are a number of important spatial concomitants to these new organisational arrangements. Some have argued that they embody a marked tendency to re-establish industrial agglomerations, with spatial proximity necessary to contain the very high transaction costs associated with this transaction-intensive system of production. From this perspective, **it can be argued that the transport system will be faced with an increasing demand for frequent, small-scale and relatively short-distance movements of components and finished goods.**

The transport demand situation is however, much more complicated than this simple 'industrial district' model of production organisation would suggest, for it ignores the considereble countervailing tendencies towards the increasing global integration of production systems, a process underpinned by the telematics innovations which have diffused so rapidly in recent years and which are the main focus of the DRIVE programme.

A further development in economic organisation which has profound implications for the transportation system concerns the development of what has been termed an "information economy". The increasing centrality of information management within organizations, the growing importance of the design and knowledge components of both goods and services, and the explosive potential associated with the new technology of information and communication have given an immense potential to the so-called "information activities". Indeed, estimates by the OECD suggest that approximately half of the total economic activity in the advanced western nations can be accounted for by these information activities (see Gillespie, 1991).

Not surprisingly therefore these activities have important impacts upon the spatial organisation of the European economies. Perhaps the most significant symbol of this impact has been the considerable expansion in office floorspace, which has affected not only the capital cities of Europe, but has also found significant expression in secondary cities and in the outer parts of metropolitan regions. Information and communication technologies again underpin many of these developments, facilitating both the integration of Europe's major centres into a system of "world cities", and permitting the decentralisation of so-called "back offices" within metropolitan regions and into non-central regions.

The implications of the growth of information activities for the transportation system is again very important. While research undertaken earlier has focussed on the substitutability of the new communication technologies for the physical movement of people, and on the prospects for a widespread dispersal of office activities as they became freed from the need to co-locate, **our understanding now is of a much more complex pattern of inter-relationships and inter-dependencies between "wheels and wires".**

11.5 The Constraints

The protection of the environment and energy conservation has long been of growing concern and is now a major policy objective for main European countries and the Community. The "environmental factor" is now incorporated into policy developments. Like other economic sectors, the transport sector has a wide-ranging impact on the environment and the environment is likely to be the major constraint in policy formulation in the future (see Masser et al., 1992). This impact is even more important given the strategic role of transport within the general economy.

Taking adequately into account the "environmental factor" without unduly impeding the economy process, requires not only technical skills, given the complex nature of the problem, but also a large amount of creative planning to turn the existing trade-off between environmental protection and development of transport activities into a "friendly" relationship. The major environmental impacts of freight transport are affecting the physical environment as well as the national heritage due to the "heavy" characteristics of freight traffic.

The effects on the physical environment come from noise, vibration, air pollution by gasses and dust, pollution of surface and ground water, the use of land for different purposes, hazards attached to the transport of dangerous goods, etc. The effects detrimental to national heritage relate to visual intrusion, spoiling of beauty spots and of archaeological sites, and irreversible damage to historical monuments and artworks. Fauna and flora may also be damaged by microclimatic effects or accidents.

Also increasing congestion creating several bottlenecks in the European road network is considered as an important environmental impact, due to time losses, operational pollution (especially CO_2 emissions adding to the greenhouse effect) and general area degradation in the vicinity of the problematic points.

Even if these indirect effects of noise and pollution on health are severe, the direct effect of traffic accidents are enormous. The cost is equal to that of the combined GNP of Portugal and Greece and the accidents on the European roads equal two crashed jumbo jets per week. It is expected that radical measures to increase safety on the roads will soon be political acceptable.

Transport policy, energy policy, environmental policy, and health policy must therefore be better coordinated as they interact with each other. Although from time to time it may be necessary to choose between conflicting objectives, these policies should when ever possible be compatible to each other.

The European Commission has so far taken the rather neutral position that the possibility of meeting energy or environmental objectives by transfers of traffic between modes should not be overestimated and that the free market competition between modes should not be distorted. In return it believes that by using new technologies and telematics it can induce some reduction in the number of empty running lorries, the development of combined transport, the reduction of obstacles at frontiers, railway cooperation etc., so that it will gain both energy and environmental benefits. Also the building of environmental factors into each criteria for infrastructural assistance will meet definite environmental objectives.

Existing EEC transport regulations that can be directly related to the environment are currently rather few and mainly aim at improving road traffic safety, to assist the movement of persons within the Community, to test the fuel quality, consumption and emissions of motor vehicles. However, it can be expected that the growing concern for environmental protection and the expected increase in commercial and passenger traffic discussed previously will lead in the future to more stringent environmental protection measures that will inevitably affect the operation of transport systems by imposing certain constraints.

For example, many ways of controlling lorry noise and nuisance have been proposed already. As mentioned above, EEC regulations deal mainly with dimension and weights, levels of noise and smoke and aspects of safety and loading. Increasing environmental problems at lorry terminals have led to necessary arrangements relating to the parking of vehicles at specified "operating centres", which are also subject to planning and development controls by local authorities.

The possibility of a system of national lorry-routes has also been examined, but no such road system has yet been found suitable. There have been suggestions by environmental and amenity groups that future numbers of lorries should be limited in some ways. But this prospect seems rather difficult to implement especially considereing the existing transport demand forecasts.

The likely areas of changes in the future due to environmental and safety constraints are: special truck design and cargo protection, routing, traffic control, incident management and training, licencing, driver working conditions and stricter enforcement of traffic regulations (e.g. the French system where the driver loses his driving licence after a certain number of violation points). Training, licencing and driver working conditions changes refer specification to freight transport and include:

- improved specification of training and examination criteria
- harmonizaton of training content
- inclusion of training for managers of road haulage companies.

Enforcement of higher standards for the reduction of vehicle emmissions, vehicle engineering and maintenance changes include the improvement of the relevant procedures and ensurance of minimum required standards by means of regulation, enforcement and control.

Routing and route maintenance is a tool available to communities that limits traffic nuisances to the general public. It refers to:

- underlying decision principles and routing models
- implications on road layout
- signaling practices
- granting exemptions and routing restrictions
- internalisation of external costs in infrastructure pricing schemes

In addition to route selection and design, maintenance of motorways, and especially traffic control devices, constitutes a complementary component of safe transportation.

The enforcement of regulations and restrictions can be greatly assisted by the use of existing and forthcoming transport informatics systems. For example, vehicle identification and tracking systems (particularly for dangerous goods), emission monitoring systems, collision avoidance systems, international EDI communication systems, and differentiated infrastructure pricing are expected to have very positive results both on controlling emissions and impacts and on reducing the total number of vehicle kilometers.

Last but not least we are likely to see increased constraints in the free access to certain heavily congested areas on purely environmental grounds. Such is the case in vehicle-free areas that are already in force in some city centers as well as restrictions in the accessibility to similar areas. A further separation of buses, trucks and private cars with respect to access and road pricing is expected.

11.6 **Policy Options and Conclusions**

When a new technology is introduced, it first substitutes for old technology and the impact is often rather limited. In the second phase innovations are also made in the surrounding systems and organisations. These organisational and institutional changes are necessary to extract the full benefit of new technologies. Therefore, research on the development and diffusion of the necessary organisational and policy changes is as important as research on the technical applications themselves.

Demand for both passenger and freight transport is expected to increase far more than the infrastructure capacity allows. Hence, a better understanding is needed of the complex interplay between spatial organisation of activities, communication, transport service provision, and infrasstructures for transport and communication. The frameworks in Capello and Gillespie (1991) and Wandel and Ruijgrok (1991) are developed for that end.

The current forecasting methodologies are mainly developed for forecasting demand for public transport and for daily trips by private cars. Further theoretical and methodological developments have to be made in order to obtain equally good forecasting methods for transport generated by tourism, freight transport and by business trips as well as for the different modes of communication. Tourism generated transport may explode and dominate certain modes of transport, and freight transport is increasing its share of vehicles on the roads. In Japan there are already more truck kilometers than car kilometers on the roads.

For passenger as well as freight movements, demand management has to be an increasingly important policy instrument. One important means will be user charges for transport and informatics infrastructure. Differentiated and flexible charges, partly based on the marginal cost principle, can considerably restore the imbalance between center and periphery, and rural and urban areas. If full external costs are included, user charges can also be an effective instrument for the more efficient use of congested networks, and to control environmental impact.

Moreover road pricing generates finances to expand capacity within the mode or in suplementary modes in the transport network, transfer gains from "winners" to "losers" in order to obtain equity, investment in activities that reduce the need for mobility, and of course, as a general tax to the government. Special attention has to be given to develop demand management instruments for the fast growing market segments: tourism, freight transport and business trips.

To sum up options concerning rural mobility, there are some priorities in policies worth emphasizing:

Firstly, public procurement and R&D support for rural or peripheral communications and transport applications are needed, because there is an urban bias in technical development in network infrastructure and services.

Secondly, the modernisation of rural and peripheral networks, especially in telecommunications, is a necessary precondition for the utilisation of their potential in rural development. This calls for special-purpose programs. Also, modernisation should be ensured as an important target in regulatory practices concerning network service operators in a more competitive setting.

Thirdly, economic development requires transport and particulary communication services to have at least an equal minimum standard all over Europe. Therefore, universal service obligations should not be abandoned as a point of reference in policies, although in practice relevant measures (e.g. subsidised tariffs, differentiated service charges etc) have to be modified according to resources, technologies and specific circumstances.

Fourthly, upgrading demand is an essential element in development strategies concerning transport and communications infrastructure and services in rural areas. It emphasizes the need to employ measures in the context of an integrative program which, for its part, presupposes co-operation between organisations at different levels.

Environmental and safety concerns seem to be the most important constraints for increased mobility of people and goods. Neither the institutional settings nor the proper incentives exist to cope with the development of clean car technology, green logistics and ecology-friendly tourisms. Innovations in incentives and institutions are called for.

Transport was once a part of engineering but as illustrated above transport is today so interrelated with other parts of society that research and development have to involve many other disciplines, i.e. economics and management, policy and systems analyses, geography and regional sciences, telematics and computer sciences, and behavioural and health sciences. However, these disciplines treat transport as one study object besides many other more central objects, which prevents true interdisciplinary transport research. The European Round Table of Industrialists therefore suggests (in Nijkamp et al., 1990) an interdisciplinary infrastructure research institute for strategic transportation research in Europe.

Acknowledgement

This paper is based on a synthesis of studies undertaken by various members of the NECTAR working group "Europe 2020"; various papers by these members are included in the References.

References

Capello, R., and A. Gillespie, Transport and Communications: Towards a New Spatial Organisation, Paper NECTAR, Group "Europe 2020", 1991.

COST project 30 bis, Electronic Traffic Aids on Major Roads - Final Report, EUR 9835, CEC, Luxembourg, 1985.

Biéber, A. and F. Potier, Transport and the Development of Tourism: Some European Long Term Scenarios, Paper NECTAR, Group "Europe 2020", 1991.

Giannopoulos, G.A., Technological Innovation in Private Road Passenger Transport, Paper NECTAR, Group "Europe 2020", 1991.

Giannopoulos, G.A., Road Guidance and In-car Communication Systems, Paper ECMT, Paris, pp.30-58.

Gillespie, A., New Forms of Production Organisation: Change, Continuity and Communication Technology, Paper NECTAR, Group "Europe 2020", 1991.

Frybourg, M., The "Imaginary" in the World of Transport From Mechanism to Virtual Networks, Paper NECTAR, Group "Europe 2020", 1991.

Eskelinen, H., Rural Areas in the High Mobility Communications Society, Paper NECTAR, Group "Europe 2020", 1991.

EUROFRET, The Evolution of Road Transport Informatics in Road Freight Operations in Europe, Deliverable 3, EEC/DGXIII, DRIVE project V.1027, Brussels, 1991.

Nijkamp, P., S. Reichman and M. Wegener (eds.), **Euromobile: Transport, Communications and Mobility in Europe**, Avebury, Aldershot, 1990.

Nijkamp, P., R.Maggi and I.Masser, **Missing Networks in Europe**, A Study Prepared for the European Round Table of Industrialists, Brussels, 1990.

OECD, **Dynamic Traffic Management in Urban and Suburban Road Systems**, Paris, 1987.

OECD, **Route Guidance and In-car Communication Systems**, Paris, 1988.

Sviden, O., Clean Fuel and Engine Systems for 21st Century Road Vehicles, Paper NECTAR, Group "Europe 2020", 1991.

Wandel, S. and C. Ruijgrok, The Freight Sector Response to Changing Spatial Organisation of Production, Paper NECTAR, Group "Europe 2020", 1991.

CHAPTER 12

REGULATORY REGIMES IN EUROPEAN TRANSPORT AND MARKET CONTESTABILITY

David Banister, Joseph Berechman, Bjorn Andersen
Sean Barrett and Ginés de Rus Mendoza

12.1 Introduction

A considerable amount of theoretical debate and empirical evidence is now available for all modes of transport and from many western countries on the impact of regulatory reform on transport markets. However, the success of attempts to liberalise one aspect of transport supply may be limited in its impact if free markets do not exist in the supply of complementary facilities. Research on the potential gains from an integrated approach to developing freer markets which would embrace all aspects of supply is still lacking. One issue which affects all modes is that of the ownership, location and access to terminal and interchange facilities. Unless competitive principles are applied to these facilities, barriers to entry will be maintained.

This paper presents the argument for the restructuring of the network and the considerable benefits to the operator of a hub and spoke network with a limited number of terminals or interchanges over which they have an effective monopoly control. This network structure is likely to minimise the costs to the operator and allow interlining of "friendly" services through the terminals, but it also makes it difficult for competitors who can only offer a disconnected network of services or a network which duplicates the incumbent operator's network. The established operator almost always seems to be in a more powerful competitive position and so can reestablish their supremacy (see Banister et al., 1992).

The theoretical argument is illustrated with empirical evidence taken from long distance bus services, from the airlines and from maritime transport for a range of European case studies. The European cases are taken from the U.K., Ireland and Scandinavian countries where various forms of competition have been introduced or are being introduced into the bus and airline markets. In urban areas there are likely to be large numbers of journeys requiring a spatially disaggregated route structure, but even here hub and spoke operations may evolve with links from the centre to the periphery. These networks may be deformed as they are influenced by the structure and form of the city. Hence, the importance of terminal facilities is more complex as it relates to both the route structure and the spatial organisation of the urban area (eg the distribution of activities and land uses). Consequently, the arguments put forward here may be less relevant for urban public transport services. Often the terminal facilities in urban areas are owned by the local public authority to ensure fair access.

In the final part of the paper a range of options are considered which might help restore competitive entry conditions to allow all operators access to terminal and interchange facilities. The organisation of the network can be used to deter entry in a competitive market. This was not possible in a heavily regulated market because the structure of the network was determined according to the principles of spatial equality, with the commitment to the maintenance of the network. All operators were able to link into that network through common interchange points with no entry barriers.

12.2 The Theoretical Arguments

Network structure in a **regulated public transport market** is concerned with maintaining an even distribution of services so that as many locations as possible are linked into the network. Services, although responding to demand in terms of higher service frequencies along certain routes, are evenly distributed spatially, and interchange can take place freely between routes and operators. The structure of the network results from the particular regulatory regime given the spatial organisation of that region and hence the levels of demand. It is dictated by political decisions, the evolution of the network and the availability of subsidy. Such a network may have a hub and spoke structure, but it is more likely to have a large number of nodes and direct links. Clear welfare objectives, such as those providing for accessibility to low income groups, or helping reduce congestion, can all be accommodated within such a network structure through the provision of (subsidised) bus, air or shipping services on routes with low demand and through the provision of additional vehicles at the peak.

Network structure in a **competitive public transport market** will concentrate on hub and spoke operations which are essentially radial in structure and require the passenger to travel greater distances but to interchange on fewer occasions. There are considerable network economies to operators from such a network structure as it helps the joint objectives of cost minimisation and entry deterrence. These network economies lead directly to economies of scale and density which allow the operator to cluster passengers for further transport, lowers operating costs per unit of output and impacts on passenger welfare (see Berechman, 1991). By reducing the number of routes operated, the transport firm can raise frequencies which will benefit passengers, but the partially connected network (as in a hub and spoke system) will increase travel times and reduce the passengers' welfare.

The reduction in the operator's unit costs results from the ability to use larger sized vehicles (scale economies), to operate services at higher frequencies (density economies) and to have access to interchange and terminal facilities (scope economies). This crucial third factor affects both the firm's cost structures and the network structure and allows for economies of scope (Table 1). A common input factor such as a terminal allows the fixed costs to be allocated to all services using that terminal. By concentrating services through a hub and spoke network into a few terminals joint costs can be reduced. At the same time, the possibility of a competitor using the same terminal can be reduced either through a prohibition if the terminal is also owned, or through a capacity limitation argument. It is also easy to add new routes through the hub, and the potential for strategic pricing is increased as new entrants to the market are unlikely.

Table 1 Terminal access and barriers to entry

Network Economies	Savings due to cost advantages arising from the production of services on different routes which belong to the same network (e.g. hub and spoke operations) - allows the interchange of labour and vehicles because of the network structure or because of different frequencies on routes - marginal costs of production on one route declines when more output is produced on another which links to the same facility - presence of common facilities influence the configuration of the network which in turn affects total costs
Scope Economies	The presence in the production process of a common input factor whose fixed costs are shared by all outputs - centralised or coordinated planning of the investment resulting in more efficient use of management skills, sales network and operational capital (see Shughart, 1990) - common facilities (terminal, interchange or maintenance) which are shared by routes belonging to one operator so that joint costs are minimised

For new entrants it becomes crucial to have access to the key interchange points in the network so that these services can link in (interline) with the incumbent operator's services, or even compete with those services. Ownership, location and access to these facilities in a competitive market are essential, and unless competitive principles are applied to terminals and interchange facilities, barriers to entry will be maintained. The explanation is that terminal facilities constitute a substantial sunk cost and a minimum provision of such a facility is required for the production of the smallest amount of a transport service. Additional units of terminal capacity can only be purchased in minimum sizes.

These two basic regulatory regimes illustrate the ends of a continuum of regulation - deregulation policies, and the actual structure of the network is modified by cost conditions, demand conditions and market competition which are all influenced by the prevailing regulatory regime. Network structure is continually changing with the direction of that change being influenced by the regulatory regime.

12.3 Inter Urban Long Distance Bus Services

In the U.K. the evidence of the impact of entry barriers to terminals is mixed. In interviews carried out with bus operators in the main Metropolitan Areas access to garage facilities and bus stations was not seen as a problem, even by the large operators when facilities were owned by a major competitor. Some operators were worried about unequal access to bus stations and information offices, and some felt that capacity constraints at bus stations and garages may influence their ability to expand (see Pickup et al., 1991).

This generally optimistic view contrasts to that of Thames Transit in Oxford (see Blundred, 1991) where exclusion from the central bus station resulted in threats of litigation, delays in entering the market and claimed unfair competition (Table 2). After three years of instability, the new entrant and the incumbent operator both compete profitably on the Oxford to London route (100 kms). But, it was only after a new bus terminal was built in central Oxford to which all operators were allowed access that real competition could take place. Prior to this, the incumbent operator was supported by the City Council who owned the old bus terminal, and they were able to prevent Thames Transit from establishing a credible threat to their established bus service.

The consequences of exclusion from terminal facilities, either to use inferior facilities or of incurring significant sunk costs, are well illustrated by the case of the main long distance bus terminal in London. When long distance bus services were deregulated in the U.K. (1980), the ownership of the Victoria Coach Station was not separated from the main operator. National Express used its ownership and control of this terminal to deny access to potential rivals, principally British Coachways which was a consortium of six major long distance operators who set up a competitive network of services. The Victoria Coach Station is widely known by the public, it occupies a prime city centre site, and some 24 percent of passengers interchange from coach to coach at Victoria (see Davis, 1984). British Coachways found it difficult to establish a presence in the market and had to terminate their services on the street (Gloucester Road) or on derelict land (Kings Cross). The net result was that competition was short lived and, for a variety of reasons including terminal access, the British Coachways consortium collapsed (Table 3).

In Norway, the express-bus routes were restructured (1988) with the creation of the Norway Bussekspress (NBE) company to market all services and to control entry to terminals. Some forty operators now participate in the NBE, but in the initial stages several operators stayed independent as membership required payment of 3.5 percent of all revenue to support the marketing and terminal services provided by NBE. Since 1988, traffic has more than doubled (640,000 passengers 1988; 850,000 1989; 1,300,000 1991) with the system as a whole operating commercially. Two important points to note are that NBE is limited in the frequencies with which services can be operated as the Ministry of Transport and Communications wants to protect the railways. Secondly, there is only one primary hub to the whole system (Oslo) and two secondary hubs (Bergen and Trondheim).

Table 2 Thames transit in Oxford

1.	Thames Transit's decision to compete with established operator (City of Oxford Motor Services) on the Oxford to London service.
2.	Thames Transit unable to find a suitable depot site within the City, partly due to the absence of appropriate locations, but mainly due to the City Council's "desire to protect the incumbent operator".
3.	Depot eventually found in the neighbouring South Oxfordshire district outside of the City. For long distance bus operators it is necessary to have frequent servicing to meet strict safety standards.
4.	City Council banned Thames Transit from using the central bus station which it owned in Oxford and the service had to operate from derelict land opposite the bus station. Patronage was poor.
5.	Litigation started by Thames Transit to gain access to the bus station, and leave given to have an expedited hearing in the High Court. Case not taken there because of the possible costs and because a new bus station was being constructed to replace that owned by the City Council.
6.	After a three year period of instability, the City of Oxford Motor Services and Thames Transit both operate out of the new Oxford Bus Terminal, and both are profitable.

In Bergen and Trondheim the express buses use the ordinary bus terminals owned by the local bus companies and the municipal authorities which are open to all competitors on the basis of a usage charge. In Oslo NBE secured the exclusive lease on a city centre site (1987) opposite the Central Railway Station and close to the urban bus terminal and the main underground terminal. NBE has built a terminal on this site which can only be used by members of the NBE system. The independent operators have no alternative express bus terminal in Oslo as there are no other suitable sites and they had to operate in the streets as in London. The net result has been that many independents (e.g. the Kristiansand-Oslo route with 40,000 passengers in 1990) have been forced to join the NBE system to gain access to the Oslo terminal. In addition, the information and marketing advantages of NBE has permitted the development of a public identity which the independents have not been able to match. An effective monopoly of express bus operations has been established by NBE in Norway, and it is almost impossible for an independent operator to compete because of this market dominance, the control of the primary hub in Oslo, and the extensive public image which NBE has established.

Table 3 Long distance bus services terminating at different types of location

Percentages

Company	BS-BS	BS-CP	BS-ST	CP-CP	CP-ST	ST-ST
National Express and SBG	83	2	13	0	2	0
Private Companies	5	7	17	5	29	37

Key : SBG Scottish Bus Group
BS Bus Station CP Car Park ST Street
Source: Barton and Everest (1984)

A similar attempt to establish a network of express buses in Denmark (1990) failed, as the licensing authority (the Passenger Traffic Council) declined to grant the necessary licenses as they wished to protect the railways and the local bus networks which are under the control of county-based transport authorities. Of the few express bus services which do operate (4), three run from Jutland to Copenhagen (from Aarhus, Aalborg and Hanstholm) with two daily return trips. However, they are not permitted into central Copenhagen and passengers have to transfer in the suburbs to travel the final part of their journey by city public transport (30 minutes) to the city centre. The hub in Copenhagen is the City Railway Station which forms the main central public transport node and the departure point for Kastrup Airport, but the express bus services are denied access. This competitive disadvantage has meant that demand for cheap express bus services has not been large.

In the inter urban bus market, the empirical evidence suggests that operators who are not already in a strong position (e.g. National Express in the U.K.) could form themselves into a cartel (e.g. Norway Bussekspress - NBE) so that they are in effect in a dominant position. However, even when many operators are in competition there are other means by which market share can be maintained. Because of the high sunk costs involved in terminal construction and because of the advantages of structuring the network on a few hubs, access to terminals becomes critical. Market dominance can be achieved by control over terminals (including booking facilities), particularly if they are located in the city centre and have a high public profile (eg Victoria Coach Station in London and the NBE Terminal in Oslo). Equally, access restrictions on operators will prevent competition. Such restrictions can be placed by competitors (Oslo or London) or by the city authorities (Copenhagen) to protect themselves, local services or the railways.

There seem to be few intrinsic benefits deriving from the ownership of both terminals and services. The control of access should be separated from the operation of services, and there should be safeguards against collusion. This strategy might work well in the bus industry where the likelihood of capacity limitations is small and where other related functions (e.g. servicing) can be carried out elsewhere. However, in the airline industry, the separation of control of access from the operation of services has not resulted in a competitive market.

12.4 The Airlines

The 1980s has seen a huge growth in the demand for air travel, and many airports are now at capacity with restrictions on the number of take off and landing slots. In these situations, it is impossible for new competitors to enter the market, and although some slots have been sold to other airlines, the problem is compounded when incumbent airlines hoard unused landing slots as part of a strategy to exclude new entrants (see Keeler, 1991).

The deregulation of the U.K./Ireland route (1986) provides an example of the benefits and problems caused by regulatory reform. The number of air passengers between the two countries increased by nearly 2.5 times (1985-1989 1.8m to 4.2m), with fares being reduced by some 40 percent in real terms. Four new entrants came into the market (Ryanair, May 1986; Virgin Atlantic, June 1987; British Midland, April 1989; and Capital Airways, August 1989) to supplement the two existing operators Aer Lingus and British Airways (Virgin Atlantic withdrew in 1989 and BA has also recently withdrawn from the London-Dublin route). The new entrants have obtained 28 percent of the expanded market. Four new international airports opened in Ireland in the three years after deregulation (Knock, Galway, Kerry and Waterford) compared with none in the period since 1961. However, there are still considerable barriers to competition (see Barrett, 1990; 1991).

Since 1977 new entrants have been banned from London Heathrow, but traffic has increased from 22m to 38m passengers with the growth being allocated to incumbent airlines. It was only in 1991 that the U.K. government modified the traffic distribution rules and allowed access to more airlines at Heathrow. The two largest airlines in the western world (United Airlines and American Airlines), with huge domestic hubs in the USA, were allowed to replace the services of the weaker PanAm and TWA. At the same time four BA slots were transferred to Virgin Atlantic so that they could operate on the Heathrow to Tokyo Narita Airport. For the new operators on the U.K./Ireland route, it was necessary to use Luton as their London airport, and it was difficult to develop interlining. A total of 25 percent of traffic on the Dublin-Heathrow and the Dublin-Gatwick routes interlines, and until British Midland gained access to these airports this market was uncontested. One other problem has also reduced the attractiveness of the new services to the public. Ground handling monopolies meant that the costs of handling baggage for the new entrants were considerably higher than those for the established airlines. British Midland estimated that the costs at Heathrow were twice those of its own handling at Birmingham (see Monopolies and Mergers Commission, 1985, p.107).

In this case deregulation opened up the market and had clear advantages for the travellers as they benefitted from a greater choice of flights and cheaper fares. However, for the new entrants there were problems with competing with the two established operators, principally in terms of access to the main London airports, but also in terms of interlining arrangements and support services.

The air transport system in Sweden is divided into a primary and a secondary network. The primary network is unsubsidised, but cross subsidisation is permitted on peripheral routes with light demand. The secondary network is commercial, with services being provided if demand is sufficient. The only subsidy is paid on some routes in Northern Sweden operated by Linjeflyg and its subsidiary Swedair. The primary network is operated by SAS and Linjeflyg (until 1990 half owned by SAS, but since then sold to

Sweden's largest freight forwarder - the Bilspedition group). Of the 22 routes in the primary network, five are operated by SAS (Stockholm - Gothenburg, Malmo, Lulea and Kiruna; and Lulea - Kiruna) and these routes carry 2.967m passengers (1989). The 17 routes run by Linjeflyg carry a further 4.711m passengers (1989). All but one of these routes are hubbed through Stockholm/Arlanda. The total traffic at this airport (1990) is 13.5m passengers of which 7.7m was domestic traffic. The secondary network has a further 22 routes and is operated by several airlines, the largest being Swedair. A further nine of these routes hub through Stockholm/Arlanda increasing its primacy to 30 of the 44 domestic routes.

In 1988 Swedish domestic air transport policy was reviewed and the existing regulated system was maintained with only two operators on the primary network. The revenue adjustment between the two operators in favour of Linjeflyg would continue until the end of 1991. It should be noted that domestic regulation contrasted with the Swedish government's desire for greater competition in international air transport. In 1989 a Commission was appointed by the Swedish government to review competition policy in general, with domestic air transport being one of the sectors identified for special attention.

The main proposals from the Competition Commission are summarised in Table 4. All restrictions would be lifted on the eight most intensively used routes and a competitive market would be created with no controls over prices. As any route reached the 300,000 passengers a year threshold it would switch from the regulated position to join the competitive market. The main problem now was to reallocate the slots at Stockholm/Arlanda airport through which all these routes hubbed. At present the coordination responsibility belongs to SAS and the allocation of times is based on "grandfather rights". As there were no spare slots at the peak, the Commission proposed a combination of administrative reallocation of slots and peak pricing of slots (Table 5).

The response of the Swedish government to these proposals was cautious, and they had concerns over the impacts of airline deregulation even though they agreed that it was likely to lead to improved accessibility and efficiency. The final policy proposed a much slower path to deregulation with the air transport and competition authorities preparing new rules for full deregulation of domestic air transport from the date when new capacity is available at Arlanda (a third runway will open in 1995/96). The argument here is that competition will not emerge until extra capacity is available at this key hub airport, and so the efficiency gains will not be made. In the meantime SAS and Linjeflyg will be able to compete on the primary network from 1 January 1992 (a temporary duopoly), and other operators will be given the opportunity to start services on new routes. The system of cross subsidisation and revenue equalisation between SAS and Linjeflyg on the Northern routes will continue, and there will be no subsidy on the primary network. Most significantly, Sweden will await EC rules on slot allocation.

The net result of this decision is that SAS and Linjeflyg have been given monopolistic protection for at least three years with the possibility of consolidating their market position before full deregulation takes place. The only opportunities for other smaller airlines (e.g. Transwede) are to try out new routes, but these are unlikely to raise much revenue. The Transwede company has claimed that it can operate on the Stockholm/Arlanda to Gothenburg/Landvetter route with a fare that is 33% lower than the current SAS fare. There seem to be direct comparisons between this route and the U.K./Ireland route which was deregulated in 1986.

The long term future of air travel in Sweden is likely to be controlled by SAS and

Table 4 Proposals for domestic airline deregulation in Sweden and the government response

Competition Commission Proposals	Government Response
Free access to routes with more than 300,000 passengers. Regulated system of monopolies on other routes with no change in operators. New routes can be operated. Loss making routes will be supported through a tendering process if they promote regional development. Subsidies to be paid by a charge on all primary domestic routes.	Partial deregulation for routes with more than 300,000 passengers would soon spread to the rest of the network and this would result in the two major airlines gaining a duopoly. A special charge on all primary routes would be against EC rules and Sweden must act in line with EC policy.
No transport duty for routes with more than 300,000 passengers, but a common system for information on service and route changes.	Not accepted
No price regulation on routes with more than one operator, and maximum prices on route monopolies.	Primary routes to be unsubsidised as a totality. This allows cross subsidy and maximum normal price control over all the primary system.
Freedom to hire capacity on all routes as long as it cannot be defined as a circumvention of the ban on cabotage.	Not accepted
Cabotage in line with EC rules (no opening up before the EC does).	Accepted
Measures to increase the number of available slots at Arlanda. Time differentiated landing charges or administrative reallocation of slots if there is no agreement on a voluntary basis.	Policy would have to include other airports as well as Arlanda to reform the present situation where airlines do not pay the full costs of landing. Deregulation at present is impossible because Arlanda is at capacity.
Swedish competition law to be introduced to domestic air transport together with increased control over monopolies.	Accepted

Linjeflyg, and it has yet to be seen whether these airlines will actually compete with each other (from 1 January 1992). Real competition may come from the new high speed train which is operating on the Stockholm to Gothenburg corridor. Since March 1991, this train has carried 150,000 passengers and some 60 percent of these have transferred from air, as there is only a marginal difference in the total time taken (15 minutes difference) and a cost saving of SEK 500 (about £50). SAS have responded by reducing their fares to compete on their internal routes with rail and the car.

Table 5 Slots at Arlanda Monday to Friday in summer 1990

Operator	Peak Totals	24hr Totals	Peak %
SAS Domestic	209	492	43
Linjeflyg and Swedair	675	1502	45
Regional Operators	258	540	48
SAS International	266	503	53
Other International	221	609	36
TOTAL	1629	3646	45

Source: SOU (1990) Konkurrens i inrikestrafiken, 58

Events in Swedish air transport policy are now moving very fast with the announcement (20 January 1992) that SAS want to "Buy Back" Linjeflyg from the goods operator Bilspedition. Final approval has been given with SAS paying Bilspedition SEK 300 million and Blidspedition will get 30 percent of the potential profit for the next four years. For an operator which lost SEK 100 million in 1991 after cost cuts of SEK 340 million, this price seems high and demonstrates the value to SAS of securing monopoly control (The original price paid for Linjeflyg was SEK 475 million). SAS argue that SEK 1 billion (some 20 percent of costs) must be saved as a result of the acquisition by reductions in the labour force (about one third of the total employees in the two companies, some 1050 persons) and economies of scope.

The case was referred to the Swedish Monopolies and Mergers Commission (Naeringsfrihetsanbudsmannen) and the Commission has approved the SAS takeover of Linjeflyg. This reverses a previous decision which prevented SAS from buying back the shares. However, some compromise has been reached with SAS giving up 50 slots at Arlanda from 18 August 1992 and a further 50 from 31 March 1993. Agreement has been reached to prevent predatory pricing to eliminate competitors, there will be no discrimination against other operators using SAS baggage handling facilities, and SAS has agreed to sell their majority share in the SMART system of distributing air tickets to travel agencies. The possibility of other operators linking into the SAS Eurobonus frequent flier programme will be discussed. The reason for this reversal can be directly explained by the dramatic reduction in air travel demand in Sweden which would have bankrupted Linjeflyg.

The Swedish government has accepted the buyback of Linjeflyg, and has speeded up the process of full deregulation in the Danish air market which took place in July 1992. There will no longer be any preference given to the enlarged SAS-Linjeflyg company, and the Swedish government is examining ways to encourage new operators entering the market. Transwede is likely to apply for licences on four Alranda routes. Despite this optimism, it is unlikely that any other airline will threaten the effective monopoly which SAS-Linjeflyg has over the domestic air market (over 95 percent control).

In Norway the situation with respect to domestic air travel is similar to that in Sweden. The domestic route network is divided between the unsubsidised primary network, a subsidised secondary network operated by STOL aircraft and an unsubsidised secondary network based on commercial operations. The regulatory regime has allowed a duopoly between SAS and Braathens Safe (SAFE), giving SAS 60 percent of the seat kms operated and SAFE the remaining 40 percent. The authorities approve capacity, timetables and prices, and there is a uniform price system in operation based on distance, making it cheaper for people living in the more remote parts of the country to travel. Even the discounted fares are identical.

Parallel licenses were introduced in 1987 on the three busiest routes (Oslo-Bergen 850,000 passengers 1990; Oslo-Stavanger 720,000; and Oslo-Trondheim 890,000), but there were still severe restrictions. The prices were still identical with the only flexibility being in the number of discounted seats available on each flight, and promotions including campaign fares for a maximum of 8 weeks. The Ministry of Transport and Communications determines the numbers and timings of flights. This limited form of competition has led to some small redistribution of passengers between SAS and SAFE. Overall load factors have been reduced (as capacity has increased but not demand), prices have fallen marginally as a result of the increased use of discount fares, and in flight and ground service has improved as this is where the only real competition has taken place. The net benefits from this limited form of deregulation have been negative as the savings to passengers from reduced prices (NOK 66m) have been more than outweighed by the increased costs of operation of the parallel service and the lower load factors to the operator (NOK 250m).

The latest stage in the gradual move to a fully deregulated market in domestic air services on the primary network is now being discussed. Decisions will be taken in 1992, but as in Sweden the question of cabotage in the EC will be a crucial factor here. Routes are being divided according to their profit levels to determine the levels of cross subsidy, and to determine the outcome of various options, particularly in light of the possible limitations on airport capacity. There are two basic types of routes. Point-to-point routes originate from the main Oslo hub and link the capital with the main regional centres (Stavanger, Bergen, Trondheim, Bodo, Evenes, Tromso and Alta). Multiple stop routes coast-jump along coastline of Southern Norway and Northern Norway, and also link the North with the South of the Country.

If deregulation takes place it seems that the network will involve increased hubbing and there will be pressures on Oslo/Fornebu airport as the multiple stop routes are replaced by direct routes from this hub. This hub will dominate services in the Southern and Western parts of Norway, and it will also form the basic links to the Northern parts of the Country. At present (1991) Oslo/Fornebu is operating at capacity for 4 hours in each weekday, with 36 flight movements per hour. Consequently, although the airport still has spare capacity, the same problems may occur here as at Stockholm/Arlanda as hub dominance is compounded by growth in demand for air travel and access is heavily weighted in favour of one or two large airlines. New entrants to the market will find it difficult to obtain attractive slots and competition will be limited to the effective duopoly exerted by the two incumbents. One possible solution is to use Oslo's second airport (Oslo/Gardermoen), but in the past this has mainly been used for charter flights, and the proposed new airport in Oslo is still being discussed in Parliament.

As with Sweden, some mechanism has to be devised to allocate slots to competitors as any new investment in runway capacity will not be available, at least in the short term.

The alternative is for the incumbent operators to maintain and strengthen their position, and deregulation in the limited form discussed in Scandinavia will help them achieve that objective. The dominance of the Stockholm/Arlanda hub is absolute and it seems that Oslo/Fornebu is following the same path to dominance. Weak regulatory reform measures also seem to help the incumbent.

12.5 Maritime Transport

International maritime transport is considered a competitive business. Low profitability and frequent entry and exit are characteristic of the industry. Low marginal costs and the high mobility of assets in the industry contribute decisively to the reduced effectiveness of market power.

It is unclear whether the industry is contestable. Tramp services are clearly competitive, and Davies (1986, 1989) argues that in the liner shipping industry all the operators have access to identical technology, there are no significant sunk costs given the ease with which ships can be leased or purchased, exit is easy through resailing or leasing, and there exists a time lag in the response of the incumbent to entrants underpricing as long as "shipping conferences" are slow to respond to outsiders. Davies (1986) supports his case with empirical evidence from the Canadian shipping lines which have frequent entry and exit as well as hit and run entry.

Jankowski (1989) challenges this position and argues the case that contestability theory is not relevant to the liner shipping industry where there is often disequilibrium between capacity and demand. He interprets the entry and exit found in the Canadian shipping lines "as an indication of lack of contestability not of its existence" as " the very idea of contestability is that the threat of entry, not actual entry which disciplines the industry".

Even if one accepts the argument that the maritime industry does not satisfy the strict conditions for a market to be contestable, at least in scheduled traffic (Section 11.2), there are clear indications which point to a highly competitive environment characterised by a lack of important entry barriers, low prices and low profitability. Although maritime transport in Europe is considered a competitive business, particularly as a result of the international characteristics of its demand and supply activities, it has experienced different types of intervention aimed at restraining competition. The main restriction to the operation of the market are the "shipping conferences", a kind of self-regulation between the operators which acts as a cooperative oligopoly setting the prices and the levels of service which would otherwise have been set by the market.

In the international arena, public intervention tends to favour national merchant fleets through subsidisation and flag discrimination. Bohme (1989) has identified the main instruments of discrimination in favour of the national fleet as:

- reservation of part or all cargo moving in a country's foreign trade.
- special levies on foreign flag ships, or preferential dues and levies for national flag ships.
- preferential treatment granted to national flag ships in national sea ports, priority allocation of berths, and so on.
- the use of the terms of shipment as a device to influence the choice of vessels by shippers.
- the establishment of cargo booking monopolies (government or semi-government)

as a means to control and allocate cargo flows, or the admission of only certain designated carriers to a country's shipping markets.

Two different factors have contributed to the reestablishment of the competitive nature of sea transport in Europe. One is the pressure of low cost fleets, particularly the use of flags of convenience and low labour cost operations from developing countries, and the other is the liberal shipping policy of the European Community. Flags of convenience consist of fleets operating under open registration systems with lower labour costs and a more favourable tax regime. Even accepting the hypothesis of lower labour quality in these open registries (see Yannopoulos, 1988), flags of convenience have contributed to the competitiveness of the industry. The shipping policy of the European Community (see Erdmenger and Stasinopoulos, 1988) is against the discriminatory cargo sharing agreements and the other anti competitive practices itemised above, as this would reduced the efficiency of intracommunity trade and permit the use of unfair pricing strategies. Although the application of competition rules (Articles 85 and 86 of the Treaty of Rome) is favoured, the European shipping policy exempts "shipping conferences" from the provision of these Articles, even though conditions have been established to avoid the use of oligopolistic powers.

Assuming that the European shipping policy and the strength of outsiders guarantee that "conferences" do not constitute barriers to entry in the industry, the recent evolution of maritime business shows similar developments to those found in the airline industry. There are network economies combined with economies of ship size. Big shipping companies have developed a form of hub and spoke operation with ships of 4,000 TEU on the main routes and feeder services from secondary ports. Concentration has been the consequence, but lower prices and low profitability suggest that a reduction in the number of firms has not led to a reduction in competition. On the contrary, concentration has increased rivalry, and, although fewer firms are now operating in the main routes, price competition is still a crude reality for shipping companies. For example, CGM (the French public company) has had to abandon services on its North Atlantic route.

This situation is similar to the airline industry, but with two very important limitations. Firstly, the development of hub and spoke operations in the shipping industry has not reduced competition as cost considerations are paramount and time plays only a limited role in the total generalised costs. Secondly, there is still considerable spare capacity at the main ports and so questions of allocation of slots is not relevant. Shipping firms do not suffer from the problems of being denied access to ports at peak times. These two differences encourage port competition and do not create problems related to access to terminals as in the European airline industry.

12.6 The Options for Increasing Access to Hubs

In this paper it has been argued that under competitive market regimes, bus, airline and maritime transport networks will be gradually restructured in a hub and spoke configuration with access to terminals becoming the key elements in maintaining competition where capacity is limited. The dominance of national hubs in European cities has a direct parallel in the USA where the dominance of many large American airports by one operator has been one of the most striking developments since deregulation. In 1978, there were only two leading airports where over half the departures were accounted for by one airline (Charlotte and Pittsburgh). However, out of the 40 leading airports, 14 are now dominated by a single carrier with more than half of the domestic departures (see Pryke, 1991). The hub and spoke system which developed after deregulation provided the airlines with the opportunity to concentrate their services on one centre, and the network economies have been added to a wide range of scope economies such as publicity, maintenance and market image. All these factors can be presented to the passenger as advantages for a particular airline.

Apart from the benefits to the operators, hub and spoke systems have to have considerable volumes of traffic before it will support two or three operators, particularly if one or two dominate the terminals at either end of the route. At the time of deregulation, American airports had a significant amount of spare capacity but no such margin exists in European airports. Airlines forecast that capacity will be reached at 17 European airports by the year 2000. But in Europe, the dominance of individual airports by particular operators is not as complete as that in the USA (Table 6).

The basic proposition made in this paper is that ownership of the terminal should be separated from the main transport operators using that facility, and that there is no collusion between particular operators and the terminal authority. Such a separation reduces the likelihood of cost complementarities and joint production costs for one operator which would give that company significant competitive advantages. This prerequisite would prevent the Victoria coach station situation and the effective monopoly control which NBE has in Oslo. Similarly, the absence of collusion would prevent the alliance between the City of Oxford Motor Services and the Oxford City Council preventing the new operator from using the terminal. For the inter-urban bus services, such a separation would allow the terminal owner to coordinate and publicise services using the terminal, and each operator would pay for the use of the terminal. Maintenance and other support functions could be carried out elsewhere. If the bus terminals were to reach capacity, then peak pricing of slots could be introduced, but in most cases efficient organisational practices would allow all buses access at desired times.

Table 6 Airport dominance in Europe and the USA

Airport	Operator	Percentage
Heathrow	British Airways	37
Charles de Gaulle	Air France	49
Frankfurt	Lufthansa	55
Dallas	American Airlines	58
Dulles	United Airlines	70
Atlanta	Delta	87

Source: British Airways (1991) Business Life, September

Notes: Heathrow figures relate to landings and take offs, whilst the figures for the other airports are for air traffic movements

For maritime transport there is less necessity to separate the ownership of terminals from their main users as there is considerable spare capacity available. It is only when capacity becomes in short supply that fair allocation procedures are required. Under other conditions, the market can easily accommodate all demand.

Thirty six US cities have open airports where no single operator has more than 39% of all domestic departures and no 2 operators have more than 59% of domestic departures.

A different situation occurs with respect to the airlines, as there are considerable advantages to the operators to both concentrate their services and their fleet of aircraft at one centre, as this gives them maximum operational flexibility and minimises maintenance costs. It also helps their public image to be associated with one airport. Unless action is taken to open up access to airports before full deregulation in Europe, it would seem that hub dominance will follow the US pattern with competition being limited to the routes with very high levels of demand (see Pryke, 1991). The other routes will remain as monopolies or duopolies.

There are four main means to allocate access to airports more equitably:

1. **Auctioning of slots** to the highest bidder on a willingness to pay basis. The auction would allow the successful bidder to run the services on that route for a specified period of time (eg three years). There are problems with the timing of such an auction and the necessity to coordinate procedures for all types of services as airline timetables would be dependent on negotiations after the auction. Slot auctions would lead to the use of larger aircraft at the most heavily used airports and it would probably be harder for new entrants to get into the market. Bass (1991) has suggested that the silence of the smaller operators on this issue seems to support the assertion that they are not advocating market pricing of slots. However, if the problems of organising such an auction can be overcome, this option forms the market solution to matching supply and demand for airport capacity. It allows all operators to compete and slots are not allocated in perpetuity, but for a fixed period. It may also be appropriate to give existing operators first refusal on slot renewal as the period of time must be sufficient to encourage investment by bus companies and airlines in the necessary support infrastructure.

2. **Administrative rationing and reallocation by the authorities.** Such an allocation process would have to be carried out by an independent authority on a set of agreed criteria. It would allow positive discrimination in favour of particular (small) operators and it could prevent effective monopoly control of airports. However, the complexity required from such an allocation process may prove difficult to solve as information would be required of all services (both domestic and international). Where capacity has been reached, such a procedure might result in a secondary market where operators would sell on or exchange their allocated slots.

3. **Buying and selling of slots** could follow on from an allocation process (Option 2), with the possibility of the larger airlines gradually acquiring monopoly control over routes and hubs. Airlines with a strong market position would buy more slots to further strengthen their position. A slot market actually exists at four congested airports in the USA (Chicago/O'Hare; Washington/National; New York/JFK; New York/La Guardia). The rules are clear and there is no bureaucracy. The expected move towards greater concentration has been modest, with United and American acquiring 250 new slots at

Chicago being the main exception. Transfers are scrutinised by the US Justice Department to conform with antitrust requirements (see Cameron, 1991). United's recent attempts to buy slots at Washington/National in the Eastern auction were blocked on competition rule because of the carrier's dominance at Dulles (70 percent of all movements: Table 6).

4. **Peak-pricing** allows scarce capacity to be allocated according to the time of day and would encourage the use of larger aircraft. International experience demonstrates that the big airlines continue to fly at the most attractive periods because of their low price sensitivity. In the US, there have been moves to flat fare charging, irrespective of aircraft size, and the British Airports Authority has introduced movement charges with a very large differential between peak and off peak use. However, as airport charges still form a small part of total operating costs, a substantial increase may be requires to reach the market-clearing level. It may be necessary to feed that excess rent back into the industry to improve capacity and air traffic control systems.

All these possible options have limitations and it is unlikely that any one will be adopted on its own. The justice of "grandfather rights" is being questioned, particularly when capacity is reached as this limits the possibility of competition and new entrants. It is also clear that slots are valuable and that they are tradeable. At present the trading can only take place within the current set of bilateral agreements. In the recent London/Heathrow case where PanAm's and TWA's slots were allocated to United and American, only US carriers could replace other US carriers. If a secondary slot market was set up, then allocated slots (Option 2) or purchased slots (Option 3) could be exchanged between all licensed carriers on a particular route. Such as system would allow increased flexibility and permit all slots to be used, rather than the present situation where unused slots are retained in the knowledge that if they were given up, they could not be reacquired.

If a pricing mechanism is used to allocate slots at airports, then the revenues raised could be reinvested in expanding airport capacity and air traffic control systems. One unresolved area of debate is over whether the airport owns the slots or whether the airlines own them. Will access rights and new licences be "grandfather rights" as with the old system of slot allocation? If so then the airlines would have acquired a significant asset with the slot, and this asset would form part of their balance sheet. In effect, this has happened with the exchange of slots at London/Heathrow. It was the airlines which benefitted and not the airport. However, the likely costs of the slot would also add to the airlines debt and cash flow problems (see Cameron, 1991).

The most likely outcome for the access to airports problem will be a compromise and a mixed solution which combines the market with some regulation. To maintain the structure of the network, some of the slots will be reserved for new entrants, particularly on the thin peripheral routes. Regulation will be maintained to protect small airlines and these thin routes, and it will also be necessary to prevent collusion between operators and airport authorities, and the possibility of predatory practices. Market principles will be introduced through forms of peak pricing to spread the load and through the buying and selling of slots in a primary and secondary market. For some of the main corridors of demand a limited form of auction may be appropriate. In all cases, the ownership of the airports must be separated from the main operators and this process must be completed before deregulation takes place.

However, certain other complications are likely to distort any reforms on the question of terminal access. **Mergers** within both the bus and the air industries may provide the means for any operator to maintain and increase their effective control over terminals. The **EC Requirements** for interlining between competitors may provide some short term respite for new and small operators, but if terminal access is not part of such an agreement then effective interlining will not take place. With respect to maritime shipping where terminal capacity is not an issue, the EC "shipping conferences" allow cooperation between operators to be maintained but new operators must also be allowed into the market. The longer term question of additional **Capacity at Airports** is still unresolved with many European airports close to capacity. This means that tradeable airport slots become the most important issue, and any pricing or auction is likely to place a premium price on the value of any slot. Airport capacity expansion seems to lag behind the steady growth in demand. Real competition in the bus and air markets may come from the **Railways**, particularly if a new generation of high speed rail investment takes place in Europe over the next decade. Similarly, there is no reason why a competitive **Inter City European Bus Network** should not be set up to compete at the cheaper end of the market. All these complicating factors are beyond the scope of this paper, but must be taken into account before a particular set of requirements are agreed upon for determining fair access to terminals for all modes of transport in Europe.

References

Banister, D., J. Berechman and G. De Rus, Competitive Regimes within the European Bus Industry: Theory and Practice, **Transportation Research**, 26A (2), 1992, pp. 167-178.

Barrett, S., Deregulating European Aviation - A Case Study, **Transportation** 16(4), 1990, pp. 311-327.

Barrett, S., Discussion of American Deregulation and European Liberalisation, **Transport in a Free Market Economy** (D. Banister and K. Button, eds.), Macmillan, London, 1991, pp. 242-248.

Barton, A.J. and J.T. Everest, Express Coach Services in the Three Years following the 1980 Transport Act, **Transport and Road Research Laboratory**, LR 1127, 1984.

Bass, T., Discussion on the Internal EC Market for Air Transport, **Transport in a Free Market Economy** (D. Banister and K. Button, eds.), Macmillan, London, 1991, pp. 216-219.

Berechman, J., Transit Deregulation and Market Structure, Paper prepared for the Second International Conference on Privatisation and Deregulation in Passenger Transportation, Tampere, Finland, June 1991.

Blundred, H., Barriers to Market Entry, Paper prepared for the Second International Conference on Privatisation and Deregulation in Passenger Transportation, Tampere, Finland, June 1991.

Bohme, H., The Economic Consequences of Restraints on Transactions in the International Market for Shipping Services, **Shipping Policies for an Open World Economy** (G.N. Yannopoulos, ed.), Routledge, London, 1989, pp.84-106.

Cameron, D., Slot Machinery, **Airline Business**, July 1991, pp 38-40.

Davies, J.E., Competition, Contestability and the Liner Shipping Industry, **Journal of Transport Economics and Policy** 20(3), 1986, pp. 299-312.

Davies, J.E., Competition, Contestability and the Liner Shipping Industry: A Rejoinder, **Journal of Transport Economics and Policy** 23(2), 1989, pp. 203-207.

Davis, E.H., Express Coaching since 1980: Liberalisation in Practice, **Fiscal Studies** 5(1), 1984, pp. 76-86.

Erdmenger, J. and D. Stasinopoulos, The Shipping Policy of the European Community, **Journal of Transport Economics and Policy** 22(3), 1988, pp. 355-360.

Jankowski, W.B., Competition, Contestability and the Liner Shipping Industry: A Comment, **Journal of Transport Economics and Policy** 23(2), 1989, pp. 190-203.

Keeler, T.E., Airline Deregulation and Market Performance: The Economic Basis for Regulatory Reform and Lessons from the US Experience, **Transport in a Free Market Economy** (D. Banister and K. Button, eds.), Macmillan, London, 1991, pp. 121-170.

Monopolies and Mergers Commission, The British Airports Authority, HMSO, London, 1985.

Pickup, L. et al., **Bus Deregulation in the Metropolitan Areas**, Avebury, Aldershot, 1991.

Pryke, R., American Deregulation and European Liberalisation, **Transport in a Free Market Economy** (D. Banister and K. Button, eds.), Macmillan, London, 1991, pp. 220-241.

Shughart, W.F., **The Organisation of Industry**, Richard D. Irwin Inc, New York, 1990.

Yannopoulos G.N., The Economics of "Flagging Out", **Journal of Transport Economics and Policy** 22(2), 1988, pp. 197-207.

CHAPTER 13

OPTIMAL POLICIES IN THE PROVISION OF PUBLIC TRANSPORT IN EUROPE

Ginés de Rus Mendoza

13.1 Introduction

In the European context, as well as in other countries in which deregulation has not been chosen as the main policy for the organization of the bus industry, it is relevant to address the issue of what policies are welfare maximizing in a regulated industry. In order to achieve the maximum benefits from the resources employed in the provision of public transport, services should be provided at minimum cost by the operators (productive efficiency); the route structure, frequencies and bus size should be set in a way that makes it impossible to increase social benefits through the reallocation of resources (allocative efficiency); the introduction of technology should be carried out in the optimal timing (dynamic efficiency); and finally, the organization of the industry should allow the achievement of these three sides of a common economic problem: to provide the service efficiently.

In Jansson (1979) and Nash (1978, 1988) optimal pricing, service level and bus size are determined in a first best world. In Nash (1988) the analysis is extended including the size of the network and considering the consequences of the introduction of a budget constraint. In this paper we follow these contributions; in the first part of the paper we introduce an objective function in which the unweighted consumer and producer surplus is maximized and first best solutions are obtained to determine the optimal price and service level; the positive economies of density associated to the use of public transport (see Mohring, 1972) appear as the crucial factor in the determination of price and service quality, and also in the distinction of economies of scale and density.

We analyse the consequences of introducing financial constraints in the second part of the paper. Optimal fare and service levels are obtained subject to a budget constraint; the welfare consequences of cross-subsidization are also discussed. Finally, we considered the determination of fares and service levels in European countries, as well as other relevant regulatory issues with the aim of contrasting optimal policy with actual practice.

13.2 Resource Allocation Decisions in the Optimization of Public Transport Provision

13.2.1 Economies of scale and density

The transport literature shows contradictory results in relation to the findings about the type of returns to scale in urban bus transport. One of the sources of these differences is the expression of the output used in the econometric estimation of the cost function. The findings point to constant returns to scale when bus-kilometres are the output measure (see Berechman and Guliano, 1985 for a review) as one could expect if we consider that the main sources of economies of scale such as the higher degree of specialization, the organization of production and changes in inputs proportion are largely exhausted when the bus company has reached the minimum optimal size which is not far from the left extreme in the range of firm sizes. This result is compatible with the presence of economies of vehicle size at a route level (see below).

In the discussion about the economies of scale a crucial issue consists of the behaviour of factor prices when firm size rises. One standard assumption in the estimation of the cost function is that firms minimize costs for a given set of exogenously determined input prices; Miller (1978) have shown that wages are sensitive to firm size; the empirical evidence in the case of public transport in Spain (see De Rus, 1989a) shows that within comparable tasks, wages are higher in large scale firms, and public ownership contributes by itself to higher wages. The information gathered for this paper from 18 European countries is consistent with these results.

In a regulated industry the measurement of economies of scale is crucial in deciding the desirable size of companies but when we deal with pricing and investment the relevant issue is the presence or absence of economies of density. In the provision of public transport services there are substantial network externalities as the average user cost of making a journey decreases with an increase in passenger flow. Existing users obtain benefits when more passengers decide to use the system.

13.2.2 Optimal price and service level

In the production of passenger-kms two main types of inputs are required: firstly, the flow of vehicle-hours, labour, fuel and materials; secondly, the time the user supplies in making the trip. The inclusion of user time as an input in the production function has allowed a deeper understanding of the industry.

In the urban context, the three main components of the user time (t) spent in making a trip are the following: walking time to and from the bus stop (t_1), waiting time in the bus stop (t_2) and in vehicle time (t_3).

t_1 depends on the route structure, the design of the network according to the spatial distribution of the population. t_2 is a function of the headway, the inverse of the frequency. In urban transport systems with frequent services it is usually assumed that passengers arrive at random at bus stops; therefore, waiting time is considered to be approximated by half of the headway. Finally, t_3 depends on the trip length, vehicle speed, and total boarding time of passengers taking the bus (we assume a two doors bus and alighting times to be less than boarding times at each stop).

The generalized cost of a journey (g) can be expressed as:

$$g = p + h(N,Q) \qquad (1)$$

and the flow of passenger-trips as a function of "g",

$$Q = f(g) \qquad (2)$$

where:

Q: passenger-trips per hour

p: fare per journey
h: total user costs per journey
N: number of buses in the route.

The generalized cost of a journey has two main components: the total value of journey time and the fare (ignoring other quality variables as comfort, security, etc.) and, though the user pays p to the operator, the total cost to him making a journey is g; the difference (g-p) is h: walking, waiting and in vehicle time multiplied by their money values. In order to increase patronage, the operator may affect g through fare reductions and quality improvements (extending the network, increasing frequencies, improving reliability, etc.). h may be considered as the money value of walking, waiting and in vehicle time ($h=v_1t_1+v_2t_2+v_3t_3$) where v_1, v_2 and v_3 are assumed constant but not necessarily equal.

Let us consider that the operator's objective function is the maximization of the user and producer's surplus. The starting point is the analysis by Jansson (1979) and Nash (1978, 1988). We consider the passenger flow as a variable which depends on the concept of generalized costs with price and frequency determining demand level. In a first best world this can be expressed in the following way:

$$W_1 = \int_0^Q f^{-1}(x)dx - zN - Qh(N,Q) \tag{3}$$

where "z" is the operating cost per vehicle-hour (assuming a constant bus size).

First-order conditions are:

$$\frac{\partial W_1}{\partial Q} = f^{-1}(Q) - \left[h + Q\frac{\partial h}{\partial Q}\right] = 0 \tag{4}$$

$$\frac{\partial W_1}{\partial N} = \int_0^Q \frac{\partial f^{-1}(x)}{\partial N}dx - z - Q\frac{\partial h}{\partial N} = 0 \tag{5}$$

Conditions (4) and (5) are partial derivatives of (3) obtained keeping "N" and "Q" constant respectively. From (4) the social surplus is maximized, for a given level of service, when price is equal to marginal cost; with "N" constant, marginal cost is the increase in total user costs when an additional passenger takes the bus.

From (1) we find:

$$p = f^{-1}(Q) - h(\Phi,N,V) \tag{6}$$

From (4) and (6) we can derive:

$$p = Q\frac{\partial h}{\partial Q}$$

(7) arises because an extra passenger does not increase operating costs as long as the service level, measured by the number of vehicles per hour on the route, is kept constant, and hence the price will be equal to time and comfort penalty imposed on the existing

users.

From (5) we obtain the optimal level of service, for a given passenger flow per hour:

$$- \left[Q \frac{\partial h}{\partial N} \right] = z \tag{8}$$

as the integral in (5) is equal to zero (for a constant level of Q). In view of (8), the objective function (3) is maximized with respect to service level, for a given passenger flow, when the user costs savings are equal to marginal operating costs.

In the real world, one of the most relevant tasks in the management of public transport services consists of attaining the highest social benefit subject to the constraint that operating revenue less operating cost has to reach a given financial target. Let us consider the introduction of a budget constraint; the optimization problem can be now expressed as follows:

$$W_2 = \int_0^Q f^{-1}(x)dx - zN - Qh(N,Q) - \mu\,(zN - pQ - D) \tag{9}$$

where D is the level of subsidy. Thus, W_2 represents a measure of net social benefit in the presence of a revenue constraint. The set of first order conditions are:

$$\frac{\partial W_2}{\partial Q} = f^{-1}(Q) - \left[h + Q \frac{\partial h}{\partial Q} \right] + \mu \frac{\partial (pQ)}{\partial Q} = 0$$

$$\frac{\partial W_2}{\partial N} = \int_0^Q \frac{\partial f^{-1}(x)}{\partial N} dx - z - Q \frac{\partial h}{\partial N} - \mu \left[z - \frac{\partial (pQ)}{\partial N} \right] = 0$$

$$\frac{\partial W_2}{\partial \mu} = pQ + D - zN = 0 \tag{10}$$

From (10) and (1) we find:

$$\frac{p - Q \frac{\partial h}{\partial Q}}{- \frac{\partial (pQ)}{\partial Q}} = \frac{- Q \frac{\partial h}{\partial N} - z}{z - \frac{\partial (pQ)}{\partial N}} \tag{11}$$

In order to attain an optimum with a budget constraint, the marginal social benefit per monetary unit due to marginal price reductions or to marginal quality improvements has to be equal. The economic interpretation of (11) is the following: the social benefit of an extra unit of subsidy is the social value of extra patronage attracted through a fare reduction or through an improvement in the level of service. $[p - Q(\delta h/\delta Q)]$ expresses the social benefit of an extra passenger attracted through a fare reduction (private benefit - the price - net of costs imposed on existing passengers, $\delta h/\delta Q > 0$ as N is kept constant). $[- Q(\delta h/\delta N) - z]$ expresses the social benefit of extra traffic attracted through an improvement in service level: the benefits are user time changes from quality improvements ($\delta h/\delta N < 0$ as Q is kept constant) net of marginal operating costs; social benefits in (11) are divided by the financial resources devoted to both policies: marginal revenue of a price cut and marginal operating cost less marginal revenue of an increase in quality.

If the constraint is binding at the optimum, relaxing the budget limit will increase social benefits ($\delta W_2/\delta D = \mu > 0$); then (11) has to be positive, hence price will go up and frequency will go down in comparison with (7) and (8), which are the conditions for an unconstrained maximum.

13.3 Cross-subsidization: An Evaluation of Ramsey Pricing

13.3.1 Cross-subsidization in public transport

Cross-subsidy has been widely criticized when it is the consequence of flat fares and marginal costs differences between market segments (areas, times of day, etc.); especially when it is a deliberate procedure to keep a particular structure of services, which otherwise should be modified. The burden of internal subsidy on consumers has been shown to be a consequence of the absence of competition. With budget constraint and different demand elasticities, cross-subsidy appears as a side effect of pricing with the aim of achieving social surplus maximization, although it has been criticized for its distributional consequences.

In the majority of European countries, public transport provision is carried out within a regulated environment with budget constraints. Generally, each city or metropolitan area has a company, either private or public, operating as the exclusive supplier. The existence of cost differences between areas, times of day, etc., which is ignored in the design of fare structures, has generated a pattern of cross-subsidy which involves the provision of some services for which the incremental revenues are below incremental costs, the difference being financed by surpluses in other services or activities of the firm, modifying in this way the structure of service provision between groups of users. This pattern of cross-subsidy has been analyzed for the transport industry (see Gwilliam, 1984, 1987).

We are interested in the pattern of cross-subsidy that appears as a consequence of maximizing consumer and producer surplus subject to financial constraints. Social surplus maximization subject to a budget constraint requires resource reallocations between market segments charging prices which deviate from marginal costs inversely proportionally to their demand elasticities. This is the accepted criterion in a second best world. The consideration of cross-subsidy as something linked to the existence of legal monopolies in the bus industry and its theoretical defence as the efficient way to satisfy budget constraints, concedes to this internal source of subsidy the role of the optimal solution for allocative efficiency under regulation. Jansson (1984) questions the application of the inverse elasticity rule in transport, particularly when the necessity of the goods and the absence of substitutes are the reasons explaining the lowest elasticities. Jansson's arguments are strongly based on equity considerations.

In this section the justification for cross-subsidy is questioned, even where it is the result of implementing Ramsey pricing. The net gain in consumer surplus derived from the application of the inverse elasticity rule is relatively small, as long as the suppression of cross subsidy does not imply route closures. A similar argument has been put forward by Brown and Sibley (1986) in the case of telecommunications and by Nelson, Roberts and Tromp (1987) in the case of electricity. In practice, a commercial objective which is used as a proxy for social welfare maximization consists of maximizing passenger-kms. We also evaluate the welfare gains of satisfying the financial constraint allowing cross-subsidy with that objective function.

According to Baumol, Panzar and Willig (1982, p.348) cross-subsidization means

> "...that the buyers of some products do not bear the costs it takes to supply those products. This may mean that those prices fall short of the corresponding marginal costs or that the revenues of those products fall short of the corresponding total (incremental) costs incurred by the supply of those products. In either case one can expect inefficiency in resource allocation to result, with excessive demand for the products that receive a cross subsidy, inadequate demand (in term of the social welfare) for products that bear the burden of the cross subsidies, and excessive demands for substitutes for the products that bear the burden, whether these substitutes are goods that would have existed in any event or are new products introduced in response to the opportunity created by the cross subsidy".

We have seen that with first best pricing incremental revenue falls short incremental cost due to the existence of external economies (Mohring effect; see Mohring, 1972). Let us suppose now that the company has to satisfy a given financial constraint and that the market is reduced to a single route used by a number of identical consumers. In view of the solution to the optimization problem in (9) the rule consists of adjusting price upwards and frequency downwards minimizing deadweight losses, and this can be done equalising the net benefit per extra unit of subsidy from fare increases and frequency reductions.

Let us assume now that the company operates two sectors with independent demands and different production costs. Two possible ways of satisfying the financial constraint are:

(i) in each sector separately.
(ii) the constraint is satisfied overall.

The case of each sector satisfying the constraint separately is similar to the single market with identical consumers. We now consider that the constraint is imposed overall; the objective function would be the following (let us assume that costs are variable with the number of buses):

$$W_3 = \int_0^{Q_i} f_i^{-1}(x)dx + \int_0^{Q_j} f_j^{-1}(x)dx - z_iN_i - z_jN_j$$
$$- Q_ih_i - Q_jh_j - \mu(z_iN_i + z_jN_j - p_iQ_i - p_jQ_j - D) \qquad (12)$$

(12) is an extension of (9) where "i" and "j" are two different sectors with independent demands (in this section Q represents passenger-kms flow; alternatively we can assume a constant average journey length). First-order conditions in this case are the following:

$$\frac{p_i - Q_i \frac{\partial h_i}{\partial Q_i}}{-\frac{\partial (p_i Q_i)}{\partial Q_i}} = \frac{p_j - Q_j \frac{\partial h_j}{\partial Q_j}}{-\frac{\partial (p_j Q_j)}{\partial Q_j}} \tag{13}$$

$$\frac{-Q_i \frac{\partial h_i}{\partial N_i} - z_i}{z_i - \frac{\partial (p_i Q_i)}{\partial N_i}} = \frac{-Q_j \frac{\partial h_j}{\partial N_j} - z_j}{z_j - \frac{\partial (p_j Q_j)}{\partial N_j}} \tag{14}$$

With a unique shadow price for public funds in (12), conditions (13) and (14) are required to maximize social welfare: on the margin an extra unit of subsidy must yield the same increase in social benefit in both sectors and with both policies (fare reductions and service level improvements). The introduction of indirect costs in (12) does not change conditions (13) and (14).

Glaister and Collings (1978) and Nash (1978) have shown that passenger-kms maximization is a reasonable proxy for social surplus maximization, when a commercial objective is required for transport operators. In this case the objective function is:

$$W_4 = f_i(g_i) + f_j(g_j) - \mu(z_i N_i + z_j N_j - p_i Q_i - p_j Q_j - D) \tag{15}$$

$$\frac{\frac{\partial f_i(g_i)}{\partial p_i}}{-\frac{\partial (p_i Q_i)}{\partial p_i}} = \frac{\frac{\partial f_j(g_j)}{\partial p_j}}{-\frac{\partial (p_j Q_j)}{\partial p_j}} \tag{16}$$

$$\frac{\frac{\partial f_i(g_i)}{\partial N_i}}{z_i - \frac{\partial (p_i Q_i)}{\partial N_i}} = \frac{\frac{\partial f_j(g_j)}{\partial N_j}}{z_j - \frac{\partial (p_j Q_j)}{\partial N_j}} \tag{17}$$

Condition (16) shows that the increase in passenger-kms on sector i per extra unit of subsidy for a fare reduction should equal the increase in passenger-kms on sector j. Similarly, in view of condition (17), the increase in passenger-kms from an improvement in the level of service per extra unit of subsidy should be the same on both sectors. In other words, an extra unit of subsidy must lead to the same increase in passenger-kms on both sectors, adjusting prices or service levels. This interpretation is similar to (13) and (14) but with a difference to be underlined: for a given financial constraint more passenger-kms can be obtained by increasing price and reducing bus-kms in routes with lower elasticities and diverting the resources to less inelastic routes as long as conditions (16) and (17) are satisfied. Nash (1978) points out this risk of overexpansion in the relatively elastic markets.

Consumer and producer surplus maximization can be achieved applying conditions (16) and (17) instead of (11) in each sector. That is, allocating resources with a global perspective and putting money in that sector or policy which yields higher marginal social benefits; this involves cross-subsidy between groups of services and what is particularly important, between groups of consumers, as incremental revenue in one sector may well fall short of incremental cost as long as differences in elasticities allow an optimal departure from the first best solution. Jansson (1984) has criticized cross-subsidy based on the equity principle, we address now the issue of the efficiency gains of cross-subsidy over average pricing in each sector as an alternative form of satisfying the budget constraint.

13.3.2 The welfare gains from Ramsey pricing

Nash (1978) has shown the fare structure, service levels and financial results which are obtained from different objective functions pursued by a transport company operating as a legal monopoly. Net social benefit maximization with budget constraint is evaluated in Nash (1978) breaking even overall, that is, admitting cross-subsidization. We now evaluate the deadweight losses of breaking even separately in each sector without cross-subsidy.

With data on cost, disaggregated flows of passenger-kms and fares for a Spanish suburban operator (see De Rus, 1989b), we have considered two differentiated sectors within the area in which this statutory monopoly provides bus services; routes are grouped according to their profitability in these two sectors. This operator provides suburban services (average passenger journey length of 15 kms); we have chosen the suburban services for the present exercise due to data availability and to the existence of two separable sectors in cost and revenue. Using Nash's non linear optimization programs, net social benefit (NSB) and passenger-kms have been obtained for different combinations of demand price and service level elasticities, both with and without cross-subsidy.

Each sector is composed of a group of routes with different level of profitability, hence even in the option of breaking even in each sector, some degree of cross-subsidy remains, and not only between routes, but time of day, different parts of a route, etc. The only aim of this application is to test, under reasonable assumptions, the consequences of satisfying the budget constraint using two alternative ways: breaking even in each sector and allowing cross-subsidy.

We have tested various combinations of fare and service level elasticities, assuming a semilog functional form and constant marginal costs in the production of bus-kms.

The computation of demand equations is straightforward once the functional form has been chosen. The exogenous values are: passenger-kms flow in each route, price (common to all routes) and bus-kms run; with these data and for particular elasticity values demand coefficients were calculated. The cost functions were obtained through a fully distributed cost approach in which producer costs are allocated according to bus-kms run, bus-hours and number of vehicles required in each sector. It is assumed that in both sectors demands are independent (cross elasticities are zero) and costs are separable (the most serious problem of joint production in some routes were overcome when they were aggregated in the same sector).

Fares, bus-kms, passenger-kms and net social benefit (NSB) have been calculated for various combinations of demand elasticities, breaking even overall and separately. Allowing cross-subsidy there are substantial fare changes. These changes mean consumer surplus reallocations among consumer groups and, according to the theory of optimal pricing with budget constraint, an increase in aggregate social surplus. Tables 1 and 2 display the net welfare gains of breaking even overall above average pricing expressed as percentages of NSB and revenue obtained with average pricing.

The net gains from adopting Ramsey prices are rather small (1.2% of NSB, 5.3% of total revenue as the best outcome). Maximizing passenger-kms, the efficiency gains of breaking even overall are lower. In 8 cases out of 32, reductions of NSB are obtained if unweighted passenger-kms maximization is pursued in each sector.

When the profitable sector has the lowest elasticities (absolute value) and the demand for the unprofitable sector is the most elastic, the implementation of Ramsey prices produces the highest efficiency gains (combinations -0.2/0.2 and -0.3/0.3). In order to test the sensitivity of this result with greater elasticity differences, the values -0.1/0.1 have been chosen for the profitable sector. The net gains are lower when expressed as percentage of NSB which corresponds to average pricing (1%) and substantially higher when expressed as a percentage of revenue (8%). The explanation rests on the shape of the semilog demand curve, with extremely high prices when quantity approaches the origin, producing a dramatic change in social surplus when the elasticity is reduced (absolute value) from -0.2 to -0.1 (with similar prices, vehicle-kms, passenger-kms and revenue, the NSB is aproximately double when the elasticity is -0.1).

Other possibilities have been tested with higher values for service level elasticities without significant changes. A particularly interesting result is the impossibility of breaking even when higher demand price elasticities are assumed for the unprofitable services. In these cases the elimination of cross-subsidy would cause service closures with losses which need a broader approach for their evaluation.

13.3.3 Cross-subsidy, equity and externality

The optimal departure from marginal cost pricing as formulated in Baumol and Bradford (1970) has been criticized, because optimal taxation (Ramsey pricing) is concerned with allocating the tax burden efficiently, considering elasticity values for different goods; on the other hand, the application of the inverse elasticity rule in transport is usually linked to different groups of consumers with strong equity implications (see Jansson, 1984).

Table 1 Net social benefit maximization. Gains (%) of consumer surplus and patronage allowing cross-subsidy with respect to average pricing in each sector

	UNPROFITABLE SECTOR -0.3/0.3		-0.3/0.2		UNPROFITABLE SECTOR -0.2/0.3		-0.2/0.2	
PROFITABLE SECTOR	Passen-ger-kms	NSB	Passen-ger-kms	NSB	Passen-ger-kms	NSB	Passen-ger-kms	NSB
-0.3/0.3	0.9	0.9 (3.2)	0.4	0.4 (1.5)	-0.8	0.2 (0.8)	-0.5	0.1 (0.3)
-0.3/0.2	1.1	1.2 (4.5)	0.6	0.4 (2.3)	-1.0	0.4 (1.5)	-0.7	0.1 (0.6)
-0.2/0.3	3.4	1.2 (4.6)	2.2	0.6 (2.6)	0.4	0.4 (2.0)	0.2	0.2 (1.1)
-0.2/0.2	3.8	1.2 (5.3)	2.5	0.6 (3.0)	0.5	0.5 (2.3)	0.2	0.3 (2.3)

Price and service level elasticities, e.g.: -0.3/0.3

Consumer surplus gains as a percentage of average pricing revenue in parenthesis.

Table 2 Passenger-kms maximization. Gains (%) of consumer surplus and patronage allowing cross-subsidy with respect to average pricing in each sector

	UNPROFITABLE SECTOR -0.3/0.3		-0.3/0.2		UNPROFITABLE SECTOR -0.2/0.3		-0.2/0.2	
PROFITABLE SECTOR	Passen-ger-kms	NSB	Passen-ger-kms	NSB	Passen-ger-kms	NSB	Passen-ger-kms	NSB
-0.3/0.3	0.9	0.9 (3.2)	0.4	0.4 (1.5)	0.4	-0.9 (-3.1)	4.8	-0.8 (-0.3)
-0.3/0.2	1.2	1.2 (-4.5)	0.6	0.4 (-2.3)	0.1	-0.8 (-3.4)	0.2	-0.6 (-2.8)
-0.2/0.3	4.9	-0.4 (-1.9)	3.7	-0.6 (-3.0)	0.4	0.4 (2.0)	0.2	0.2 (1.1)
-0.2/0.2	5.4	-0.2 (-0.9)	3.9	-0.1 (-0.7)	0.5	0.5 (2.3)	0.3	0.2 (1.3)

Price and service level elasticities, e.g.: -0.3/0.3

Consumer surplus gains as a percentage of average pricing revenue in parenthesis.

We have considered the optimization problem in the provision of public transport in an area in which two groups of services with independent demands are supplied by the same operator subject to a budget constraint with two alternative ways of satisfying that constraint: admitting cross-subsidy, and through price differentiation exclusively according to cost differences. The gains of cross-subsidy have been calculated in efficiency terms under reasonable assumptions, with results showing an insignificant superiority with respect to average pricing.

The pattern of price differentiation without cross-subsidy, derived from the application of average pricing in each sector, appears as an acceptable solution if there were not a strong social interest based on equity grounds to benefit one of the sectors, or significant externalities to be taken into account. Practical decisions about the extent and the structure of internal subsidy are taken in a second best world in which budget limitation is not the only constraint. Equity considerations and private traffic interactions may be crucial when taking the decision on how to satisfy the budget constraint.

If it is socially desirable to give a higher weight to one of the sectors in the welfare function to be maximized, the resulting price structure will differ from that corresponding to the maximization of unweighted social surplus; however, the final set of prices could reduce or increase cross-subsidization depending on distributional weights, demand elasticities and cost differences.

Even assuming that the introduction of a social welfare function which includes distributional weightings is preferred to income taxation and direct subsidization (when choosing prices and service levels), it seems difficult to justify the deviation from average pricing in each sector, as distributional pricing is in each case applied within the bus transport users' group, which might possibly be more efficiently segmented through self selection in a second degree price discrimination scheme and standard third degree schemes (OAP, students, etc.).

The elimination of cross-subsidy through average pricing in each sector also has advantages over Ramsey pricing when public and private transport externalities are considered. Although the efficacy of public transport subsidy as a policy to relieve traffic congestion and environmental externalities is open to question, there are specific situations in which public transport subsidy is required as a second best policy (see Gwilliam, 1987). Compared with low density and rural services, in dense populated areas the cost of public transport provision will increase due to the reduction in average speed; however, this effect is most probably overcome by the reduction of average cost per passenger-trip produced by the higher load factor in these areas. It may well be that the most profitable local bus services tend to be those on congested corridors, and the least profitable tend to be services operating at uncongested places or times. If those services cross-subsidize rural routes (or residential) in sparsely populated areas, an inefficient set of prices and frequencies will be the outcome, unless negative externalities in the busiest routes (among passengers and with respect to traffic congestion) offset the benefits of higher frequencies associated to higher traffic flows (value of time savings plus diversion of traffic to public transport).

13.4 Current Regulatory Regimes in Europe

There exist different regulatory regimes in Europe for the provision of public transport with a varying degree of integration and public control. For the purpose of this paper, and with the exception of U.K., several common characteristics seem to underlie this industry (see Tables 3 and 4):

(i) statutory monopolies provide transport services protected by absolute barriers to entry.
(ii) local, provincial or regional authorities control the size of the network, frequencies and fare structures.
(iii) the existence of public and private ownership in different cities within the same country and a wide range of company sizes are common.
(iv) though some operators break even, public financial support is widespread.

Public transport services are generally provided by an operator in each European city (a group of operators in some of the metropolitan areas). In the majority of the cities, the type of ownership is private. Nevertheless, public operators are responsible for the provision of services in largest cities. In general, public operators seem to operate with higher costs and lower productivity than private operators. The regulatory regimes for public transport in Europe combine the following systems:

(i) exclusive rights to public companies
(ii) franchising
(iii) quantitative restrictions depending on local assessment of necessity.

Leaving aside Great Britain, where the elimination of the barriers to entry makes this experience unique, the usual systems in Europe are (i) and (ii), particularly in the case of local transport. The right to be the exclusive supplier (license holder or franchisee) varies from 3 years to practically no limit. More than 5 years is common, and it is fairly frequent that operators renew automatically their licences or franchises. Switzerland has a 3 years trial before a 10 years is given. Denmark has introduced contracts of 5 years.

Although tendering appears as a widespread system in European cities, the length of the exclusive right in many cities (10 years in Norway, 8 to 20 in Spain) seems too long to speak of competition for the road. The unlimited length in practice seems to be a common system of regulating the industry. Some countries are introducing a more market oriented system through contracts and tendering (minimum of 3 years in Sweden through tendering or agreement), with a significant impact on costs. There is empirical evidence of important costs savings when bidding for tendered services is introduced (see Glaister and Beesley, 1989). We have gathered information which points to 20 percent cost reduction on average when competition is introduced through a bidding process.

At present in Europe, regulated monopolies with contract or franchises too long to make potencial competition a real threat, operate without well defined commercial objectives (2 countries out of 17 report that there exist clear objectives for local public transport). Practically every operator benefits from network subsidies and, in some cases, from subsidies to cover concessionary fares and capital investment. Fuel tax rebates is not very common. The extended formula appears to be the blank subsidy without specific targets (see Table 3). Subsidy route by route is also reported in Finland (rural areas), France (for intercity services), Spain (intercity low traffic corridors) and Great Britain (non commercial services offered through a bidding process).

Revenue/cost ratio varies from country to country and between cities. It is not unusual to break even in intercity services. In local services cost coverage with commercial revenue is usually higher than 50 percent with a high coefficient of variation. It does not appear to be a systematic behaviour of revenue/cost ratios and countries. Although it seems that more developed countries devote in general more public money to public transport, there is not a well defined pattern to be associated with different revenue/cost ratios. Finland has a ratio of 57% for 25% of the network but 92% for the 75%. Switzerland ranges from 56% to break even; Spain and Portugual show a relatively high revenue/cost ratio, nevertheless in the case of Spain there are significant variations. Italy shows one of the lowest coverage of cost from commercial revenue. In this situation of long contracts and high subsidies, the degree of public control is a crucial issue. The answers to those questions directed to obtain information of public control mechanisms show a more effective control of prices and frequencies than costs. A large majority of countries report extensive control in the fulfilment of regulated frequencies and prices but only some or little control of operator costs.

Table 3 Degree of public control in public transport in Europe (Urban and intercity)

Prices and frequencies: F
Operator costs: C

Country	absence of control	little	some	extensive	full control	revenue/cost (%) urban	intercity
Denmark			C		F	56	
Finland			C	F		57(c) 92(c)	
France	C (in intercity)		C	F		53	
Greece			C	F			
Ireland			C	F			
Israel			C	F		66	66
Italy		F,C (in intercity)				24	28
Netherlands	F (private operators)	C (private operators)		F (public operators)	F (both)	≈30	≈40
Norway			C	F		50-60	b.e.(*)
Portugal (changes with new law)			C	C		67	b.e.(*)
Spain	C (in intercity)	C	F (in intercity)	F		70-90	b.e.(*)
Sweden			C		F	50 70(d)	b.e.(*)
Switzerland			C	F		(e)	
Turkey			F (in intercity)		F (in urban)	95	
U.K.	F,C (a)			F (b)		(f)	b.e.(*)
West Germany			C	F		54	
Yugoslavia				F,C			

(a) for commercial services subject to six weeks advance notice
(b) for tendered services
(c) 57% for 25% of the network (public operators or private monopolies) 92% for 75% of the network (private operators)
(d) Stockholm
(e) between 56 and break even
(f) break even + subsides through tendering
(*) b.e.: break even or profits

Table 4 Price structure in public transport in Europe

Urban: U
Intercity: I

Country	flat fare	distance related	zonal system	travel card and multiple ride tickets	peak pricing	different prices for different routes
Denmark		I	U,I	U,I		
Finland	U(a)	U,I	U	U		
France	U	I	U	U		
Greece	U(f)	U(f)	U,I(f)	U(g)		
Ireland		U,I			U(b)	I(c)
Israel	U(d)	I	U(d)	U		
Italy	U	I		U		
Netherlands		U,I	U,I			I(e)
Norway	U	U,I	U(g)	U,I	U(g)	
Portugal	U	I	U			
Spain	U	I	U(g)	U(g)		
Sweden	U	U,I	U,I	U,I		
Switzerland	U	I	U	U,I		
Turkey	U(h)	I		U(g)		
U.K.		I	U	U	U	
West Germany		I	U	U		
Yugoslavia		I	U(g)	U		

(a) Large zones only in Helsinki Metropolitan Area (e.g. a zone is one city; three zones for an area with 850.000 inhabitants). Within each zone flat fare.
(b) Little use of city centre off-peak shopper discount.
(c) Lower fares charged to compete with independents from non scheduled sector.
(d) One of the largest cities (Jerusalem) and all small cities have a flat fare. The two other metropolitan areas (Tel-Aviv and Haifa) have a zonal system.
(e) Private operators only
(f) In large cities flat fare. In medium and small cities, distance-related or zonal, given that the service area is extended.
(g) In largest towns
(h) In small towns

Note: Concessionary fares are of general use in every country.

Finally, the price structure is similar throughout Europe: flat fare in urban areas with some kind of non uniform pricing (multiple-ride tickets and travelcards) and zonal systems in the largest towns. Distance related fares are more frequent in intercity services. Peak pricing or off-peak discounts are only reported for three countries.

A quick picture of the pattern of public transport provision in a medium European city may be described as follows: A public or private operator provides the service in markets protected by legal barriers to entry. Potential competition does not put pressure on the operator cost structure, on the pattern of service and on the combination of price and frequency, as long as the contract or franchise is too long to worry about it, or the procedure of renewal is practically automatic. Once the route network, fare structure, frequency and level of subsidy is determined, costs are not properly controlled by public agencies, so it is fairly possible the presence of technical inefficiency, x-inefficiency and uncompetitive factor payment. The price structure based mainly on a flat fare without peak charges or route by route pricing points to the development of cross-subsidization. The existence of a zonal system in the largest cities does not rule out this possibility as long as zone sizes allow relevant cost differences to exist.

13.5 Optimal Policies and the Present Regulatory System in Europe

In this section we compare some relevant features of the functioning of urban transport markets in Europe with the criteria obtained in the first part of the paper where unweighted social surplus maximization was chosen as the objective to be pursued.

It is important to remember that we compare here actual operators' behaviour and industry performance with optimal policies that may well be impossible to precisely apply in the real world. This does not mean, however, that the derivation of a set of optimal policies lacks of practical interest; on the contrary, from that background we can carefully detect inefficiencies, deviations that could be corrected to improve industry performance.

There are some results that contrast with the present situation:

(i) It seems that the production of local bus transport services shows constant return to scale, so firm size does not affect bus-kilometer average cost. Nevertheless, there exist density economies as the generalized cost per passenger declines when traffic volume increases. Marginal cost falls short of average cost and first best pricing does not allow to cover total costs with commercial revenue using marginal cost pricing. Neither first best or second best policies require to produce with a single operator. Economies of density are not in conflict with the existence of several companies providing a set of services publicly planned. The present regulatory framework in European cities does not contribute to cost minimization. The existence of statutory monopolies, the lack of commercial objectives and the presence of network subsidies as the main formula of public support are not a suitable environment for the achievement of productive efficiency. To introduce competition for the right of providing bus services could lead to a reduction in average costs. The evidence is not limited to the reduction of 20% in costs in the U.K. as a consequence of deregulation. Recently, competitive tendering has allowed reductions of 20% in USA, London and Israel, and 10-15% in Sweden. In Australia private operators are 11 to 24% more cost efficient than public operators. In Spain, labour costs are on average 20% higher in public companies working in similar operating conditions than private companies (see Hensher, 1987; Andersen, 1992; Glaister and Beesley, 1989; De Rus, 1989a).

(ii) When producer and user costs are considered, the social benefits of changes in price or the level of service should be equal in each route and service; therefore, the relative price increase in each market must be higher the lower (absolute value) the fare elasticity, and the higher (absolute value) the elasticiy of demand with respect to user costs. When demand shows a relatively high sensitivity to changes in waiting time, cutting services would imply higher social costs than increasing the price. Given the present pattern of regulation in the bus industry there is no reason to expect an optimal balance between the level of fares and frequencies. Glaister (1987), Dodgson (1987) and De Rus (1990) have shown that in British, Australian and Spanish cities there exist an imbalance between fares and the level of service, which suggest that economic efficiency could be increased changing the price-quality combination. When market forces do not account in the decision about the level of quality to be provided, an economic evaluation is needed taking into account the cost of service provision and users' preferences. Moreover, in present conditions, it may well be possible that bus size is above the optimum, as long as producer costs may have a higher weight than user costs.

(iii) In local bus transport the relevant setting is a second best world in which first best policies are not attainable or desirable, mainly due to the existence of financial constraints, prices below social marginal costs in private traffic, and equity considerations. Even in the case in which cross-subsidy derives from Ramsey pricing, efficiency gains applying the "inverse elasticity rule" are too small to justify by themselves the introduction of a fare structure that has an important impact on income distribution. Average pricing in each relevant set of services or routes should not be discarded.

13.6 Policy Conclusions

Keeping the basic regulatory system unchanged several policies could be introduced in the majority of the European cities in order to change the behaviour of the operators with the aim of improving performance (for the assement of the possible effects of deregulation of local bus transport in Europe, see Banister et al., 1992).

- **Entry, ownership and operator size**

In a regulated system it is vital to introduce some incentives to keep costs as low as it is technically feasible. The empirical evidence shows that cost reductions around 20 percent are possible when bidding for tendered bus routes is introduced. Given the relatively low share of fixed costs in the industry, franchising length should be reduced substantially in order to make entry a real threat to the incumbent. The presence of constant return to scale in the production of bus-kilometres makes possible to offer routes or set of routes to tender in order to reduce operator's size below a level in which the strategy position of incumbents would reduce the effectiveness of the bidding process.

Once the public control of the network is combined with competitive tendering, there are no economic reasons to keep public companies providing transport services in those countries and/or cities where there is evidence of low productivity and higher costs associated to public ownership. Privatization would be desirable in these cases as long as competitive tendering is effective. To summarize, the key idea is to introduce the discipline of market forces without losing public control of the transport network.

- **Public control**

To reduce costs is not enough. In the provision of public transport a fare structure, frequencies and the size of the network have to be decided. Minimizing producer costs combined with different frequencies, early morning and late night services and route coverage.

Commercial objectives should be made clear to operators and network subsidies should give way to the financing of particular routes, services or groups of users, with clear targets that should be monitored. Public control should be reinforced in order to make competition more effective and privatization a socially desirable policy.

- **Cross-subsidization**

Cross-subsidization should not be accepted as a mechanism of financing uncommercial services without a careful evaluation of its consequences on those services supporting the burden. Direct subsidies to specific targets (rural routes, low income groups, etc.) would take the place of network subsidies, and price differentiation in relevant pieces of the network or at different times of the day should be considered against the present discriminatory policy consisting of flat fares for the whole network with acute differences in production costs for different routes and services. This does not mean that cross-subsidization should be eliminated. Some degree of internal subsidization might be desirable, but a much more critical view of this source of financing could improve performance.

Acknowledgement

This research was supported by the European Science Foundation. The author thanks Chris Nash, Peter Mackie, Joseph Berechman, David Bannister and members of the Network for European Communications and Transport Activity Research (NECTAR) for their useful comments.

References

Andersen, B., Factors Affecting European Deregulation and Privatization Policies in Local Public Transport, **Transportation Research B**, vol. 26A, no. 2, 1992, pp. 179-192.

Banister, D., J. Berechman and G. De Rus, Competitive Regimes within the European Bus Industry: Theory and Practice, **Transportation Research B**, vol. 26A, no. 2, 1992, pp. 167-179.

Baumol, W.J. and D.F. Bradford, Optimal Departures from Marginal Cost Pricing, **American Economic Review**, vol. 60, 1970, pp.265-283.

Baumol, W.J., J.C. Panzar and R.D. Willig, **Contestable Markets and the Theory of Industry Structure**, New York: Harcourt Brace Jovanovich, 1982.

Berechman, J. and G. Guliano, Economies of Scale in Bus Transit: A Review of Concepts and Evidence, **Transportation**, vol. 12, 1985, pp.313-332.

Brown, S.J. and D.S. Sibley, **The Theory of Public Utility Pricing**, Cambridge

De Rus, G., El Transporte Público Urbano en España: Comportamiento de los Costes y Regulación In de la Industria, **Investigaciones Económicas**, vol. 13, 1989a, pp.207-225.

De Rus, G., **The Economics of Urban Bus Transport in Spain: An Analysis of Costs, Demand, and Pricing**, School of Business and Economic Studies, Institute for Transport Studies. Ph.D. thesis, University of Leeds, 1989b.

De Rus, G., Public Transport Demand Elasticities in Spain, **Journal of Transport Economics and Policy**, vol. 24, 1990, pp.189-201.

Dodgson, J., Benefits of Changes in Urban Public Transport Subsidies in the major Australian Cities, **Transport Subsidy** (S. Glaister, ed.), Policy Journals, 1987, pp.52-62.

Glaister, S., The Allocation of Urban Public Transport Subsidy, **Privatization and the Welfare State** (J.L. Legrand and R. Robinson, eds.), George Allen and Unwin, London, 1987, pp.177-200.

Glaister, S. and M. Beesley, Bidding for Tendered Bus Routes in London, Paper Conference on Competition and Ownership of Bus and Coach Services, Thredbo, Australia (mimeo), 1989.

Glaister, S. and J.J. Collings, Maximization of Passenger Miles in Theory and Practice, **Journal of Transport Economics and Policy**, vol. 12, 1978, pp.304-321.

Gwilliam, K.M., **Aims and Effects of Public Financial Support for Passenger Transport**, Round Table on Transport Economics, European Conference of Ministers of Transport, Paris, 1984.

Gwilliam, K.M., Market Failures, Subsidy and Welfare Maximization, **Transport Subsidy** (S. Glaister, ed.), Policy Journals, 1987.

Hensher, D., Productive Efficiency and Ownership of Urban Bus Services, **Transportation**, vol. 14, 1987, pp.209-225.

Jansson, J.O., Marginal Cost Pricing of Scheduled Transport Services, **Journal of Transport Economics and Policy**, vol. 13, 1979, pp.268-294.

Jansson, J.O., **Transport System Optimization and Pricing**, John Wiley and Sons, New York, 1984.

Miller, F., The Extent of Economies of Scale: The Effects of Firm Size on Labour Productivity and Wage Rates, **Southern Economic Journal**, vol. 44, 1978, pp.470-487.

Mohring, H., Optimization and Scale Economies in Urban Bus Transportation, **American Economic Review**, September 1972, pp.591-604.

Nash, C.A., Management Objectives, Fares and Service Levels in Bus Transport, **Journal of Transport Economics and Policy**, vol. 12, 1978, pp.70-85.

Nash, C.A., Integration of Public Transport: An Economic Assessment, **Bus Deregulation and Privatisation** (J.S. Dodgson and N.Topham, eds.), Gower, Aldershot, 1988, pp.121-138.

Nelson, J.P., M.J. Roberts and E.P. Tromp, An Analysis of Ramsey Pricing, in Electric Utilities, **Regulating Utilities in an Era of Deregulation** (M.A. Crew, ed.), MacMillan Press, New York, 1987, pp.78-98.

CHAPTER 14

PASSENGER AIR TRAFFIC AT THE REGIONAL LEVEL IN EUROPE: A TRANSPORT STRATEGY TOWARDS INTEGRATION

Cristina Capineri

14.1 The Conceptual Framework

In the last forty years the world economy and in particular the European economy has shown increasing tendencies of integration which involve people, goods and information and create wider territorial perspectives. Even though exchanges are a common element in human history, today they show some distinctive traits which make them different from those of the past, especially from a quantitative perspective in terms of the intensity and the reach of territorial relationships, the range and volume of goods and information exchanged and the speed of movement. This has produced an increase in transport infrastructures which enable the relations to take place in space. Infrastructures have their immediate expression in networks (transport, telecommunications, energy, etc.) which in turn give way to traffic flows and establish relations between the place of production and the markets (see Dupuy, 1990; Capineri, 1990).

In the past much importance was attached to growth poles (Perroux's development theory) which were considered fundamental in a regional economy; nowadays the attention has shifted to those elements which encourage links between regions: networks create a "networked space" which enables an interaction process among uneven areas due to their basic territorial property, i.e. connectivity. Due to the role networks generally play in social and economic dynamics, no analysis at regional development can leave them aside.

In conclusion, the complex frame of network systems requires an analytical context which considers the synergy created by both the infrastructure and its service rendered; in this way the traditional sectoral analysis of the technical network aspects should be overcome; the analysis must be dedicated to the networked space which is formed by the technical network and which develops according to social and economic factors (population distribution, industrial activities, amenities, national and international policies, etc.). Moreover, this is validated by a geographical approach based on the study of relational space, where networks are a traditional subject of enquiry and a fundamental feature.

14.2 The Research Aims

Our paper aims to give a survey - at the European level - of regional air links in the context of recent developments in fast means of transport and their integration. As is observed in preliminary studies on the Transport Master Plan of the EC: "a system of urban nodes should be identified and a system of fast networks (rail and air) should be related to it. A high-speed railway network should provide intercity services; the air network should create regional services at communitarian levels".

The paper addresses four issues:

i) general aspects of airline networks;
ii) the development of regional air services in some western European countries;
iii) the identification and classification of nodes and networks;
iv) the role of regional air traffic at a national and international level.

14.3 Statistical Sources

The data employed in the research refer to the latest (1989-1990) passenger traffic flows and aircraft movements in their static context (entity of the flows), their relational aspect (origin-destination matrix) and qualitative aspects (domestic, international, scheduled and non-scheduled flights). The information has been collected from the Civil Aviation Authorities in each country, from international institutions (ICAO, IATA, AEA), and from official time-tables (ABC World Airways Guide). Unfortunately the available data are not always comparable and in some case the necessary information has not been obtained; so the survey is limited to those countries which have kindly cooperated. Moreover, a questionnaire have been sent to ninety European airline companies to get direct information from the carriers about trends of regional air traffic in Europe (the results are still preliminary).

14.4 Regional Air Traffic in Europe: a Definition

Regional and interregional air traffic in EEC countries has been defined in many ways; nevertheless, they refer to similar phenomena. First of all, we must distinguish between regional and interregional traffic; the first generally refers to either domestic links or to links inside wide geographical regions (Europe, America, Africa, etc); the latter to international links. We will refer to interregional links in a general sense as to traffic between different areas (at a European level); and to regional air links as domestic or international traffic on medium-short distances which show the following features:

(1) regional air links play a subsidiary role to scheduled air links at the national and international level;
(2) they provide links mainly between non-metropolitan areas or big cities;
(3) they offer connections between large cities and other centres of economic

interest (commuter and business traffic);

(4) they link small towns to large cities connected by international or intercontinental flights (feeder links).

In the framework of air transport interregional links play a double role in passenger traffic: first, they redistribute flows which are centred on main airports towards small towns and areas with a distinctive role (industrial, touristic, cultural, technical, scientific) at a local or regional level; second, they offer a fast means of transport which is particularly useful when other fast links are lacking (e.g., high speed railways or motorways). Third, they offer the advantage of short waiting and boarding times, as airports are generally small and located not far from the city centres. From a functional point of view these interregional links are the expression of intensive hierarchical relations between centres of a different rank; in fact the links between small towns show interaction processes at a peripheral level which might avoid large cities and validate the assumptions of less polarized networked territorial systems and of the existence of economic potentials at a local level.

From an administrative point of view the EC regional airline services were regulated by an EC regulation (n.83/416/1983) which established the rules to be observed for the issuing of authorization to the airline companies. According to this rule, the interregional services should have the following features:

(1) the links must be operated by small aircrafts (max 70 seats);
(2) the links should take place between EC airports for regular international traffic;
(3) the flights should cover distances of more than 400 km (or less only if the link would enable to overcome natural barriers (sea, mountains, etc.) more easily than other means).

In order to limit the competition among airports and the duplication of similar services, the authorization would not be given if there was already a regular service within 50 km from the airport which required a travelling time of less than 90 minutes. and an increase of total flying time of less than 50% than the interregional service suggested. Since 1989 most legislation has been repelled and the interregional air traffic is now regulated by annual authorization and it is part of scheduled air traffic. In the sequel of this paper we will give a consice description of regional air traffic in various European countries: Italy, the U.K., Germany, France, The Netherlands, Denmark, Portugal, Spain and Greece. Based on this survey we will discuss European policy issues.

14.5 **Airline Connections in Italy**

14.5.1 **Introduction**

Since the late 1970s, passenger air transport in Italy has acquired a growing role compared to other means of public transport. The long shape of the Italian peninsula, the many islands in marginal position, and the geographical position of the country at the centre of the Mediterranean area, between the West and the East of Europe, near the African coast, have definitely improved air traffic. This is shown by traffic trends (aircrafts and passengers) in the last ten years. In 1979 passenger public transport was carried out by rail (90,3%), by water (3,2%) and by air (6,5%); after ten years rails have decreased to 85% and air transport has reached 10,5% of total national passenger/km produced. In the same span of time (1979-1989) domestic traffic has nearly doubled (from 11 to 21 million pax) and international traffic has increased from 14 to 18 million pax. It is interesting to note that the average flight length has decreased for international links from 1359 km to 1225 km, while for domestic links it has increased from 498 km to 519 km[1].

The Italian air network consists of 101 airports 42 of which are used for commercial traffic. In the Piano Generale dei Trasporti (1986) five groups have been distinguished on functional criteria: intercontinental, international, domestic, regional and local airports. The intercontinental airports deal with long-haul traffic (viz. Milan and Rome); the international airports deal with medium or short-haul scheduled and charter traffic; the domestic airports have a large proportion of domestic traffic while the international traffic is generally carried out by charter flights and it is concentrated in the summer; the regional airports have a limited traffic and the services are carried out by small aircrafts; the local airports are used for general aviation and aerotaxis services.

The flow patterns are strongly polarized on two nodes: Rome and Milan which deal with nearly the 50% of total national traffic. They are followed by a group of smaller airports (Napoli, Catania, Venezia, Pisa, Palermo, Cagliari, Torino, Bologna, Genova, Olbia and Bari) which make up 30% of the traffic. Some airports, which are mainly situated in attractive tourist areas, deal with large proportions of charter flights (Crotone, Rimini, Roma-Ciampino, Grosseto, Treviso, Bergamo, Forlì, Milano/Malpensa, Napoli, Pescara, Venezia).

In 1989 the domestic flows were 54% and the transit passenger were mainly engaged in international links (84%); charter flights have recently increased and account for the 10% of total passenger traffic (9,3% of aircraft movements); they are mainly operated by foreign carriers.

14.5.2 The regional air traffic

The regional and interregional flights are defined by the Italian Civil Aviation Authority as "regular regional and interregional regular traffic at a domestic and international (European) level operated with aircrafts of no more than 70 seats". In 1989 these flows were mainly on domestic routes and accounted for 61% of aircrafts movements, 60% of passenger traffic and 20% of transit passengers; they were concentrated on 61 links which can be grouped as follows:

---

[1] A **link** is the connection between two airports carried out by a direct or non-direct flight; a **flight-section** is the distance covered by the aircraft from take-off to landing; a **flight** is the service offered by the carrier between two towns.

a) links between medium-sized and large cities in the north-south direction, generally feeder connections on international flights;
b) links between the main land and the islands (peripheral links);
c) transversal links between medium or small towns which are not connected with other fast means of transport (intercity service or motorway network) (e.g. Perugia-Milano; Bergamo-Roma).

From a functional point of view the airports involved in this kind of traffic are mainly national and regional with a traffic factor from ranging 100,000 to one million passengers (pax)[2]. Moreover, most of the airports are situated in the fringe of urban areas, general at a distance of 10-20 mins from the town centre which can be reached by local means of transport (bus, taxi) or private cars. Although this location is particularly attractive as it enables short travelling times between home/work and the airport, nonetheless it requires efficient connections (frequent, fast, accessible) as regional flights are generally short, so that boarding times and other dead-time must be reduced to minimum[3].

From the origin/destination matrix it can be observed that in 1989 the nodes involved in regional traffic were Bologna, Firenze, Alghero, Bari as origins; Torino, Milano, Roma, Napoli, Olbia, Cagliari and Catania as destinations. With reference to the entity and directions of the flows, in 1989 the main links (more than 20 thousands passengers), have been Bergamo-Roma, Firenze- Milano; other minor links (5000<pax<20.000) Alghero-Genova, Alghero-Torino, Bari-Bologna, Bari-Cagliari, Bari-Catania, Bari-Palermo, Bologna-Napoli, Catania-Cagliari, Firenze-Catania, Firenze-Roma, Perugia-Milano, Tremiti Islands-Foggia, Rimini-Roma[4]. These services are strongly concentrated in the summer (from August to September) and at the beginning and end of the week (Mondays and Fridays) as they generally comply with touristic, commuter and business movements.

As regards flows to European countries, they are mainly directed to bordering countries (France, Germany, Switzerland[5]) followed by Great Britain, Belgium and Luxemburg. They have reached an volume of 284.448 pax (19.783 aircrafts movements) from only 12 Italian airports (six in the North, four in the central regions, one in the south and one on the islands) and the strongest relations (more than 10.000 pax) have been Venice-Lugano, Milan-Marseille, Rome-Marseille, Florence-Lugano, Florence-Munich, Milan-Tolouse, Milan-Lyon. Other important flows (5.000<-pax<10.000) are directed to European capital cities and centres of economic, touristic

---

[2] According to the ICAO classification, the airports belong to groups A, B and a few to C group, none to D.

[3] In Great Britain, for example, the shuttle services between major towns offer immediate boarding conditions in order to favour the users (businessmen, commuters).

[4] The flights are carried out by small aircrafts from 7 seats (AGH and BNI) to 48 seats (ATR) and 65 (F28).

[5] Though Switzerland is not a member of the EC, it is included in the analysis due to its geographical position and functional attractiveness.

and cultural interest (Lyon, Birmingham, Malaga).

The first interregional services started at the end of the sixties and they often failed due to a limited demand, lack of connections with other modes, or the use of large and costly aircrafts. In 1985 there were three national carriers (Aligiulia, Transavio, Cadabo) and a few foreign carriers (Air Littoral, Crossair, Nuernberger Flugdienst). The links were concentrated in North and central Italy and they connected towns as Torino, Milano, Venezia, Trieste, Genova, Pisa, Firenze, Grosseto, Perugia and Elba Island. After five years - in 1989 - the authorised interregional flights have significantly increased: 121 on domestic routes and 72 to EEC countries. The main carriers are Alitalia, Areo Trasporti Italiani (ATI), Alisarda and minor carriers (Air Dolomiti, Avianova, Tas Airways, Air Capitol, Aliadriatica) which have obtained about 20 authorizations on domestic links.

14.6 Airline Connections in the United Kingdom

14.6.1 Introduction

Air transport in Great Britain plays the role of the main means of transport to European and extra-European countries; in fact only a very small portion of domestic traffic is by air (1% against 92% by car/coaches and 7% by rail) (HMSO, 1989, p.13). The competition with other means is fairly strong, as the main direction is North--South which is also well equipped with motorways and a good intercity service. Moreover, due to the limited extension of the country many airports suffer from the vicinity to other airports. For example, Liverpool and Leeds/Bradford are negatively influenced by Manchester which offers a wider range of services.

The air traffic in the U.K. has reached in 1989 a volume of 1,5 mil aircraft movements and over 100 mil pax and it has registered an increase of 41% between 1980 and 1989. In particular, a growth of 75% can be observed for international traffic and of 65% for scheduled flights (35% on charter flights). The domestic traffic is mainly carried out by scheduled services (96%).

Like in many other countries, the air traffic is polarized on the two airports (London and Manchester) which are linked to the whole national network and to international and intercontinental destinations. Other important airports are Glasgow, Birmingham, Edinburgh, Belfast, Aberdeen, Newcastle, East Midlands, Leeds, Bristol, Cardiff, Isle of Man Southampton, Belfast City, Liverpool, Sumburgh, Teesside, Prestwick, which play an important role in international air transport. There are many other small airports mainly situated on the islands which attract tourist, business and transit traffic at a subregional level. Their traffic is limited (less than 10.000 pax), but they play a social role as they offer links between marginal regions and the main land; their structures are often oversized; so they need governmental or local subsidies.

Due to the strong polarization of air traffic, recent British airline policies aim at a decentralization of flows from the London area to minor airports in order to exploit the existing infrastructures and the incentives which airports can induce.

The main domestic routes include links between London, Glasgow, Edinburgh, Belfast, Manchester (mainly by shuttle flights operated from 1975 by British Airways); links with Northern Ireland (Belfast) and the islands (Orkney, Shetland, Isle of Man).

The traffic with Europe has strongly increased between 1980 and 1989: Austria (+260%), Portugal (+158%), Spain (+125%), Ireland (+119%), Greece (+91%), France (+85%), Switzerland (+83%), Netherlands (+61%), Belgium (+61%), Germany (+52%) Italy (+23%).

The strongest relations at the European level are with Spain (more than 11 mil pax), France (6 mil), Ireland (4 mil), Germany(4,5 mil), Italy (3,6 mil), and The Netherlands (3 mil).

The strong increase of tourist movements, which privilege air transport, has raised the number of charter flights. In particular British holiday-makers who go abroad have tripled since 1978 thanks to the development of inclusive tours. This is shown by the main international destinations: Palma, Malaga, Tenerife, Naples, Lisbon, Faro. On the other hand, much air transport is used for business (50%) and holidays (30%) by visitors to the United Kingdom (HMSO, 1989, p.13).

14.6.2 **The regional air network**

The British regional network has developed since the 70s and in particular between 1973 and 1980 when several domestic and international links were authorized by the Civil Aviation Authority[6]. At the beginning of the 80s the regional traffic was regulated by the White Paper on Airline Competition Policy (1984) according to which British Airways should not compete with independent carriers. Then in 1984, 15 services to Europe were created from airports where British Airways mostly operated (Manchester, Birmingham, Newcastle, Glasgow, Aberdeen, Edinburgh). The regional carriers do not receive subsidies from the central government except for a few companies such as the Scottish Logan Air which has recently increased its fleet and flights to Ireland. The regional traffic is generally limited to those nodes where it is possible to exploit scale economies, or to improve load factors and connections with other modalities. In order to improve regional traffic some infrastructural adaptations have been carried out; at London airports reserved runways have been planned.

The passenger traffic at regional airports has increased in the past twenty years; in particular international traffic has risen from 18% to 25% in 1988 (CAA, 1989). In 1988 there were 70 international links and 206 domestic links; routes were of an average distance of 300-500 km. The regional links mainly operate connections between the main island and the minor islands or between medium-sized towns and important centres in the Continent (Netherlands, Germany, France and Spain). According to the number of flights the principal regional airports are Jersey, Glasgow, Guernsey, Belfast, Aberdeen, Manchester, Gatwick, Stansted, Isle of Man, Edinburgh, Humberside, Norwich, Newcastle, Leeds, Kirkwall, Cardiff, Bristol, East Midlands and

---

[6] The CAA supported the policy of deregulation and encouraged more competition on major routes and transversal links from peripheral areas to the London area.

TeesSide. The main domestic routes are Jersey-Southampton, Alderney-Guernsey and Jersey, Guernsey-Southampton, Birmingham-London, London-TeesSide, Belfast-London. The international routes are directed to Amsterdam, Bruxelles, Paris, Cork, Dublin, Bruxelles, Copenhagen, Düsseldorf, and Milan.

14.7 **Airline Connections in Germany**

Before analyzing air regional transport in Germany, we will consider some general aspects of the national airline network. It consists of 12 international airports (Berlin, Hannover, Frankfurt, Hamburg, Stuttgart, Munich, Düsseldorf, Bremen, Nuernberg, Koln, Muenster and Saarbrucken) which take care of the main international connections, and several regional airports. The airports defined as regional are 28 but those which show a considerable regional traffic are: Dortmund, Paderborn, Friedrichshafen, Kiel, Augsburg, Hof, Bayereuth, Mannheim, Monchengladbach, and Essen.

Regional air services in Germany are defined as "all routes where at least 50% of all flights are operated by small aircrafts"[7]; they work as feeder links to Lufthansa's major services and are generally in competition with the well organized intercity rail system which has recently been enlarged. In 1990 more than 150 regional links were authorised: 57 on domestic routes and 100 on international ones. Passenger traffic has shown a considerable increase compared to the beginning of the 80s when the domestic links were about 10 and the international ones 16. The flows have increased from 200.000 and 500.000 on domestic and international flights to 1.200.000 and 2 million in 1990, respectively. The highest increase took place between 1987 and 1988 on both domestic and international routes. The percentage of regional passengers on total scheduled traffic was of 7,6% in 1989 (against 2,6% in 1984), 8,5% on domestic flights, 9,8% on European and 6,7% on total international flights.

The services are operated by the flag carrier and other carriers (NFD, RFG, Delta Air, Crossair, KLM, Hamburg Airlines) and by Lufthansa partners. In 1990 the regional carriers carried out 620 weekly flights and Lufthansa 252 (against 212 and 256 in 1985) which show a considerable increase of non flag carriers. Regional traffic is also operated at international airports (3 mil pax in 1989) and at regional airports (286.000 pax). The international airports that are most interested in regional traffic are Muenster, Saarbrucken, Bremen, Hamburg, Nuernberg, Stuttgart and Berlin.

Domestic regional traffic plays the role of connecting medium-sized towns to large cities and generally takes place in the northern part of the country, that is the traditional industrial core-region. The main European destination are Amsterdam, Zurich, Basel, Luxembourg, Vienna, Paris, Bruxelles, Jersey Island, Copenhagen, Florence, Lyon, London/Stansted, Manchester, Turin and Nice.

---

[7] There are other additional regional flights on other routes operated by bigger jet aircrafts.

14.8 **Airline Connections in France**

The French airline network shows a large number of nodes which can be distinguished into: Paris airports (Orly and Charles de Gaulle); domestic airports that deal with 50% of the passenger traffic (Marseille, Lyon, Toulouse, Bordeaux, Bale-Mulhouse, Fort de France, Strasbourg, Nantes, Montpellier, Ponte à Pitre); provincial airports which can be subdivided in large airports which deal with radial services to/from Paris and transversal domestic services; medium airports which offer links with major regional centres; small airports which accept small aircrafts and deal with regional traffic; service and general aviation airports (excluded in this study).

The passenger flows are concentrated on Paris airports (53%), on provincial airports (39%) and on overseas airports (8%). The domestic traffic is a little higher than the international (42 mil against 34 mil international). The international traffic is operated mainly at Paris airports (72%), while 51% of domestic traffic is carried out by provincial airports and 40% by Paris airports. The flow pattern is distinguished in official statistics into radial routes and transversal routes: the former include links with the capital city, the latter links other centres in the country. The radial links to/from Paris have been 48 in 1989 and the transversal 51, with origins in Lyon, Bordeaux, Marseille, Nice, Toulouse, Bastia, Ajaccio, Lille and Calvi, and destination to Lyon, Marseille, Nice, Nantes, Lille, Strassbourg, Bale-Mulhouse and Montpellier.

The flows with Europe have a volume of more than 21 mil pax of 16 mil which among EEC countries in 1989; the main relations are with Great Britain (35%), Italy (15%), Germany (14%), Spain (12%), Greece (5%), Netherlands (5%), Belgium (3%) and Denmark (2%)[8].

The regional services, which are operated by several regional carriers (Aeromaritime, Air Caledonie, Air Caledonie International, Air Jet, Air Liberté, Brit'Air, Air Littoral, Europe Aero Service, T.A.T)[9], aim at connecting minor centres, often situated in a marginal position (Bretagne, Pyrenees, etc.), to the main nodes of the national network. Most of the carriers operate on routes concentrated on a few poles. For example, Air Littoral connects centres in southern France (Angoulème, Agen Perigueux, Bergerac, Pau, Beziers, Perpignan, Biarritz) with major nodes (Paris, Toulouse, Marseille, Lyon, Clermont-Ferrand); Air Vendée mostly links Le Havre and Rouen to the national and international networks; while T.A.T. services cover most of the national area. The routes cover an average length of 430 km on domestic flights and more 700 km on international links. In 1989 the regional traffic - defined as "traffic out of the Paris area" - reached 6 mil pax[10]. The principal international

[8] It is not possible to obtain a complete origin/destination matrix for French airports and European airports since only data about the South-East and South-West regions are available at the moment.

[9] The regional carriers which operated regular services, were 13 in 1973 and about 25 in 1989.

[10] In 1980 the "Schema Directeur de l'equipement aéronautique" identified 80 centers privileged for regional air trafic according to the following features: more than 50.000 inhabitants; lack of air services within 50 km or 60 mins. by car; minimum annual traffic of 50.000 passengers.

destinations are situated in bordering countries (Madrid, Lisbon, Barcelona, Saragossa, Bilbao, Milan, Turin, Venice, Bologna, Florence, Roma, Frankfurt, Düsseldorf, Bruxelles and Amsterdam) and the United Kingdom (London, Manchester, Birmingham, Edinburgh and Dublin).

14.9 Airline Connections in The Netherlands, Denmark and Portugal

14.9.1 The Netherlands

Among the countries considered in our enquiry there are a few which, due to their limited size or geographical position, present air patterns that are strongly internationally-oriented. We refer to the Dutch, Danish and Portuguese networks.

The Dutch airline network consists of five main airports (Schiphol, Rotterdam, Groningen, Maastricht and Eindhoven) and twelve minor airports (Ameland, Budel, Drachten, Enschede, Hilversum, Hoogeveen, Lelystad, Midden-Zeeland, N.O. Polder, Seppe, Tenge and Texel). The domestic traffic is mainly directed and generated among the major airports. The strongest flow is between Amsterdam/Schiphol and Maastricht. The latter is linked with almost all minor airports; Amsterdam/Schiphol is linked with Beloodjing; Rotterdam with Borei.The international traffic is mostly linked with Europe and mainly with Great Britain (35%), Spain (14%), Germany (13%), France (10%), Greece (8,5%), Italy (7%), Portugal (5%), Denmark (3,4%), Ireland (1,4%), Belgium (0,2), and Luxembourg (0,1%). The main destinations are the capital cities, industrial towns and tourist areas in Spain, Greece and France.

14.9.2 Denmark

The regional air traffic in Denmark takes place between Copenhagen and other minor towns in the North of the country, in the Jutland peninsula and other islands; it is generally of limited dimension and charter. Moreover, it will be definitely influenced by the new Fixed Link of the Great Belt which is meant to solve the present traffic problems in the Copenhagen area. In fact, a new link between Copenhagen and Funen Island will be created with fast branches towards Arhus, Albay, Odense, Holstebro, Esbjerg, Sonderby, Vejele, so that the travelling time will be reduced on major routes (Arhus-Esbjerg 2,5 hrs; Copenhagen-Aalborg 3,5 hrs)[11]. Another connection between Copenhagen and Malmo, in Sweden, will help to improve exchanges between Denmark-Europe and the Scandinavian country through Copenhagen airport.

The total passenger traffic exceeds 11 mil in 1989 and it is mainly international (80%) and for a small proportion domestic (20%). The connections within Europe

---

[11] For a long time the creation of a new underground link between Copenhagen and the railway has been discussed in order to improve traffic problems with the metropolitan area of Amager.

are over 2 mil pax and the largest flows are towards Great Britain (26,1%), Greece (24,6%), France (13%), Netherlands (9%), Italy (8,5%), Belgium (5,6%), Germany (3,5%), Portugal (2%) and Spain (6%). The domestic traffic is carried out by three regional carriers (Cimber Air, Maersk Air, Danair/S.A.S.) which mainly connect the capital city with minor centres (Aarhus, Ronne, Aalborg and Thisted). Other relevant flows are on the domestic routes Odense-Ronne; Ronne-Aalborg, Ronne-Aarhus, Ronne-Billund, Sondeborg-Copenhagen and Thisted-Copenhagen.

14.9.3 **Portugal**

The Portuguese air network consists of 5 major airports (Lisbon, Porto, Bragança, Faro and Vila Real) and other minor airports situated in Acores and Madeira islands (Chaves, Funchal).

The main air services are offered by the flag-carrier TAP between national airports (Faro, Ponte del Gada, Porto)and with Europe (London, Madrid, Paris); other less intensive services are with Amsterdam, Barcelona, Aberdeen, Bruxelles, Copenhagen, Rome, Frankfurt, some of them from Porto.

The regional air services are operated by three regional carriers: LAR (Linhas Areas Regionais), which is part of TAP, Portugalia and Sat/Air Acores. The latter operates almost exclusively among airports of Acores Islands (Ponte del Gada, Santa Maria, Terceira, Graciosa, Pico, Horte, Flores, Sao George). The domestic links are between Lisbon and Porto, Faro, Vila Real and Braganca; the international ones with nearby towns ("transfrontalier" links) Bilbao, Bordeaux, Vigo, Sevilla, Santiago and Malaga.

14.10 **Airline Connections with Spain and Greece**

The Spanish and the Greek airline patterns show a common feature which is characterized by large incoming flows from northern European countries (directed to popular seaside and cultural resorts and strongly concentrated in the summer period) and by a weak domestic air traffic.

14.10.1 **Spain**

The Spanish airline network consists of 39 airports, six of which account for more than 70% of total traffic (Madrid 19%, Palma de Mallorca 17%, Barcelona 10%, Las Palmas 9%, Malaga 7%, Tenerife Sur 7%). The passenger traffic has been more than 68 mil (43% domestic and 57% international). There are several airports which operate almost exclusively at a national level (Sevilla, Bilbao, Tenerife Norte, La Palma, Jerez de la Fra, Asturias, Vigo, Granada, Vittoria, Melilla, Santander, Zaragoza, Pamplona, San Sebastian, Hierro, Vallalodid, La Coruna, Salamanca, Badajoz, Cordoba, Sabadell, Cuatro Vientos). Other airports have a large portion of traffic with European destinations (in rankorder of traffic intensity): Palma de Mallorca, Madrid, Barcelona, Malaga, Tenerife Sur, Las Palmas, Alicante, Ibiza; moreover, Gerona and Reus are mainly international airports.

As regards domestic links it is possible to identify radial links towards Madrid (26 links), Barcelona (25), Palma de Mallorca (16), Las Palmas (16), Tenerife (13), Valencia (13), Santiago (13); and transverse connections among the main Spanish towns (Siviglia, Granada, Valencia, etc.). In particular the minor airports are strongly connected with Madrid, Barcelona and the islands (Las Palmas, Tenerife, Mallorca). The main airports are intensively connected with them and with the islands as a confirmation of strong tourist traffic.

The air traffic with the European countries has been over 36 mil in 1988 of which 31mil within the EEC and it involved 33 out of the 39 Spanish airports.

The most important relationships are with the United Kingdom (47%), Germany (24,8%), the Netherlands (5,5%), Denmark (3,7%), France (6,6%), Italy (5,5%), Ireland (1,3%), Portugal (1,1%), Greece (0,5%) and Luxembourg (0,4%). It is interesting to note that the traffic with the United Kingdom, Denmark, The Netherlands and Ireland is mostly charter (80%), while 95% of the flights to Portugal and 75% to Greece are scheduled flights.

The development of regional traffic has in general been very slow, as the monopoly has been kept by Iberia and Aviaco for a long time; only in the past few years new services have been operated by regional carriers (Aerovalencia, Air Sevilla, Eolo Catalunya, Lineas Aeres Canarias, Ten Air).

14.10.2 **Greece**

The airline network consists of 38 airports of which Athens, Thessalonikis, Iraklion, Rodos, Corfu, Mykonos and Mytilini are major nodes also connected to the national and international networks.

The passenger traffic has exceeded 22mil in 1989, and has suffered from a decrease of -9% (generally in the domestic traffic), while the international flows have remained unchanged. The air traffic is internationally oriented (63%) and it is linked to strong incoming tourist flows.

As regards domestic traffic, some airports operate only at a national level (Alexandroupolis, Kasson, Kastelorizon, Kastorias, Kythiron, Leros, Limnos, Skiathos, Skiros). The flag carrier, Olympic Airrways, does not perform regional services in the traditional meaning of the term; nevertheless, the domestic services (33 routes in 1991) may be considered as such, since they feed the international routes. Other minor regional carriers are partners of the flag carrier and they cover short connections between the main towns and the islands, in particular Rodos, Mykonos and Mytilini.

The traffic with EC countries accounts for 61% of foreign traffic; the airports involved in European exchanges are Athens, Iraklion, Rodos, Corfu, Thessaloniki, Kos and Ghania. The main relationships are with northern European countries such as the United Kingdom (38%), Germany (25%), The Netherlands (9%), France (9%), Italy (7%), Denmark (4%), Belgium (3%), Spain (1%), Luxembourg (0,3%), Ireland (0,4%) and Portugal (0,1%). The East-West flows are rather weak compared to the North-South flows.

14.11 Towards an Identification of European Regional Airline Patterns

Regional airline services in the 70s were generally meant to cover connections of limited traffic volume on short-medium haul routes, mostly operated by small aircrafts. Recently, services operated by most regional carriers are acquiring are more internationally-oriented ("transfrontalier links"). This is mostly due to changes in traffic patterns, as trends of European air transport show in the 80s and the 90s. The air passenger traffic in Western Europe in the past ten years has shown an increase of 10%, in particular in southern countries (Italy, Spain, Portugal); a lower increase is shown in Switzerland and The Netherlands. The highest increase (12%- 18%) has been registered on medium and short-haul routes of 100.000-50.000 pax, while major routes (>500.000 pax) have shown a change +4,4% (Association of European Airlines, 1990)[12]. The trend is demonstrated by a wider usage of small and large aircrafts and by a decrease of medium capacity planes (120-140 seats). With reference to the volume (in terms of number of passengers), the largest flows are between Great Britain, Spain and Germany; less strong but equally intense flows do exist between Great Britain, France, Ireland, and France-Germany; of a medium intensity of flows can be formed between France/Italy, France/Germany, France/Spain, Great Britain/Greece, Greece/Germany, Netherlands/Germany.

Nevertheless, the European air traffic is threatened by congestion (20% of European flights are generally delayed more than 15 minutes), so that companies which operate at a regional level need to be highly competitive in order not to raise air fares. Thus regulations and provisions should avoid additional burdens so that smaller companies, such as regional carriers, do not need to be dependent on the State, as other modes of transport are. In fact regional carriers show strong ups and downs in their activity as they are heavily limited and regulated by official air transport policies.

From the analysis developed in this research, it is possible to identify some common features about regional air traffic in most western European countries, as regards both the nodes and the links. The nodes involved in regional traffic are characterized by a traffic factor of 3 (100.000<pax<1mill) or 4 (10.000<pax<100.000) and they are generally situated in towns with a popolution of about half a million or less; or centres in core regions or with specific functions (science parks, tourist towns, etc). Moreover the distances covered are on average 250-500 km on domestic routes and 700-1000 km on international routes. Although at a national level regional services may not be competitive with high-speed railway services, they may be so at an international level.

A glance at the pattern of the main interregional links reveals that they mostly operate between economically important areas of central and northern Europe, i.e. the traditional core-region (see Parker, 1984). At the domestic level most of the countries show strongly polarized flow patterns which may be described by bipolar or

---

[12] The AEA aims at improving European air transport by encouraging cooperation among airline companies, and by informing communitarian associations (such as ECAC and GATT) about problems of the European air traffic. At the moments it comprises 22 airline companies. In 1991 the Ceskoslovenske Aerolinie joined the Association.

three-polar models formed by radiant crowns originated by the main pole. Nevertheless, with reference to the rank of centres linked it is possible to identify at least three patterns:

(1) polarization patterns with flows directed/originated by large cities; often of feeder charcter on continuing flights (international and intercontinental);
(2) complementary or transversal patterns between medium-sized towns often of a transfrontier character;
(3) a non-hierarchical pattern among minor centres caused by morphological reasons (traffic between the mainland and the islands) or for tourist reasons.

Regional air transport appears - according to the features emerged from an research - a privileged means to face new territorial developments which most of the industrialized countries are showing: functional and urban development of small and medium towns, counterurbanization processes, decentralized and endogenous development often accompaned by the increase of high-tech sectors (e.g. science parks), short-term tourism (e.g. weekend-holidays) which requires short travelling times, trips for qualified economic operators where face-to-face contacts are required and a decrease in old strong industrial core regions and new emerging areas (e.g. Southern Italy and France, Bavaria, etc.).

14.12 The Role of Regional Air Transport in the European Integration: Some Concluding Remarks

The spreading of networks, the emerge of integration processes and European intermodality have had strong geographical effects since the functional coordination - which may be defined as an interconnection process - increases the interaction level and works on place hierarchy. The modernization of transport and communication techniques, from which only a few places benefit (modal-split nodes as specialized stations, intermodal centres, etc.), introduces strong elements of nodality and polarization potential rather than factors of flow diffusion, which are dependent on them[13].

The regional air transport, together with the high-speed railway services, seem to be fundamental in the increase of interaction processes at a European level, as they enable contacts between distant areas creating "positive discontinuities" in regional devolpment. Like in the past railway and motorway networks created processes of time-convergence between privileged areas (the intercity network retraces the motorway network in most European countries), nowadays the airline network creates - and puts in motion - more opportunities of development. The concepts mentioned

[13] The concept of interconnection refers both to the structural and the functional aspect of the network. Interconnection takes place between different networks (rail-road; rail-air) or in the same network (multifunctional network): the structure is used for different services (high-speed rail services, eurocity trains, charter flights). Structural adaptations are frequently required in order to ensure compatibility between existing infrastructures and specialized networks (e.g. the Shinkansen in Japan).

above may be confirmed by recent developments of railways and airline networks: once they have reached a wide territorial extension, they have established contacts and have created places of interchange where "break-of-bulk" and modal-splits take place. The interconnection poles become fundamental nodes in a new integrated network; they may be defined "commutateurs sociaux, des dispositifs spatiaux qui facilitent la selection des partenaires et le passage rapide de l'un à l'autre" (see Claval, 1990). The value of such poles should be studied with reference to the range of the relationships established (hinterland) and to the functions performed rather than in the volume of the flows managed[14].

In this context the role and the future of regional air traffic must be considered: a complementary role with rail transport - expecially with intercity services - that will play an important part in future European transport[15]. Then, barriers removal and the creation of a free trade within the Community offer development issues to the whole transport system. As regards regional air traffic, the removal of frontier control will speed up air travel operations and increase passenger amenities[16].

Nevertheless, the structural changes, that inevitably will take place with the creation of a common market, might have negative drawbacks on the sector. In fact, the high-speed railway networks and new European projects (for example, Channel Tunnel, link from France to Spain, Portugal and Germany) seem a very interesting solution for rapid passenger links at the European level, as major European towns are at a distance between 200-1000 km that can be covered by trains in 4-6 hrs[17]. Railways have the advantage of eliminating traffic on major nodes (saturation problems at large airports)[18]. Thus the air carriers will have to face a stronger mutual competition with other modes of transport (rail and road) and with the telecommunication system, while having to cope with higher running costs which could be solved by establishing equal development opportunities for the different modes (infrastructure adaptations, less taxes on added value).

In conclusion, the interconnection process, of which regional air transport is a part, may be considered as a starting point of mobility changes at a regional and inter-European level as an element which enable a decentralized development and a functional adaptation of the urban network. In this context, geography may have the task to show "voluntary" choices that are adequate for development promotion with a man-environment perspective in mind.

---

[14] In the past the interconnection poles were defined traffic-ganglia (see Toschi, 1959) and recently gateways. A hierarchy of interconnection poles should be based on the function performed at a regional level.

[15] In order to avoid priorites among the networks and to develop integration, the existing structures are generally adapted and renewed (new vehicles, signalling systems, etc.).

[16] The creation of reserved runways (third channels) has been proposed in many major airports (Heathrow and Gatwick, for example).

[17] Distances over 2500 km may be covered in 8-12 hrs.

[18] Lufthansa affirms to have lost 50mil DM due to delays in 1987.

References

Association of European Airlines, **Yearbook, May 1991**, Brussels, 1991.

Beitrage zur Osterreichischen Statistik, **Zivilluftfahrt in Osterreich 1989**, Wien, 1990.

Capineri, C., **Una Categoria di Analisi Geografica: le Reti di Trasporto Ferroviario,** Dip.to di Scienze Economiche, n.69, Univ. degli Studi di Firenze, 1991.

Cattan, N., Une Image du Réseau des Métropoles Européennes par le Trafic Aérien, **L'Espace Géographique**, n.2, 1991, pp.105-115.

Civil Aviation Authority, **UK Airports, Annual Statements of Movements Passengers and Cargo 1989**, London, 1990

Civil Aviation Authority, **UK Airlines, Annual Operating, Traffic and Financial Statistics 1989**, London, 1989.

Civil Aviation Authority, **Passengers at the London Area Airports and Manchester Airports in 1987**, London, 1989.

Civil Aviation Authority, Planning Division, **Greek Airport Traffic**, 1990.

Claval, P., La Mise en Réseau des Territoires, **Communications et Territoires** (H.Bakis ed.), La Documentation Francaise, Paris, 1990, pp.35-46.

Copenhagen Airports, **Scheduled Traffic, Origin/Destination**, Copenhagen, 1990.

Copenhagen Airports, **Air Traffic Statistics**, Copenhagen, 1990.

Direction Général de l'Aviation Civile, **Bulletin Statistique, Année 1989**, Ministère de l'Equipement, du logement, des transports et de la mer, Paris, 1989.

Dupuy, G., **Système, Reseaux et Territoires, Principes de Réseautique Territoriale,** Paris, Ecole Nationale des Ponts et Chaussées.

Federal Office for Civil Aviation, **L'Aviation Civile Suisse en 1989**, Berna, 1990.

Frishkorn, G., Der Wettbewerb zwischen der Deutschen Bundesbahn und den Luftverhrsgesellschaften im Innerdeutschen Personenfernverher unter Beruck-sichtigung Verkehrsgeographischer Aspekte, Heft 32, **Frankfurte Wirtschafts und Sozialgeographische Schriften**, Frankfurt, 1980.

Heynen, T.C., Ordunungs und Strukturpolitische Gestaltungselemente zur Erstellung eines Neun Luftverkehrspolitischen Konzepts unter Besonderer Berucksichtigung des Luftverkehers in Europa und Nordamerika, Heft 48, **Frankfurte Wirtschafts und Sozialgeographische Schriften**, Frankfurt, 1985.

IATA, **World Air Transport Statistics**, 34, 1990.

Maltby, D. and H.P. White, **Transport in the United Kingdom**, Macmillan, London, 1982.

Ministerio de Transportes, Turismo y Comunicaciones, Direccion General de Aviacion Civil, **Anuario Estadistico del Tranporte Aereo, Espana 1988**, Madrid, 1989.

Ministerio de Transportes, Turismo y Comunicaciones, Direccion General de Aviacion Civil and Comunidad Economica Europea, **Anuario Estadistico del Tranporte Aereo, Espana 1988**, Madrid, 1989.

Ministero dei Trasporti e dell'Aviazione Civile - Direzione Generale dell'Aviazione Civile, **Ammodernamento e Ampliamento della Rete Aeroportuale Civile Nazionale, Piano Regolatore degli Aeroporti**, Roma, 1969.

Ministero dei Trasporti e dell'Aviazione Civile - Direzione Generale dell'Aviazione Civile, **Piano Generale Aeroporti, II Fase, Sintesi della Ricerca**, Italairport, Milano, 1986.

Ministero dei Trasporti - Direzioni Generali - Programmazione, Organizzazione, Coordinamento - Aviazione Civile, **Gli Aeroporti Italiani, Cenni Sugli Eliporti e le Aviosuperfici**, Roma, 1988.

Nodari, P., I Trasporti Aerei in Italia, **Geografia del Trasporto Aereo** (K.Sealy, ed.), F.Angeli, Milano, 1977, pp.237-240.

Parker,J., **The Logic of Unity**, Macmillan, London, 1984.

Ruggiero,R., La Pianificazione del Sistema Aeroportuale Italiano, **Nord e Sud**, XXVI, n.31-32, 1977, pp.65-139.

Ruggiero, R. and G. Skonieczny, Aviazione Civile Italiana e Trasporto Aereo Internazionale, **Nord e Sud**, XXVI (1977), n.7, pp.133-200.

Russo Frattasi, A. and R. Grisoglio, **Rapporto sul Trasporto Aereo Regionale in Europa, Rapporto Finale 1984**, CNR, Progetto Finalizzato Trasporti, Sottoprogetto Trasporto Aereo (VIII), dattil.,1984, pp.27.

Scherrer, F., Transport Interurbain, l'Interconnexion T.G.V., **Cahiers du Groupe Reseaux**, n.4, Paris, 1986, pp.89-104.

Taafe, E.J., The Urban Hierachy, an Air Passenger Definition, **Economic Geography**, 1962, pp.2-14.

CHAPTER 15

TRANSPORT MOBILITY, SPATIAL ACCESSIBILITY AND ENVIRONMENTAL SUSTAINABILITY

Veli Himanen, Peter Nijkamp and Juraj Padjen

15.1 **Euro-mobility**

In a recent publication (see Nijkamp et al., 1990) it has been conjectured that the spatial development of Europe (and of all developed and industrialized countries) can be characterized as the 'geography of movement'. There has been an unprecedented rise in both passenger and freight transport. This observation can be confirmed by a recent publication of the European Conference of Ministers of Transport (ECMT, 1990), where it has been shown that from 1970 to 1987 passenger car transport as well as road freight transport almost doubled in OECD Europe countries (see for details also Fig. 1 and 2). And it is foreseen that - in the absence of radical changes in social and economic conditions - current transport trends are likely to continue. Furthermore, it is shown that in OECD Europe annual investment in transport infrastructure has fluctuated (see Björnland, 1991), so that road investments have decreased from 1975 to mid 80's and have thereafter increased but still remained in 1989 under the level of 1975. Investments in rail infrastructure have however increased all the time.

The above figures on mobility are remarkable in that so far no saturation level has been reached. Apparently we are still observing the rising part of a logistic growth curve.

Traffic increase in Europe has mainly been caused by the rise in the number of cars, vans and lorries as well as by the rising number of air flights. The higher speeds obtained by new vehicles and new networks have been used for more travelling. Various recent forecasts still foresee a considerable increase in European traffic. However, the forecasts differ very much from each other. It should also be noted here that the forecasts are usually related to the economic development in the western part of Europe; economic growth and its related traffic are still uncertain in many former socialist countries in the eastern part of Europe.

The International Road Federation (IRF, 1990) expects a 35 percent increase in passenger-kilometres in Western Europe from 1988 to the year 2000. If this pace of increase would continue, car traffic would double early next century. This kind of development has been forecasted in the United Kingdom where 82 (low GDP growth) to 134 (high GDP growth) percent increase (from 1988 up to the year 2025) is expected in car traffic (cf. Goodwin et al., 1991).

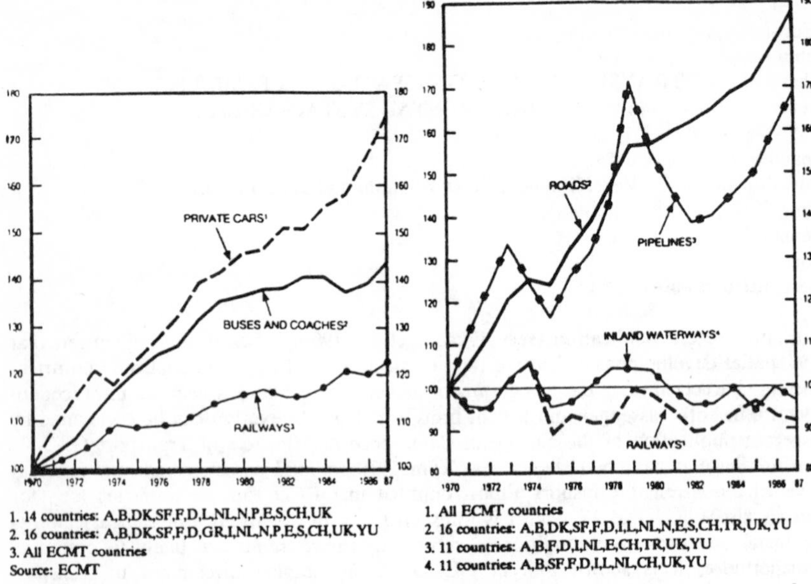

1. 14 countries: A,B,DK,SF,F,D,L,NL,N,P,E,S,CH,UK
2. 16 countries: A,B,DK,SF,F,D,GR,I,NL,N,P,E,S,CH,UK,YU
3. All ECMT countries
Source: ECMT

Figure 1 Passenger Traffic Trends
1970 = 100 (passengers-kilometres)

1. All ECMT countries
2. 16 countries: A,B,DK,SF,F,D,I,L,NL,N,E,S,CH,TR,UK,YU
3. 11 countries: A,B,F,D,I,NL,E,CH,TR,UK,YU
4. 11 countries: A,B,SF,F,D,I,L,NL,CH,UK,YU

Figure 2 Freight Traffic Trends
1970 = 100 (tonne-kilometres)

In other forecasts somewhat lower expectations are presented. For example, in Finland car traffic is expected to reach a maximum in 2010 and then to decline because of decreasing population (Tie-ja vesirakennushallitus & Taloudellinen suunnittelukeskus, 1987). Before that period an increase of 50% from the end of the 1980's is forecasted. A similar increase, 54 percent, has been foreseen for Sweden (see Svidén, 1983), although another study (see Jansson, 1989) gives somewhat lower estimates, viz. 23 percent (1984-2010). Also in the Netherlands various forecasts have been made. According to De Jong (1988) a 70 percent increase up to the year 2010 in car traffic is possible, compared to a 40 percent rise indicated by Vleugel et al. (1990). Also De Jong (1988) points out the possibility of a reduced increase in car traffic because of restrictive governmental actions.

Theoretically, the upper limit of car ownership per capita might be reached when almost all adult persons would own a car. However, Californian figures showed that this 'natural' limit can easily be exceeded. Whether such a situation would ever become reality in Western European countries is still an open question. The total number of cars depends naturally on the number of people, but this is apparently not leading to a fixed saturation level. In any case, in countries with still an increasing population the increase of car traffic will undoubtedly still continue after the saturation of car ownership has been obtained.

If we assume a saturation level of one car per adult person, then in many European countries a saturation of car ownership has approximately already been obtained for males. For example, in the Oslo area during the years 1977-1990 the share of car owners has been fluctuating around 80 percent for males between 25 - 54 years old (see Vibe, 1991). This figure has been reached in 1990 also by older males (55 - 74 years old). If we would exclude the oldest generations, only a minor increase may be foreseen resulting in a situation where about 85 percent of adult males own a car. For females however, car ownership has been increasing very fast for all generations. However, still in 1990 the share of car owners stayed just over 60 percent for females of 25 - 54 years old. The same phenomenon can be observed in Swedish forecasts (see Jansson, 1989), where male car ownership is expected to grow only by 3 percent at the same time when female car ownership will likely grow by 70 percent.

Theoretically, the limits of car traffic might be calculated with the aid of behaviourial data. The average daily travel time seems to be very stable over time (cf. Brög 1991, and Himanen et al., 1992)[1]. The average daily travel distance per capita has increased with higher average journey speeds obtained by cars (see Himanen et al., 1992). However, when calculated separately, the average daily journey distance for car users and for non-car users has also been rather stable, 51 km for car users and 27 km for non-car users in Finland from 1974 to 1986. These figures are very close to Swedish figures, viz. 53 and 25 km for 1984/1985 (see Vilhelmson 1990)[2]. When we would know demographic features and suppose that female car ownership will probably remain somewhat below male ownership, the maximum traffic might in principle be calculated. It has to be added that the number of average kilometers can be made with different cars (e.g., one for long distances and one for intra-urban traffic), so that the saturation level for car ownership is still difficult to identify.

The development of freight transport is influenced amongst others by the number of people and the level of consumption. IRF (1990) expects a 30 percent increase in freight ton-kilometres in Western Europe in the year 2000, compared to the 1988 level. If this increase would continue, the freight transport would also double early next century. ECMT (according to the European Round Table of Industrialists (ERTI), 1990, p. 31) forecasts a somewhat lower increase, by which European freight transport would obtain the same 30 percent increase ten years later.

It is evident that the share of road transport is all the time increasing. ECMT (1985) supposes that freight transport on rails and inland waterways would not increase at all; the predominant expansion would take place on roads with a 70 percent increase in ton-kilometers between 1988 and 2010. A similar development has been forecasted in the United Kingdom (1988-2025); heavy lorry traffic will go up by 67 - 141 percent and light goods traffic by 101 - 215 percent (cf. Goodwin et al.,

---

1 Vilhelmson (1990) has presented a thorough discussion about the theory of the stable daily travel time. He also noticed that the average daily travel time is independent of household characteristics, except for old people. Prendergast and Williams (1980) have however, found that travel time is related to various socio-economic characteristics.

2 The journey distances given above were averages for the whole country. The journey kilometers inside an urban area are lower.

1991). In Finland a more moderate increase is expected, viz. 23 percent for lorry traffic and 70 percent for van traffic (Tie-ja vesirakennushallitus & Taloudellinen suunnittelukeskus, 1987).

Demand for air travel and air freight transport will likely continue to expand well into the next century. This growth is expected to be supported by the coming liberalization of regular air services and scheduled flight routes.

Clearly, much information is still needed to offer reliable and convincing traffic forecasts and mobility pattern estimates.

Interesting information about the variation in mobility patterns between (nine) EC countries can be found in a recent study by Van Maarseveen and Kraan (1991). Differences in car densities are noteworthy: Germany is approaching 500 cars per 1000 inhabitants, but Ireland just got over 200. Annual increase in passenger kilometers by car has been over 4 percent in Belgium and France (1971 - 1986) but only 1.5 percent in Denmark and not much higher in the United Kingdom. Also in rail transport there are big differences. Ireland, France and Denmark have had a clear increase in passenger kilometers but in Belgium and United Kingdom there has been a decrease.

Given the above observations, it is plausible to state that 'Euro-mobility' has become a widespread phenomena in all European countries, not only for local traffic but also for international traffic. This mobility drift is clearly not exclusively technology-driven, but also a result of far reaching changes in our ways of living, thinking and working. Our welfare societies have apparently generated a complex array of contact patterns (material and immaterial) which require physical interaction at an unprecedented scale. Nevertheless, it is noteworthy that the daily travel time per person has hardly increased as stated before; this 'law of conservation of travel time' means essentially that the average travel speed - and hence distance - has increased. Apparently there is an intrinsic human resistance against unlimited travel time, so that the need for efficiency rise of transportation networks (i.e., higher speeds) has become predominant.

Clearly, similar observations emerging from social science research can be made in the context of changes in labour force participation, life styles, demographic development etc. In this context, it is interesting that social science research provides convincing empirical evidence that changes in our societies are major driving forces for the intensification of spatial mobility (persons and goods) in our Western world.

In addition, the awareness of the limits to growth in mobility - as a result of high social costs involved - has also dramatically increased. Environmental and safety considerations have become major determinants in the declining social acceptance of our mobile society. Thus new transport solutions and technologies will have to be implemented within increasingly narrower limits imposed by our society and the environment (i.e., ecologically sustainable socio-economic development). The range of such solutions is further influenced by the simultaneous behaviour of all actors in a transport system generating congestion effects and thus causing additional social costs.

The previous observations also provoke an intriguing policy dilemma in transport planning: transport is a necessity for economic and budgetary reasons, and at the same time it is a social evil for environmental and safety reasons (see Himanen et al., 1992). This dilemma evokes the important question: is there a case for co-evolutionary mobility policy that reconciles the positive and negative aspects of the Euro-mobility phenomena? This question will be addressed in the next sections. First, the nature of the above dilemma will be spelt out in greater detail in Section 15.2.

15.2 The Triangular Relationship of Sustainable Spatial Development, Mobility and Accessibility

Conventional economic policy has to face in general a conflicting relationship between **allocative efficiency** and **distributional equity**. In recent years also a third element, i.e. **environmental sustainability**, has gradually been added, following the spirit of the World Commission on Environment and Development (1987) report on 'Our Common Future" (the so-called Brundtland report) (see also Nijkamp et al., 1991). Applying the previous concepts to transportation planning there is clearly an equivalence between the following concepts:

. spatial mobility - allocative efficiency
. accessibility - distributional equity
. sustainable spatial development - environmental sustainability

Each of these three concepts will now successively be described (see for details also Vleugel and Van Gent, 1991).

(a) Spatial mobility

Mobility concerns the spatial movement of people and goods. Efficient transport is a sine qua non for a balanced economic development: it ensures that production factors be brought together for the production processes and that final products be distributed to the markets. Both passenger and goods mobility will concisely be discussed here.

(i) Mobility of persons

Mobility of persons has steadily increased in the past years (see Fig. 1), with the private car as the most important vehicle. The following factors can be mentioned for this mobility growth:

- **demographic** factors: not only population rise in absolute sense, but also (and more importantly) the decline in family size, the rise in the number of small households and the increased female labour force participation.
- **technological** factors: the emergence of increasingly more 'footloose' activities, accompanied by drastic improvements in infrastructure and car technology.
- **spatial** factors: suburbanisation and des-urbanisation trends accompanied by lagging investments in public transport, as well as separation of work and home locations.
- increase in **car ownership** and **drivers's licence ownership**: the trend towards one car per adult person.

- general **income rise** per capita: removal of financial barriers for purchasing a car.
- rise in **leisure** time: a trend toward recreational and social mobility.
- **stable costs** of the car: a tendency in the past 40 years to keep the real costs of a car at a modest level.

It is quite clear that, if all these explanatory factors will follow more or less the same trend in the next years, also passenger traffic will continue to rise.

(ii) **Mobility of goods**

Freight mobility has also dramatically risen in the past decades (see Fig. 2), while a considerable share of freight transport is taken by trucks (approx. 80 percent in many EC countries).
The following factors may explain the freight traffic trends:

- **flexibility** in delivery: a trend towards new logistic concepts and just-in-time door-to-door transport systems (where the truck has an advantage compared to rail or inland waterways).
- competitive transport **costs**: trend towards high-value low-volume goods transportation.
- **speed** of transport: a tendency towards high accuracy and reliability of freight transport.
- **containerisation**: a trend to use for short- and medium-distances the truck rather than container-oriented modes which are more long-distance oriented.
- **government policy**: a tendency to favour truck transport (e.g., by low diesel tax) compared to other modes.
- **suburbanisation** and **spatial deconcentration** of firms: a new geographic pattern where - apart from trucks - other transport modes do not have much potential.

From the previous observations it seems plausible that commodity transport in Europe - in particular after the completion of the internal market - will significantly rise in the next years.

(b) **Accessibility**

Accessibility refers to the ease with which people can reach desirable facilities (e.g., schools, hospitals, work, recreation areas etc.), and has as such direct distributional aspects. Equal access for everyone to all facilities is however at odds with the necessary economic efficiency of a transport system. But this access to facilities is often regarded as a public good, governments have decided to develop and maintain transport systems for mobility-deprived groups (e.g., special population groups such as elderly, handicapped people or children) or isolated areas (thus subsidizing public transport), even though this is financial-economically not profitable.

Accessibility is often threatened by **congestion**, which is a social cost borne by the infrastructure user. In this context mobility rise - as a result of the drift toward higher economic performance and efficiency - is in contrast with the accessibility goal.

(c) Sustainable spatial development

Sustainable spatial development in relation to the transport sector concerns a variety of environmental aspects, ranging from the construction of new infrastructure to car production and car use. Besides, there are significant and dramatic impacts on human health, not only via noise annoyance and exhaust gases, but also - and mainly - as a result of accidents: in Europe approx. 50.000 people are killed annually because of traffic accidents! Furthermore, there is the change in climate caused by the greenhouse effect to which also exhaust gases from transport vehicles contribute significantly.

In view of the mobility drift, it seems plausible to expect that spatial sustainable development will be seriously threatened in the next decades. In order to provide a framework for a policy analysis of the above triangular relationship we will in the next section pay somewhat more attention to the environmental issue.

15.3 Environmental Sustainability

Transport is a part of our necessary livelihood system. In developed countries transport is also a part of mass consumption and at the same time transport is necessary to facilitate mass consumption. Our economy uses energy and raw materials from our natural environment and - after its use in production or consumption processes - returns these as waste and heat back into the natural system (the so-called materials balance system, based on the law of conservation of matter and energy; see for more details Nijkamp, 1981).

Human life is dependent on an uninterrupted and balanced functioning of natural ecosystems. These systems do not always react immediately to distorting human activities, since they can - because of their resilience - continue to function for a long time by means of stabilizing feedbacks, but they cannot resist structural and intensive environmental disruptions (see also Stutz, 1986 and Knoflacher and Himanen, 1991).

Exhaust fumes form the most important part of the waste generated by a transport system, although also liquid and solid wastes are noteworthy. Both exhaust gases and other wastes have an impact on the quality of air, water and soil (and hence indirect implications for our well-being and health).

The various impacts of the spatially dispersed transport system lead to a complicated process together with waste impacts from sources outside the transport system. It is evident that the future of the mass consumption system in developed countries depends - besides the development of the system itself - also on the limits set by nature. In Europe, the environmental hazards caused by the mass consumption system are accumulating in such a manner that many changes in the production and consumption system are needed (see Stigliani et al., 1989). Being a part and a facilitator of the mass consumption system, there is no doubt that transport is likely to change as well.

Ecological sustainability and the carrying capacity of the environment are threatened by the transport sector in various forms and at different geographical levels. Examples are: local health risks in urban areas triggered by exhaust fumes on or nearby busy streets; regional health risks triggered by photochemical smog (a mixture of gases and particles oxidized by the sun); forest damage, damage to buildings and destruction of soil quality caused by acid rain (generated especially by sulphur dioxide, nitrogen oxides, and hydrocarbons); climatic changes activated by atmospheric concentrations of greenhouse gases (carbon dioxide, methane, nitrogen oxides, chlorofluorhydrocarbons (CFC), and tropospheric ozone); depletion of the ozone layer caused by greenhouse gases - mainly CFC but also nitrogen dioxide - pushing up to the stratosphere. Also various solid wastes from the transport sector form a part of general accumulation of toxic materials in soils. The above mentioned traffic accidents have to be added as well.

Thus in many respects the transport sector has a negative impact on environmental sustainability. The main question now is whether the transport sector - and other parts of a mass consumption economy as well - is able to minimize the use of non-renewable energy and raw materials and to keep the amount of hazardous waste and pollutants inside the compensation possibilities of the natural environment (thus ensuring an improvement of environmental quality and hence ecological sustainability).

The amount of exhaust gases and other wastes as well as the use of fossil energy and raw materials depends primarily on the number of vehicle kilometres driven and the number of vehicles used. Fuel consumption depends also on various characteristics of vehicles and on cruising speeds. The amount of harmful components in exhaust gases is influenced by possible exhaust cleaning mechanisms, e.g. catalytic converters and by the type and quality of fuel used (e.g., unleaded petrol, content of sulphur in diesel fuel etc.).

Clearly, the precise implications of measures stimulating or improving ecological sustainability are difficult to assess, especially because the effects of transport cannot easily be separated from effects emerging from the other parts of our mass consumption society. In the so-called Brundtland Report (1987), where ecological sustainability was discussed, no clear goals for reducing the environmental effects of the transport system are given. King and Schneider (1991), in a report by the Council of the Club of Rome, propose for the industrialized countries a carbon dioxide reduction of 30 percent by the year 2005. It should be noted here that atmos-pheric concentrations of greenhouse gases adjust only slowly to changes in emissions. The longer emissions continue at high rates, the larger the eventual reduction would have to be. According to Döös (1991) an immediate reduction of over 60 percent of net emissions of long-lived gases (carbon dioxide, CFC, and nitrogen oxides) from human activities would stabi-lize concentrations at today's levels.

Unfortunately, no international agreement for limiting the emissions of carbon dioxide has been approved, although some recommendations were made in Toronto in June 1988. The obvious problems with limiting carbon dioxide emissions are related to mass consumption in developed countries and rapid population increase in many developing countries. The mass consumption system is in many ways closely connected with the massive use of fossil fuels. The need for economic development in developing countries will call for even more consumption of fossil fuels.

Governmental actions regarding CFC have been much more stringent. According to the decision of 93 nations in June 1990, CFC will not be used after 2000 in industrial countries and after 2010 in developing countries. Even more stringent decisions have been prepared in 1992 because of alarming news of ozone layer.

European nations have agreed to lower emissions of sulphur and nitrogen oxides by 30 percent, however all nations have not signed the contract. According to Döös (1991) these commitments are far from sufficient to stabilize the harmful effects of acid rain in Europe. According to Kauppi et al. (1990), a 90 percent decrease of annual sulphur and nitrogen deposits would be needed (compared to the year 1987) in order to stop acidification of forest soil in southern Finland. In order to meet the less stringent requirement that forest land acidification would be allowed to the extent that forests are not in danger, a 75 percent decrease of deposits would be sufficient. Similar figures are also obtained in Sweden (Eriksson and Hesselborn, 1990). Other gases responsible for the acidification problem are mainly produced outside the transport sector; sulphur dioxide in energy production and ammonia in agriculture.

It should be noticed that the European transport sector is only a fraction of the global system responsible for worldwide environmental problems. Its share is however, not negligible. According to King and Schneider (1991) at present there are four predominant cases of macro pollution at a global scale:

(1) Diffusion of toxic substances in the environment.
(2) The acidification of lakes and the destruction of forests.
(3) Depletion of ozone layer.
(4) Greenhouse effect.

It is clear from the above observations that the road towards co-evolutionary mobility is not easy to find. A free movement of people and commodities is apparently hard to integrate in a conventional price and market system, so that the existence of negative environmental externalities causes a major concern to governments. This is an issue to be discussed in the next section.

15.4 Transport and Environment: Is Policy a Matter of Taste?

Transport has a wide variety of negative environmental consequences: noise, particulates, vibration, risk, accidents, fuel emissions, depletion of natural resources, urban sprawl, damage to built environment, commune severance, congestion, visual intrusion, aesthetics etc. Formally speaking, transport causes a qualitative and quantitative reduction in scarce commodities (or aspects thereof) thus affecting negatively individual and social well-being . Under normal conditions, where all sacrifices and benefits would be incorporated in the price of a good, the allocation of scarce resources would - in view of a conventional economist - lead to an equilibrium between wish and possibility (or between demand and supply) via the intermediate tool of the market mechanism. This mechanism is giving price signals as a way of generating adequate responses of economic actors. One of the critical assumptions in the economist's view of the world is that all costs and revenues are reflected in the price mechanism. Failure to do so leads to biased signals and hence to inappropriate behaviour. For instance, if certain social costs (e.g., noise annoyance of cars) are not adequately calculated in from the source, an over-consumption of the activity will take place. This shortcoming in the price system is often called marked failure, although a more appropriate term may perhaps be a **signal failure**.

There is, however, also a related problem which may intensify the impacts of signal failures. Biased behaviour of economic actors as a result of signal failures has in many countries led to government responses in order to cope with negative externalities of economic activities. Given the above mentioned exposition, it is clear that a government intervention will only restore the balance, if the measures imposed on actors ensure that all social costs are fully reflected in the price signals of a market system. Such measures may be financed in money terms (e.g., charges, subsidies or taxes), but may also include non-financial instruments (e.g., regulations, standards or prohibitions). In all cases, the effects of such measures should be such that they charge economic actors with all marginal social costs (either directly or indirectly). Otherwise an efficient market equilibrium will not be reached, or in the worst case the government response may even lead to a further deviation from a social optimum. Such **response** failures may emerge, as public decision-makers are often unable to collect reliable information on the behaviour of actors in case of externalities (or of measures coping with externalities). Thus often they are not in a position to interpret the behaviour in case of biased signals. And indeed in many countries we have witnessed the existence of response failures of government (see Barde and Button, 1991).

Two examples may clarify this case. Parking policy in the Dutch city of Utrecht has aimed at reducing car use by restricting the number of parking places, but as a result most car-drivers were driving more kilometres (and hence causing more air pollution) in order to find a parking place (see Vleugel et al., 1990). Traffic restraint policy in Athens has tried to reduce car use by introducing the system of even and odd number plates for entering the inner city circle on a given day, but as a result car-drivers were making many more kilometres in order to reach the circular ring around the city as close as possible (thus causing even more traffic annoyance) (see Damianides and Giaoutzi, 1991).

It is thus clear that public intervention is a risky matter, as most actors appeared to have creative talents in circumnavigating intervention measures. Given the rigidity in government behaviour, in various countries severe response failures appeared to emerge. The transport sector is a glaring example of the existence of a great many of such response failures.

The combination of signal and response failures may lead to high social costs of the transport sector. However, a precise assessment of externality costs in the transport sector is fraught with many difficulties. Such an assessment has to take into consideration two types of costs, viz. **actual damage costs** (e.g., costs to human health, decline in market value of houses) and **prevention (or abatement) costs** (e.g., the construction of anti-noise screens, the manufacturing of new catalytic converters in cars). In most cases, it is possible to gauge the prevention costs, as these are based on expenses actually make. The quantification of damage costs is much more difficult, as this includes a mix of psychological elements, actual market repercussions, and multi-source effects. Various methods have been developed to assess the order of magnitude of such costs (e.g., multivariate regression analysis, hedonic price assessment, contingent valuation etc.), but a reliable outcome is still extremely difficult to obtain. In general, the damage costs show a spatial variation depending on the location of the amenity affected, the welfare level of people, the way of financing public goods etc. This estimation is once more complicated because of the above mentioned interference of signal and response failure.

Nevertheless, there is a growing awareness that the social costs of the transport sector have grown dramatically in the past years, so that there is an urgent need for a critical look at the applications of the transport sector in terms of environmental externalities. Despite the strong deregulation trend in the transport sector, governments begin to realize that these externalities have sometimes become unacceptable, so that there is a new trend starting with more public concern regarding social costs of the transport sector.

It is noteworthy that the above mentioned response failures of governments are often caused by mutually conflicting objectives aimed at in public policy. In general, the government tries to pursue mainly two objectives in the transport sector, viz. **economic** objectives (in view of the socio-economic importance of the transport sector, both as a source of economic growth and of fiscal revenues) and **social** objectives (in view of both environmental interests and the interests of the mobility-poor). In various situations these two objectives are conflicting, for instance, in the case of a joint application of two governmental fiscal instruments one favouring public transport through subsidies and another one favouring truck traffic via a low diesel tax. Such conflicting objectives form also one of the backgrounds of the above mentioned public response failures.

It is often claimed that the best way to avoid such failures would be to introduce a system of user charges, so that all people using transport will have to pay the full price (including external costs) of their mobility. Various countries have indeed taken measures to charge external costs to the users of transport, but the degree of success so far has been fairly modest.

A main problem inherent in such road pricing schemes is the fact that the financial revenue accruing to the government tries to cover a set of mutually conflicting options:

- user charges can be used - in the form of tolls e.g. - to finance new expansion of infrastructure;
- user charges can be collected from car drivers in order to be used to cover expenses in new public transport;
- user charges can be used as an economic instrument in order to reduce congestion and to ensure that traffic will remain within the capacity limits;
- user charges can be levied in order to compensate for external costs (environmental decay, lack of safety etc.), both from signal and response failures.

It is clear that the use of a single instrument for so many purposes is almost bound to fail, in particular as these objectives are mutually conflicting.

The previous discussion has clearly indicated that there is a need for a balanced representation of all (social and private) costs and benefits of a transport system in all its modalities. The costs are already hard to assess, but the benefits are even extremely difficult to estimate, as this includes also access to all public and private facilities, social contact patterns, competitive production and distribution etc.

In order to create some structure in the assessment of social costs and benefits of transport modes from a public policy viewpoint, it makes sense to make a distinction into four categories of social costs (see Grupp, 1986):

* infrastructure costs
* environmental costs
* accident costs
* government subsidies

A careful screening of all items and (public and private) expenses would then lead to a more ambiguous conclusion on the environmental sustainability costs and benefits of various transport modes. Diekmann (1991) concludes in this context that a user charge principle would make the viability of public transport dubious, but this statement would require more rigorous empirical research. In any case, it is clear that governments cannot play a passive role in the environment-transport sector. This will be further discussed in section 15.5.

15.5 A Confluence of Mobility, Accessibility and Sustainability?

It has become clear from the above considerations that the mutual relationships between economic interests, social equity and environmental sustainability are by no means a priori mutually compatible. In this context it is somewhat surprising that the modern transport problem - notably accidents and pollution - is essentially the result of solving an old historical problem: how to get from one place to another. The solution found by modern societies includes an enormous use of materials and energy. At the end transport policy is hampered between the demand for more mobility and worries about negative side-effects of traffic. It is also frustrating that after the modern transport problem we have also got a postmodern transport problem. Traffic volumes in bigger cities and on main roads of the European core area have reached the available road capacity resulting in severe congestion. It is obvious that it is hardly any more possible to expand road infrastructure or urban parking space to meet forecasted demand (cf. Button and Gillingwater, 1986, Plowden, 1983, and Goodwin et al., 1991). Congestion has reached such dimensions that many are waiting for the final gridlock (see Banister, 1989). Although evidently, in many European countries physical limits for transport have been reached, there are still many other countries where people enjoy an ever increasing mobility. The question confronting us is now whether we are able to cope with such seemingly irresistible processes. According to Goodwin (1990) one may distinguish six different approaches to solve traffic congestion:

1. Classical road-building; more roads for more traffic.
2. Neo-classical traffic engineering; optimal use of existing capacity of the road

system.

3. Public transport; increased use of public transport.
4. Traffic calming; reduced mobility.
5. Laissez-faire; transport corrects itself.
6. Road pricing; with right prices the system organizes itself efficiently.

Although even nowadays all such policy measures do exist, it is remarkable that transport policy has never resolved the conflict it has provoked. And actually the problem can hardly be solved inside the transport sector. The obvious failure of transport policy can be interpreted as a symptom of the above mentioned failing governing. This kind of problematic can be found in many areas. Capra (1983) noticed as a striking sign of our time that people who are supposed to be experts in various fields can no longer deal with the urgent problems that have arisen in their area of expertise.

The research into complex systems has produced results, which at least partly brought to light why transport policy has been unable to solve transport problems. According to Forrester's first law (see King and Schneider, 1991) we may take for granted that: "In any complex system, attack - however apparently intelligent - on a single element or symptom generally leads to a deterioration of the system as a whole."

This can be illustrated on the basis of urban transport policy (cf. also Hanson, 1986). When regarding urban transport policy we can see that at least four main items ought to be handled in a consistent and co-ordinated way:

1. Public transport
2. Road network
3. Parking in city centres
4. Pedestrian zones in city centres

These transport items are closely correlated to land use planning, which also must be included in a comprehensive policy strategy.

Wärnhjelm (1990) has investigated transport problems, measures, and results in 25 European cities. According to his material it is obvious that the cities which have had a broad approach have been able to avoid congestion and environmental problems much better than other cities. However, no city can be claimed to have found a permanent solution. Hannover can be taken here as an example. In Hannover a new transport policy was established already in 1967. Its main objectives were: improvement of public transport (especially light rail) and removing of through traffic from the city centre. These objectives were mainly obtained already in 1976. Also in the city centre a large pedestrian zone was established and car parking was concentrated outside the city centre in connection with public transport terminals. The results from Hannover compared to Essen, which represents a more common development, are striking (see Table 1).

The modal split in 1976 was very similar in both cities. In 1990 Essen is much more car oriented than Hannover. However, also in Hannover car traffic is increasing and resulting negative effects are felt. The same phenomenon can be found in

Helsinki. Strict parking policy and rather well developed public transport have kept the share of public transport high. However, a small increase in car traffic to the city centre can be observed, viz. on average 0.8 percent per year, which is very similar to the situation Hannover has observed.

According to a recent study (see Himanen et al., 1992) it seems possible, with rigorous traffic restrictions, to prevent people from undertaking certain trips. These restrictions are obviously directed to urban areas and especially to city centres. Outside city centres some restrictions might also be imposed, so that the total effect might be a maximum of a 10 percent decrease of total national car traffic. It must be remembered however, that the impacts of actually implemented restraint measures have been much more modest (see also Webster and Bly, 1980).

Table 1 Modal split in Hannover and Essen in 1976 and 1990

MODE	MODAL SPLIT (%) IN 1976/1990	
	HANNOVER	ESSEN
Foot	36/23	39/27
Bicycle	9/16	3/5
Mot. two-wheeler	1/0	1/0
Car driver	26/30	27/42
Car passenger	12/9	13/11
Public transport	16/22	17/15

Source:Brög (1991).

There are also many technical possibilities (see Alppivuori and Himanen, 1990) to decrease fuel consumption, e.g. smaller cars, smaller engines, new diesel engines, electric engines, etc. Here the theoretical reduction in fuel consumption may be 30 percent in passenger cars. To achieve this, strict national and international standards and pricing mechanisms must be established. Smaller cars will also need less raw material. Supposing that half of the car stock consists of small cars weighting 600 kg, the average reduction in raw material for the whole car stock would be about 20 percent.

When combining the above mentioned impacts of various measures with a moderate 40 percent increase (compared to the late 1980's) in car ownership and car traffic in western parts of Europe, the following assessments are plausible for the next twenty to thirty years:

(i) Car production, ownership, and mileage will still increase with 20 to 30 percent;
(ii) Raw materials needed for car production may remain at its current level;
(iii) Fuel consumption by cars would decrease with at least 10 percent;

(iv) Exhaust emissions from car traffic could be reduced with more than 40 percent (CO), 50 percent (HC), and 85 percent (NO_x).

Next, assuming an average of 70 percent increase (compared to late 1980's) in car traffic, the corresponding impacts would be as follows:

(i) Car production, ownership, and mileage would increase with more than 50 percent;
(ii) Raw materials needed for car production would increase with 20 percent;
(iii) Fuel consumption by cars would increase with almost 10 percent;
(iv) Exhaust emissions from car traffic could be reduced by 30 percent (CO), 40 percent (HC), and 80 percent (NO_x).

When comparing the above mentioned objectives with the results of various measures, it may be noticed that the reduction in nitrogen oxides is near the target. The major effect has been obtained here by obligatory catalytic convertors. According to a recent review (see Mäkelä et al., 1990), exhaust emissions per kilometer from new private cars using gasoline in 2010 will be 30 percent carbon monoxide (CO), 10 percent (HC), and 18 percent (NO_x) of the emissions of the year 1989 in city streets. On highways the corresponding figures will be approximately 25, 50 and 6 percent.

Production of carbon dioxide is directly correlated to fuel consumption. The impact of the measures in carbon dioxide fall short of the possible targets, even in case of a scenario with a moderate increase in car traffic.

Similar conclusions have been obtained by Eriksson and Hesselborn (1990) in a Swedish study. They noticed that regarding nitrogen oxides, hydrocarbons, and carbon monoxide it is possible to reduce the emissions according to very far reaching targets with the aid of emission limits and technological development. However, regarding carbon dioxide, the difficulties in obtaining targets are much more severe.

It should be added that these estimates are made for private car traffic. The increase in freight traffic is also considerable, but its share in total traffic will also in the future be minor compared to that of cars. However, the possible reductions in exhaust emissions per kilometre for diesel engines will be considerably less than those obtained by cars (cf. Mäkelä et al., 1990)

Possibilities to shift freight transport by means of various transport policy measures from road to rail have been studied by PROGNOS (see ERTI, 1990). However, very strong efforts in the field of the organization and realization of cross-frontier railway transport are then needed.

The future position of the railways in European cross-frontier transport is fairly debatable. On the one hand, the railways have suffered from the highly unsatisfactory functioning of European co-operation, technological stagnation, relatively low technical and commercial speed, strong centralization and bureaucracy, and insufficiently effective government policy. On the other hand, the rising problems of transport capacity and environmental restrictions may give a relative advantage to railways for long-distance consignments of goods which could partly influence transfer from lorries to rail haulage (see Kristiansen, 1990).

The situation in former socialist countries in the eastern parts of Europe is different. The vehicle stock is old, unleaded gasoline is not or hardly used, emission reduction standards include only a small proportion of vehicle use, governments have insufficient means to check and enforce maintenance of emission standards, etc. For example, according to Mäkelä (1991) old trucks using gasoline are the major pollution producers in road traffic in Estonia. Even though car traffic in Estonia is only 7 percent of Finland's car traffic, emissions from road traffic in Estonia range from 20 percent (particles) to 150 percent (HC) of Finland's emissions.

The above discussed measures are only examples of the possible actions. Even though some of the actions far exceed current policy actions, they are quite well possible to obtain and are including well-known technology. In fact, there is a variety of possibilities open. Himanen (1991) has calculated that the transport sector has 4800 possible futures. This figure is obtained by observing that we have six different ways to solve traffic congestion (see above) and five system keeping principles found in the ecosphere (cf. Knoflacher and Himanen 1991) which can be assimilated also to transport systems. These must be combined with four main groups of objectives (socio-economic efficiency, equity, aesthetic and cultural values, and ecological sustainability), each one with at least four different aspects, and ten different transport modes.

Despite the above expositions, given the high socio-economic value attached to mobility, transport policy has in reality only a limited range of possibilities. In the **short and medium term**, it can only to some extent influence the volume of traffic, the use of transport modes, the way cars and modes are used, and the direct impacts on the environment. Examples of policy measures are road pricing (including urban cordon road pricing), emissions pricing (e.g., via fuel tax), technical emission standards for vehicles, zoning (e.g., pedestrian shopping zones), intermodal transport, public transport enhancement. There is nowadays a general tendency not to look for single measures, but for policy packages in order to offer a more comprehensive transport policy.

In the **long** run transport policy would have to take resort to new car technologies, road transport informatics and telematics, more environment-oriented physical planning and urban design, new ways of transport (e.g., subterranean transport, perhaps in vacuum tubes).

It is clear that in all cases there is a need for both transport users and suppliers to pay the full external costs of their activities, including appropriate costs for environmental damage, resource depletion, human health and congestion. The extent to which such measures will be accepted depends also by individuals and group choices made in a democratic society. In line with the triangular relationship discussed above three 'ideal types' of scenario's can be imagined; viz. an environmental scenario, a car mobility scenario and an accessibility scenario (see also Vleugel and Van Gent, 1991).

(a) **Environmental scenario**

This scenario aims at strictly reducing transport mobility, especially car mobility (by both pricing regimes and regulations based on polluter pays principles), the design and introduction of new 'best technical' vehicle technologies, a strict shift towards environment-friendly transport modes, a ban on expansion of road infrastructure, new urban design and physical planning etc.

(b) **Car mobility scenario**

The car mobility scenario takes for granted sufficient investments in new road infrastructure, a moderate pricing policy for transport, no strict traffic-ban regulations, limited substitution towards other transport modes, and development of car technologies that ensure enduring car mobility.

(c) **Accessibility scenario**

This scenario is based on sufficient investments in all infrastructure types, intra-urban access roads, separation of passenger and commodity transport, a moderate transport pricing regime, sufficient infrastructure for isolated areas, adequate and reasonably priced public transport, and use of 'best available' car technologies.

All these scenario's play implicitly or explicitly a role in each transport policy and hence the search for a co-evolutionary mobility policy ensuring a confluence of interest is fraught with many and diverse difficulties. From an analytical research perspective it would make sense to investigate policy measures that would be in agreement or at odds with each of these scenario's. This would require a more systematic typology of policy options. A useful typology seems to be according to demand-side transport policy, supply-side transport policy, and coordinated demand/supply-side policy (see also Louw et al., 1991). A systematic screening of various policy options against the attributes of the above scenario's brings to light main items on a research agenda for co-evolutionary mobility policy:

* identification of all relevant (micro and macro, individual and social) costs and benefits of transport
* analysis of effectiveness of policy measures in terms of mobility, accessibility and sustainability
* design of new packages of policy instruments with a particular view on attaining co-evolutionary mobility patterns (e.g., location policy, marketing, price differentiation)
* development of new technologies favouring a more efficient and environment-friendly transport system (not only vehicle technology but also telematics and road informatics technology)
* societal acceptance of policies aiming at behaviourial change of transport users (using both social and economic stimuli)
* institutional reorganisation of the transport system in which more market-oriented stimuli (ranging from local to international transport movements and for all modes and all users) are given.

15.6 Concluding Remarks

Transport policy has never escaped from the conflict between the historical and modern transport problem. Now, faced with the emerging postmodern transport problem (heavy congestion without any space to enlarge the capacity) in major European cities and motorways of the European core area, the identification and acceptance of a solid and fruitful transport policy is still more difficult.

The design and implementation of transport policy is embedded in general policy making with - from the environmental viewpoint - two unresolved long-term problems: the future of mass consumption in developed countries and dramatic population explosion in developing countries. In fact Europe has just now a special public planning problem in view of the great many development needs in former socialist countries in the eastern part of Europe.

Clearly, there are many possibilities to obtain environmentally more friendly transport systems when combining governmental actions and technological development. However, some questions are still left unresolved, e.g. how to decrease carbon dioxide emissions. Also the necessary effective governmental actions are mainly still on the waiting list. Decision-makers cannot only be blamed here, because there is even no general agreement among transport professionals regarding solutions to urgent transport problems.

References

Alppivuori, K. and V. Himanen, Energiansäästö liikenteessä, tekniset mahdollisuudet (Energy conservation in traffic, technological possibilities), Technical Research Centre of Finland, Road and Traffic Laboratory, Research Report 805, Espoo, 1990.

Banister, D., The Final Gridlock, **Built Environment**, vol. 15, 1989, pp. 163-165.

Barde, J.Ph. and K.J. Button (eds.), **Transport Policy and the Environment**, Earthscan, London, 1991.

Björnland, D., Trends in Transport Infrastructure Investment, Maintenance and Capital Assets in the ECMT Countries in the 1980's. Paper presented in TFBs Symposium om Infrastrukur Och Samhällsekonomi, Sjudarhöjden, Sweden, 1991.

Brög, W., Behaviour Begins in the Mind, Marketing and Service Quality in Public Transport, Round Table 91, ECMT, Paris, 1991.

Button, K.J. and D. Gillingwater, **Future Transport Policy**, Croom Helm, London, 1986.

Capra, Fr., **The Turning Point**, Bantam Books Inc., New York, 1983.

Damianides, L. and M. Giaoutzi, Transport and Environment: Experiences with Greek Policies, **Transport Policy and the Environment** (J.Ph. Barde and K. Button, eds.), Earthscan, London, 1991, pp.157-176.

Diekmann, A., **Stichting Weg Mobiliteitsschrift**, July/August 1991, pp.37-45.

Döös, B.R., Environmental Issues Requiring International Action, IIASA, RR-91-16, Laxenburg, 1991.

ECMT, 33 rd Annual Report - 1986, Activity of the Conference, Resolution of the Council of Ministers of Transport and Reports Approved in 1986, Paris, 1985.

ECMT, **Transport Policy and the Environment**, Paris, 1990.

Eriksson, G. and P.O. Hesselborn, A Transportation System Adapted to the Environment, TFB Report 1990:15, Stockholm, 1990.

ERTI, **Missing Networks, a European Challenge**, Brussels, 1990.

Goodwin, P.B., Understanding Congestion, **Recherche - Transport - Sécurité, Revue de L'INRETS**, English issue no 5, 1990, pp.75-80.

Goodwin, P.B., S. Hallett, F. Kenny and G. Stokes, Transport: The New Realism, Transport Studies Unit, University of Oxford, Report to the Rees Jeffreys Road Fund, Oxford, 1991.

Grupp, H., Die Sozialen Kosten des Verkehrs, **Verkehr und Technik**, vol. 39, no. 91, 1986, pp.359-366.

Hanson, S. (ed.), **The Geography of Urban Transportation**, Guildford Press, New York, 1986.

Himanen, V., Transport Policy, Infrastructure Assessment, and Future in Urban Areas, **Proceedings of the Seminar on Future Road Transport Systems and Infrastructures in Urban Areas**, 4-6 June 1991, OECD and Japanese Ministry of Construction, Chiba, 1991, pp.171-182.

Himanen, V., P. Nijkamp and J. Padjen, Environmental Quality and Transport Policy in Europe, **Transportation Research**, vol. 26A, 1992, pp.147-157.

IRF, AIMSE, The Motorway Project for the Europe of Tomorrow, Geneva, 1990.

Jansson, J.O., Car Demand Modelling and Forecasting, **Journal of Transport Economics and Policy**, vol. 23, 1989, pp.125-140.

De Jong, G.C., An Indirect Utility Model of Car Ownership and Private Car Use, **European Economic Review**, vol. 34, 1989, pp.971-985.

Kauppi, P., P. Anttila and K. Kenttämies (eds.), **Acidification in Finland**, Springer Verlag, Berlin, 1990.

King, A. and B. Schneider, **The First Global Revolution, A Report by the Council of The Club of Rome**, Simon & Schuster, London, 1991.

Knoflacher, H. and V. Himanen, Transport Policy between Economy and Ecology, Technical Research Centre of Finland, Research Notes 1221, Espoo, 1991.

Kristiansen, J., The Transport Infrastructure in Western Europe - A Conceptual Approach, Dept. of Development and Planning, Aalborg University, Aalborg, 1990.

Louw, E., P. Nijkamp and H. Priemus, **Sturingssystemen voor Infrastructuur en Mobiliteit**, Delftse Universitaire Pers, Delft, 1991.

Maarseveen, M. van, and Kraan, M., A Comparative Analysis and Reconstruction of Mobility Developments in EC Countries 1970-1985, **De Prijs van Mobiliteit en Mobiliteitsbeperking** (P. Tanja, ed.), CVS, Delft, 1991, pp. 207-225.

Mäkelä, K., Kanner, H., Himanen, V., Laurikko, J., Salusjärvi, H. and Anila, M. Tieliikenteen pakokaasupäästöt, Ennustava tietojärjestelmä, LIISA II (Road traffic exhaust emissions in Finland, year 1989 and forecasts) Technical Research Centre of Finland, Research Report 82, Espoo, 1990.

Mäkelä, K., Finnish Pilot Project in Estonia, Lorries Dominate in Emissions, **Nordic Road & Transport Research**, vol. 3, 1991, pp.8-11.

Nijkamp, P., **Theory and Application of Environmental Economics**, North-Holland Publ. Co., Amsterdam, 1981.

Nijkamp, P., S. Reichman and M. Wegener (eds.), **Euro-mobile**, Gower, Aldershot, 1990.

Nijkamp, P., J.C.J.M. van den Bergh and F. Soeteman, Regional Sustainable Develop ment and Natural Resource Use, **World Bank Economic Review** (Proceedings World Bank Annual Conference 1990), 1991, pp.153-187.

Plowden, S., Transport Efficiency and the Urban Environment, **Transport Review**, vol. 3, pp. 363-398 (1983).

Prendergast, L.S. and R.D. Williams, An Empirical Investigation into the Determinants of Travel Time, TRRL Supplementary Report 555, Crowthorne, Berkshire 1980.

Stigliani, W.M., F.M. Brouwer, R.E. Munn, R.W. Shaw and M. Antonovsky, Future Environments for Europe: Some Implications of Alternative Development Paths, IIASA, RR-89-5, Laxenburg 1989.

Stutz, F.P., Environmental Impacts, **The Geography of Urban Transportation**, (S. Hanson, ed.), Guilford, New York, pp.329-351, 1986.

Svidén, O., Automobile Usage in a Future Information Society, **Futures**, vol. 15, 1983, pp.261-274.

Tie- ja vesirakennushallitus and Taloudellinen suunnittelukeskus, Lükenne- ja autokantaennuste 1986-2010, TVH 713092, Helsinki, 1987.

Vibe, N., Reisevaner i Oslo-omradet, endringer i reisevaner i Oslo og Akershus fra 1977 til 1990, Transportokonomisk institutt, TOI-rapport nr 0096/1991, Oslo, 1991.

Vilhelmson, B. Vår daglig rörlighet. Transportforskningen, TFB-rapport 1990:16, Stockholm, 1990.

Vleugel, J.M., H.A. van Gent and P. Nijkamp, Transport and Environment: Experien ces with Dutch Policies, **Transport Policy and the Environment** (Ph. Barde and K.E. Button, eds.), Earthscan, London, 1990, pp.121-156.

Vleugel, J.M. and H.A. Van Gent, **Duurzame Ontwikkeling, Mobiliteit en Bereikbaarheid**, Delftse Universitaire Pers, Delft, 1991.

Webster, F.W. and P.H. Bly (eds.) The Demand for Public Transport, Report of the International Collaborative Study of the Factors Affecting Public Transport Patronage, Transport and Road Research Laboratory, Crowthorne, 1980.

World Commission on Environment and Development (Brundtland report), **Our Common Future**, Oxford University Press, Oxford, 1987.

Wärnhjelm, M., Trafiksystem i europeiska städer, TFB-meddelande 150, Stockholm, 1990.

PART D

MODELLING SPATIAL INTERACTION BEHAVIOUR

CHAPTER 16

STATIC AND DYNAMIC SPATIAL INTERACTION MODELS: AN INTEGRATING PERSPECTIVE

Peter Nijkamp and Aura Reggiani

16.1 Introduction

The evolution of sciences is based on the rise and decline of scientific 'mental constructs'. For many decades scholars from various disciplines have been intrigued by the question whether there are unifying principles or models that have a validity in different disciplines. The building of such analytical frameworks bridging the gaps between different scientific traditions is a very ambitious task and has not been very successful up till now.

In the past - in a static context - several such principles have been defined and advocated at the edge of the natural sciences on the one hand and social sciences (in particular, economics and geography) on the other hand, mainly based on the paradigm of 'social physics'. Some important contributions to the integration of the spatial systems sciences and physics can be found in gravity theory and entropy theory, which have formed the corner stones of interaction models in space. The present paper is about spatial interaction models. It summarizes the correspondence of such models from a 'social physics' perspective. It is noteworthy that such models need a behavioural underpinning as a sine qua non for a valid use in spatial systems analysis. This view also explains the use of micro-based disaggregate choice models as a tool for analyzing spatial systems. This is mainly analyzed in Section 16.2.

In recent years much attention has been devoted to qualitative (structural) changes in dynamic systems, evolutionary theory, morphogenesis, bio-social science and the like. Also here the question emerges as to the validity of such approaches in social sciences in general and in spatial systems in particular. Is it, for instance, possible to design models that describe indigenous behavioural shocks in spatial systems models?

In this context, non-linear dynamics has many important lessons to offer to the analysis of the dynamic behaviour of spatial systems. Especially modern chaos theory, which has gained much popularity in recent years, presents fascinating new analytical departures. At the same time the need for a behavioural explanation in such qualitative structural change models has to be emphasized. Therefore, Section 16.3 contains a critical overview of non-linear types of models, with a particular emphasis on their applicability in dynamic spatial systems.

We postulate here that spatial interaction models - interpreted in a broad sense from a logistic perspective - may offer a general framework for many (static and dynamic) phenomena in interconnected spatial systems (Section 16.4). They appear to be compatible with 'social physics' and chaos principles. Clearly, a major challenge is to generate a more solid empirical basis for such models. For the time being we have to take resort to simulation experiments. The past development of spatial interaction models in a dynamic environment suggests also various items for a research agenda, and therefore an outline of such a research ambition is sketched in the concluding section of this paper.

16.2 Relevance of Spatial Interaction Models in a Static Context

The relevance of Spatial Interaction Models (SIMs) was clearly and significantly outlined by Olsson (1970, p.233) in the following statement: "The concept of spatial interaction is central for everyone concerned with theoretical geography and regional science... Under the umbrella of spatial interaction and distance decay, it has been possible to accommodate most model work in transportation, migration, commuting, and diffusion, as well as significant aspects of location theory".

Similar observations were also made by Fotheringham and O'Kelly (1989, p.1), who claimed: "Spatial interaction can be broadly defined as movement or communication over space that results from a decision process. The term thus encompass such diverse behaviour as migration, shopping, travel-to-work, the choice of health-care services, recreation, the movement of goods, telephone calls, the choice of a university by students, airline passenger traffic, and even attendance at events such as conferences, theatre and football matches. In each case, an individual trades off in some manner the benefit of the interaction with the costs that are necessary in overcoming the spatial separation between the individual and his/her possible destination.... It is the pervasiveness of this type of trade-off in spatial behaviour that has made spatial interaction modelling so important and the subject of such intense investigation".

In this paper we will proceed along these lines by showing how SIMs play nowadays a fundamental role as the common basis for many other models widely used in transportation studies and related applications, in both a static and dynamic context.

To this purpose we will briefly give here a presentation of SIMs, which may also be useful for a better understanding of our subsequent considerations. We will start from the general formulation of a doubly-constrained SIM, whose role is more predictive than explanatory, since it takes the propulsiveness of origins and the attractiveness of destinations as exogenously given and allocates a known number of outflows and inflows to links between these origins and destinations (see Fotheringham and O'Kelly, 1989).

Consequently, a doubly-constrained SIM depicts the flow T_{ij} (flows of people, goods, messages, etc.) from some origin i to some destination j as follows:

$$T_{ij} = A_i B_j O_i D_j \exp(-\beta c_{ij}) \tag{1}$$

with:

$$A_i = [\Sigma_j B_j D_j \exp(-\beta c_{ij})]^{-1} \quad (2)$$

and

$$B_j = [\Sigma_i A_i O_i \exp(-\beta c_{ij})]^{-1} \quad (3)$$

where:

T_{ij} = the (unknown) trips from origin zone i to destination j
O_i = the (given) trips generated from origin zone i
D_j = the (given) trips attracted to destination zone j
c_{ij} = a measure of the (given) unit cost of transport between zone i and zone j
$\exp(-\beta c_{ij})$ = a (non-linear) function of transport costs, where β is a parameter to be determined by means of a calibration process for the whole model.

A_i and B_j are so-called **balancing** factors ensuring the additivity condition that the total activity leaving origin zone i is equal to O_i, and the total activity attracted to destination j is equal to D_j, respectively.

To calibrate model (1) at some base year, with data on a given set of origin zones O_i and destination zones D_j, a parameter value for the transport cost function $f(c_{ij})$ has to be found that 'best' reproduces the known base year trip pattern T_{ij} (see, e.g., Foot, 1986). Since the balancing factors A_i and B_j form a set of simultaneous non-linear equations (see equations (2) and (3)), an iterative procedure is necessary to solve the model. For this purpose Hyman's method (see Hyman, 1969) is usually applied.

Particular cases of model (1) are the singly-constrained SIM and the unconstrained SIM. The former class provides information only on the destination characteristics (the so-called production-constrained SIM) or on the origin characteristics (the so-called attraction-constrained SIM), while the latter class (the unconstrained SIM) provides information on the attributes of both the origins and the destinations of the interactions. Thus these three types of models are more 'explanatory' in nature, since they determine, by means of model calibration, the attributes of locations giving rise to the flows of people, goods, etc. (see again Fotheringham and O'Kelly, 1989). In particular the production-constrained SIM can be represented by the following equation:

$$T_{ij} = A_i O_i D_j \exp(-\beta c_{ij}) \quad (4)$$

where the balancing factor A_i now has the following specification:

$$A_i = [\Sigma_j D_j \exp(-\beta c_{ij})]^{-1} \quad (5)$$

The value of A_i serves to ensure that model (4) reproduces the volume of flows originating from zone i, so that:

$$O_i = \Sigma_j T_{ij} \tag{6}$$

The inverse of A_i in (5) is often interpreted as a measure of the accessibility of zone i (see, among others, Weibull, 1976).

It is interesting to recall that in a static context SIMs have various origins:

- The most common specification of a SIM originates from gravity theory (see e.g., Ravenstein, 1885, and for a review, Isard and Maclaren, 1982).
- A second, macro-oriented approach from which SIMs can emerge is the entropy concept. Even though the entropy model has its roots in statistical mechanics (see Wilson, 1967, 1970), the entropy concept can be interpreted in terms of a generalized cost function for transport behaviour, thus offering a macro-behavioural context to SIMs (see Nijkamp and Reggiani, 1992).
- A further utility background of entropy is offered by programming (or optimization) models, since entropy can be regarded as a specific type of the latter models. Consequently, the family of SIMs can be derived from different formulations of an entropy (or utility) maximizing macro-approach and hence viewed as an optimum system's solution. Once again, the entropy concept results are compatible with a macro-behavioural interpretation of spatial interaction (see Nijkamp and Reggiani, 1992). It should be noted that in this framework SIMs are essentially considered as **aggregate models** describing the **macro-state of a system** and based on **macro** data.
- A further, very interesting derivation of SIMs, is also the one emerging from random utility theory in economics (see, for example Anas, 1983). In particular the formal analogy between Multinomial Logit (MNL) models belonging to the class of Discrete Choice Models (DCMs) and SIMs has often been stressed in recent years (see, for a review, Nijkamp and Reggiani, 1989).

In fact, if we examine the structure of a production-constrained SIM in its probabilistic form, i.e.:

$$P_{ij} = T_{ij} / O_i = A_i D_j \exp(-\beta c_{ij}) \tag{7}$$

where P_{ij} represents now the probability of moving from origin i to destination j, it is clear that, if we introduce in equation (7) the expression of the balancing factor A_i like in (2), the following equivalence results:

$$P_{ij} = D_j \exp(\beta u_{ij}) / \Sigma_j D_j \exp(\beta u_{ij}) \tag{8}$$

where D_j can be interpreted as a weighting factor reflecting the attractiveness of a point of destination j, and where $u_{ij} = -c_{ij}$ can be considered as the deterministic part of the individual random utility underlying an MNL model (see, for the derivation of an MNL model, the seminal work of McFadden, 1974 and Domencich and McFadden, 1975).

Expression (8) is clearly an MNL model. For the sake of convenience we suppose here that the reader is familiar with the basic literature on MNL models and DCMs.

Consequently, we will summarize here some basic considerations related to the equivalence between (7) and (8):

- If a singly-constrained SIM can be considered equivalent to an MNL model, it also means that SIMs embed the limits inherent in MNL models such as the so-called IIA property.
- Secondly, since << the same model without any aggregation error may be derived in disaggregate form from both entropy and utility maximization >> (see Batten and Boyce, 1986, p.378), it follows that entropy and SIMs are not inherently less behavioural than stochastic utility models of DCMs (and MNL models in particular). Therefore, in this perspective, SIMs can be considered as aggregate models of human behaviour.
- SIMS can also emerge from the maximizaton of a micro-economic (deterministic or random) utility function. In particular, the latter analysis illustrates that SIMs are formally analogous to DCMs; consequently, depending on the type of available data (aggregate or disaggregate) SIMs can provide a similar behavioural background as DCMs. In particular, a singly-constrained SIM can be considered equivalent to an MNL model thus embedding also the limits inherent in MNL models such as the IIA property. Only a doubly-constrained SIM - and more generally an Alonso model - with a sequential choice process may be associated with a nested MNL model, thus overcoming the IIA axiom. It then follows that entropy can also be interpreted as a measure of interaction between economic individuals and consequently as a social/collective utility function (including cost elements) (see Nijkamp and Reggiani, 1992).

It should be noted that the above mentioned SIMs mainly deal with the demand side in a transportation system (or more generally in a spatial interaction system). However, it has also been pointed out (see Florian and Gaudry, 1983) that a phenomenon designated as supply at one particular level for a transportation system may become demand at another level. Consequently, relationships among different levels can be considered as input-output interactions, so that a precise distinction between supply and demand side can be made only at one particular level of the system. It turns out that the same SIM can be used in both demand and supply side analysis (see, for example, the concept of accessiblity derived from spatial interaction analysis and applied to infrastructure systems; see Rietveld, 1989).

However, most models developed in the sixties and seventies and ending up with a SIM structure are still static/deterministic equilibrium models and to not consider the time paths followed by the transportation system components as well as the uncertainty of the system and its network (see the special issue of Transportation Research; Boyce, 1985).

In this context it is interesting to emphasize the formal connections between SIMs and MNL models, since this link can place more emphasis on the analysis of individual motives and on the impact of micro random behaviour upon the functioning of transport and spatial interaction systems (in view of the need to a better understanding of the stochasticity of systems).

A further connection is also offered by the integration of SIMs with rational screening methods related to risky alternatives (e.g., the stochastic dominance approach). This unifying approach, which also shows the possibility of linking models of choice behaviour under certainty and models of choice behaviour under uncertainty (see Reggiani and Stefani, 1986), has recently also been applied to modal choice problems in a transportation system (see Reggiani and Stefani, 1989) by considering the attributes of the alternatives according to different states of nature.

Having now briefly reviewed the connections between SIMs and behaviourial models, the next step will be to draw our attention to the broad category of dynamic models (DCMs) developed more recently in transportation systems, in order to take into account newly emerging relevant aspects of system dynamics, such as slow and fast dynamics, uncertainty, bifurcations, catastrophic changes, chaotic behaviour, fractal structures, etc. In particular we will point out a common similarity in these DCMs - despite their different theoretical sources - viz. their close association, under particular conditions, with dynamic SIMs.

16.3 **Relevance of Spatial Interaction Models in a Dynamic Context**

16.3.1 **Dynamic properties of SIMs**

16.3.1.1 **Prologue**

It has recently been shown (see Nijkamp and Reggiani, 1992) that also in a dynamic framework SIMs emerge from various roots. In particular a dynamic analysis of SIMs has led to the following main results:

- The formal parallel between SIMs and DCMs can be extended also in a dynamic and stochastic context. Moreover, a SIM can be shown to be the optimal solution of a dynamic spatial interaction problem. Consequently, the interrelations between entropy and SIMs exist also in a dynamic framework. This indicates that dynamic SIMs are able to capture also the evolutionary patterns of a dynamic interaction system and that a dynamic entropy can be viewed as a cumulative utility function concerned with generalized cost minimization (see Nijkamp and Reggiani, 1992).
- SIMs also have the possibility of explaining the interaction activities in a stochastic dynamic framework. In fact, a stochastic (doubly-constrained) SIM can be shown to emerge as an optimum system's solution to a dynamic entropy optimal control problem subject to random disturbances. Furthermore, a singly-constrained SIM shows a structural stability even in the presence of such small perturbations. This has been shown in an illustration of catastrophy behaviour in the field of mobility (see Nijkamp and Reggiani, 1992).

The relevance of stochastic (exogenous) fluctuations (according to which the usual form of a SIM varies) then leads to the issue of analyzing SIMs in the context of states of disequilibrium, causality and unpredictability; in other words, in the context of potentially chaotic behaviour.

The discovery of 'chaos' seems to have created a new paradigm in scientific modelling. However, chaos models in economic and social sciences are often theoretical or illustrative rather than empirical, given the lack of available data. In particular, SIMs in the framework of chaos theory show that irregular dynamic behaviour is a possibility depending on initial conditions and on critical parameter values. More specifically (see Nijkamp and Reggiani, 1990a) SIMs have the possibility of showing chaotic features in their MNL formulation, in particular for high values of the marginal utility function. Consequently, a great deal of attention has to be paid to the speed of change of the utility function (or to the distance decay), since some critical parameter values can lead to a chaotic movement with unfeasible values for the socio-economic variables considered. This interesting result essentially derives from the mathematical interrelationships between SIMs and logistic structures, as will be shown in the next subsection.

16.3.1.2 Relationships between SIMs and logistic function

If we consider, in a dynamic framework, the equivalence between SIMs and MNL models, we get the following logit form:

$$P_j = \exp(u_j) \,/\, \Sigma \exp_\ell (u_\ell) \tag{9}$$

which is equivalent to a dynamic SIM and which represents the probability of choosing alternative j at time t.

In this context we may recall a recent result, i.e., that the rate of changes of P_j (formulated in 3.1) with respect to time (i.e., $\dot{P}_j$) can be expressed by a structure of the Volterra-Lotka type (see Sonis, 1988, and Nijkamp and Reggiani, 1990a), as follows:

$$\dot{P}_j = \dot{u}_j P_j (1-P_j) - P_j \sum_{\ell \neq j} \dot{u}_\ell P_\ell \tag{10}$$

It is also interesting to note that a particular case of the above dynamic MNL, i.e. a binary case, obtained by deleting the last term in (10) (i.e. the interaction term), is a **logistic growth model**. It is also well-known that the difference version of the standard logistic growth model has been thoroughly discussed in the literature for its capability of generating bifurcations and chaos for certain critical values of the growth parameter (see, e.g., the seminal work by May, 1976). Therefore, a 'binary' logit model, belonging to the family of May models, shows the same 'chaotic' properties, i.e. a cascade of bifurcations leading to chaos for certain values of its dynamic utility function u_j which represents the growth parameter of the variable P_j (see Figure 1).

Given the above mentioned link between logistic functions, dynamic SIMs and dynamic MNL models, we will give in the next section a more thorough overview of the most frequently used dynamic interaction models in order to show their connection with a logistic structure and hence with SIMs.

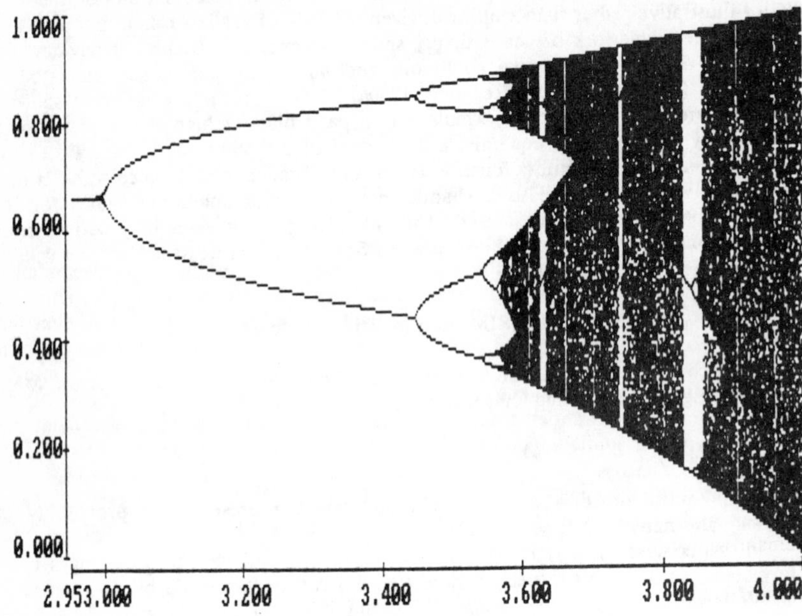

Figure 1. Bifurcation diagram for a dynamic - binary - logit model

Legend: y - axis = P_j

x - axis = $\dot{u}_j$

16.3.2 Relevance of the logistic form in dynamic spatial models

16.3.2.1 Introduction

As noted above the last decade has shown a boom in the interest in the development of both behavioural and dynamic models, as it is generally expected that such models are capable to describe and represent the behavioural mechanisms underlying the evolutionary changes in complex transportation and network systems (see, e.g., Ben-Akiva, 1985). Consequently, a wide variety of multi-temporal or dynamic transportation models has arisen in the past decade with the aim of providing a stronger and more useful analytical support to planning processes than conventional static tools (such as static spatial interaction models, linear programming models, etc.). In this context it is noteworthy that **SIMs tend to become again a focal point of analysis**, since they can deal with the complicated and interwoven pattern of human activities in space and time.

However, despite all progress made in this new research direction (mostly from a theoretical viewpoint), still some important research questions remain, which largely concern the applicability of these dynamic models in relation to the scale of analysis at which various operational developments of these models are taking place. In particular, this important field of reflection concerns the advantages and disadvantages related to the use of macro-meso-micro approaches.

On the one hand, it is evident that aggregate representations may become extremely cumbersome and inefficient when it is necessary to represent complex systems, especially where there is considerable heterogeneity amongst the actors in those systems (see Clarke and Wilson, 1986). On the other hand, it is clear that the problems of data availability and computational processing requirements are often in contrast with the need to use a micro-oriented approach. Moreover, the response of population in aggregated models does not always correspond to an aggregation of the individual responses obtained from a micro model, so that it seems evident that the phenomena being studied require a careful consideration as regards the nature of their level of analysis (see again Clarke and Wilson, 1986). This problem has also been treated in analytical attempts focusing attention on the interdependiencies between micro- and macro-responses, which also depend on the interaction between demand and supply.

16.3.2.2 Logistic forms in macro-dynamic approaches

Several dynamic models of spatial structure have recently been developed at a macro level. We will give here a few illustrations. An example is the model developed by Allen et al. (1978), in which the evolutionary growth of zonal activities is assumed to follow a **logistic pattern**. Allen et al.'s model is a comprehensive model incorporating urban activities such as employment and residential population. A major finding in this model is that random fluctuations (e.g., changes due to infrastructure constructions) may alter the related urban evolution.

Another dynamic model of the **logistic type** is the one developed by Harris and Wilson (1978) and Wilson (1981). In this case the standard static spatial interaction model for activity allocation has been embedded into a dynamic evolutionary framework, again of a logistic type. Bifurcations and catastrophe behaviour emerge from this model, depending on particular values of the parameters. Obviously, owing to this logistic structure also oscillations and cycles may occur.

These two important models have induced a wide spread production of related models both from theoretical and empirical viewpoints, also in a stochastic framework (see also Nijkamp and Reggiani, 1988a). However, it should also be noted that the above mentioned two models primarily focus on the supply side, without clear dynamic equations at the demand side.

Another stream of research at the macro-level is the series of models based on ecological dynamics of the Volterra-Lotka type (see Dendrinos and Mullally, 1981); in this formulation of interacting biological species, each species is characterized by a birth-death process of the **logistic** type. Recent papers on this topic show the integration between ecological models and optimal control models (see Nijkamp and Reggiani, 1990b), between ecological models and random fluctuations of a white noise type (see Campisi, 1986) or between ecological models, SIMs of a gravity type and turbulence (see Dendrinos, 1988).

Obviously, since a Lotka-Volterra system is a system of interrelated equations, we get by necessity here interaction mechanisms of supply and demand. Furthermore, given the related logistic form, it is also here again possible to get - for critical parameter values - oscillations and complex behaviour.

The last group of macro approaches in the area of SIMs are represented by models based on **optimal control** approaches or **dynamic programming** analysis (see, for example, Nijkamp and Reggiani, 1988b). Also here different forms of equilibrium/disequibrium may emerge (e.g., saddle points, borderline stability), which show the possibility of unstable motions.

As a synthesis we may conclude that a common trend in these groups of macro-approaches is the development of models that are able to exhibit (under certain conditions) complex or chaotic behaviour and hence outcomes which are hardly foreseeable by modellers and planners. This lack of predictability of future events is clearly also a major concern in transportation planning and reflects analytically - in terms of a scientific paradigm - essentially the beginning of a new phase of a research life cycle. Here another important research problem is emerging, i.e., the relevance of critical parameter values, such as their speed of change in a geographic or planning context in order to understand whether the system at hand is moving towards a predictable or complex (unpredictable) evolution.

16.3.2.3 Logistic forms in micro-meso dynamic approaches

In this subsection we will briefly pay attention to the considerable body of literature based on micro simulation models (see Clarke and Wilson, 1986). Given the above mentioned drawbacks related to a macro-approach, a mixture of aggregate dynamic models in conjunction with micro-simulation (the micro-meso approach) has recently been advocated and adopted for various spatial applications (see also Birkin and Clarke, 1983). In this way also an integration between demand and supply results is possible. In other words, micro-meso dynamic approaches utilize individual data in conjunction with aggregate equations.

Another interesting micro-meso approach is the well-known logit model, based on a micro-economic foundation. In Section 16.3.1.2 it has been shown that the growth over time of people choosing such alternatives as travel choice mode, destination, etc. according to a logit procedure follows again a logistic pattern. Thus development can also lead to a chaotic or irregular behaviour for particular values of the underlying utility function. The most important consequence of this result is the link between DCMs - and hence the equivalent SIMs - and logistic formulation of these models. Since most of the models referred to end up with a logistic shape, it is clear that

SIMs can be considered as a comprehensive framework incorporating many advanced models also at a dynamic level.

In this area also the **master equation/mean value equation** models (see Haag and Weidlich, 1984; Haag, 1989) have to be mentioned. These models have been used extensively in spatial flow analysis. This framework models the uncertainties in the decision process of the individuals via the master equation approach. The mean values are then obtained from the master equation by an aggregation of the individual probability distributions. Thus this approach provides the link between micro-economic aspects and the macro-economic equation of motions for aggregate mean values.

In this context also compartmental analysis should be mentioned (see De Palma and Lefèvre, 1984) which consists of equations which are the approximate mean-value equations. It has recently been shown (see Reiner et al., 1986) that also these meanvalue equations may display chaotic behaviour with strange attractors, given particular conditions for the group interaction. On the other hand, this result is not surprising, since the mean value equations are strongly related to logit models. Hence it is plausible that interrelated logistic functions cause the emerging chaotic motions.

After this brief review based on a typology of dynamic models and their potential in transportation planning, we will now incorporate them in the framework of a life-cycle (evolutionary) pattern.

16.4 Evolution of Spatial Interaction Models

The models discussed in the previous section can be unified in the broad area of DMs and then compared, in their evolution, to the groups of static SIMs and DCMs, in the light of life cycle concepts. As a synthesis, we can represent the series of the transportation models studied and adopted so far according to the scheme of overlapping generations illustrated in Figure 2.

In Figure 2 we have essentially depicted the generation and diffusion of the three main families of models which have received a great deal of attention in the last century, i.e., Spatial Interaction Models (SIMs), Discrete Choice Models (DCMs) and Dynamic Models (DMs).

From Figure 2 we can see that - while SIMs present a smooth development at the beginning of the century with more emphasis after the sixties - DCMs and DMs exhibit a rapid growth (from both a theoretical and empirical point of view). It should be noted that in DMs we have included the whole group of dynamic models treated so far, so that we can observe that after the mid seventies a large number of mathematical models emerged.

Altogether we observe an overlapping generation of models: in particular we can unify all these models in a unique general logistic shape where the points A and B mean the theoretical conjunction of DCMs and DMs with SIMs, respectively. However, it seems plausible that a saturation level of the development of the above mentioned models will be approached. Probably, from this upper level, new tools will emerge in the next century, in response to new activity patterns. This upper level can likely be linked to the analytical structure of the models, since there are inevitable constraints in their formulation, so that also from a mathematical point of view the potential of such models will certainly reach a limit.

Evolution of models

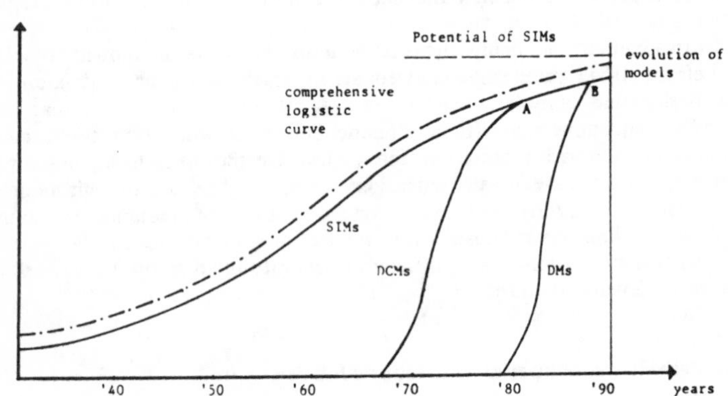

Figure 2 Overlapping generations of models

Legend: SIMs = Spatial Interaction Models
DCMs = Discrete Choice Models
DMs = Dynamic Models

Since it has been underlined in the previous section that most of these models can be reformulated in terms of a logit-logistic formulation - and hence can be interpreted in a SIM structure - the broad potential of SIMs can be considered as such a limit.

16.5 Towards a Research Agenda for Dynamic Spatial Interaction Systems

It is clear from the previous arguments that the field of transportation and communication research is increasingly dominated by dynamic systems considerations. Bifurcation, catastrophe and chaos theory have become critical components of a new framework for investigating the long term evolution of spatial interaction flows.

At the same time it is also evident that still a long trajectory has to be followed before the 'new dynamics' movement will have led to operational and testable analytical propositions which can also be used in empirical research. For the time being, various new research directions are necessary in order to complement the tools developed in the past decades.

A systematic listing of such new tools leads directly to the design of a research agenda for dynamic spatial interaction systems. The following items are central in such a research agenda.

(1) **Specification theory**
The formulation of dynamic spatial systems models which are compatible with plausible behavioural hypotheses on the one hand and which lend themselves for empirical testing on the other hand is a difficult methodological task which so far has not yet been very successful. The extent to which a dynamic SIM is a satisfactory mapping of highly dynamic real world processes is a formidable research effort, mainly since empirical tests are lacking.

(2) **Verification analysis**
The question whether (theoretical) model results are in agreement - in a qualitative or quantitative sense - with non-linear patterns incorporated by an underlying data set is another important research challenge. So far it has been very difficult to find statistically satisfactory parameter estimates in non-linear models whose value at the outset is falling in the chaotic domain. Besides, the statistical tools for identifying non-linear dynamic (and possibly chaotic) patterns are not very well developed, although the value of the Liapunov exponents, the Brock-Dechert-Scheinkman test, and the use of recurrence plots may provide analytical support.

(3) **Behavioural analysis**
The identification of chaos behaviour in the decisions of actors is to a large extent dependent on the degree of aggregation of observed time series. In a very short time span (e.g., on an hourly basis) the possibility of chaotic patterns in behaviour is much higher than in a longer time span (e.g., on a yearly basis), as in the latter case a smoothing amendment has taken place. Furthermore, in the longer run rational expectations of actors would generate negative feedback reactions, so that wild fluctuations would be prevented. Altogether, it is difficult to separate random shocks, measurement errors, impacts of time series and behavioral feedbacks in a given data set.

(4) **Impacts of time delays**
Although it was sometimes assumed in the past that the inclusion of more time lags would destabilize a growth trajectory, it has recently been recognized that this is not necessarily true (e.g., in the rational expectations model the probability of occurrence of chaos diminishes if the weight of the past increases). In recent publications it has been demonstrated that an increase in time lags may increase the probability of chaos, but on a much smaller domain. Two research directions might be interesting in this context, viz. the relevance of **fractal theory** (which takes for granted that phenomena at a given scale level are replicated at lower levels) and of **percolation theory** (which analyzes the time trajectory of a dynamic phenomenon in case of unstructured barriers).

(5) **Impacts of chaos modules**
This question focuses on the overall stability of a non-linear dynamic systems model, if this model incorporates one smaller module which may exhibit chaotic

behaviour. This leads to the intriguing research question whether lower order chaos may affect overall stability and vice versa. In this context there is much scope for innovative research strategies, viz. **niche theory** (which deals with partly overlapping and interwoven sets of populations in a dynamic system) and **autopoièsis** (which addresses the issue of self-organization in dynamic social-cybernetic or self-organizing systems).

It is clear that in all above research suggestions the behavioural aspects of actors are of decisive importance. This once more emphasizes the need for an integration of behavioural modelling along the lines of discrete choice theory with meso/macro dynamic spatial interaction modelling. In this context - and given the usual lack of appropriate time series data - the recent trend towards **experimental social science research** is undoubtedly an important step forward.

Acknowledgement

The second author gratefully acknowleges the NECTAR grant from the European Science Foundation (ESF) as well as CNR grant No. 91.02288. CT11.

References

Allen, P.M., J.L. Deneubourg, M. Sanglier, F. Boon and A. De Palma, The Dynamics of Urban Evolution, Final Report of the U.S. Department of Transportation, Washington D.C., 1978.

Anas, A., Discrete Choice Theory, Information Theory and the Multinomial Logit and Gravity Models, **Transportation Research**, vol. 17B, 1983, pp.13-23.

Batten, D.F. and D.E. Boyce, Spatial Interaction, Transportation and Interregional Commodity Flow Models, **Handbook of Regional and Urban Economics** (P.Nijkamp, ed.), North Holland, Amsterdam, 1986, pp.357-406.

Ben-Akiva, M. and A. De Palma, Analysis of a Dynamic Residential Location Choice Model with Transaction Costs, **Journal of Regional Science**, vol. 26, 1986, pp.321-341.

Birkin, M. and M. Clarke, Comprehensive Dynamic Urban Models: Integrating Macro and Micro Approaches, **Evolving Geographical Structures** (D.A. Griffith and A.C. Lea, eds.), 1983, pp.164-191).

Boyce D.E. (ed.), Transportation Research: the State of the Art and Research Opportunities, **Transportation Research: Special Issue**, vol. 19A, 5/6, 1985, pp.349-542.

Campisi, D., Lotka-Volterra Models with Random Fluctuations for the Analysis of Oscillations in Urban and Metropolitan Areas, **Sistemi Urbani**, 2/3, 1986, pp.309-321.

Clarke, M. and A.G. Wilson, A Framework for Dynamic Comprehensive Urban Models: The Integration of Accounting and Microsimulation Approaches, **Sistemi Urbani**, no. 2/3, 1986, pp.145-177.

Dendrinos, D.S. Volterra-Lotka Ecological Dynamics, Gravitational Interaction and Turbulent Transportation: An Integration, Paper presented at the 35th North American Meeting of the Regional Science Association, Toronto, Canada, 1988.

Dendrinos, D.S., and H. Mullally, Evolutionary Patterns of Urban Populations, **Geographical Analysis**, vol. 13, no. 4, 1981, pp.328-344.

De Palma, A. and C. Lefèvre, The Theory of Deterministic and Stochastic Compart mental Models and its Applications: the State of the Art, **Sistemi Urbani**, no. 3, 1984, pp.281-323.

Domencich, T.A. and D. McFadden, **Urban Travel Demand: A Behavioural Analysis**, North-Holland, Amsterdam, 1975.

Florian M. and M. Gaudry, Transportation Systems Analysis: Illustrations and Extension of a Conceptual Framework, **Transportation Research**, vol. 17B, no. 2, 1983, pp.147-153.

Foot, D., Spatial Interaction Modelling, **Models in Urban Geography** (C.S. Yadav, ed.), Concept Publ., New Delhi, 1986, pp.51-69.

Fotheringham, A.S. and M.E. O'Kelly, **Spatial Interaction Models: Formulations and Applications**, Kluwer Academic Publishers, Dordrecht, 1989.

Haag G., Spatial Interaction Models and Their Micro Foundation, **Advances in Spatial Theory and Dynamics** (Andersson A.E., D.F. Batten, B. Johansson and P.Nijkamp, eds.), North-Holland, Amsterdam, 1989, pp.165-174.

Haag, G. and W. Weidlich, A Stochastic Theory of Interregional Migration, **Geograp hical Analysis**, vol. 16, 1984, pp.331-357.

Harris, B. and A.G. Wilson, Equilibrium Values and Dynamics of Attractiveness Ter ms in Production-Constrained Spatial Interaction Models, **Environment and Planning A**, vol. 10, 1978, pp.371-338.

Hyman, G.M., The Calibration of Trip Distribution Models, **Environment and Planning A**, vol. 1, 1969, pp.105-112.

Isard, W. and V.W. Maclaren, Storia e Stato Attuale delle Ricerche nella Scienza Regionale, **Problematiche dei Livelli Subregionali di Programmazione** (Bielli, M. and A. La Bella, eds.), Franco Angeli, Milano, 1982, pp.19-35.

May, R., Simple Mathematical Models with Very Complicated Dynamics, **Nature**, vol. 261, 1976, pp.459-467.

McFadden, D., Conditional Logit Analysis of Qualitative Choice Behaviour, **Frontiers in Econometrics** (P.Zarembka, ed.), Academic Press, New York, 1974, pp.105-142.

Nijkamp, P. and A. Reggiani, Dynamic Spatial Interaction Models: New Directions, **Environment and Planning A**, vol. 20, 1988a, pp.1449-1460.

Nijkamp, P. and A. Reggiani, Analysis of Dynamic Spatial Interaction Models by Means of Optimal Control, **Geographical Analysis**, vol. 20, no. 1, 1988b, pp.18-29.

Nijkamp, P. and A. Reggiani, Spatial Interaction and Discrete Choice: Statics and Dynamics, **Urban Dynamics and Spatial Choice Behaviour** (Hauer, J., H. Timmermans and N. Wrigley, eds.), Kluwer Academic Publishers, Dordrecht, 1989, pp.125-151.

Nijkamp, P. and A. Reggiani, Logit Models and Chaotic Behaviour: A New Perspective, **Environment and Planning A**, vol. 22, 1990a, pp.1455-1467.

Nijkamp, P. and A. Reggiani, An Evolutionary Approach to the Analysis of Dynamic Systems, with Special Reference to Spatial Interaction Models, **Sistemi Urbani**, vol. 1, 1990b, pp.95-112.

Nijkamp, P. and A. Reggiani, **Interaction, Evolution and Chaos in Space**, Springer-Verlag, Berlin, 1992.

Olsson, G., Explanation, Prediction and Meaning Variance: an Assessment of Distance Interaction Models, **Economic Geography**, vol. 46, 1970, pp.223-233.

Ravenstein, E.G., The Laws of Migration, **Journal of the Royal Statistical Society**, vol. 43, 1885, pp.167-235.

Reggiani, A. and S. Stefani, Aggregation in Decisionmaking: A Unifying Approach, **Environment and Planning A**, vol. 18, 1986, pp.1115-1125.

Reggiani, A. and S. Stefani, A New Approach to Model Split Analysis: Some Empirical Results, **Transportation Research B**, vol. 23, no. 1, 1989, pp.75-82.

Reiner, R., M. Munz, G. Haag and W. Weidlich, Chaotic Evolution of Migratory Systems, **Sistemi Urbani**, vol. 2/3, 1986, pp.285-308.

Rietveld, P., Infrastructure and Regional Development. A Survey of Multiregional Economic Models, **The Annals of Regional Science**, vol. 23, no. 4, 1989, pp.255-274

Weibull, J.W., An Axiomatic Approach to the Measurement of Accessibility, **Journal of Regional Science and Urban Economics**, vol. 6, 1976, pp.357-379.

Wilson, A.G., A Statistical Theory of Spatial Distribution Models, **Transportation Research**, vol. 1, 1967, pp.253-269.

Wilson, A.G., **Entropy in Urban and Regional Modelling**, Pion, London, 1970.

Wilson, A.G., **Catastrophe Theory and Bifurcation**, Croom Helm, London, 1981.

CHAPTER 17

SCHOLARY COMMUNICATION IN EUROPE STATED COMMUNICATION MEDIA CHOICE AND CONTACT DECISION MODELS BASED ON LABORATORY CHOICE EXPERIMENTS IN UNIVERSITIES

Manfred M. Fischer, Rico Maggi
and Christian Rammer

17.1 Introduction

The term **scholarly communication** has gained increasing acceptance over the past decades as an umbrella term covering a wide range of issues, including the refereeing and publication of journals and books, the use of informal systems for the exchange of ideas and information, the application of new technology to teaching, research and publishing, the governmental system of policies and regulations affecting scholarship, such as the funding of higher education and research, and restrictions on the free flow of information (see Morton and Price, 1989). Although scholars are the central figures in the system, surprisingly there is a significant lack of conceptual and operational models to explain how communication media choices are made and how knowledge based networks are formed. Research undertaken within the ESF-Network on European Communication and Transport Activity Research (NECTAR) made a modest attempt to fill this gap in pursuing three major objectives:

- **first**, to develop a conceptual framework and a methodology for analyzing the context-specific nature of communication behaviour at the individual level,
- **second**, to identify key factors and barriers influencing media choice and contact decision behaviour, and
- **finally**, to understand the role of cross-national differences in communication media choice behaviour in the function of communication networks.

The paper summarizes some of the major outcomes of these research activities. In contrast to earlier contributions by the authors (see Fischer et al., 1990, 1992) this paper relies on a much broader European data base, including information on academic scholars from nine universities located in Austria, Great Britain, The Netherlands and Switzerland.

For the study, universities have been chosen as focus of research mainly due to two reasons. First, there is an increasing proportion of knowledge makers in information societies. Universities play an important role in the production, dissemination and exchange of academic and scientific knowledge. Thus, a study of communication networks in a university setting may provide a model of the way professionals in other knowledge intensive fields function effectively. Second, we do not know the key factors determining the use of sophisticated telecommunication media (such as electronic mail), and resulting network developments. Such aspects are of utmost relevance in the academic community which relies so strongly on communication at large. Research collaboration across universities are intellectual resources (see Galegher et al., 1990).

The paper is organized as follows. In Section 17.2 the conceptual framework which underlies the study is set out. Section 17.3 outlines the methodology used in the enquiry. The methodology is based on a micro-level approach which combines discrete choice theory with laboratory choice experiments to develop stated media choice and contact decision models devised with following features: The models treat media choices and contact decisions as particular forms of discrete choices, they are based on the individual decision makers, they rely on experimental or stated (preference) data obtained from laboratory choice experiments rather than on revealed (preference) data, and they emphasize the influence of the decision context on choice formation. Empirical results of these models are presented in Section 17.4. Factors and barriers influencing communication media choice and contact decision behaviour as well as country specific variations are discussed in some detail. The final section presents some general conclusions.

17.2 The Framework

The main features of the conceptual framework which underlies the study of communication behaviour in academia is shown in Figure 1. It is a development of ideas first proposed by Moore and Jovanis (1988) and modified by Fischer et al. (1990, 1991). A key element of the integrated framework is the interaction of a department's supply of communication facilities (such as telephone, facsimile, electronic mail, physical mail media, courier services, etc.) with the demand for communication.

The demand for communication evolves from the organizational structure of the department including its objectives and ambitions (especially with respect to research) as well as formal and informal rules governing individual behaviour. Supply and demand result in the need for a certain quantity and type of communication activity. Most of the communication needs are met by communication within the existing contact network, either by using communication media or by travel to face-to-face meetings (conferences, workshops, seminars, etc.), while others may be satisfied only by establishing new direct contacts. An important feature of the conceptual framework is the feedback from communication outcomes to both the supply of communication facilities and the demand for communication.

In this paper major emphasis is laid on the media choice and the contact decision components of the conceptual framework. The media choice process is conceptualised as including the following stages (see Fischer et al., 1990):

- **First**, the communication initiator becomes aware of a need to communicate in a specific context. The initiator has individual characteristics (especially characteristics such as profession and status, age, keybord and typing skills, attitudes towards computer technology) and works in a department with specific characteristics (especially concerning cost control norms, media access and usage rules, etc.).
- **Second**, given the initiator's awareness of the communication context it is postulated that characteristics of the message to be communicated (such as its complexity, volume, urgency and confidentiality) and characteristics of the initiator-recipient relationship (such as status effects, location of the recipient, famili-

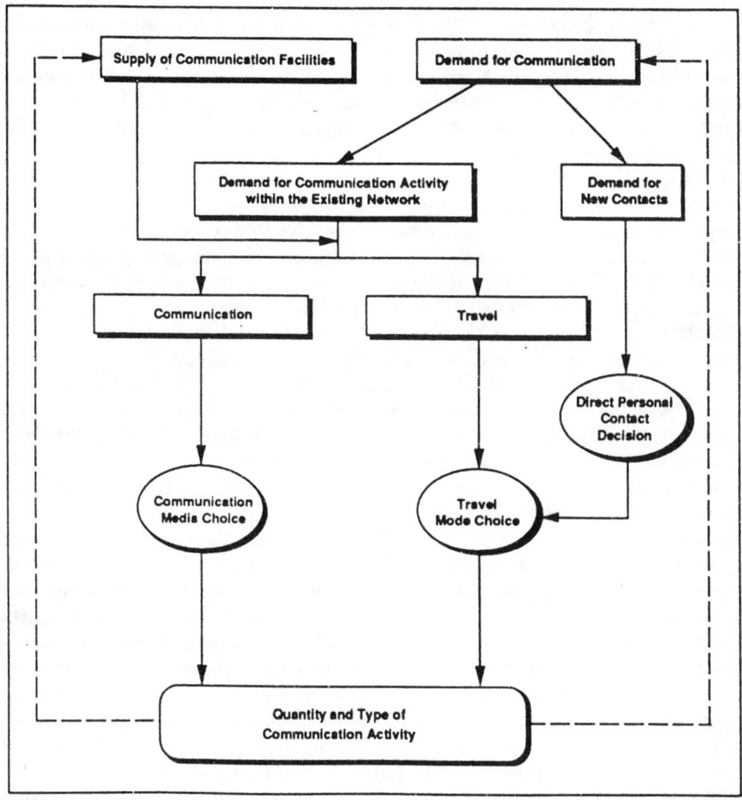

Figure 1 **Integrated framework for communication behaviour within a university setting**

arity with the recipient, awareness of recipient's media dislikes) influence the formation of communication media preference.

- **Third**, the initiator is assumed to have knowledge of the characteristics of the communication media. The conceptualisation focuses on perceptions and feelings related to media characteristics rather than objective characteristics (such as cost of use, accessibility, ease of use, reliability of time delivery, reliability of success delivery). The link between objective and perceived characteristics is very difficult to analyse and outside the scope of the study.
- **Finally**, there are three types of constraints acting on the preferences, namely institutional constraints, time and cost related constraints.

The contact decision component is conceptualized in a similar manner. Contact decision in this context refers to the situation where an individual (termed contact decision maker) decides on a possible new face-to-face contact which is conceived as a necessary, but not sufficient condition to extend his/her personal (knowledge based) contact network. The choice process is conceptualized as including the following stages (see Fischer et al., 1991):

- **First**, the contact decision maker becomes aware of a need to cooperate in a specific context and expects a productivity gain from cooperation with a potential contact partner, where awareness and expectations strongly depend upon his/her own stock of knowledge, research activities and ambitions. The decision maker has individual characteristics (such as profession and status, reputation, scientific ambitions, etc.) and works in a specific institutional environment. Two extreme types of institutional environments may be distinguished: Competitive environments with several incentives in which quality of academic output is rewarded, and bureaucratic environments where constraints rather than incentives dominate the scene and where the reward system is only loosely related to the quality of academic output. Thus, not only personal characteristics, but also the institutional setting may have strong implications for the formation of contact decision preferences in specific contexts.
- **Second**, given the academic's awareness of the contact decision context it is assumed that he/she evaluates the fellow scholar's knowledge potential in relation to his/her own human capital stock. Consequently, individual characeristics of the potential contact person (such as his/her reputation in the academic field, his/her professional status, but also his/her language skills) as well as the reputation of the institution with which he/she is associated, and additionally the attractivity of the city in which the institution is located may be considered as important factors influencing the formation of contact decision preferences.
- **Third**, the contact decision is assumed to depend not only upon the contact decision maker's own knowledge potential, but also upon the knowledge accessible in his/her existing personal contact network. Personal contact networks are conceived as informal immaterial knowledge-based networks where nodes represent academic scholars and links personal relationships.
- **Finally**, the decision maker is subject to restrictions which relate to rules and norms (culture) of the institution in general, refer to time and cost budgets allo-

cated to travel by the decision maker and the academic's level of mobility in particular.

The refinement and empirical testing of the two components of the integrated framework will be achieved via the development of stated communication media choice and contact decision models.

17.3 Methodology: Stated Choice Modelling and Experimental Design

The development of media choice contact decisions models is based on a micro-level approach which combines discrete choice theory with laboratory choice experiments based on design theory.

17.3.1 Revealed versus stated choice models

Much recent progress in the field of behavioural modelling relates with discrete choice models, their extension and refinement, experimental work with decompositional preference models, and the creation of statistical procedures for better inference (see Fischer et al., 1990). The development of empirical random utility choice models consists of estimating and testing a parametrically specified model using data on choices made by a sample of individuals, attributes of the decision makers, and characteristics of the choice options among which the choices are made (see, for more details, Hensher and Johnson, 1981; Ben-Akiva and Lerman, 1985; Fischer and Nijkamp, 1985).

The data may come from either of two sources. One source is observations of choices made by individuals in real environments. The second source is observations of choices made by individuals in laboratory choice experiments carried out in hypothetical choice environments (see Horowitz and Louvière, 1990; Louvière and Timmermans, 1990; Wardman 1988; Louvière and Woodworth, 1983). The data obtained from observations of choices in real environments are called **revealed (preference) data** and choice models based on such data **revealed choice models**, while data obtained from laboratory choice experiments are termed **experimental** or **stated (preference) data** and choice models based on such data **stated choice models**.

Revealed choice and stated choice models have complementary advantages and disadvantages. Revealed choice models have high face validity in that they are callibrated to real data while stated choice models based on scenario responses have lower face validity in that choices are made in hypothetical choice environments. Revealed data, however, are uncontrolled and, thus, may suffer from collinearity and limited ranges of variations of variables. These conditions often make it difficult to identify the separate effects of individual variables on choice (see Horowitz and Louvière, 1990). Such difficulties can be greatly mitigated by stated choice models. Choice experiments control or eliminate collinearity. There is no problem in extending the ranges of variable to include values beyond those currently observed in real environments (see Horowitz and Louvière, 1990).

17.3.2 The stated choice modelling approach

Stated choice models owe their current popularity to two major sources: The development and refinement of random utility based discrete choice theory, and significant advances in the design of statistical experiments that allow to analyse individual decisions under rigorously controlled conditions (see, for example, Louvière and Timmermans, 1990; Wardman, 1988; Louvière, 1988; Louvière and Hensher, 1983).

The stated choice modelling approach is used in this study because there are significant difficulties in collecting data on observed choices for a consistent set of communication activities. Unlike travel choices which are made relatively infrequently, an individual may make many separate communication decisions per day. Acquiring detailed information on each choice implies enormous data analysis resources and time commitments from participants (see Moore and Jovanis, 1988). From a theoretical perspective, stated and revealed random utility choice models share common theoretical underpinnings. Both assume that individuals arrive at some choice by integrating partsworth utilities associated with the attribute levels of choice options according to simple decision rules.

Let us assume that the preferences of an individual in the laboratory environment can be described by a utility function **U** which depends on attributes of both the available choice options and the individual. Let $\mathbf{x}_{ia}$ denote the vector of attributes of the individual **i** and the alternative **a** relevant to choice task at issue, and **A** the choice set. An individual maximizes its utility by choosing the alternative with the highest utility $\mathbf{u}_{ia}$. Thus, choice alternative $\mathbf{a} \in \mathbf{A}$ is chosen if $\mathbf{U(x_{ia}) > U(x_{ib})}$ for all $\mathbf{b} \in \mathbf{A}, \mathbf{b} \neq \mathbf{a}$.

If the utility functions and attribute vectors would be known with certainty, choice could be predicted with certainty. But in practice this never occurs due to several reasons. For example, an individual's preferences may vary from one choice occasion to another due to uncertainty by the individual about his preferences, mistakes caused by poor concentration, etc. The standard procedure for dealing with this kind of problems is to express the utility function as the sum of a systematic component accounting for the systematic effects on preferences and a random component accounting for random variation in preferences and any attributes that participants in the experiment input to the alternatives (see Horowitz and Louvière, 1990). Mathematically, the utility $\mathbf{u}_{ia}$ for individual **i** and alternative **a** may be written as

$$\mathbf{u}_{ia} = \mathbf{V}(\mathbf{x}_{ia},\Theta) + \epsilon_{ia} \tag{1}$$

where **V** is the systematic component of utility, ϵ_{ia} is a vector of observed characteristics of individual **i** and alternative **a**, and Θ a vector of parameters.

In stated - like in revealed - random utility choice models, choice cannot be predicted deterministically because the utilities are random. Rather, stated random utility models predict the probabilities that a particular choice option is chosen, conditional on the observed atrributes. Let $\mathbf{P(a \mid x_{ia},\Theta,A)}$ denote the probability that a randomly selected individual **i** chooses alternative $\mathbf{a} \in \mathbf{A}$ in the laboratory environment given the attribute vector $\mathbf{x}_{ia}$ and choice set **A**. Then

$$\mathbf{P}(a \mid \mathbf{x}_{ia},\Theta,A) = \Pr(V(\mathbf{x}_{ia},\Theta)+\epsilon_{ia}>V(\mathbf{x}_{ib},\Theta)+\epsilon_{ib}, \text{ for } b\neq a;a,b\in A). \tag{2}$$

The choice probabilities $\mathbf{P}(a \mid \mathbf{x}_{ia},\Theta,A)$ depend on the joint probability distribution of the random components of utility. Different distributions generate different choice functions.

An explicit functional relation between the choice probabilities and the deterministic components of utility can be obtained if the probability distribution of the random components are known or assumed. The simplest assumption that leads to useful stated choice models is that the random terms of the laboratory utility function are independently and identically (IID) distributed with the Gumbel Type I extreme value distribution $\mathbf{F}(\epsilon)=\exp(-\exp(-\epsilon))$. The choice probabilities are then related to the deterministic component of utility through the well-known multinominal logit (MNL) model

$$\mathbf{P}(a \mid \mathbf{x}_{ia},\Theta,A)=\exp(V(\mathbf{x}_{ia},\Theta))/\sum_{b\in A}\exp(V(\mathbf{x}_{ib},\Theta))=:\mathbf{P}_{ia} \tag{3}$$

In this paper, the function **V** is specified to be linear in the set of unknown parameters Θ that are estimated by fitting the choice function to experimental data, that is

$$V(\mathbf{x}_{ia},\Theta) = \Theta_{oa} + \sum_{k=1}^{K} \Theta_k \, x_{iak} \tag{4}$$

where Θ_k is the **k**-th component of Θ, x_{iak} the **k**-th component $\mathbf{x}_{ia}$, and Θ_{oa} the alternative-specific constant for alternative **a**.

17.3.3 Questionnaire and laboratory choice experiments

In this study the data collection was done in survey form and consisted of four sections of interest:

- an **introductory section**, in which respondents were asked to provide relevant background information (socio-economic characteristics, availability and use of communication media, perceptions of and feelings about the media, etc.),
- a **media choice experiment**, in which respondents were asked to indicate communication media choices for hypothetical scenarios where conventional communication services (physical mail media, courier services), traditional telecommunication services (telephone and telex) and new electronic telecommunication services (facsimile and electronic mail) were alternatives to complete information communication tasks,
- a **contact decision experiment**, in which respondents were asked to indicate contact decisions (i.e. decisions whether to establish a new face-to-face contact

which is conceived as a necessary, but not sufficient condition to extend their personal knowledge-based contact-networks) for hypothetical scenarios, and a **current behaviour section** in which respondents were asked to supply information about their current knowledge-based communication networks.

The design of the experiments is outlined in Fischer et al. (1990, 1991) and will not be repeated in great detail here. With four key variables (confidentiality of communication, urgency of communication, complexity of the content of communication and volume of the message, each with two predefined levels) used in the design of the media choice experiments, a 2^4 fractorial design was selected, with 8 units of 2 each. This meant that each questionnaire contained two media choice experiments designed such that there is no correlation between the context variables and the characteristics of the individual. Concerning the contact decision experiment, the location of the potential contact partner with five predefined attribute levels, his/her reputation (two levels), his/her professional status (two levels) and his/her language skills (two levels) were incorporated into a (reduced) fractional factorial design with 32 different hypothetical choice evironments (16 units of 2 each) (see Fischer et al., 1991). Thus, each simulation section contained only two different scenarios. In this way the so-called problem of 'respondent fatigue' may be avoided which refers to factors such as learning, boredom, or anchoring to earlier choice tasks and might distort the measurements (see Bates, 1988).

Choice designs are difficult to control if self-administered. Thus, face-to-face interviews were conducted to ensure that the choice tasks were fully understood. Interviews lasted for between twenty minutes and thirty-five minutes. Identical surveys were undertaken at three Austrian universities (University of Vienna, Technical University of Vienna, Vienna University of Economics and Business Administration) and at two Swiss universities (University of Zürich, Swiss Federal Institute of Technology at Zürich) between November 1989 and February 1990. Due to organizational problems the Swiss Federal Institute of Technology survey could be accomplished only in 1991 (January to March). Virtually identical surveys were carried out by Piet Rietveld and Hans Ouwersloot at two Dutch universities (University of Amsterdam, Free University Amsterdam), by Kenneth Button at the Loughborough University (both in spring 1991) and by Peter J.B. Brown at The University of Liverpool (summer and autumn 1991). In the Dutch and British surveys the contact decision section of the questionnaire was skipped.

The sample design used for all the university surveys relied on exogenous stratification. The dimensions for stratification were the status of the subject (full professor and assistant professor/lecturer) and the discipline (natural sciences; social and economic sciences, and humanities; engineering). The sampling fractions were chosen to be equal to the population shares. The drawing of observations out of each stratum was done randomly (see Table 1). It is worthwhile to note that the sample likelihood of this proportionately stratified sample reduces to that of random sampling and greatly facilitates the maximum likelihood estimation of stated choice models (see Fischer et al., 1990; Ben-Akiva and Lerman, 1985; Lerman and Manski, 1979). The surveys produced a total of 616 questionnaires generating 1669 media choice observations and 618 contact decision observations.

Table 1 Proportionate stratified samples of academics in nine European universities

University	Target Population (Sample Size)	Uniform Sampling Fractions in Strata						Choice Experiments Repeated Measurements on Individuals	
		A	B	C	D	E	F		
		(in per cent)						Media Choice	Contact Decision
Austria									
Univ. of Vienna	540 (75)	17.0	29.4	- -	50.6	22.0	- -	2	2
Technical Univ. of Vienna	699 (82)	12.6	3.1	10.2	35.2	7.2	31.7	2	2
Vienna Univ. of Economics and Business Administration	202 (31)	- -	25.2	- -	- -	74.8	- -	2	2
Switzerland									
Univ. of Zurich	931 (55)	13.3	8.4	- -	48.1	30.2	- -	2	2
Swiss Federal Institute of Technology Zurich	1226 (66)	8.4	- -	- -	91.6	- -	- -	2	2
Great Britain									
Loughborough Univ.	501 (77)	2.8	8.2	8.0	12.6	34.3	34.1	4	-
The Univ. of Liverpool	577 (81)	10.2	3.4	9.0	26.2	39.9	11.3	2	-
The Netherlands									
Univ. of Amsterdam	115 (50)	- -	20.0	- -	- -	80.0	- -	4	-
Free Univ. Amsterdam	441 (99)	3.5	12.2	- -	17.2	67.1	- -	4	-

A: Full Professors in Natural Sciences
B: Full Professors in Economic and Social Sciences, and Humanities
C: Full Professors in Engineering
D: Other Academics in Natural Sciences
E: Other Academics in Economic and Social Sciences, and Humanities
F: Other Academics in Engineering

17.4 Model Estimation and Results

Börsch-Supan's HLOGIT program was used to estimate the stated choice models. HLOGIT estimates maximum likelihood parameters, utilizing a Marquardt-type modified Newton-Raphson procedure. Three scalar measures of performance on fit were used: Rho-squared (at market shares) and the adjusted rho-squared (at market shares) indicate how well the model at issue explains preferences relative to the so-called market shares model where all parameters in the stated choice model except the alternative-specific constants are set to zero; and the prediction success which measures the percentage of correct ex-post predictions.

17.4.1 The stated media choice model

The stated media choice model developed emphasizes the influence of the context of the communication activity on media choice. Media characteristics are explicitly considered, along with variables characterising the communication activity itself. Two types of variables enter the indirect utility function U. The **first type** (uncontrolled interpersonal variables) attempts to measure the influence of feelings about the perceptions of communication media characteristics. The generic variable and familiarity with the communication media and the alternative-specific variable (perceived) accessibility specific to e-mail are included. The **second type** of variables refers to characteristics of the communication context, such as the context-specific variables confidentiality and volume of communication as well as urgency and complexity of communication.

The model was empirically tested using experimental data obtained from the media choice experiment (see Section 18.3), in which physical mail media, courier services, telephone, facsimile and electronic mail were choice alternatives to complete information communication tasks. Physical mail media has deliberately been chosen as the base alternative serving as a base (or origin) of the utility scale. With the availability of the British and Dutch surveys carried out in 1991, the empirical database could be greatly broadened in comparison to earlier papers of the authors (see Fischer et al., 1990, 1992).

Table 2 presents coefficient estimates, asymptotic t-statistics and summary statistics of the model. The country-specific results relying on national segments of the data are summarized in table 3. The model achieves a high prediction accuracy in terms of all three measures of fit in spite of the simple specification. The rho-squared-values, for example, range from 0.28 (British stratum) to 0.44 (Dutch stratum). All the coefficients have the anticipated sign. Positive (negative) coefficients reflect positive (negative) marginal utilities.

Analysis of the media perceptions showed that physical mail media, with 38.1 percent of the preferences, was the dominant communication medium. Facsimile was preferred in 27.6 percent and telephone in 17.9 percent of the cases, while courier services (10.5 percent) and especially electronic mail (5.9 percent) were preferred relatively infrequently. However, there were significant cross-national variations in preferences as indicated in table 3.

Table 2 Coefficient estimates for communication media choice

Variable	Generic or Alternative Specific to	Parameter Estimate	t-Value
Familiarity with the Communication Media	generic	0.36	8.24*
Accessibility to the Media (1 if located in the organisational unit, 0 otherwise)	electronic mail	0.85	2.07*
Confidentiality of the Message (1 if confidential, 0 otherwise)	courier services	1.07	2.01*
	telephone	0.10	0.36
	facsimile	-1.71	-7.11*
	electronic mail	-0.76	-1.00
Urgency of the Message (1 if urgent, 0 otherwise)	courier services	3.81	5.59*
	telephone	3.41	9.84*
	facsimile	4.09	13.97*
	electronic mail	2.93	4.21*
Complexity of the Message (1 if complex, 0 otherwise)	courier services	-0.33	-1.29
	telephone	-2.87	-7.84*
	facsimile	0.06	0.31
	electronic mail	-1.13	-2.83*
Volume of the Message (1 if long, 0 otherwise)	courier services	1.09	3.69*
	telephone	-3.82	-5.20*
	facsimile	0.04	0.16
	electronic mail	-0.36	-1.22
Alternative Specific Constant	courier services	-3.30	-6.84*
	telephone	-0.31	-1.28
	facsimile	-0.89	-3.19*
	electronic mail	-1.66	-4.09*
Log-Likelihood at Zero		-2686.15	
Log-Likelihood at Constant		-2329.40	
Log-Likelihood at Convergence		-1496.12	
Rho Squared at Market Shares (adjusted)		0.36 (0.35)	
Prediction Success (in %)		68.2	
Stated (Predicted) Media Preferences (in %):			
Courier Services		10.5 (11.8)	
Telephone		17.9 (20.1)	
Facsimile		27.6 (24.0)	
Electronic Mail		5.9 (0.1)	
Physical Mail Media		38.1 (44.0)	
Number of Observations		1669	

* Significant at the 0.05 level

Table 3 Coefficient estimates of the stated communication media model by country (t-values in parentheses)

Variable	Generic or Alternative Specific to	Strata: Austria (Vienna)	Netherlands (Amsterdam)	Great Britain (Liverpool, Loughborough)	Switzerland (Zurich)
Familiarity with the Communication Media	generic	0.38 (4.36)*	0.40 (-4.77)*	0.34 (4.41)*	0.37 (3.43)*
Accessibility to the Media (1 if located in the organisational unit, 0 otherwise)	electronic mail	1.93 (2.99)*	1.08 (1.93)	0.42 (1.27)	1.07 (1.36)
Confidentiality of the Message (1 if confidential,0 otherwise)	courier services	0.72 (1.19)	1.04 (2.41)*	1.02 (1.87)	0.70 (0.84)
	telephone	1.48 (3.28)*	0.06 (0.16)	-1.00 (-1.77)	0.59 (0.97)
	facsimile	-1.88 (-4.32)*	-2.06 (-5.97)*	-1.61 (-4.45)*	-2.31 (-3.05)*
	electronic mail	-1.18 (-2.25)*	-0.36 (-0.78)	-1.05 (-1.26)	-0.46 (-0.60)
Urgency of the Message (1 if urgent,0 otherwise)	courier services	4.34 (6.43)*	4.63 (10.04)*	3.54 (6.54)*	3.62 (4.24)*
	telephone	3.61 (7.25)*	3.45 (7.89)*	4.49 (6.96)*	2.57 (3.73)*
	facsimile	4.51 (9.87)*	4.53 (12.18)*	4.07 (9.13)*	5.49 (6.06)*
	electronic mail	2.82 (5.40)*	3.30 (6.55)*	3.30 (5.04)*	2.32 (3.26)*
Complexity of the Message (1 if complex, 0 otherwise)	courier services	0.52 (0.95)	-0.37 (-0.96)	-0.60 (-1.46)	0.65 (0.88)
	telephone	-3.45 (-6.91)*	-3.95 (-8.10)*	-1.76 (-3.52)*	-3.62 (-5.14)*
	facsimile	0.59 (1.39)	0.24 (0.74)	-0.17 (-0.56)	1.03 (1.82)
	electronic mail	-1.85 (-3.60)*	-1.30 (-2.63)*	-0.59 (-1.01)	-0.37 (-0.61)
Volume of the Message (1 if long, 0 otherwise)	courier services	1.68 (2.28)*	0.97 (2.31)*	1.63 (3.34)*	1.06 (1.32)
	telephone	-5.54 (-7.81)*	-4.93 (-6.54)*	-2.61 (-3.85)*	-3.40 (-4.96)*
	facsimile	0.59 (1.33)	0.25 (0.74)	-0.17 (-0.56)	1.14 (1.82)
	electronic mail	-0.55 (-1.09)	0.05 (0.10)	-0.41 (-0.58)	-0.71 (-1.15)
Alternative Specific Constant	courier services	-4.93 (-4.92)*	-3.47 (-5.14)*	-2.64 (-3.30)*	-4.68 (-4.01)*
	telephone	-0.28 (-0.76)	-0.03 (-0.11)	-1.01 (-1.66)	-0.37 (-0.77)
	facsimile	-1.89 (-3.40)*	-1.36 (-3.42)*	0.18 (0.53)	-4.50 (-4.30)*
	electronic mail	-1.61 (-2.16)*	-2.52 (-3.37)*	-1.38 (-1.92)	-2.42 (-2.85)*
Log-Likelihood at Zero		-597.10	-957.62	-748.39	-383.04
Log-Likelihood at Constant		-538.56	-844.20	-647.62	-312.56
Log-Likelihood at Convergence		-287.52	-454.93	-443.74	-191.78
Rho Squared at Market Shares (adjusted)		0.47 (0.43)	0.46 (0.44)	0.31 (0.28)	0.39 (0.32)
Prediction Success (in %)		71.2	71.6	65.2	69.3
Stateded (Predicted) Media Preferences (in %):					
Courier Services		7.5 (8.9)	12.4 (16.5)	12.3 (7.7)	7.1 (6.3)
Telephone		23.2 (27.5)	17.5 (21.0)	11.6 (9.3)	22.7 (26.0)
Facsimile		24.0 (20.8)	25.4 (21.2)	30.1 (36.8)	28.5 (20.2)
Electronic Mail		8.4 (4.0)	4.5 (0.0)	4.5 (2.2)	8.4 (2.5)
Physical Mail Services		36.9 (38.8)	40.2 (41.3)	33.5 (46.0)	43.3 (45.0)
Number of Observations		371	595	465	238

* Significant at the 0.05 level

Tables 2 and 3 clearly indicate the influence of context on preferences for communication media through varying levels of significance and magnitude of the parameter estimates of the explanatory variables. The first media characteristic attempts to measure the influence of accessibility to electronic mail as perceived by the recipients. This alternative specific variable is significant, highly significant for Austrian scholars and least for British and Swiss scholars. The second media characteristic, familiarity with the communication media, is strongly significant in all strata, but much less important compared to communication context variables. To gain some intuition for the magnitudes of the coefficient, and measure the effects of this explanatory variable on media choice separately, the elasticities $\partial \log (P_{ia}) / \partial \log (x_{ia})$ were calculated. Familiarity elasticities refer to a percentage change of the fraction of individuals choosing a medium when the variable familiarity of each individual with this medium is raised by 1 unit. Concerning electronic mail and facsimile, the following patterns emerge: The probability that an individual will choose facsimile (electronic mail) increases from 0.343 (0.058) to 0.428 (0.111). The elasticities in the rarely chosen alternative electronic mail are of very large magnitude. As a regional pattern, the stratum of British scholars is at least familiarity-responsive with respect to electronic mail.

The **context variables** have an important influence on preference formation. One major substantial result is the significance of and the great weight given to the alternative-specific urgency variables in all strata. The complexity variables are much less significant. Only complexity of the communication activity specific to telephone is (highly) significant and important in all countries considered. The negative signs of the parameter estimates indicate a decrease in the odds of choosing telephone if the message is complex. Complexity specific to electronic mail shows a significant and negative effect only in the Austrian and Dutch samples. Volume of the message (specific to telephone) has - in accordance with a priori expectations - a strongly negative effect, regardless of the different national environments. Confidentiality specific to facsimile has a significant and negative influence across all countries while confidentiality specific to electronic mail is significant only in the Austrian case, with a negative effect. The coefficients point to the existence of barriers to communication. Barriers can be diagnosed for transmitting complex messages via telephone or electronic mail. The extra time-cost incurred in the case of using these media for complex communication tasks results in a negative shift in utility. The same holds true in the case of using the telephone for long messages (the example used in the experimental design was a 10-pages paper). Another barrier can be diagnosed for the transmission of confidential messages via facsimile and electronic mail. Again significant user costs occur, if one wants to make sure that the recipient gets the message confidentially.

The empirical results clearly indicate that communication media choice behaviour is very context-dependent. Several cross-national differences in choice behaviour indicated through varying levels of significance and magnitude of the parameter estimates could be identified. **First**, the media characteristic accessibility to electronic mail was found to be important in explaining preferences in Austrian universities rather than in British and Swiss universities. **Second**, complexity of the communication activity (specific to telephone) is a highly significant variable with a strong and negative effect in all countries considered, while complexity specific to electronic mail shows a significant and negative effect only in the strata of Austrian and Dutch scholars. **Third**, confidentiality specific to facsimile has a strong negative influence on preference formation in all national contexts, but confidentiality specific to courier services only in the Dutch universities, and confidentiality specific to telephone and specific to electronic mail only in the stratum of Austrian scholars.

17.4.2 The stated decision model

The stated contact decision model developed emphasizes the influence of the decision context on contact decision. Individual and organizational characteristics of the decision maker are explicity considered, along with variables characterising the potential contact person and his/her location. Three types of variables enter the indirect utility function. The **first type** attempts to measure the effect of individual and institutional characteristics of the contact decision maker. Basically the variables included reflect the differences in preferences for establishing a new direct contact as a function of age interacting with the professional status, the technical orientation, and cooperation incentives (measured in terms of contact intensity) of the organizational environment. The **second type** of variables measures the influence of the existing knowledge-based contact network of the decision maker on the contact decision. The **third type** of variables refers to context specific variables. A first subgroup relates to individual characteristics of the potential contact person, such as his/her professional status, his/her reputation and his/her language skills. A second subgroup of context specific variables including travel costs and location specific dummies measure locational characteristics as well as barriers to establish a new contact. For the five locations (Munich, Prague (in the case of the Austrian stratum)/Paris (in the case of the Swiss stratum), Lisbon, Los Angeles, Tokyo) used in the scenarios four location specific dummies (excluding Munich) have been constructed which take the value 0 if the perceived costs are prohibitive for realising a contact with a scholar at the corresponding location, and the value 1 otherwise. The location specific dummies may be viewed to reflect the perceived attractiveness of the contact place in face of cost considerations.

The stated binary logit model was empirically tested using experimental data from the contact decision experiment (see section 17.3.3) in which respondents were asked to indicate contact decisions (yes/no) for a number of hypothetical scenarios. The contact decision experiments were undertaken only in the Austrian and Swiss university surveys.

Table 4 presents coefficient estimates, asymptotic t-statistics and summary statistics of the model. The country-specific results relying on the Austrian and Swiss segments of the data are summarized in Table 5. With an adjusted rho-squared (at market shares) of 0.25 and a prediction success of 77.7% the model performs reasonably well in spite of the simple specification. The model performs much better in the stratum of Austrian scholars (rho-squared: 0.33, prediction success: 80.3%) than in the stratum of Swiss scholars. All the significant coefficients have the anticipated sign. Positive (negative) coefficients reflect positive (negative) marginal utilities.

Table 4 Coefficient estimates for contact decision

Variable	Parameter Estimate	t-Value
Individual Characteristics of the Contact Decision Maker		
Age and Status (1 if older than 50 years and full professor, 0 otherwise)	-0.77	-2.58*
Individual Knowledge-Based Contact Network		
Orientation (1 if international, 0 otherwise)	0.97	4.46*
Organisational Environment of the Contact Decision Maker		
Co-operation Incentives (average contact intensity)	0.19	2.19*
Institutes of Technology (1 if school of technology, 0 otherwise)	-0.71	-2.77*
Characteristics of the Potential Contact Person		
Professional Status (1 if full professor, 0 otherwise)	0.24	1.17
Reputation (1 if high, 0 if low)	0.63	3.11*
Language Skills (1 if perfect in English or German, 0 otherwise)	0.79	3.34*
Location of the Potential Contact Person and Perceived Attractiveness of the Place		
Prague (Austrian strata)/Paris (Swiss strata)	1.59	4.82*
Lisbon	2.49	6.61*
Los Angeles	4.00	6.31*
Tokyo	6.07	7.16*
Travel Costs	-0.29	-5.63*
Alternative-Specific Constant	-2.06	-3.63*
Log-Likelihood at Zero	-428.37	
Log-Likelihood at Constant	-415.84	
Log-Likelihood at Convergence	-300.15	
Rho-Squared at Market Shares (adjusted)	0.28 (0.25)	
Prediction Success (in %)	77.7	
Stated (Predicted) Positive Contact Decisions	60.0 (74.6)	
Number of Observations	618	

* Significant at the 0.05 level

Table 5 clearly indicates the influence of different institutional environments in Austria and Switzerland for the contact decision through varying levels of significance of the variables characterising the contact decision maker and his/her institution. International orientation of the personal knowledge-based contact network is the only variable belonging to the first type of variables which is significant in both, the Austrian and Swiss strata. This variable, however, gets a considerably greater weight in the Austrian case. All the other individual and institutional characteristics are only significant in the stratum of the Austrian scholars. Age interacting with the professional status negatively influences the contact decision behaviour. Full professors older than 50 years are less likely to realise a new contact. Technical orientation of the university has a strong negative influence. This may look strange at the first glance, but can be explained by the fact that scholars in the engineering field tend to be strongly nationally oriented and if internationally then primarily towards German speaking countries. Cooperation incentives have a significant positive influence. In the Swiss stratum there is a negative effect which is, however, insignificant at the 0.05 level.

Table 5 Coefficient estimates of the stated preference contact decision model by country (t-values in parentheses)

Variable	Strata			
	Austria (Vienna)		Switzerland (Zurich)	
Individual Characteristics of the Contact Decision Maker				
Age and Status (1 if older than 50 years and full professor, 0 otherwise)	-0.95	(-2.46)*	-0.54	(-0.97)
Individual Knowledge-Based Contact Network				
Orientation (1 if international, 0 otherwise)	1.22	(4.05)*	0.67	(1.97)
Organisational Environment of the Contact Decision Maker				
Co-operation Incentives (average contact intensity)	0.74	(2.24)*	-1.70	(-1.35)
Institutes of Technology (1 if school of technology, 0 otherwise)	-2.52	(-2.59)*	0.14	(0.24)
Characteristics of the Potential Contact Person				
Professional Status (1 if full professor, 0 otherwise)	0.16	(0.59)	0.22	(0.98)
Reputation (1 if high, 0 if low)	0.54	(1.91)	0.80	(2.50)*
Language Skills (1 if perfect in English or German, 0 otherwise)	0.65	(2.03)*	0.79	(2.00)*
Location of the Potential Contact Person and Perceived Attractiveness of the Place				
Prague (Austrian strata)/Paris (Swiss strata	0.88	(1.99)*	2.22	(3.79)*
Lisbon	5.20	(2.86)*	4.55	(2.47)*
Los Angeles	9.99	(2.95)*	8.00	(2.15)*
Tokyo	13.73	(2.80)*	13.97	(2.36)*
Travel Costs	-0.69	(-2.63)*	-0.90	(-2.16)*
Alternative-Specific Constant	-4.56	(-2.32)*	8.29	(1.31)
Log-Likelihood at Zero	-260.63		-167.74	
Log-Likelihood at Constant	-255.15		-160.23	
Log-Likelihood at Convergence	-158.48		-119.40	
Rho-Squared at Market Shares (adjusted)	0.38	(0.33)	0.25	(0.17)
Prediction Success (in %)	80.3		75.6	
Stated (Predicted) Positive Contact Decisions	58.5	(70.2)	62.4	(75.2)
Number of Observations	376		242	

* Significant at the 0.05 level

The decision context variables show an important effect on preference formation, across the two countries. The variables appear to be much more important than the individual and organizational characteristics of the contact decision maker and his/her organizational environment. The travel cost variable is highly significant, has the expected negative sign, and is rather robust across the two strata. The same is true for the location specific dummies where considerably greater weight is given to Tokyo as contact place, followed by Los Angeles, Lisbon and finally Prague/Paris. The relatively low parameter value of Prague (Austian stratum) evidently points to the barrier of the iron curtain which was still present at the time of the survey. Language skills are found to be important characteristics of the potential contact partner which positively influence the contact decision. His/her professional status - in contrast to the reputation - does not play a significant role at all.

In summary, the results clearly indicate the importance of the context variables in general and in particular the importance of the location specific dummies reflecting the perceived attractiveness of specific contact places in different cultural regions, the cost variable, as well as the language skills and the reputation of the potential contact partner. Several cross-national differences in decision behaviour were identified. **First,** international orientation of the personal knowledge-based contact network and cooperation incentives of the institutional environment were found to be important in explaining preference formation of Austrian scholars. In the Swiss stratum considerably less weight is given to the first variable, while the second one shows even a negative, but very weak influence. **Second,** the individual characteristics older than 50 years and full professor as well as the technical orientation of the organizational environment negatively influence the contact decision in Austrian universities, while they are insignificant in Swiss academia. **Finally,** the reputation of the potential contact person or in other words the expected increase in the knowledge potential associated with a new link in the personal contact network tends to have a stronger effect on preference formation of Swiss than Austrian scholars.

17.5 Summary and Conclusions

The paper makes a modest attempt to develop a conceptual framework and a methodology for analyzing the context-specific nature of communication behaviour at the individual level. Two particular forms of communication are dealt with: communication media choice and contact decision behaviour in academia. The methodology suggested is based on a micro-level approach which combines discrete choice theory with laboratory choice experiments to develop stated media choice and contact decision models devised by the following features: the models treat media choices and contact decisions as particular forms of discrete choices, they are based on the individual decision maker rather than on aggregates, they rely on stated (preference) rather than on revealed (preference) data.

Stated choice models owe their current popularity to two major sources: the development and refinement of random utility choice theory, and significant advances in the design of statistical experiments which allow to analyse individual decisions under rigorously controlled conditions. From a theoretical perspective, stated and revealed choice models share common theoretical underpinnings. Both assume that individuals arrive at some choice by integrating partsworth utilities associated with the attribute levels of choice options according to simple decision rules (see Louvière and Timmermans, 1990). The main difference lies in the way data are collected and analyzed. Revealed choice models are based on strong assumptions among individuals, errors in variables, correlations among the random explanatory variables, etc. Stated choice models are more flexible because one can control for many of these problems which occur with observational data. One major caveat of stated choice models, however, needs to be mentioned: the problem of external validity. In contrast to revealed choice models stated ones suffer from lower prima facie validity in that choices are made in hypothetical rather than in real choice environments.

The data were obtained from laboratory media choice and contact decision experiments carried out in nine universities (Austria: University of Vienna, Technical University of Vienna, Vienna University of Economics and Business Administration; The Netherlands: University of Amsterdam, Free University Amsterdam; Great Britain: Loughborough University, The University of Liverpool; Switzerland: University of Zürich, Swiss Federal Institute of Technology at Zürich). Four contextual variables were incorporated into fractional factorial designs with 16 different hypothetical media choices and 32 different hypothetical contact decision environments, respectively. The sample design for the surveys relied on proportionate exogenous stratification. With this sample design the maximum likelihood estimation of the stated choice models could be greatly facilitated.

The models perform well in terms of fit and prediction accuracy. The signs of the coefficient estimates have a fairly stable pattern across the countries considered. This gives us confidence in the robustness of the models and the validity of our conclusions. Significant variations in the levels of significance and magnitude of the explanatory variables provided evidence of the strong influence the context has on media choices and contact decisions.

The results demonstrate that an experimental design approach to communication behaviour analysis can yield sensible and useful results when combined with discrete choice models such as the MNL model approach. When revealed data are lacking, suspect, or otherwise deficient, laboratory choice experiments represent an attractive alternative to revealed choice analysis.

Acknowledgement

The work in this chapter forms part of a wider study, generously funded by the 'Fonds zur Förderung der wissenschaftlichen Forschung' (P7516). We are extremely grateful to our colleagues and friends Peter J.B. Brown, Kenneth J. Button, Hans Ouwersloot and Piet Rietveld for their cooperation in the joint venture of undertaking the surveys and for permission to use their records of survey data, as well as to all members of the NECTAR-Core Area 'Barriers to Communication' for helpful comments and suggestions on our research efforts. The views expressed and any errors in this chapter, however, remain our own.

References

Bates, J., Econometric Issues in Stated Preference Analysis, **Journal of Transport Economics and Policy**, vol. 22, 1988, pp.59-69.

Batten, D.F., K.Koboyashi and A.F.Anderson, Knowledge, Nodes and Networks: An Analytical Perspective, Working Paper 19, CERUM, University of Umea, 1988.

Ben-Akiva, M. and S.R.Lerman, **Discrete Choice Analysis: Theory and Applications to Travel Demand**, The MIT Press, Cambridge, MA, 1985.

Brown, S.R. and L.E.Melamed, **Experimental Design and Analysis**, Sage Publications, London, 1990.

Cicarelli, J. and L.Spitzman, The Production of Economic Knowledge, **Quarterly Review of Economics and Business**, vol. 24, 1984, pp.41-50.

Fischer, M.M. and P.Nijkamp, Development in Explanatory Discrete Spatial Data and Choice Analysis, **Progress in Human Geography**, vol. 9, 1985, pp.515-551.

Fischer, M.M., R.Maggi and C.Rammer, Context Specific Media Choices and Barriers to Communications in Universities, **The Annals of Regional Science**, vol. 24, 1990, pp.253-269.

Fischer, M.M., R.Maggi and C.Rammer, Stated Preference Models of Contact Decision Behaviour in Academia, WSG-Discussion Paper 13, Vienna University of Economics and Administration, Vienna, 1991.

Fischer, M.M., R.Maggi and C.Rammer, Telecommunication Media Choice Behaviour in Academia: An Austrian-Swiss Comparison, **Geographical Analysis**, vol. 24, 1992, pp.1-15.

Fischer, M.M., P.Nijkamp and Y.Y.Papageorgiou (eds.), **Spatial Choices and Processes**, North-Holland, Amsterdam, 1990.

Galegher, J., R.Kraut and C.Egido, **Intellectual Teamwork: Social and Technological Foundations of Cooperative Work**, Erlbaum Associates, Hillsdale, NJ, 1990.

Hengevoss, T. and R.Maggi, Barriers to Production and Distribution of Swiss Economists' Output, Paper Presented at the 29th European Congress of the Regional Science Association, Cambridge, August 29 - September 1, 1989.

Hensher, D.A. and L.W.Johnson, **Applied Discrete-Choice Modelling**, Croom-Helm, London, 1981.

Horowitz, J.L. and J.J.Louvière, The External Validity of Choice Models Based on Laboratory Choice Experiments, **Spatial Choices and Processes** (Fischer, M.M., P.Nijkamp and Y.Y.Papageorgiou, eds.), North-Holland, Amsterdam, 1990, pp.247-263.

Kalton, G., **Introduction to Survey Sampling**, Sage Publications, London, 1983.

Lerman, S.R. and C.F.Manski, Sample Design for Discrete Choice Analysis of Travel Behavior, **Transportation Research A**, vol. 13A, 1979, pp.29-44.

Louvière, J.J., Conjoint Analysis Modelling of Stated Preferences. A Review of Theory, Methods, Recent Developments and External Validity, **Journal of Transport Economics and Policy**, vol. 22, 1988, pp.93-119.

Louvière, J.J. and D.A.Hensher, Using Discrete Choice Models with Experimental Design Data to Forecast Consumer Demand for a Unique Cultural Event, **Journal of Consumer Research**, vol. 10, 1983, pp.348-361.

Louvière, J.J. and H.Timmermans, Stated Preference and Choice Models Applied to Recreation Research: A Review, **Leisure Sciences**, vol. 12, 1990, pp.9-32.

Louvière, J.J. and G.Woodworth, Design and Analysis of Simulated Consumer Choice on Allocation Experiments: An Approach Based on Aggregate Data, **Journal of Marketing Research**, vol. 20, 1983, pp.350-367.

Manski, C.F. and D.McFadden, Alternative Estimators and Sample Designs for Discrete-Choice Analysis, **Structural Analysis of Discrete Data with Econometric Applications** (Manski, C.F. and D.McFadden, eds.), The MIT Press, Cambridge, MA, 1981, pp.2-50.

Moore, A. and P.P.Jovanis, Modelling Media Choices in Business Organizations: Implications for Analyzing Telecommunications-Transportation Interactions, **Transportation Research A**, vol. 22A, 1988, pp.257-273.

Morton, H.C. and A.J.Price, **The ACLS Survey of Scholars. Final Report of Views on Publications, Computers and Libaries**, University Press of America, Boston, 1989.

Nijkamp, P., P. Rietveld and I.Salomon, Barriers in Spatial Interactions and Communications. A Conceptual Exploration, **The Annals of Regional Science**, vol. 24, 1990, pp.237-252.

Ungerer, H. and N.P.Costello, **Telecommunication in Europe**, Office for Official Publications of the European Communities, Brussels, 1990.

Wardman, M., A Comparison of Revealed Preference and Stated Preference Models of Travel Behaviour, **Journal of Transport Economics and Policy**, vol. 22, 1988, pp.71-91.

CHAPTER 18

TELECOMMUNICATIONS DEMAND: THE ROLE OF BARRIERS

Piet Rietveld and Fabio Rossera

18.1 Introduction

Telecommunication is among the most rapidly growing fields of spatial interaction. Average annual growth rates of 10% per year are not uncommon in various countries. The costs of long distance, international and intercontinental telecommunication decreased substantially in real terms. A downward tendency in the real tariffs of long distance and international telecommunication can be observed, although cross subsidies from international (and long distance) to short distance calls continue to exist in many countries.

There are several tendencies which are expected to lead to a further growth of international telecommunication. In several parts of the world economic integration stimulates international trade. A special tendency is that international trade in services - which is communication intensive - grows at a high rate compared with trade in commodoties. International interwovenness in the financial system increases. International cooperation between governments is expected to grow. The same holds true for tourism, migration and long term labour contracts abroad.

Nevertheless, it must be recognized that international telecommunication traffic is only a small part of total telecommunication traffic. Even in relatively small countries the share of calls to other countries is usually smaller than 1 or 2%. Communication networks usually have a domestic or even local orientation. Distance appears to play an important role as a communication discouraging factor, even though the role of distance in the determination of communication tariffs has considerably decreased. In a country as The Netherlands where all calls between 30 and 300 km fall in the same tariff zone, one can still observe a very clear distance decay effect in telecommunication (see De Ben et al., 1990).

The present paper addresses the question whether in addition to distance decay other factors can be identified which discourage communication. This will be done by investigating so-called barrier effects. Barrier effects are espacially important in the case of national borders. Borders are lines in space which separate areas ruled by different governments. They often coincide with differences in language, culture, institutions, etc. The barrier effect of a border is defined as the degree to which the existence of the border leads to a reduction in telecommunication across the border. An effort will be made to relate the barrier effect of a border to the features of the border (e.g., separator of language groups, separator of economies with/without trade agreement). This may yield insight into the question to which extent economic integration will reduce barrier effects of borders.

Barrier effects are not confined to national borders, however. Within countries there may be notable spatial differences in language or culture which will reduce telecommunication demand between various parts.

This paper is related to analyses of barriers in the international trade literature (e.g., Bikker, 1987; Bröcker and Rohweder, 1990). It differs from these since it focuses on telecommunication rather than trade. Besides, in addition to international flows, also interregional flows will be taken into account.

This paper reviews recent studies on the role of barriers in telecommunication both at the intra- and international level. It brings together work of researchers from Switzerland (see Donzé, 1990; Rossera, 1990), Austria (see Fischer et al., 1992), Greece (see Giaoutzi and Stratigea, 1992) and The Netherlands (see Rietveld and Janssen, 1990; Rietveld et al., 1991).

This paper is organized as follows. In Section 18.2 we discuss various types of barriers in relationship with demand and supply of telecommunication. Section 18.3 is on modelling barrier effects. Data issues are discussed in Section 18.4; empirical results are shown in Section 18.5. Section 18.6 concludes.

18.2 Barriers to Telecommunication: Demand Versus Supply

Barriers influence the level of telecommunication between regions. They may do so both via **demand** and **supply** factors.

Figure 1 gives an example of a **demand** oriented barrier effect. The figure depicts downward sloping demand functions for communication between a certain region A and two other regions: B and C, where B is separated from A by a barrier, and C is not. The regions B and C are assumed to be identical for all other relevant features. In this example the occurrence of a barrier leads to a downward shift of demand. Assuming that supply behaviour is represented by a given cost of communication which is equal for B and C, a reduction occurs in the volume of telecommunication due to the existence of the barrier.

The shift in the telecommunication demand curve may be due to several reasons (see also Nijkamp et al., 1990):

(1) Barriers to telecommunication per se

- **Language differences**
  Language differences may, or may not coincide with national borders. They tend to reduce the utility of communication.
- **Information barriers**
  Lack of information about destination elsewhere reduces actual telecommunication. On the other hand, telecommunication creates information on regions elsewhere. Thus, there is an important **historical** element in information exchange patterns.

- **Cultural differences**
  These differences correspond to a certain extent with national borders, but also within countries cultural differences may be subsytantial (compare , for example, the Southern and Nothern part of Italy).

(2) Barriers to other types of cross-border interaction

Demand for telecommunication depends on (or is complementary to) other types of interactions such as trade, travelling, tourism, migration and activities of trans-national corporations and agencies. Barriers to these types of spatial interactions will indirectly appear as barriers to telecommunication. Below we list certain examples:

- **Barriers to international trade**
  Fiscal barriers and quota systems are often a serious disincentive to international trade. This also holds true for institutional differences leading to divergent product specification standards among countries.
- **Barriers to international migration**
  Most countries of the world discourage immigration. Some countries discourage outmigration. It is much easier to migrate within a country than from one country to another.
- **Barriers to transport**
  Physical barriers such as mountains, rivers or lakes may be severe barriers of road transport. In addition, borders may lead to time losses for cross-border transport due to customs formalities. Quota systems for cross-border freight transport may induce ralatively high transport costs. Infrastructure networks are usually designed from a national perspective: for international traffic they are relatively inefficient. Frequences of domestic air and rail connections tend to be higher than for international connections leading to higher time losses.

The second group of barrier effects discussed above is based on the strong complementary between information flows and physical flows. There are also examples of substitution effects, however, especially between different information transmitting media. For example, a barrier in telephone traffic may lead to a more than average use of telex. This underlines the importance of interdependencies between communication networks (see Batten and Törnqvist, 1990).

The case of a **supply** oriented barrier effect is shown in Figure 2. Here the communication costs to the foreign region B are higher than to the domestic region C. Such a pattern is quite usual in telecommunication. In many countries the charge for a domestic long distance call is lower than the charge for an equidistant international call (see Rietveld et al., 1991).

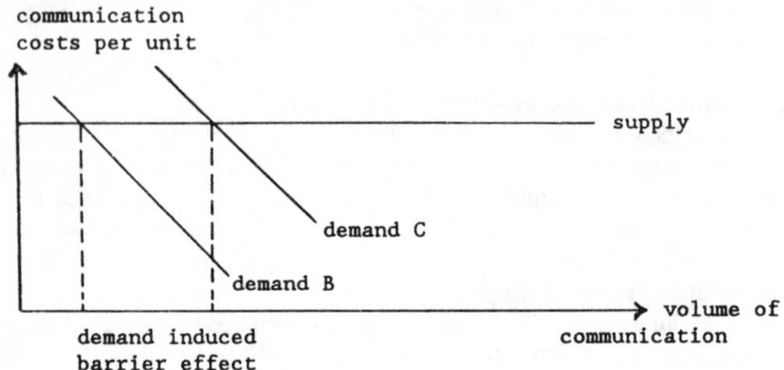

Figure 1 Demand oriented barrier effect on communication volumes

One must not exaggerate the importance of discontinuities in telephone tariffs on telecommunication demand, however. Tariffs are not the only component of the full costs of telecommunication. Time costs often play a dominant role as a cost component (see Dunn and Oh, 1990). They will have a dampening effect on the tariff elasicity of telecommunication demand. It is interesting to note that Healy and Baker (1990) mention **quality** (not just tariffs) of telecommunication as one of the major location factors of large European firms.

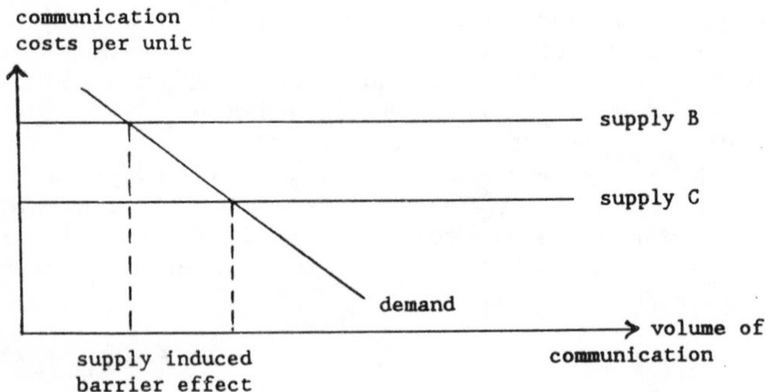

Figure 2 International - domestic - tariff differentials and their communication volumes

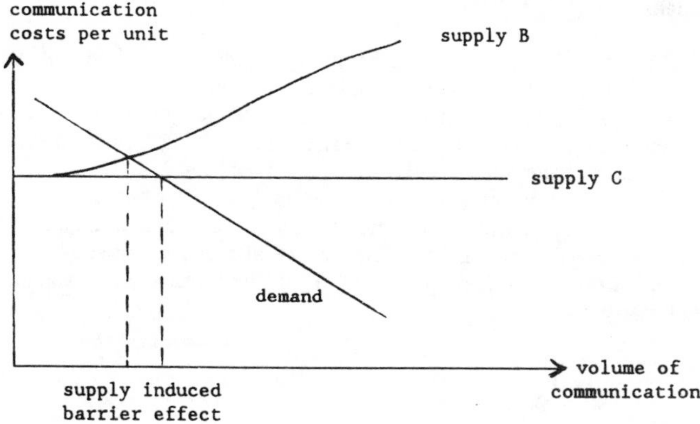

Figure 3 Effects of bottlenecks in international infrastrcuture on communication volumes

Lack of capacity in international telecommunication connections (for example to Eastern Europe) may be another supply oriented communication barrier. It is common practice that the national perspective dominates in the provision of infrastructure for transport and communication. As a result, bottlenecks might appear in international communication, leading to time losses and hence higher user costs compared with domestic communication (see Figure 3).

A third supply related type of barriers to telecommunication is that particular facilities are not provided at the cross-border level. For example, cross-border mobile telecommunication facilities were very bad in Europe due to a lack of standardization.

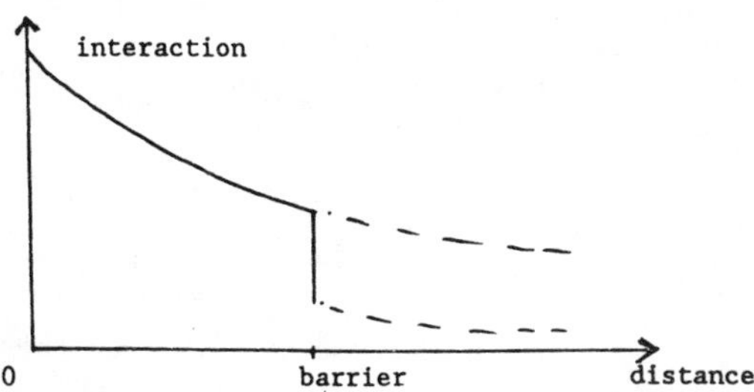

Figure 4 Impact of barrier on spatial interaction

18.3 Modelling Barrier Effects in Space

A barrier can be defined as a discontinuity in the marginal cost of communication which leads to a discontinuity in the intensity of communication.

As indicated in Figure 4, distances (or communication costs) exert a negative impact on communication. A spatial barrier exists when adding a small distance leads to a sudden fall in the communication level.

The gravity model provides a useful way to analyze and estimate the impact of barriers in space. Let X_{rs} denote the volume of calls between spatial units **r** and **s**. Let M_r and M_s denote variable representing the masses of **r** and **s**. Futher, let c_{rs} denote the cost of a call from **r** to **s** (per unit time). Then the unconstrained version of the gravity model reads:

$$X_{rs} = a\, M_r^{\alpha_1}\, M_s^{\alpha_2}\, c_{rs}^{\tau} \tag{1}$$

where $\alpha 1$, $\alpha 2 > 0$ and $\tau < 0$. A barrier effect can be added by introducing a dummy variable e_{rs}. For example, when the barrier relates to language differentials, it may be defined as:

e_{rs} = **0** if r and s are part of the same language area
= **1** otherwise

Then, the original model can be extended as:

$$X_{rs} = a\, M_r^{\alpha_1}\, M_s^{\alpha_2}\, c_{rs}^{\tau}\, \exp(\beta e_{rs}) \tag{2}$$

where β is expected to be negative. Thus, **exp** (β), the so-called **barrier factor** is expected to be smaller than 1. The specification can also be extended to study several barrier effects simultaneously. For example, for border related barrier effects one could define

g_{rs} = **1** if r and s are part of the same country
= **0** if r and s are separated by a border

Then the extended model is:

$$X_{rs} = a\, M_r^{\alpha_1}\, M_s^{\alpha_2}\, c_{rs}^{\tau}\, \exp(\beta e_{rs} + \eta g_{rs}) \tag{3}$$

This model allows one to distinguish the case of a national border which is no language border (barrier factor **exp** η) from the case of a national border which is also a language border (barrier factor **exp** ($\beta+\eta$)).

Another direction into which the interaction model can be developed concerns the impact of distance. One might argue that distance should not play a role in the analysis of telecommunication demand once the tariff c_{rs} is included. Indeed, a major difference between physical transport and telecommunication is that the user costs of the first depends on both tariffs and distance, whereas the user cost of the second depends on tariffs only.

Nevertheless, there is a strong reason why distance will play a role in telecommunication demand: the complementarity between telecommunication and other types of spatial interaction where distance does play a role makes also telecommunication distance dependent. There are two directions to formalize this idea of complementarity.

The first way is to state that the importance of a destination is not only dependent on its mass M_s, but also on the extent to which this destination is part of the contact network of people/firms residing in r. The latter is assumed to be distance dependent. Therefore, the idea of complementarity can be introduced by replacing $(M_s)^{\alpha 2}$ by $(M_s\, d^{\epsilon}_{rs})^{\alpha 2}$. Thus, one arrives at:

$$X_{rs} = a\, M_r^{\alpha_1}\, M_s^{\alpha_2}\, d_{rs}^{\mu}\, c_{rs}^{\tau}\, \exp(\beta e_{rs} + \eta g_{rs}) \tag{4}$$

where $\mu = \epsilon\, \alpha_2 \leq 0$. In this formulation, distance plays a role in two ways: a direct one via d_{rs}, and an indirect one via c_{rs} since telephone tariffs are to a certain extent distance dependent (see however Salomon and Schafer, 1991; Rietveld and Janssen, 1990, who indicate that in certain countries distance dependence of tariffs is low or even absent).

The second way to take into account complementarity of telecommunication and other forms of spatial interaction is to formulate it explicity in a multi equation model. For example, when Y_{rs} denotes trade between r and s, a model based on complementarity can be written as:

$$X_{rs} = f\,(Y_{rs}, c_{rs}, e_{rs}, g_{rs}) \tag{5a}$$

$$Y_{rs} = h\,(M_r, M_s, d_{rs}, e_{rs}, g_{rs}) \tag{5b}$$

Thus, use is made of an ordinary gravity model for trade with distance as an indicator of transport costs; telecommunication is assumed to be dependent on trade and communication tariffs. It is not difficult to see that equation (4) can be interpreted as a reduced form of equations (5).

This interpretation of equation (4) as a reduced form of equations (5) is not only important for the distance factor, but also for the barrier factors. The barrier factors in (4) do not only reflect the barriers to telecommunication per se as included in (5a), but also the barriers to trade implied by (5b).

We finish this section on model specification with two remarks of a more technical nature. The first one concerns the specification of the distance decay formula. In formula (4) we have used the power function d^{τ}_{rs} rather than the exponential form $\exp(\tau d_{rs})$. The reason is that according to common experience (see, for example, Fotheringham and O'Kelly, 1989) the exponential form performs better with short distances. In our context of interregional and international telecommunication, the power function is more promising, accordingly. This choice is confirmed by estimation results of Rietveld and Janssen (1990), and Giaoutzi and Stratigea (1991), who find that results with the power function are superior to those of the exponential form.

A final remark concerns the fact that the interaction models described above are specified in an unconstrained form. A feature of unconstrained models is that the volume of interaction between regions **r** and **s** does not depend on the situation in region v. However, when the mass in region **v** increases, this may not only induce a higher interaction between **r** and **v**, but also a decrease in the interaction between **r** and **s**. To take such effects into account one can make use of constrained interaction models (see Fotheringham and O'Kelly, 1989). An example is the **origin constrained** model which deals with outgoing flows in terms of shares of the total outgoing flow x_{rs}:

$$x_{rs} = X_{rs} / \Sigma_{s'} X_{rs'} \tag{6}$$

The origin constrained version of equation (1) is:

$$x_{rs} = (M_s^{\alpha_2} c_{rs}^{\tau}) / (\Sigma_{s'} M_{s'}^{\alpha_2} c_{rs'}^{\tau}) \tag{7}$$

In addition to origin constrained models one may also formulate destination constrained, and doubly constrained models. The latter type requires that one knws the totals of all incoming and outgoing flows. This is usually not the case in telecommunication, however, given the lack of complete and coherent data sets. This will be the subject of the next section.

18.4 Telecommunication Data

A major difficulty in telecommunication research is the quality and availability of data. The present wave of deregulation and privitization threatens the monopoly position of many national telecommunication companies. As a result many of these companies are reluctant to provide data for research purposes. The following difficulties had to be faced in our efforts to arrive at a compatible data set at the international level.

(1) Incomplete coverage of countries

Some countries only report infrequently, and/or do not provide data on important variables, or they do not report at all. For example, among the countries which do not report about outgoing international calls are: USA, U.K. and USSR. Another example concerns the destinations of outgoing international calls. The statistical yearbook of AT&T (The World's Telephones) contains data on outgoing international calls for a reasonable number of countries. However, only the ten most frequently called countries are mentioned in this source. This is a serious draw-back since in an analysis of barriers one is especially interested in the destinations with low numbers of calls.

(2) **Lack of standardization**
Telephone traffic can be measured in pulses, minutes, calls and erlangs. For most countries only one of these is available. Another difficulty is that interregional (long distance) traffic may be measured in another dimension than international traffic. For an integrated analysis one is forced to arrive at a common unit of measurement.

(3) **Limited range of variables**
A major draw-back is that data on telephone traffic by purpose (business, private) is not generally available at the interregional or international level. Another difficulty is that data on (international) telephone tariffs are not generally provided in statistical yearbooks with an international orientation such as the ones of the International Telecommunication Union (ITU) or AT&T.

(4) **Unreliability of data**
Data reported by national telecommunication companies and published by ITU or AT&T are sometimes unreliable. For example, sometimes the ITU and AT&T data are mutually inconsistent. In addition some countries report implausible data. For example, Ireland does not mention the U.K. among the ten most frequently called countries in the world.

(5) **Lack of coherence in data**
Lack of coherence often occurs at the regional level. The spatial division of telecommunication areas is usually not consistent with spatial delimitations used for socio-economic variables. This problem must be solved when one wants to link telecommunication data with socio-economic data. Another sign of lack of coherence may occur when one compares the levels of spatial aggregation for communication within countries and between countries. Within countries one usually will have data on communication flows between regions of fairly small size, whereas between countries data are often not available at the interregional level (i.e., region 1 in country A to region 2 in country B).

In Figure 5 a number of cases are shown of data availability when one wants to study barriers in telecommunication.

In case A one only has interregional data without an international dimension. In this case one may study barrier effects related to language differentials in multilingual countries such as Belgium (see Klaassen et al., 1972) and Switzerland (see Rossera, 1990). One may also use data of this type to study the effects of physical barriers on telecommunication flows. An example would be the impact of a separation by the sea between Greek regions.

Data of type B can be used to estimate the impact of national borders on telecommunication flows. A limitation is that barrier effects relate to only one country of origin. When data are available on a sufficient number of countries of destination one can estimate barrier effects for various types of countries. For example, countries which belong to the same trading area, countries which have the same language as the country of origin, etc. Data of this type have been used for The Netherlands by Rietveld and Janssen (1990) and for Greece by Giaoutzi and Stratigea (1991).

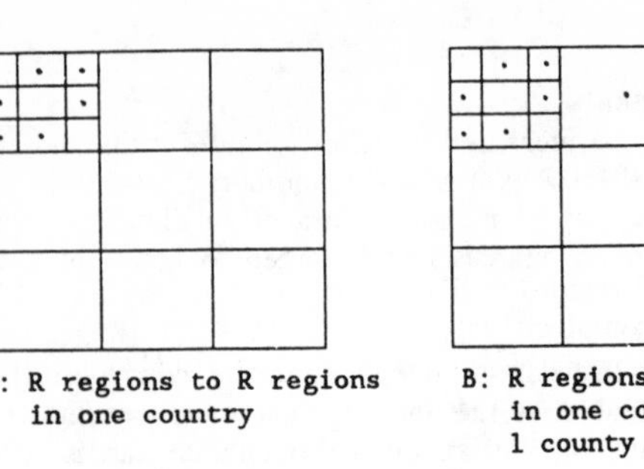

A: R regions to R regions in one country

B: R regions to R regions in one country, combined with 1 county to N countries

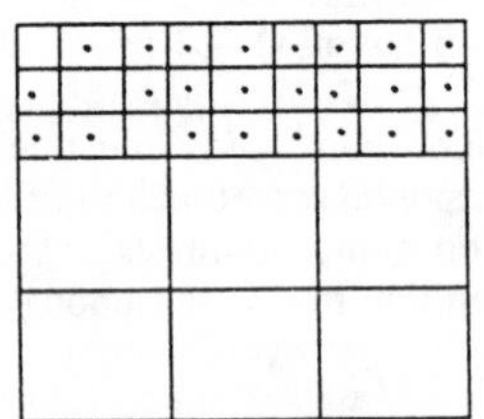

C: R regions to R regions in one country, combined with R regions to S regions in other countries.

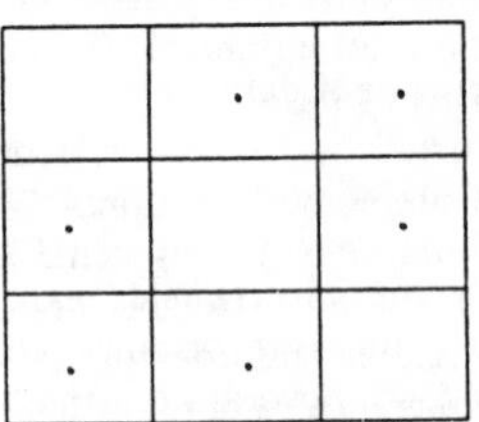

D: N countries to M Countries

Figure 5 Configurations of data availability

In case C data are available on interregional telephone calls, both within a country and between regions in different countries. Data of this type have certain advantages above case B. First, the number of observations is larger. Second, the variance in independent variables (such as distance), is larger, which enables one to arrive at more reliable estimates. Third, in case C one may study differences in international orientation of various regions, which allows one to analyze spatial hierarchical patterns of communication. Fourth, compared with type B, data of type C are more adequate to disentangle the effects of language barriers and other border related barriers in the case of multilingual countries. Data of type C have been used in Donzé (1991) and Fischer et al. (1992).

In case D, the regional dimension is no longer present. A difference with the other cases is, that data are no longer based on only one country as an origin, but on many countries. Data of this type cannot be used to estimate the overall effects of borders on telecommunication per se, but rather the effects of different types of borders on communication. For example, certain borders coincide with language differences while others do not. In adition, borders may have various meanings as separators of countries in different trade preference areas, ideological blocks or cultural groups.

18.5 Empirical Results

We will follow the typology of data availability presented in the preceding section:

(1) Interregional data (R regions to R regions in one country)
(2) Interregional data combined with international data (R regions to R regions combined with 1 country in N countries)
(3) Cross-border interregional data (R regions to R regions in one country, combined with R regions to S regions in other countries)
(4) Interregional data (n countries to M countries)

18.5.1 Interregional data

Switzerland with its four languages (German, French, Italian and Romansh) is an interesting case for an interregional analysis of language barriers. Rossera (1990) details the divergencies existing in contacts between regions of different language. Data on long distance communication between districts - measured in erlang - were used. Several adjustments have been carried out to rule out the effects of concomitant factors. The findings are summarized in Table 1.

A disparity of language reduces the intensity of contacts between two regions by 30%. The impact is however far from being uniform, if we consider the individual associations of language. The most important outcome relates to the fact that Switzerland is not primarily subdivided among German and Latin regions, as along a vertical line separating the western from the eastern part. By this, the cultural distance separating linguistic areas is intermingled as an explanatory factor with components relating to other phenomena. The relationships of economic dependence existing between the German part - by far the dominant one - and the Italian and Romansh periphery takes to a lower level and sometimes obliterates the language effects. This is particularly evident in the case of the Romansh community - limited to 5% of the population of the country - which is in danger of loosing its cultural identity.

Some remnants of the language affinities persist among Latin regions, In fact, light preferences in the contacts of Italian and Romansh regions are visible, among themselves and with French regions compared with those between German and French regions.

18.5.2 Interregional data combined with international data

Interregional data combined with international data have been used by Giaoutzi and Stratigea (1991) for Greece, Rietveld and Janssen (1990) for The Netherlands, Fischer et al. (1992) for Austria, and Donzé (1990) for Switzerland.

Table 1 Barrier effect of language disparities in Switzerland (1985)

Language at origin	Language at destination	Barrier factor
German	French	0.45*
	Italian	.64*
	Romansh	1.60*
French	German	0.43*
	Italian	.48*
	Romansh	.54*
Italian	German	.63*
	French	.54*
	Romansh	1.20*
Romansh	German	1.30*
	French	.50*
	Italian	1.23*
General level of language disparity:		.70*
Number of observations:		2550
R^2:		0.915

* Significantly different from 1 at 5% level

Because of the type of data used, only an unconstrained version of the gravity model has been estimated. A summary of the findings is given in Table 2. There is a strong similarity in most of the results. The barrier factors found for EC and EFTA countries is about .30 to .40. This means that reduction in telecommunication flows which makes them only 30 to 40% of the volume one would expect when no borders exist. It is interesting to note that the difference between barrier factors for EC and EFTA is negligible which implies that no impact of trade areas on telecommunication can be observed in Europe (both Greece and The Netherlands are EC members). The relatively high outcome for the Dutch-Belgian border suggest that language is an important factor. This is also suggested by the outcome for communication between Greece and Cyprus (although it is difficult to believe that in this case the barrier effect is so much higher than 1).

Table 2 Barrier effects of national borders for The Netherlands (1983) and Greece (1988)

The Netherlands		Greece	
Belgium	.40*		
Germany	.36*	EC	.31*
Rest of EC	.31*		
Scandinavia	.31*	EFTA	.28*
Central Europe	.36*		
Eastern Europe	.05*	Eastern Europe	.04*
USA, Canada, Japan	.34*	USA, Canada, Japan	.22*
Developing countries	.08*	Africa	.13*
Indonesia	.88	South America	.06*
		China, India, Hongkong	.05*
		Middle East	.30*
		Turkey, Yogoslavia	.22*
		Austalia/New Zealand	1.05
		Cyprus	9.84
Number of observations: interregional: 22x21 international: 1x27 R^2: .812		Number of observations: interregional: 43x42 international: 1x53 R^2: .613	

* Significantly different from 1 at 5% level

Telecommunication interactions with Eastern Europe are very low for both Greece and The Netherlands. Also with most developing countries telecommunication is low for The Netherlands and Greece. An exeption is telecommunication between Indonesia and The Netherlands, which suggests that former colonial relationships play an important role.

18.5.3 Cross-border interregional data

Cross-border interregional data provide new insights into the structure of preferences to be bound in regional interaction. A study by Donzé (1992) analyzes the telephone flows from Switzerland to its neighbour countries, i.e. France, Italy, Germany and Austria. Data on the volume of communication between Swiss dialling areas have been pooled with those concerning flows from the same areas to the bordering countries subdivided into regions.

The analysis rests on a modelisation in terms of gravity type models. Two specifications have been proposed. The first one is in form of a traditional gravity model, while the second one incorporates income and telephone tariff as additional explanatory variables, more in line with usual demand models.

A second particularity of this model lies in the use of the maximum quasi-likelihood method for estimation (see also Bröcker and Rohweder, 1990). It is shown how better results in terms of goodness of fit can be achieved than by the ordinary least squares method.

On the empirical level, the tariff and income seem to represent important variables which one has to take into account. The distance variable is very sensitive to the type of specification and is not always significant. On the whole set of estimates computed, the elasticities of these three variables are approximately, resp.-3.0, 0.25, and 0.04.

Table 3 Barriers to communication between Switzerland and neighbouring regions (1989)

General border effect	0.28*
Reduction of contacts in relation to:	
- Germany	0.23*
- France	0.26*
- Italy	0.43*
- Austria	0.73*
- Lyon	0.66*
- Stuttgart	0.22*
Number of observations:	4524
Proportion of variance explained (estimates are taken from different adjustments):	0.81-0.89

* Significantly different from 1 at 5% level

In Table 3 we recapitulate some further points. The general impact produced by the presence of a political border separating Switzerland from the neighbouring countries is important. It reduces the traffic to about a fourth of its usual level. This impact may be further detailed, by considering in turn the individual countries involved. The most important reductions are found in relation to Germany and France. The communications with Austria are least influenced. It may be also interesting to consider contacts to particular foreign metropolitan centers. Only the cases of Lyon and Stuttgart are reported. An important difference is visible. There is a deviation from the general national level in the intensity of communications with Stuttgart, which represents the main reference of Germany for all German speaking regions in Switzerland. The case is different for Lyon: Geneva had strong contacts with this bordering region, although its main reference in France is Paris.

A similar data set has been used by Fischer et al. (1992) for Austrian regions. They arrive at an average border factor of about .15 to most European countries which would imply that for Austria cross-border telecommunication is substantialy hampered by the existence of national borders.

18.5.4 International data

International telecommunication data have been analyzed by Rietveld et al. (1991). These data do not allow one to compare domestic and international traffic in order to assess the impact of borders. Instead, these data can be used to disentangle the impact of various aspects of borders such as language differences and membership of different trade preference areas. Data have been published for bilateral telephone communication flows by AT&T, and for bilateral telex communication flows by ITU. The type of data available allow one to use an origin constrained spatial interaction model.

Estimation results are shown in Table 4. As a reference case we take two countries without any special linkage in terms of language, historical links, common, membership of a trade preference area, etc. It appears that historical links (operationalized as the existence of colonial ties in the year 1914) have a strong impact on international communication by telephone: the level of interaction between countries with a former formal linkage is about 3.25 times as high compared with countries without such linkage. This effect can be observed especially in many African countries where the former colonial powers France and the U.K. dominate international calls. More than 50% of the outgoing international calls of Senegal go to France, for example.

Neighbour countries have telephone interactions which are about 20% higher than other countries according to the gravity model. The main reason why the neighbourhood variable is introduced is to correct for the inaccuracy created by the way of measuring distance between countries. Using distance between countries may lead to an underestimate of spatial interaction. The reason is that short distance between regions along the same border may give rise to relatively high levels of spatial interaction which is not taken into account in the way the aggregate distance is measured.

The estimation results in Table 4 indicate that trade preference areas do not have a significant influence on telephone calls in most cases. Exceptions are the CACM (a group of four Central American countries) and the Commonwealth. It is especially striking that for an important trade preference area such as the EC no significant impact can be observed.

Table 4 Effects of communication stimulating factors on international communication (1986)

	Telephone	Telex
Neighbour country	1.21*	1.36*
Language correspondence	1.63*	1.31*
Historical linkage	3.25*	2.23*
Common membership of:		
- EC	.95	1.08
- EFTA	1.07	.53*
- COMECON	1.49	3.85*
- CACM	4.35*	1.70
- LAFTA	1.15	1.27
- Andes Group	1.55	.96
- ASEAN	1.20	.88
- Commonwealth	1.46*	1.20

* Significantly different from 1 at 5% level

The analysis has been repeated with telex data by Rietveld et al. (1992). Results are shown on the righthand side of Table 4. The results for telex and telephone appear to be rather similar. For telex again language, historical linkage and neighbourhood relations are significant. For only two of the eight preference areas a significant effect is observed.

Another study on international telephone communications was carried out by Rossera (1991). The data used were taken from a statistical monograph by ITU. All European nations were considered, including those of Eastern Europe, as well as the non-European countries of the Mediterranean basin. For confrontation purposes with results from the study presented previously, one should keep in mind some divergence existing between the two. The masses used here for calibration refer to total incoming ang outgoing flows. By this, differences existing in the level of infrastructure endowment between individual countries are mainly ruled out. The analysis concentrates on preferences and barriers discovered.

Estimation results are reported in Table 5. Where a comparison with those of Table 4 is possible, one can find parallelisms as well as divergences. The importance of historical adjustment, and the magnitude of the impact is impressive: a five-fold increase is resulting in traffic between countries belonging to old colonial empires.

The effects of language similarities are established only in the case of peripheral areas. We note that these variables have been given a broader definition than in the study previously mentioned. The affinity is not based on the usage of an identical language but on that of language belonging to the same historical root.

Table 5 Effects of stimulating and restrictive factors in communication between countries (1986)

Language correspondence:	
- German	1.04
- Slavian	3.06*
- Latin	1.30
- Arab	1.82*
Common membership to groups of more developed countries	1.42*
Historical linkage	5.31*
Area of conflict: Arabs-Israel	.45*
Common membership of:	
- EC	1.75*
- EFTA	1.25
- COMECON	4.31*
N:	1332
R^2:	.76

* Significantly different from 1 at 5% level

Slavonic people still have strong ties of association between them. Also between Arab nations, those included in this sample, preferential relationships are evident; their impact is however more contained. On the other side, coefficients relating to reciprocal contacts with the German and Latin area are near to unity and statistically not significant. The divergences between the two studies regard the parameters relating to the contacts inside the areas of economic preference. Before coming to them, let us point to the fact that the strong degree of association between COMECON countries is quite in evidence also here.

The membership of EEC or EFTA - we come here to the divergence of results - have favoured reciprocal contacts between member countries. This is more evident, and statistically significant, in the case of EEC. We may find perhaps an explanation in the difference with the estimates of Table 4 in the particular composition of the samples. In the case of the first study, the composition is rather heterogeneous. In this way, European countries are more evidencing their similarities than their differences. The variability in the study reported here is more limited, and so divergences may better stand out.

18.5.5 Other estimation results

In accordance with the model presented in Section 18.3, distance has been included as a force reducing telecommunication in all studies reviewed above. In addition to distances, tariffs are only included in some of the studies. The reason is that some smaller countries such as The Netherlands only have one tariff zone for non-local calls. Another reason is that no general data source exists for international telephone tariffs. It appears that in all studies reviewed, distance plays an important role in explaning telecommunication. The parameter in equation (4) usually varied between -.60 and -1.30. This means that telecommunication is strongly sensitive to distance. For example, a value $\mu = -1$ means that communication with a place at a distance of 1000 km is only 10% of what it would be if distance was only 100 km. These results underline the strong complementarity between telecommunication and physical flows.

Another way to study complementarity between telecommunication and physical flows would be to estimate functions of the type (5a). This approach has been followed for example by Rietveld and Janssen (1990) for international telecommunication. It appears that communication indeed is closely linked to physical flows: trade and migration flows together explain about 97% of the total variance in Dutch international outgoing telecommunication. Similar results were found by Fischer et al. (1992) for Austria. Trade and tourism, can explain 95% of the variance of outgoing international calls for Austria.

18.6 Concluding Remarks

The empirical results in this paper clearly show that national borders exert a strong influence on telecommunication flows. Colonial dominance, political conflicts, cultural differences and language all play a role. International cooperation in the field of trade and network infrastructure will have a dampening effect on the border effects of communication, but one may not expect that the above mentioned factors such as culture and language will soon disappear as limiting factors to international communication.

Acknowledgement

The authors express their thanks to the members of the NECTAR group "Barriers to Communication" (and their associates) for their cooperation without which this paper could not have been written. We want to mention especially Manfred Fischer, Helmut Gassler, Laurent Donzé, Maria Giaoutzi and Tasia Stratigea.

References

AT&T, **The World's Telephones**, various years.

Batten, D. and C.Törnqvist, Multilevel Network Barriers, **The Annals of Regional Science**, vol. 24, 1990, pp.271-288.

Bikker, J.A., An International Trade Flow Model With Substitution: An Extension of the Gravity Model, **Kyklos**, vol. 40, 1987, pp.315-337.

Bröcker, J. and H.C.Rohweder, Barriers to International Trade, **The Annals of Regional Science**, vol. 24, 1990, pp.289-306.

De Ben, L.J.C., L.H.Immers and R.Hamerslag, De Weerstandsgevoeligheid van Communicatiemedia, **Meten, Modelleren, Monitoren** (Jager, J.M., ed.), Colloquium Vervoersplanologisch Speurwerk, Delft, 1990, pp.83-102.

Donzé, L., **Analyse des Flux Téléphoniques Suisses**, Université de Fribourg, Fribourg, 1991.

Donzé, L., **Le Traffic Téléphonique International Suisses: Les Barrières à la Commu nication**, Université de Fribourg, Fribourg, 1990

Donzé, L., **Barriers to Communication in Swiss Telephone Flows**, Université de Fribourg, Fribourg, 1992.

Dunn, D.A. and H.S.Oh, The Effect of User Cost on the Demand for Telecommu nication service, **Telecommunication Demand Modelling**, (De Fontenay, A., M.H.Shugard and D.S.Sinley, eds.), North-Holland, Amsterdam, 1990, pp.67-86.

Fischer, M.M., J.Essletzbichler, H.Gassler and G.Trichtl, **Interregional and Internati onal Telephone Communication, Aggregate Traffic Models and Empirical Evidence for Austria**, Vienna University of Economics, Vienna, 1992.

Fotheringham, A.S. and M.E.O'Kelly, **Spatial Interaction Models**, Kluwer, Dordrecht, 1989.

Giaouzti, M. and A.Stratigea, **Telephone Calls and Communication Barriers in Greece**, National Technical University, Athens, 1992.

Healy and Baker, **European Real Estate Monitor**, London, 1990.

ITU, **Yearbook of Common Telecommunication Statistic**, various years.

Klaassen, L.H., and S.Wagenaar and A. van der Weg, Measuring Psychological Distance Between Flemings and the Walloons, **Journal of the Regional Science Association**, vol. 29, 1972, pp.45-62.

Nijkamp, P., P.Rietveld and I.Salomon, Barriers in Spatial Interactions and Communi cations, **The Annals of Regional Science**, vol. 24, 1990, pp.237-252.

Rietveld, P. and L.Janssen, Telephone Calls and Communication Barriers; The Case of The Netherlands, **The Annals of Regional Science**, vol. 24, 1990, pp.307-318.

Rietveld, P., J.L.M. van Nierop and H.Ouwersloot, **Barriers to International Telecom munication**, Free University, Amsterdam, 1991.

Rietveld, P., F.Rossera, J.L.M. van Nierop and H.Ouwersloot, **Technology Substitution and Diffusion in Telecommunication, the Case of the Telex and Telephone Network**, Free University, Amsterdam, 1992.

Rossera, F., Discontinuities and Barriers in Communications, the Case of Swiss Communities of Different Language, **The Annals of Regional Science**, vol. 24, 1990, pp.319-336.

Salomon,I. and J.Schofer, Transportation and Telecommunication Costs, Some Implications of Geographical Scale, **The Annals of Regional Science**, vol. 25, 1991, pp.19-40.

Taylor, L.D., **Telecommunications Demand: A Survey and Critique**, Ballinger, Cambridge (Mass.), 1980.